DISSENT OR CONFORM?

DISSENT OR CONFORM?

War, Peace and the English Churches 1900-1945

ALAN WILKINSON

Lutterworth Press

The Lutterworth Press
PO Box 60
Cambridge
CB1 2NT
UK

www.lutterworth.com
publishing@lutterworth.com

First published by SCM Press Ltd, 1986
Corrected edition by The Lutterworth Press, 2010

ISBN: 978 0 7188 9207 4

British Library Cataloguing in Publication Data
A catalogue record is available from the British Library

In grateful memory of my parents

JOHN THOMAS WILKINSON
(1893–1980)

MARIAN WILKINSON
(1892–1980)

Fine representatives of the
Dissenting Tradition

Those to whom evil is done
Do evil in return.

W. H. Auden, 'September 1, 1939'

Christ . . . who, when he was reviled, reviled
not again; when he suffered, he threatened not;
but committed himself to him that judgeth
righteously.

I Peter 2.23

Be not conformed to this world . . .

Romans 12.2

The Church . . . is not the State's spiritual
auxiliary . . .

George Bell, November 1939

CONTENTS

FOREWORD

by Robert Runcie, former Archbishop of Canterbury

It is notoriously difficult for today's historians to write about war in their own century without bias, haste or nostalgia. Yet Alan Wilkinson has managed admirably to do so. His account of the churches' role is persuasive, yet never polemical; detailed yet never dull; evocative yet never sentimental.

It will encourage readers 'to move away from the encapsulated and often idealized world of "church history" to the study of "the church *in* history" '. For beneath the historical cameos (including the sectarian Liverpool of my own childhood), and the personalities, minds, and movements which the author so vividly describes, are embedded some vital messages.

One is the strength and continuity of Christian determination to ensure that, as one of my predecessors Randall Davidson put it, 'God helping us, there shall be no "next time" '. A second is the unassailable fact that war itself is no longer what, in 1916, a Nonconformist minister could call 'a stupendous interlude . . . a tragic episode, separable from the main currents of human experience'. Instead it is now part of an apocalypse which demands no less than a global response from Christians everywhere.

Finally, for our British churches, today's dissent – like yesterday's – can have its creative edge blunted so easily by worldliness, respectability and *Realpolitik*. Such a message, like the book itself, is sobering, stirring and timely.

Robert Cantuar
November 1985
Remembrance Sunday

PREFACE

The overt theme of this book is how the English churches reacted to, and were affected by, the international crises of the first half of this century. (I have not attempted to describe the reactions of churches in other parts of the United Kingdom.) The underlying question is: 'How can the church be a creatively dissenting community in the modern world?' On the one hand, it is easy for the church to become a conforming community – as Martin Luther King put it, to become a thermometer registering the temperature of society rather than a thermostat seeking to alter it. In Britain, or at least in England, the consensual forces which begin to operate in church and state, immediately that dissent appears, are extremely subtle and powerful. On the other hand, it is fairly easy for at least groups within the churches to be uncreative dissenters – that is people who criticize those in power, but have no experience of exercising power, and have often neither the wish nor the ability to do so. Their natural *attrait* is opposition. By contrast with both the conformist and the uncreative dissenter, those who try to exercise a ministry of creative dissent are ready to be critical of political policies and social mores in order to be true to the subversive character of the biblical message – one thinks (for example) of Jeremiah, the Magnificat or the questions put against established authority by the fact that Jesus was crucified. But the creative dissenter knows at first hand what it means to exercise authority and power, what compromises and patient negotiations are necessary to produce change and where the levers of power are situated and how best to use them. The paradigm of creative religious dissent in England in the first half of the twentieth century was Bishop George Bell.

Nevertheless, as I hope to show, and as Edward Norman has frequently reminded us, dissent is usually a much more ambiguous phenomenon than the populist version of history inculcates. What looks like courageous dissent at the time, may turn out, in retrospect, to be itself a type of conformity, for example to the dominant ideology of the intelligentsia. And within the total dialectic, there is a role for the anarchic clown figure, who with some (but not total) justification can trace his ancestry back to Jesus himself. The clown's laughter at the pretensions of the powerful is an eschatological sign, an anticipation of the hilarity of heaven. In part, Dick Sheppard fulfilled this role between the wars.

There are other sub-themes, for example: the interaction between various forms of liberalism and orthodoxy; the complex relationship between theological stance and political attitudes; the erosion of church allegiance and religious faith by secularization (which included the spread of leisure), modernity and pluralism; the failure of most church leaders to listen to the poets, unless (like Browning) they seemed to provide useful propaganda material. By 1945 it was clear that both the just war and pacifist traditions had been so battered since 1914 that they needed drastic redefinition, if either was to be of any use as a source of moral guidance about questions of war and peace. It was also after 1945 that the Christian basis of much anti-semitism was gradually realized, as anti-Judaism was traced, first back through the history of the church, and then to the New Testament itself. The painful process of recasting Christianity in the light of the holocaust has only really just begun, and no one can forecast where this may lead both Christianity and Judaism in the future.

'Christ is literally in no man's land' wrote the poet Wilfred Owen, from France in May 1917.[1] This was one of the most crucial theological discoveries of the twentieth century. If it were taken seriously it would drastically alter the whole perspective of the church's structures, ministry and liturgy. What Wilfred Owen realized in 1917, Dietrich Bonhoeffer also discovered in his prison cell between 1943 and 1945. During this half century, the most authentic Christians were those who, in different ways, lived on the frontiers and found Christ there – Studdert Kennedy, George Bell, Dick Sheppard and Reinhold Niebuhr among them.

The first three chapters examine some of the features of English Nonconformity in the first quarter or so of this century. The Noncon-formist attempt (and ultimate failure) to produce an 'alternative society' is of considerable religious and social importance, and has been neglected by Anglican and many secular historians. These chapters concentrate on how the Nonconformist churches – and particularly Primitive Methodism, the most radical of them – reacted

to, and were affected by, the First World War. I have not in these
chapters included material about the Church of England as I examined
this in detail in my earlier book, *The Church of England and the First
World War* (SPCK 1978). Thereafter, the focus shifts to the Church
of England, though I include a good deal of evidence about both the
Free Churches and the Roman Catholic Church. In any case, the most
interesting conflicts between conformity and dissent after the First
World War took place, not between the Free Churches and society,
but within the Church of England itself. One of the many paradoxes
of dissent throughout this period is that the hierarchical structures of
the Church of England and the Roman Catholic church enabled them
to participate more effectively in the decision-taking process of modern
democratic government than the democratic structures of the Free
Churches. Whereas in the episcopal churches Archbishop Temple,
Bishop Bell and Cardinal Hinsley (for example) had plenty of time to
get to know their jobs and to be known by the general public and by
government departments, Free Church Presidents and Moderators,
who held office for a year or two, were transitory figures, able to
concentrate only on short-term aims, having to leave continuity in the
hands of connectional departments. Thus Bishop Bell's dissenting
ministry was inseparable from his membership of the House of Lords
and his familiarity with Government ministers and departments. In
relation to the public, an Archbishop or a Cardinal is potentially better
press-copy, because he and his office are more widely known than a
President or Moderator whose name is probably unknown and whose
office means little to the nation.

Inevitably my treatment of such a large area of religious, social and
political history is selective, so this book can be read as a series of case
studies on the themes already stated, and others to be discovered by
the reader. Though some of the topics in this book have been previously
examined by others, this is the first attempt to cover the whole ground
in one book. Certain aspects have not, as far as I am aware, been
written about before. Some of the source material has not been
published before, like that from the papers of Archbishops Lang,
Temple and Fisher which have only recently become available at
Lambeth Palace Library. Undergirding the first three chapters is a
good deal of contemporary newspaper material from Free Church
journals and my father's diaries and press-cuttings. The staple background material for the rest of the book is the weekly Anglican
newspaper *The Guardian* (not to be confused with the *Manchester
Guardian*) – an intelligent, middle-of-the-road journal. It has been

supplemented at some points by the *Church Times*, then pugnaciously and waspishly Anglo-Catholic, *The Times* and other newspapers, popular as well as serious.

The plan of the book is chronological. But it does not progress along a straight line. Rather it is like a series of waves, each one of which recedes before the next wave moves forwards.

Except at intense crises, people have a lot of other things to think about and do, apart from attending to international events. For most people, including church leaders, these are pushed into the background by the ordinary demands and enjoyments of life and work. It is essential to remember this when we seek to understand how the people of this period thought about peace and war.

I am deeply grateful to the Archbishop for finding the time to read the typescript, and for his generous commendation. In July 1982, many were thankful (though some were angry) when he refused to make the Falklands service a nationalist celebration and said: 'War is a sign of human failure and everything we say and do in this service must be in that context . . . People are mourning on both sides of this conflict.'

Throughout the last decade of research for this and my earlier book, I have been sustained by the encouragement and advice given to me by both the Rev. Dr F. W. Dillistone and Canon Dr Robert Winnett. I wish also to express my gratitude to Dr E. G. Bill, the Librarian of Lambeth Palace Library, for permission to consult and use material from the Lang, Temple and Fisher papers and from the Diaries of Dr A. C. Don. The Bishop of Ripon (the Rt Rev. David Young) kindly permitted me to use and quote from two 1939 files of correspondence belonging to the then Bishop. I am grateful to the Rev. Tony Shepherd, the Bishop's Chaplain, for drawing my attention to these files.

To several people I am indebted for writing special material at my request. Mr Jackson Page wrote about some of his first war experiences which I have quoted in Chapter 3. Dr J. R. H. Moorman, formerly Bishop of Ripon, provided an account of his resignation from his parish in Manchester in 1942 in order to become a farm worker. This material is used in Chapter 9. My sister, Mrs H. M. Dormer, my brother, Dr J. L. Wilkinson and the late Rev. Frank Kelley kindly amplified my recollections of my father.

I owe much to many others who have helped in various ways in the making of this book. Among them are: the Rev. A. M. Barton; Dr David Bebbington; the Rev. James Bentley; Professor Günther Bornkamm; Dr Richard Byrn; Dr Martin Ceadel; former staff and students of Chichester Theological College; the Rev. Owen Conway;

Mr Michael Foot MP; Dr M. P. Hornsby-Smith; Canon David
Hutton; the Imperial War Museum; the Rev. and Mrs. T. Garnett
Jones; the Rev. R. A. Jupp; Miss Elaine Kaye; Canon J. S. Kingsnorth;
Dr Christopher Knight; the Rev. Kenneth Leech; the Ven. Lancelot
Mason; the Rev. Peter Mayhew; the Rev. Peter Midwood; Professor
Dennis Nineham; the Rev. C. W. Odling-Smee; 'Pax Christi'; Mr
John Peart-Binns; the Rev. M. C. Prescott; Lady Peggie Richardson;
the Royal Army Chaplains Department Centre; Dr E. Royle; Dr Eric
Southworth; the Rev. Dr A. R. Vidler.

I first explored the subject of this book in the Passiontide Lectures
at Lincoln Theological College which I gave in 1981 under the title
'Leaves from the Deciduous Cross' (a phrase from 'The Prayer' by R.
S. Thomas). I am grateful to Canon Henry Richmond, the Warden,
for inviting me, to staff and students for stimulating comments and to
the Bishop of Lincoln and Mrs Phipps for their generous hospitality.
In 1982 I repeated the lectures at St Matthew's Study Centre, Sheffield,
by invitation of the vicar, the Rev. A. V. Longworth. Material now
contained in Chapter 11 was also used for theological seminars for
clergy of the Wakefield diocese and for a lecture at York Minster.

It is nearly forty years since, as a sixth-former, I first used the
resources of the Manchester Central Reference Library and pondered
the words from Proverbs 4 which encircle the great dome ('Wisdom
is the principal thing, therefore get wisdom . . .'). The Library staff
there and also at the Methodist Archives of the John Rylands Library,
Manchester have been unfailingly helpful.

Dr Haddon Willmer, of Leeds University, and the Rev. J. Munsey
Turner, the Methodist church historian, read the first three chapters
of this book and the Ven. Francis House read the whole manuscript.
I greatly profited from their comments and suggestions, and express
my deep thanks for all the help they have given so generously.

Through the long gestation of this book, my wife Fenella has not
only been a constant source of support and judicious advice, but has
also provided the peaceful atmosphere which enabled me to research
and write. In the final stages of the preparation of this book she has
been an invaluable collaborator, typing and checking the whole
manuscript.

Darley Vicarage   A.W.
Harrogate

ACKNOWLEDGMENTS

I am grateful to the following for permission to quote from copyright material: Allen and Unwin for Alun Lewis, 'All Day It Has Rained' from *Raiders Dawn*; Faber and Faber Ltd for 'Transfiguration' from *Collected Poems of Edwin Muir*, T. S. Eliot, 'The Dry Salvages' and 'The Rock' from *Collected Poems 1909–1962*, W. H. Auden, 'In Memory of W. B. Yeats' from *Collected Poems*, and 'September 1, 1939' from *The English Auden*, and Louis MacNeice, 'Autumn Journal' from *The Collected Poems of Louis MacNeice*; Grafton Books for R. S. Thomas, 'The Priest' from *Not that He Brought Flowers*; Macmillan, London and Basingstoke, for R. S. Thomas, 'The Chapel' from *Laboratories of the Spirit*; Oxford University Press for David Gascoyne 'Farewell Chorus' from *Collected Poems*, edited by Robin Skelton (1965) and Keith Douglas, 'How to Kill' and 'Sportsmen' from *The Complete Poems of Keith Douglas*, edited by Desmond Graham (1978); and to Mrs Anne Ridler for her poem 'Now as Then' originally published in *The Nine Bright Shiners*, Faber and Faber 1943.

A.W.

PART I

THE FREE CHURCHES AND
THE FIRST WORLD WAR

1

THE DILEMMAS OF DISSENT

'Come out from among them and be ye separate, saith the Lord' (II Cor. 6.17). 'Not many mighty, not many noble, are called . . . God hath chosen the weak things of the world to confound the things which are mighty' (I Cor. 1.26–27). 'We ought to obey God rather than men' (Acts 5.29). Texts such as these have been a constant inspiration to those Christians who have regarded Christianity as essentially a dissenting movement against the wiles of surrounding culture. Did not the prophets thunder against the rich for oppressing the poor? Was not Jesus a dissenter who was put to death by the religious and social establishment? Did not the birth of the church inevitably lead to a schism within Judaism? How otherwise could the church have maintained the purity of the gospel? The call of God is more important than the appeal to tradition, succession and office. Amos was not a prophet's son, but 'a simple herdsman'. Jesus was not a priest but 'a simple carpenter'. 'Think not to say within yourselves, We have Abraham to our father: for I say unto you, that God is able of these stones to raise up children unto Abraham' (Matt. 3.9). Dissenters have also often looked back longingly to the pre-Constantinian era when the church was a persecuted sect, and have denounced the Constantinian concordat between church and state as the beginning of a long process of the betrayal of the gospel by mainstream Christianity. Within this dissenting tradition we might include not only English Nonconformity, but also pristine monasticism, missionaries encouraging converts to reject 'heathen' customs, various sects, elements within Anglican conservative Evangelicalism and Anglo-Catholicism, Marxist Christians in South America, pietist Christians in Soviet Russia. In this sense we can see Don Cupitt as a modern Anglican dissenter, rejecting incarnation, and regarding Jesus as 'world-denying': 'As eschatological prophet, he shows the true God because

he stands spiritually at the end of the world, where everything but
God has passed away.'¹

But a second group has sought for an alignment of Christ with
culture. In Christ (this group believes) all true human aspirations
find their fulfilment. Coronations, Midnight Mass, carol services,
ceremonies at war memorials, Commemoration of Benefactors (with
the reading from Ecclesiasticus 44, 'Let us now praise famous
men . . .') are some expressions of this tradition. Such Christians are
often drawn to the more serene and affirmative Psalms (for example
Ps. 19: 'The heavens declare the glory of God . . .'); to Wisdom
literature; to the comparatively untroubled and inward Jesus of the
Fourth Gospel; to the 'natural theology' of Acts 17; to the cosmic
Christ of Colossians and Ephesians. For such Christians, creation and
incarnation rather than redemption are the starting points for theology.
Yet Christians of this tradition, faced with a catastrophe like war or a
violently anti-Christian regime, can be forced back to consider the
apocalyptic and eschatological elements in the Bible which normally
they neglect.²

The larger churches have learnt in recent times how to maintain
within the same framework and in fruitful tension, both dissenting
and affirmative elements. The Church of England, for example, has
bishops in the House of Lords, but also monastic orders. By contrast
with the churches, the sect includes *only* those who totally accept its
particular programme of dissent. No other type of membership is
possible.³ The English Nonconformist churches have never been sects
in that strict sense, though they have displayed some sectarian features,
partly because the comparatively small size of each church gave it a
distinctive intimate family atmosphere, partly because Nonconformity
was concentrated in a particular area of the class system, partly because
many chapels lived an intensely local and congregational life. In the
late nineteenth and early twentieth centuries Nonconformists were
shedding some of these sectarian characteristics and were struggling
to find a new identity as broader and more heterogeneous churches.

Or one can express these tensions within Christianity in another
form. The church has been pulled this way and that between
Jerusalem, Athens and Rome: Jerusalem standing for passionate,
eschatological faith; Athens standing for the detached contemplation
of the ideal and a certain elitism (though the Anglican public school
attempts to teach the philosopher-king to descend the mountain to
serve the world below); Rome standing for political power, law, order,
organization, hierarchy.

As we begin to understand the sociology of knowledge, we discover the ways in which particular cultures have interacted with Christianity.[4] We cannot, as did neo-orthodoxy, draw a simple distinction between a transcendent, unconditioned Word of God in the scriptures and the relativities of human cultures. We have not only discovered the dialectical element within scripture, but ways in which scripture itself is a product of interaction with surrounding culture. So we are impelled to move away from the encapsulated and often idealized world of 'church history' to the study of 'the church in history' and to try to understand the way in which the Word emerges through a complex dialectical process, both within the church itself, and between church and world.[5] So (for example) the changed understanding of marriage and sexuality evident in the 1928 revision of the 1662 Prayer Book, can be largely explained, not by some shift in 'pure' theology, but by the impact of the feminist movement which won crucial public recognition during the First World War.[6] The growth or decline of churches in Britain (we are told) is less determined by church policies, than by external forces such as secularization, industrialization, urbanization, trade fluctuations, political changes and war.[7] Professor W. R. Ward considers that in the nineteenth century, 'Bad years for business were almost always bad or indifferent years for Methodism'.[8]

In these first three chapters I want to outline and discuss the intensification during the twentieth century of the already strong external and internal pressures upon the Nonconformist churches towards a greater conformity with the attitudes of both English society and the Church of England. During the First World War, the pressures upon Nonconformity to conform were (as we shall see) particularly strong and crucial, and to a large measure Nonconformists succumbed to them. Though the story includes an element of oscillation between conformity and dissent, the pressures upon Nonconformity which prevailed during the whole period were those towards cultural, ethical, political and religious conformity. In short, the chapels became churches, and dissenters became Free Churchmen. The painful dilemmas which the Nonconformist tradition has faced in the last hundred years are not only an important aspect of the Free Church experience, they are also a particular version of tensions within Christianity and indeed within the Bible. For example, Old Testament scholarship in the nineteenth century identified the prophets as the creative source of true religion and set them in opposition to the priests and the cult: an antithesis once very congenial to Nonconformists, but now largely abandoned by modern biblical scholars. Nonconformists used the prophets as a prime but dangerous model for ministry. If the example of the prophets has often saved the church from pietism, uncritical recourse to the prophets sometimes has led church leaders to conclude that a truly prophetic ministry was chiefly characterized by an inexhaustible capacity for emotional denunciation.[9]

It is significant that the Labour Party (which until recently had strong links with Nonconformity) has experienced similar tensions – for example, between the moderate reformists who enjoy government and are prepared for the compromises that this involves, and the natural dissenters whose *métier* is perpetual opposition. Moderates are prepared to overcome their embarrassment and mouth 'The Red Flag' on platforms, even if they hardly know the words nor believe in them. But the dissenters not only know the words and believe in them, but are emotionally fixated by the period which produced them. The Free Churches, Anglo-Catholics and conservative Evangelicals all have their equivalents of the Militant Tendency and 'The Red Flag', and much of their emotional energy, like that of the Labour Party, is derived from the battles and martyrs of earlier eras.

Nonconformist culture

I shall tell the story of the dilemmas and decline of the dissenting tradition of the Free Churches partly within a framework provided by the diaries, press cuttings and correspondence which belonged to my father, John Thomas Wilkinson (1893–1980), a Methodist minister. My parents' lives spanned the whole of the period covered by this book. However much they changed, they continued authentically and movingly to the end to represent the values, aspirations and attitudes of the late Victorian dissenting tradition in which, as Primitive Methodists, they were reared. My father began his work as a minister in 1917. After many years in circuit ministry, from 1946 to 1959 he was a tutor, then Principal of Hartley Victoria College, Manchester, where he himself had been trained for the ministry. He was an authority on the seventeenth-century Puritans, particularly Richard Baxter, three of whose works he edited for the modern reader. He wrote biographies of the two founders of Primitive Methodism, Hugh Bourne and William Clowes, and a biography of his old tutor, A. S. Peake, the notable Primitive Methodist layman and biblical scholar. My father was regarded as one of the last great expository preachers.

Within my father's life there was, as for other scholarly Free Churchmen, a constant, unresolved but creative tension between Jerusalem and Athens. As a young man he had experienced an evangelical conversion, yet he told a reporter in 1929:

I am always seeking to keep an open mind for the truth, and always seeking to teach the idea of the Bible as a record of the progressive revelation of God in human history and experience, and to make the idea the background of my preaching. I hold that the fundamental ground of religion is neither in the authority of the church, nor in the authority of an infallible book, but in the verdict of man's own inward, personal experience. I think that there is a good deal of the Quaker strain in me.

This credo reflects the liberal protestant theology of the time. But it is interesting to note that the liberal Anglo-Catholic symposium *Essays Catholic and Critical* (1926) was also marked by a much greater emphasis upon the appeal to experience than had been usual in that tradition. Undoubtedly here my father was influenced by a passage in Baxter's *Autobiography* in which he wrote that as he grew older he realized the supreme importance of 'internal experience' and 'the witness of the indwelling Spirit'.[10] Nevertheless, my father, who had been through the winnowing experience of biblical criticism, and who had read history as part of his university course, believed that the Christian faith could appeal to a solid substratum of historical fact beneath later (inauthentic) accretions. Like Charles Raven, the Anglican theologian whose friendship he greatly valued, he was drawn to thinkers whose main aim was synthesis and reconciliation – the Cambridge Platonists, John Ray and (later) Teilhard de Chardin. My father quoted Ruskin: 'At every moment of our lives we should be trying to find out, not in what we differ from other people, but in what we agree with them.'[11]

It was this eirenic attitude to life which was the basis of his pacifism and ecumenism and the source of his unease about the strident elements in Nonconformity. The favourite text of the leader of the Cambridge Platonists, Benjamin Whichcote, was often on his lips: 'The Spirit of a man is the candle of the Lord, lighted by God and lighting us to God.' It was characteristic therefore of my father that what he most admired in Baxter was his endeavour for religious comprehension in the seventeenth century. When in 1962 he edited Baxter's *The Saint's Everlasting Rest*, he excluded most of Baxter's vivid descriptions of the torments of hell 'having in mind the changed theological concepts of our time' (Preface). For he regarded those passages in the New Testament upon which Christians have based a doctrine of hell, as later, inauthentic additions to the original eirenic Jesus. My father believed that a minister could hardly commit a graver sin than to lose his temper. He was a life-long pacifist. Yet he admired Cromwell and was a dramatic, even aggressive, preacher. Early in his

ministry, when preaching at a harvest festival, he made an emotional
gesture with his fist and propelled one of the grapes on the pulpit on
to a nearby wall. The tell-tale stain was there for some time, and was
an object of awe and wonderment to visitors. Nevertheless, if pressed,
he might have granted that he would have found the company of
George Herbert (whom he deeply admired) temperamentally more
congenial than that of Cromwell or Hugh Bourne (whose life he wrote).
Hugh Bourne, the dour moorland carpenter and earnest itinerant
preacher and co-founder of Primitive Methodism, represented the
rock from which my father was hewn. But for my father, George
Herbert represented a more adequate synthesis between Jerusalem
and Athens. Indeed there were times in the middle of his ministry
when my father talked of becoming a country parish priest in the
Church of England. But to have accepted the re-ordination required,
would have been a betrayal of his own and Baxter's principles. To
have been confined in worship to the Book of Common Prayer (which
he loved, but chiefly as a quarry) would have been an intolerably
restrictive yoke, for he always preferred to keep the design and conduct
of services within his own hands. This was not only a reflection of his
own temperament, but was also an expression of the Primitive
Methodist tradition, which unlike Wesleyanism, was strongly a-
liturgical. He was uninterested in the Liturgical Movement, and was
too much of a Quaker and a Platonist to regard the sacraments as
having much more than an illustrative and marginal function. He
agreed with his tutor, A. S. Peake: 'I recognise the place of the two
sacraments in the life of the Church. But I cannot concede the
dominant position often claimed for them.'[12]

A vivid picture of many aspects of Nonconformity between 1912
and the early 1920s emerges from my father's diaries. They reflect
some of the tensions between Jerusalem and Athens in Free Church
life. During my parents' courtship (they were engaged in 1915)
they gave each other copies of their favourite poets – Tennyson,
Wordsworth, Keats and Browning. They listened to oratorios and
visited exhibitions at the Art Gallery in Hull where they lived. But
they were brought up to believe that theatres were dangerous to
morality – even attendance at performances of Shakespeare was
forbidden. They did not go to a play until they were in their early
thirties. But in January 1914 they enjoyed a film of David Copperfield
and in 1915 one about Scott of the Antarctic. A typical evening
together included reading poetry to one another, discussing Ruskin
or George Eliot, and ended round the piano singing hymns. When my
father was nineteen, his mother died. He found lasting consolation in

Tennyson's 'In Memoriam' – as also did many bereaved by the First World War. In consequence, throughout his life, he regularly lectured about the poem and quoted from it in sermons. His diaries contain many detailed descriptions of nature in a style owing much to Ruskin, Keats, Wordsworth and the moralizing use of literature and experience in the sermon tradition of the time. He was eighteen when he wrote the following in 1912 about a walk with Marian Elliott (whom he married in 1920):

> Tonight Marian and I had a walk along the Cottingham Road. The evening – a typical spring dusk, with a slight mist from a fine day – was superb and as we stood and gazed through some thickets we were profoundly impressed by the stillness, the silence of all: indeed was not the Spirit of Beauty, that Element which forms so much of our lives, upon everything; and Marian and I fittingly turned our thoughts to the place of the Beautiful in our lives, feeling that so long as our lives are beautiful, then will they be great, for Beauty is greatness, culminating in the highest, in the divine Beauty. I told Marian of my intention of writing a paper on 'The Beautiful – a Philosophical Study', for some literary Society, and I asked her to accept the MSS when completed, in dedication. She graciously accepted. My prayer is that both of us shall . . . mould our lives, sculpture our natures to the pattern of the Divine Beauty.

In tune with the spirit of that passage was a quotation he cited from Ruskin on another occasion: 'Do not think it wasted time to submit yourselves to any influence which may bring upon you any noble feeling.'[13] The diary entry was also a romantic version of one of my father's favourite texts from St Paul: 'Whatsoever things are true . . . honest . . . just . . . pure . . . lovely . . . of good report . . . think on these things' (Phil. 4.8). In the light of his romantic valuation of the role of beauty, it is not surprising that he sometimes felt ill at ease with the more graceless aspects of Nonconformist worship and architecture. Later he enjoyed making lantern slides to use in lectures to his congregations. When the subject was 'Hymns' or 'The Pilgrim Fathers' this was acceptable, but when he turned to 'Cathedrals' or 'The Story of our English Monasteries' some shook their heads and wondered whether he wasn't more of an Anglican than a Nonconformist.

At the beginning of this century it was still possible to live almost the whole of one's leisure life – personal, social and educational – through the chapels and churches. Both my parents ran classes for young people for the local chapel. In his late teens and early twenties, my father regularly spoke to meetings organized by the Band of Hope,

Sons of Temperance and the Christian Endeavour. Five to six hundred children attended one Band of Hope meeting which he addressed. He spoke to young people on such topics as 'Character in relation to our Friendships', 'The Great Principles of True Art' and 'The Thermometer': to one adult group on 'Militarism and Tyrannical Aristocracy', to another on the evils of gambling. He attended a talk on 'Alcohol and the Human Body' and worked the lantern for a lecture on 'Wandering in the Alps'. Sermons were both educational and religious events of considerable significance, and he recorded them in detail. Each time he preached, he carefully noted the feelings engendered in himself and the congregation. In the closing hour of 1913 he attended a watch-night service at which several signed the pledge. Early next year he went to a crowded meeting arranged by the Alliance of Honour, a purity organization: 'the object was to secure purity of life and chivalry for womanhood. I became a member.' Later in life my father was deeply indignant when biographies of Ruskin and his wife appeared which uncovered Ruskin's infantile sexuality, for my father was greatly influenced by the celebration of 'the stainless sceptre of womanhood' in the writings of Ruskin and in the paintings of the pre-Raphaelites.[14]

The admiration for academic distinction by Victorian and Edwardian Nonconformity is revealed by this entry for 1912: 'I attended a lecture at night by the Rev. F. Ballard M.A., D.D., B.Sc., F.R.M.S.' Even today, the Free Church chapel is more likely to advertise the degrees of visiting preachers than is the parish church. A. S. Peake, as a boy, was given a story book with the title *Learning Better Than Houses or Lands*, which greatly impressed him. Peake's father wrote frequent exhortatory letters to him while at Oxford giving practical hints about how to achieve academic success. Peake wrote to his father in 1891: 'Our people (sc. Primitive Methodists) have failed to keep pace with the advance of the nation in education and general culture.'[15] Peake was the first Nonconformist layman to be elected to a theological fellowship at Oxford,but he had a deep concern that Free Church ministers should be better trained. So, after a time, he gave up a promising career at Oxford to devote himself to the much less glamorous work of teaching Primitive Methodist ordinands at Hartley College, Manchester. The winning of academic recognition from the establishment was a particular expression of a widespread desire by Nonconformists to claim that they did or could wield considerable influence in every sphere of national life. Hugh Price Hughes, the Wesleyan minister and a fervent supporter of Empire, was constantly discovering beneficient Methodist influences in even the most unexpected places. He ascribed the glories of the monarchy to the fact that Queen Victoria's nurse was 'a godly Methodist'.[16]

By 1905, Samuel Smiles's *Self-Help* (1859) had sold over a quarter of a million copies. He taught the aspiring that it was not genius which transformed society but the energetic use of simple means and ordinary qualities. My father was the first generation of the family to go to university; he eagerly read the works of Smiles as a young man and was re-reading his *Autobiography* (1905) when he died in 1980.[17] My father constantly strove for personal, religious and educational improvement. He had few keener pleasures than rummaging through second-hand bookshops. When he appeared through the door carrying a pile of sometimes bedraggled books which he had saved from pulping, the family would sing the then popular hymn: 'Rescue the perishing'. When he first got to know his fiancée, he gave her *Adam Bede*, and wrote inside:

> Great is the ministry of noble books,
> Each line of which will surely add
> That which will mould our lives.

In 1913 he attended a meeting on education addressed by Dr John Clifford, the Baptist and the Rev. A. T. Guttery, later President of the Primitive Methodist Conference. Both were prominent in the Campaign of Passive Resistance against the 1902 Education Act. In his speech Guttery expressed attitudes to society and education common among Nonconformist Liberals. He said that the squire, the parson and the socially ambitious wished to keep the masses in their place through religious and social control, thereby resisting 'the onward march of democracy'. Control by priests must be replaced by 'civic control of education'. We must vigorously oppose conscription, military training in schools, and the evils of apathy, vice and drink:

> We plead that education is precious because of its ministry to character; it opens up the worlds where markets do not rule and dividends are not reckoned. It gives grace to the soul and vision to the spirit. We want to see England more than a workshop; we would have her to be the lighthouse and sanctuary of the world. In this faith we meet the ratepayer who regards money spent on education as wasted.[18]

My father loved the country, longed to live there and like Wordsworth, Ruskin, William Morris and other romantics, detested industrial life. Travelling up to Scotland by night train he saw the glare of the furnaces around Newcastle and wondered whether all the struggle and hardship of industrial life was really worthwhile.[19] Going round Hull delivering boots and shoes to his father's customers in 1913, he mused, echoing passages in Ruskin whom he so admired:

> The thought occurred to me whilst out: how different from the classical Greek civilisation. No bricks and mortar and town terraces: the old alabaster pillars, temples of marble, statuary and vast gardens; people lovers of art and dressed in the beauty of simplicity; no women 'hanging' around terrace-ends in groups; no men loafing and smoking, swearing and drinking; no weaklings feeding an orange peel and fish heads. Truly the finest civilisation the world has ever known.[20]

Shortly after the outbreak of war in August 1914 my father went to Hartley College to train as a Primitive Methodist minister. He recorded taking his first Communion Service – the right of lay preachers to preside was a principle of Primitive Methodism. The war did not appear very often in his diary. But he described how the Principal (the Rev. H. J. Pickett) assured his students in chapel on 4 September that the war was in a righteous cause. Later my father was often worried about the safety of his family and his fiancée whenever the Zeppelins raided Hull. To the anger of pacifist students, a recruiting officer, who was also a layman at the local Primitive Methodist chapel, was allowed by the Principal to visit the college and to talk to groups of students. By the end of 1915 nearly thirty had left – most of them to join the RAMC, but two or three to become combatants. In 1915 my father became a pacifist and remained a pacifist for the rest of his life. He was troubled that his fiancée did not agree with his pacifism, but was grateful that she promised to stand by him if ever his pacifism led him into conflict with the state. She had two brothers at the front. He was an only son. He refused to stand for the National Anthem at this period, which distressed and baffled her. Early in 1916 he and other pacifists in college were deeply worried by the government's measures for conscription. He met regularly with other members of the local branch of the Fellowship of Reconciliation (an inter-denominational pacifist organization formed in December 1914). It met at Dalton Hall (founded by Quakers) under the leadership of John Graham, its Principal. (Graham produced in 1922 *Conscription and Conscience*, a passionate, but one-sided account of the treatment of conscientious objectors during the war.[21]) 'Tonight', my father wrote in his diary, 'we had a Pacifist Prayer Meeting in Frank's den. [i.e. study] The cloud of compulsion is dark now, and our gathering strengthened us.' Because it was uncertain whether ordinands would be exempt from conscription, he wondered whether to stay in college or to appeal to a tribunal. However, in March they heard that those training for the ministry were exempt, and the Principal celebrated a special Communion of rededication. When my father, visiting his home in Hull, saw a Zeppelin raid, watched the searchlights and heard the guns, he felt his commitment to pacifism strengthened. In October 1916 he attended a series of lectures in Manchester given by Bertrand Russell on 'Social Reconstruction after the war'. The lecture on 30 October was raided by the police. (Russell had been deprived of his lectureship at Trinity College Cambridge in July after a conviction for prejudicing the recruitment and discipline of the forces).[22] A strong force of military and police arrived and examined the papers of all men who appeared to be of military age. The operation went off quietly apart from a small group which began to sing 'The Red Flag'. Five young men were arrested as deserters.[23]

In the diaries, religious and academic activities loomed much larger than the war. Each Sunday he summarized the sermons he preached, the atmosphere they created, and their length – forty, forty-five, even fifty minutes. Prayer meetings were still common after the evening service. At one such prayer meeting, after my father had preached, the chapel steward thanked God for 'the feeble efforts of thy young and inexperienced servant'. Visiting preachers were usually expected to give a lecture during their weekend engagement. As a student, my father lectured on such subjects as Browning, Tennyson, George Eliot, Christina Rosetti and Leonardo da Vinci. One Sunday afternoon he spoke to a Ladies Class on Isaiah as a political prophet. He compared Isaiah with those two politicians beloved of Nonconformity, Cromwell and Gladstone. In those days, chapel people expected to be provided not only with a weighty religious diet, but also to receive culture, education and political guidance through the chapel. Chapel religion was closely interwoven with, and expressed through, Victorian culture and the political ideology of Liberalism. So closely were they interwoven, that when Victorian culture and Liberalism both ebbed, Nonconformity never recovered.

The influence of Browning on the churches and chapels at the turn of the century is a revealing example of this interweaving of religion and culture. Several books, many of them by preachers (and much used by other preachers) were published about Browning's religious teaching. Some were based on lectures given to adult classes in churches and chapels. In addition, books about religion and literature often included a chapter on Browning – for example *The Theology of Modern Literature* (1899) by a Scottish Minister, the Rev. Dr S. Law

Wilson. The cult of Browning the thinker and religious guide was at its height between about 1890 and the mid-1920s.[24] William Temple, like Westcott, counted Browning as one of the three master influences on his thought, described 'A Death in the Desert' as the best commentary on the Fourth Gospel and regarded Browning as the greatest product of the nineteenth century. Hastings Rashdall, the Anglican theologian, considered Tennyson and Browning as two of the greatest theological teachers of their generation.

Why were the devout so attracted to Browning? Whereas they detested what they regarded as the pessimism, fatalism and sensuality of Hardy's novels, Browning's optimism and his celebration of married love were deeply reassuring for preachers, believers and seekers. The Rev. Dr John Hutton, Editor of the Free Church *British Weekly* from 1925–1946, wrote that Browning proved to be of the greatest value when 'something bitter has befallen us, and we are on the point of angrily blowing out our light. He is a real friend to any one who has been defeated, or who has been left behind in the race . . . When you would like "to curse God", Browning can break in upon your narrow passion, with a strong, hopeful word; and behold the narrow walls fall flat as did the walls of Jericho, and you see the things that compensate.'[25] A reviewer (quoted on an end-paper) described it as 'The kind of book to take up with confidence in Bible-class work'. Browning spoke to believers and searchers during this period because he gave expression to doubts which Christians would hardly have dared to articulate in their own strength. Because he seemed to wrestle with the doubts of the age he was able to speak authentically with the accents of hard-won faith. So Law Wilson asserted that more than anyone else Browning had helped to turn the tide back to religion and away from rationalism and scepticism. Browning's appeal to the heart and to the authority of personal experience was attractive to evangelicals, and his impatience with dogma and ecclesiasticism was congenial to romantics, platonists and liberal protestants. When simple appeals to biblical authority were being undermined by biblical criticism and science, preachers were grateful to be able to appeal to the writings of a contemporary figure whose importance was everywhere acknowledged. Browning's assurance that evil was only apparent and temporary was welcome news to all believers in progress. Optimistic preachers of the period often quoted such passages as this:

There shall never be one lost good! What was, shall live as before;
The evil is null, is nought, is silence implying sound;
What was good shall be good, with, for evil, so much good more;

On earth the broken arcs; in the heaven, a perfect round.

('Abt Vogler', ix)

To those struggling with doubt, Browning brought a release from guilt:

> With me, faith means perpetual unbelief
> Kept quiet like the snake 'neath Michael's foot
> Who stands calm just because he feels it writhe . . .
> No, when the fight begins within himself,
> A man's worth something . . .

('Bishop Blougram's Apology')

'Just when we are safest, there's a sunset touch' from the same poem was used by preachers to remind congregations of human insecurity. The Anglican symposium *Foundations* (1912) cited Browning no less than eighteen times. But if he was constantly quoted by Anglicans, Free Churchmen felt positively proprietorial towards him. R. F. Horton (Chairman of the Congregational Union in 1903) wrote that Browning's 'rejection of forms and externals in favour of the inner kernel of religion . . . untroubled by what the world says, or what as a matter of convention the world does' – this is the essence of Browning and dissent alike.[26]

Here was the paradox of dissent: a deep conviction that the true Christian must be a dissenter from the world, combined with a compulsive need to seek and win approval from the powerful and famous. Hugh Price Hughes in his presidential address to the first meeting of the National Council of Evangelical Free Churches in 1896 quoted this often cited and consolingly all-inclusive declaration from the one he called 'our own great Nonconformist poet'.[27]

> I say, the acknowledgment of God in Christ
> Accepted by the reason, solves for thee
> All questions in the earth and out of it . . .

('A Death in the Desert')

Since Browning's writings were thought to demand intellectual effort this quietened the consciences of puritans who could not justify literature as relaxation or entertainment. Law Wilson believed that Browning deepened belief in the divinity of Christ. Temple asserted that for Browning the incarnation was the climax of history. 'Browning's conception of heaven is very beautiful and encouraging' the *Wesleyan Methodist Magazine* told its readers in December 1882.

But Browning was also attractive to those who could not express their faith through allegiance to institutional Christianity. One of the leading Browningites, Dr Edward Berdoe, had trained for the dissenting ministry, lost his faith and been reconverted to Christianity by hearing a lecture on 'Paracelsus' at a Unitarian chapel. This led him not to attend chapel, but the meetings of the London Browning Society through which he expressed his veneration of the one he called his 'Master'. By 1887 nearly every meeting of the Society had become a pitched battle between believers and agnostics, both claiming Browning as their own.[28] The density of Browning's thought ensured that he could be construed by a wide variety of people as supporting their quite contradictory positions.[29]

During the First World War, even in the trenches and the officers' mess, Browning was avidly read. Bishop Stephen Neill writes that the poems which helped people most during the war were those like 'Abt Vogler' 'with their firm conviction that good must prevail, and that God is in charge'.[30] Towards the end of the war J. H. Shakespeare, Secretary of the Baptist Union, quoted these comforting words from the end of 'Paracelsus':[31]

> If I stoop
> Into a dark tremendous sea of cloud,
> It is but for a time; I press God's lamp
> Close to my breast – its splendour, soon or late,
> Will pierce the gloom: I shall emerge one day!

F. R. Leavis' dismissive judgment – 'Browning would have been less robust if he had been more sensitive and intelligent' – seems wholly just to many of my generation; 'the characteristic corrugation of his surface is merely superficial, and not the expression of a complex sensibility' he added.[32] Complexity, ambivalence and a suspicion of rhetoric were virtues for many in the post-1918 period, because they were convinced that millions had gone to their deaths deluded by the naive, romantic grandiloquence of the leaders of church and state.[33] But as early as 1881, Gerard Manley Hopkins had written about Browning:

> Now he has got a great deal of what came in with Kingsley and the Broad Church school, a way of talking (and making his people talk) with the air and spirit of a man bounding up from table with his mouth full of bread and cheese and saying that he meant to stand no blasted nonsense.[34]

Browning's combativeness, self-assurance, sweeping generalizations and emotional optimism had a particular appeal to rhetorical Free

Church preachers, who (as we shall see) engaged zestfully in organized campaigns of fervent denunciation which came to their climax in the hysterical diatribes against Germany voiced by those Nonconformists who were desperately anxious to prove their patriotism during the First World War.

The Nonconformist Conscience

Religious dissent has been politically influential during two periods of English history – the period of Cromwell (whose example was frequently evoked by nineteenth- and early twentieth-century Free Churchmen) and the period between the Reform Act of 1867 and the Franchise Act of 1918. The former Act opened the political system to organized pressures by groups like chapel-goers; the latter enfranchised the unskilled workers whose allegiance to the churches was particularly weak.[35]

The phenomenon known as the 'Nonconformist Conscience' has been subjected to a good deal of critical scrutiny by Free Churchmen in recent years. 'Was the conscience of Nonconformity chiefly a way of stating and fighting for social objectives, a form in fact, of social aggression rather than of outraged morality?' asks John Kent.[36] Henry Rack discusses Hugh Price Hughes' implicit decision to give the destruction of Parnell a higher priority than the support of Gladstone's efforts for an Irish settlement, Hughes' imperialism and his rabble-rousing campaigns against church schools (in which concern for education seemed to take second place to his desire to take a swipe at the established church). Rack concludes that the moral quality of the Nonconformist Conscience was 'poor and narrowly conceived'.[37] Nevertheless the Nonconformist Conscience did represent a deeper sensitivity to social need and an awareness (which had Anglican parallels) that voluntary effort was by itself inadequate to solve social problems. Thus the arch apostles of voluntaryism were pushed towards a more positive attitude to the state. D. W. Bebbington points out that the moral crusades of late Victorian and early twentieth-century Nonconformity were in a tradition which dated back to the anti-slavery campaigns. This tradition expressed itself in a great variety of campaigns in the nineteenth century – ranging from those against the toleration of idolatry in British India and against Sunday railway travel, to those against atrocities in Bulgaria and Armenia.

Inevitably the most effective way to whip up mass indignation was to present every issue in simple antitheses. So Hughes denounced the Irish Coercion Bill in the *Methodist Times* on 7 April 1887 in self-indulgent aggressive language modelled on the less desirable features of Old Testament prophecy. It was he said a religious controversy 'in which we must take part or sacrifice all claim to be thoroughgoing disciples of JESUS CHRIST . . . O that GOD would send some brave ELIJAH to awaken the national conscience! Shall we worship JEHOVAH OR BAAL?' Bebbington makes a number of telling criticisms of the methods adopted. The technique of mass indignation was quite unsuited to the aim of affecting the legislative processes at Westminster. Those running the campaigns were usually better at emotional denunciation than at suggesting carefully thought-out, practical alternative policies. Not more than one issue could be kept at white heat at any one time, so sometimes one issue was dropped when another appeared. No wonder that politicians soon learned that they could safely ride each storm as it arose or (as in the case of Lloyd George) manipulate it to their own advantage. To their own detriment, Nonconformists seemed perpetually cast in a negative role. 'Compromise was essential if Nonconformists were to gain the substance of their aims, but the whole inspiration for Nonconformist political effort was the belief that with unrighteous policies there could be no compromise. The resulting tension was a fatal flaw in the politics of the chapels.'[38]

Significantly, Nonconformist opinion over the Boer War was divided. Though the majority of Free Churchmen vigorously led by Hughes, supported the war, a notable (though fairly small) minority led by John Clifford, the Baptist campaigner for many causes, protested against it so noisily that it was widely believed that Nonconformist opinion was more hostile to the war than was actually the case. When Clifford's church was threatened by a mob which smashed the nearby Liberal and Radical Club, he wrote: 'I can enter into the heart-anguish of Jeremiah as I never could before.' Though 5,270 ministers signed a manifesto against the war it was expressed in vague and mild language. Clifford's 'Stop the War Committee' formed in January 1900, drawing on Quaker and socialist support, was a forerunner of many similar organizations in Britain in the twentieth century. Its moral absolutism was an authentic expression of the traditional campaigns of dissent.[39]

The divisions about the Boer War reflected the growing identification of an important section of Nonconformity with the moral argument for imperialism. Missionary societies believed that beneficent British imperialism enabled the gospel to be preached, and races still in their 'childhood' would be given the opportunity to mature under the benefits of Christian civilization. The radical change from the 1870s when Free Churchmen were among the most severe

critics of Empire, to the Edwardian period when the majority had
become moral imperialists, is another example of the way in which
Free Churchmen felt more and more able to assent to, rather than
dissent from, the norms of British society. This shift in opinion was
accompanied by the development of a version of the Nonconformist
Conscience for application to international affairs. Though Nonconformists remained lovers of peace, there were several campaigns
advocating British intervention when Christian minorities were
persecuted by Muslim powers. Atrocity stories similar to those circulated about the Germans in the First World War, seemed to justify
force because they enabled the enemy to be depicted as the enemy
of Christianity.[40] The Free Church Council in 1896 expressed its
unanimous detestation of Turkish treatment of Armenians in a
resolution proposed by Dr Charles Berry, the ex-President. The
seconder, Dr Bowman Stephenson, exclaimed 'Oh, for one hour of
Cromwell's might'. He argued that if the fleet could be used solely for
the righting of wrongs and the protection of life, the money spent on
it would be amply justified.[41]

If Nonconformists were divided about the Boer War, the Education
Act of 1902 (which gave financial assistance to church schools through
the rates) seemed to provide a traditional set of enemies against which
they could unite. (The Wesleyans, the most conservative of the
Methodist groups, however refused to commit themselves officially to
the cause.) The agitation against the Act known as Passive Resistance,
mobilized all the aggressive instincts of Nonconformity which always
came to the surface when it believed itself fighting for the weak against
the mighty. In the years up to 1914, thousands received summons for
refusing to pay rates; some were fined, others suffered distraint of
goods or imprisonment. It was exhilarating to fight a just war on behalf
of oppressed children against the forces of reaction represented by
peers, bishops and clergy (the latter usually called 'priests' to add a
dash of 'No Popery' to heighten the fervour). Clifford led the campaign.
'It seemed to take one back to the days of Bunyan, Baxter and Fox'
exulted his biographer. Clifford wrote in 1906: 'It is the eternal fight
between the intolerant and grasping holders of privilege and the
incalculable human soul that is at stake . . .'[42] He always travelled
third class to remind himself of his working class origins. With the
outbreak of the First World War, the movement virtually came to an
end, when after momentary but agonized hesitations, the majority of
Free Churchmen gave enthusiastic support to the war. So, like the
suffragettes and the Liberation Society (dedicated to the overthrow of
the Anglican establishment), Nonconformists abandoned dissent for

the sake of national unity. However, Clifford went on protesting against the Education Act, an isolated representative of a tradition of dissent that seemed increasingly anachronistic. In 1922, the year before he died, he appeared before the magistrates for the fifty-seventh time.

Passive Resistance was the last great battle of dissent. The movement had several important consequences. It kept alive the language of sweeping denunciation so that it was immediately to hand for use against the Kaiser and the Germans during the war. Paradoxically it also provided a recent model for the Free Church pacifists who used it to argue that defiance of the state was the traditional stance of dissent. Initially it cemented relations between the Free Churches and the Liberal Party. But, as Bebbington argues, various efforts by the Liberal Government to amend the 1902 Act came to nothing, largely because Free Church leaders found denunciation more congenial than the painstaking processes of negotiation that would have been necessary to produce a settlement. 'When nonconformity to present conditions and an aspiration to new and better things are not determined rationally nor translated into constant resolute action, they will be a devouring fever, not a life-giving warmth. Sterile turbulence, like a sluggish somnolence is a disease of the will.'[43] Nonconformists discovered to their chagrin that they possessed less leverage with the Liberals than they had imagined. As early as 1910 there was a steady seepage of Free Churchmen into the Labour and Conservative parties. Whereas the Free Church Council in 1906 openly ran campaigns in support of Liberal candidates, in 1910 its political activity was more muted. Passive Resistance gave Lloyd George his first opportunity to ally himself with radical Nonconformists and established him as someone (whom they supposed) they could trust, a position which he used to the full during the First World War when he unmercifully manipulated the often naive leaders of the Free Churches for his own ends.[44] 'Politics are one of the organs and instruments by which true Christians hasten the coming of the Kingdom of God' wrote Clifford in 1894.[45] But effective political action demanded a degree of sophistication that was beyond the capabilities and contrary to the moral tradition of dissent.

2

DISSENT AND THE
FIRST WORLD WAR

'Was the Edwardian period an era of successive crisis or a golden age?'
asks Professor Donald Read. Taking his clue from Philip Larkin's
poem 'MCMXIV', with its line 'never such innocence again', he
concludes that while it would be too sweeping to call it an age of
innocence, it was a period in which innocence could still be enjoyed,
even if it was being painfully disturbed.[1] Certainly there was a good
deal of innocent optimism about the prospects for peace among
Christians, particularly among those Free Churchmen who saw history
as a pageant of human progress. The various peace groups of the
period drew much of their support from the Free Churches, Quakers
and socialists. These societies were peace-loving rather than strictly
pacifist, though they included some pacifists.[2] Many Christians
preached the ideal of a new internationalism derived from missionary
expansion, moral imperialism and Christian and socialist visions of
world brotherhood. The adoption of arbitration by the nations was
surely the next stage in human progress towards a more rational and
brotherly world society organized on federal principles. So Hughes
urged arbitration for disputes, both international and industrial, at
the first National Council of Free Churches in 1896.[3] W. T. Stead,
Congregational layman and editor of the *Pall Mall Gazette* from 1883
to 1889, attained notoriety when in 1885, in order to publicize his
campaign against juvenile prostitution, he disguised himself as a
potential procurer, and went to prison. In 1898 he launched an
International Crusade of Peace and founded and edited a weekly with
the characteristically belligerent title of *War Against War*. He wrote
to Clifford in 1900: 'what we wish to do is to create a fertile propaganda
in favour of the principle of Arbitration, and to vindicate and popularise
the Hague Conference among the masses of the population who know
nothing at all about it.'[4] The Lambeth Conference of 1908, 'while
frankly acknowledging the moral gains sometimes won by war',

rejoiced in 'the growth of higher ethical perceptions which is evidenced by the increasing willingness to settle difficulties among nations by peaceful methods', and expressed its 'deep appreciation' of the work of the Hague conferences.[5] Free Churchmen wholeheartedly joined in the inter-denominational exchanges between German and British churchmen in 1908 and 1909 which resulted in the creation of 'The Associated Councils of Churches in the British and German Empires for Fostering Friendly Relations between the Two Peoples' in 1910.[6] Apart from the Anglo-German exchanges, there were few ecumenical contacts across the frontiers of Europe. On the other hand, the widely quoted watchword 'The Evangelization of the World in this Generation' (adopted by the Student Volunteer Movement in 1896), reflected the optimism of the churches about their prospects. But it was not until 2 August 1914, with the first meeting at Constance of what became known as the 'World Alliance for Promoting International Friendship through the Churches' that an enduring ecumenical organization was created which drew European churchmen together. Only half the delegates arrived. Those who managed to reach Constance had to disperse on 3 August as frontiers were closing. Clifford was only able to buy a German sausage and a piece of bread during the journey in a packed train from Constance to Cologne, and reached the frontier between Holland and Germany on 4 August.

Optimism about the prospects for peace among English Christians between the end of the Boer War and August 1914 was reflected in and promoted by the Anglo-German exchange visits, and by such books as *The Great Illusion* (1910) by Norman Angell, and *The Passing of War* (1912) by Canon W. L. Grane of the Church of England Peace League. The dominance of the incarnation in theology and the notion of progressive revelation both undergirded the belief that the human race was gradually climbing upwards to the point where all would accept that war was now an anachronism. In the months leading up to the war, the Free Churches became more fervent for peace than for twenty years. They felt buoyant because at last they seemed to be numerically equal in committed membership to the established church. They had also been immensely heartened by the Welsh Revival of 1904–5. One hundred and eighty Nonconformist MPs had been elected in 1906. Free Churchmen believed that the progress towards freedom and democracy in England was largely their own work. So we can only account for the *volte-face* of most Free Church leaders at the outbreak of war, if we see their pacific stance in the preceding decade or so as a temporary phenomenon. The militant temper adopted by most Free Churchmen in the early days of the war was a reversion to the belief that force was justified in the support of the weak and down-trodden. In the 1890s it was the Sultan and the Turks who were the object of Nonconformist aggressive crusades. From August 1914, the crusading temper of Nonconformity was turned against the Kaiser and Germany.

The outbreak of war

We now look more closely at Free Church attitudes to the outbreak of the First World War. The case of John Clifford is particularly instructive, because he represented the older dissenting tradition. In Emerson's essay on 'Self Reliance', given to him by his Sunday School teacher, he underlined the aphorism, 'Whoso would be a man must be a Nonconformist'. His faith was deeply nourished by the optimism of Browning, his favourite poet, and expressed itself in an evolutionary view of history in which the Free Churches represented the progressive forces in religion and politics. In 1911 he wrote: 'though progress, if viewed for the year and the day, seems unutterably slow, yet looked at in decades and even wider spaces, it is rejoicingly fast and solid'. But it was clear that progress could only be secured by a strenuous struggle with the forces of reaction. So he described the battle of 1910 with the House of Lords as 'Armageddon' and their powers of veto as 'murderous'.[7] Though he refused to stand for Parliament, his constant speaking from platforms influenced his preaching style, as happened with other Free Church leaders. In his boyhood, his father had bidden him emulate the Chartists whose battles had surrounded his youth. His New Year's message to his congregation in January 1914 was euphoric: 'A new era is coming nearer and nearer every year . . . Militarism belongs to the dark ages; it is not fit for our time. It must go. It is going. Priestism . . . is a waning force.' Nationalism and imperialism 'must broaden into internationalism and through that into brotherhood'.[8] Soon after the outbreak of war, he told his congregation that he had framed a letter for the press advocating neutrality, but when he read a newspaper at Holborn Viaduct on his return from Constance, he could not send it. 'War is anti-Christian', but this was a fight between 'the forces of freedom and those of slavery . . . The progress of humanity in my judgement hinges upon this war . . . We were forced into it.' There were murmurs of 'Hear. Hear' from every part of the chapel.[9] Soon after, he joined the jingoistic Bishop of London (Winnington Ingram) and others in contributing to a collection of essays entitled *Kaiser or Christ?*. On 11 September, together with representatives of the parties (Winston Churchill, F. E. Smith and Will Crooks), he addressed a great recruiting rally at the

London Opera House. Crooks (a Labour MP) declared that 'he would rather see every living soul blotted off the face of the earth than see the Kaiser supreme anywhere'. Clifford's entry was greeted with applause by the Tories who had hitherto regarded him as their foe. War is 'the Great Uniter' commented the *Baptist Times*.[10] To Baptists, including Clifford, the social and military establishment had been particularly antipathetic. Yet the Council of the Baptist Union asserted in September: 'We believe the call of God has come to Britain to spare neither blood nor treasure in the struggle to shatter a great anti-Christian attempt to destroy the fabric of Christian civilisation.' But it also called for national repentance, warned against a vengeful spirit, pleaded for a Christian treatment of aliens and gratefully recalled links with Christians in Austria and Germany. 'We rejoice that many of the young men of our Churches have dedicated themselves, with the consent of their parents, to the service of their country, and have been among the foremost to offer themselves for the defence of the liberties of Europe.'[11] We note that when so much that Baptists held dear was being swept away, deference to parents remained unshaken! Thus Baptist leaders, like those of other Free Churches, reacted to the crisis with a few distinctively Christian insights. But much of the Baptist statement was expressed in the hyperbolic political rhetoric which Free Churchmen had become accustomed to employ against those identified by the Nonconformist Conscience as enemies to be fought to the death.

Robertson Nicoll, editor from 1886–1923 of the *British Weekly*, the leading Free Church journal, had supported the Boer War and Passive Resistance. A minister of the Free Church of Scotland, he was recommended for a knighthood in 1909 by Asquith as a recognition of his services to literature and the Liberal Party. On 30 July 1914, the *British Weekly* argued that 'the quarrel in no way concerns us and we are fortunately unbound by any engagements that would require us to intervene . . . It is believed that the Kaiser is using his great influence on the side of peace.' But on 6 August under a banner headline, Nicoll declaimed 'United We Stand'. The Free Churches had worked for disarmament, but Sir Edward Grey's sober and lucid speech now demonstrated that there was no honourable course for Britain except war. Others may disagree, but only 'very grave reasons could justify the breaking of national unity when the nation is fighting for its life'. We love Germany, but she has changed and now wants to subjugate Europe. The Kaiser now resembles Napoleon. The nation must be united in a common sacrificial spirit, but must forswear jingoism. Already the war has united Britain and Ireland, Ulstermen and Catholics. Employers must be content to live on very little rather than dismiss employees. 'We must draw together as a family . . .' On 3 September Nicoll invoked the two of the most sacred names in the Nonconformist martyrology – Bunyan and Cromwell – in a leader headed 'Set Down My Name, Sir', a fervent appeal to Nonconformists to join the colours. (The title of the article evoked the incident in *Pilgrim's Progress* when 'a man of very stout contenance' asked for his name to be entered in the book, and then rushing upon the armed men, 'fell to cutting and hacking most fiercely'.) Cromwell was 'perhaps the greatest man of the English race'. 'It was Cromwell and his like who protected both culture and religion in the hour of their direst need.' He went on to laud both Kitchener and French and paid tribute to British soldiers ('the best in the world') as well as to 'our magnificent Navy'. Recruiting must be enthusiastically promoted (in this women must play their part) otherwise conscription will be necessary. The second part of the article recapitulated a paper commissioned from him by the War Office, explaining why young men, particularly Nonconformists, should volunteer. 'The war was thrust upon us' because we must be true to our sacred obligations. The Kaiser is a 'tyrant' whose whole life is a lie. We are fighting against him and against all who have been 'baptised into the same communion of corruption'. He is brutally arrogant, a war god whose 'egotism' is 'hardly compatible with sanity'. It is a war for the common people, for democracy, for our children, for 'our glorious Empire'. Robertson Nicoll thus established himself as the super-patriot of Nonconformity, the Free Church equivalent of Winnington Ingram.[12]

Dr Campbell Morgan was the leading expository preacher of the period, and Congregational minister at Westminster Chapel 1904–17, with a congregation of 2,500. On Sunday 2 August he prayed earnestly that if the nation could be only purged and redeemed by suffering, that God would grant 'a quietness and resignation of spirit that shall make us strong in the hour of our chastisement'. Applause (almost unknown in that chapel) broke out when he declared that anyone in Europe who wanted war was 'accursed'. A week later, he told his people that war was the result of man's wickedness, but that it could result in 'the renewal of moral consciousness and the re-birth of the soul'. He had preached peace for years, but not to have intervened would have disregarded 'the obligations of national morality'. The congregation broke into cheers. In other sermons at that time he said: 'Never again must a handful of men be able to speak the word that will involve the slaughter of millions'; he believed that 'the sign of the Cross is on every man that marches to his death', but reminded his congregation that our enemies are also our fellow-men. Yet this was the pacifist who would not even allow toy soldiers in the nursery. The strain of the war broke his health.[13]

Nonconformists felt that they could trust a Liberal Government, especially as it included Lloyd George. Surely, argued the *British Weekly* on 13 August, pacifists must have been convinced of the justice of the cause by the publication of the State Papers. The Rev. Thomas Phillips of Bloomsbury Baptist Church, a great admirer of Lloyd George, praised Nicoll's recruiting appeal in the letter columns on 10 September. He was proud that fifty of his 'young fellows' had enlisted. The Rev. S. F. Collier, Wesleyan minister at the Manchester and Salford Mission, reported that scores from the Mission had volunteered, including three of his own sons. Readers were informed that a Congregationalist football club was unable to play because eight of the team had volunteered. The *Methodist Times*, organ of Wesleyanism, edited by Scott Lidgett, founder of the Bermondsey Settlement, in a leader of 20 August expressed delight that so many Wesleyan Methodists had enlisted: 'those who bear the name of Wesley have always exhibited a loyalty to King and Country equal to that of their founder' it added proudly. Leyton Richards, a pacifist, was the Congregational minister at Bowdon Downs, near Manchester from 1914 to 1916. The church had 296 communicants. During the war, 160 men from chapel and institute served in the forces.[14] As one would expect, many Anglican clergy, particularly evangelicals, were also enthusiastic recruiting agents. The Rev. Arthur Sinker, evangelical vicar of St George's, Newcastle-under-Lyme, ran a league table for the streets of his parish to publicize those with the highest (and lowest) number of enrolments.[15]

Lloyd George played an important role in the manipulation of Free Church opinion towards whole-hearted support of the war effort. On 10 November 1914 three thousand Free Church people crowded into the City Temple, the 'cathedral' of Nonconformity, to hear him address a meeting organized by the National Free Church Council. His speech, said the *Manchester Guardian* was 'an appeal to Nonconformists to show their sympathy with the cause of justice and the small nationalities in the recruiting offices'. It reported that 60,000 Free Churchmen had already volunteered. The audience rose to cheer the leader of whom they were so proud, and frequently punctuated his speech with applause. He arrived with the Chief Whip and was flanked by Nonconformist leaders – Dr Scott Lidgett (Wesleyan), Dr John Clifford (Baptist) and the Rev. R. J. Campbell (Congregationalist). Robertson Nicoll declared from the chair: 'If we had not been

Christians, we should not have been in this War. It is Christ . . . Who has taught us to care for small nations and to protect the rights of the weak, over whom He has flung his shield . . . The devil would have counselled neutrality, but Christ has put His sword into our hands.'

Lloyd George showed that he knew instinctively how to twist a Nonconformist audience round his little finger. What a 'wrench' it was (he said) for him and for his hearers to be supporting war when they had detested militarism all their lives. He recalled addressing a meeting 'with my good friend Dr Clifford' against the Boer War. He paid tribute to the sufferings of genuine pacifists, but spoke with 'scalding scorn' about shirkers and cowards who were prepared to let others make the sacrifices. Biblical allusions laced his speech. Belgium was 'that little country bleeding on the roadside' (implying that Britain was the Good Samaritan). He thumped the pulpit cushion as he declared 'as the Lord liveth we had entered into no conspiracy against Germany . . . We are in the war from motives of purest chivalry to defend the weak.' He appealed for sacrifice, renunciation, self-denial. He quoted a French General who had described the Kaiser as having 'the soul of the devil'. 'Hear, Hear' greeted his claim that he had never read 'a saying of the Master's which would condemn a man for striking a blow for right, justice, or the protection of the weak . . . We are all looking forward to the time when swords shall be beaten into ploughshares . . .' The brave men who have died need not fear judgment, because it is our faith that 'sacrifice is ever the surest road to redemption.' (Cheers.) He reminded his audience of their own fight against persecution, quoted Cromwell and celebrated the voluntaryism of the army. To those who argued that war was never justified, he retorted that this was not the attitude of either their Puritan forefathers or of the Christian faith. Belgium was 'a poor little neighbour whose home was broken into by a hulking bully' (echoes of Luke 12.39 and Ahab's seizure of Naboth's vineyard). He so roused his audience by his scornful denunciations of Turkey, the traditional enemy of Free Churchmen, that there were cries of 'Let 'em have it'. Afterwards Nicoll was elated. He reported to the editor of the Tory *Spectator* (an Anglican) his relief that the demonstration 'showed a far more militant spirit in English Nonconformity than I had dared to hope for. No name was cheered louder and longer than the name of Lord Kitchener. Dr Clifford, our Grand Old Man, who was a keen pro-Boer, appeared as a Cromwell Ironside, taunting the shirkers and urging that the War should be pursued with our whole force and brought to an end as soon as possible.'[16]

Free Churchmen were proud to have an acknowledged Noncon-

formist in high office, and later celebrated him as the first Nonconformist Prime Minister. In 1906 it was Lloyd George who unveiled
the portrait of Clifford presented by the Baptist Union. My father
remembered hearing A. T. Guttery, the Primitive Methodist leader,
preach during the war about Lloyd George from II Samuel 5.10: 'And
David went on, and grew great, and the Lord God of hosts was with
him.' During 1915–16, Nicoll campaigned for Lloyd George to replace
Asquith as Prime Minister. In 1915, Lloyd George by his vehement
denunciations of intemperance as damaging to the war effort, by his
legislation to restrict the supply of alcohol and his enrolment of the
King's support for war-time abstinence, strengthened his hold on
Nonconformity and largely assuaged their wrath about the postpone-
ment of the disestablishment of the Welsh church. Ironically (in fact)
the King on doctor's orders continued to drink his normal amount of
alcohol, though in private. Lloyd George admitted to a colleague that
shortages of shells and ships were due, not to intemperance, but to
government mismanagement.[17] Some Anglicans disliked the use of
the war by temperance campaigners to further their ends, but there
were others like Sinker, evangelical vicar of St George's Newcastle-
under-Lyme, who saw a commitment to the King's Pledge as a
'sacrament, an outward and visible sign, that is, of an inward readiness
for self-sacrifice'. For prosperity had sapped the nation's virility, and
we were in danger of becoming 'a lesser breed than that of the men of
Waterloo'.[18]

Lloyd George knew how to flatter Free Church leaders. Sensing
their waning confidence, in 1917 he invited one hundred of them to
breakfast on 26 October. Clifford noted in his diary that they still
trusted him, but were afraid of the influence of Conservatives on him
and disapproved strongly of his acceptance of the scheme for state
purchase of the drink trade. They found him 'keen and bright, and as
usual, a master of strategy'. He reminded them that never before had
that room contained so many Nonconformists, insisted that the
majority of the War Cabinet were Nonconformists, and eulogized at
great length the contribution of Nonconformity to the war.[19] In
January 1918, Free Churchmen were suitably rewarded in the New
Year's Honours List.

But of course it was not only Nonconformists who dramatically
changed their minds at the outbreak of war. So did Gilbert Murray
and such Anglican neutralists as Bishop Edward Hicks of Lincoln and
Bishop John Percival of Hereford.[20] But the Church of England had
not been so identified in the public mind with peace movements as
had the Free Churches. Those who rejoiced to be called 'Noncon-

formist' and 'Dissenter' had thereby identified themselves as opponents of the religious and social establishment, however much they had become part of the Liberal establishment in recent years. The *volte-face* of the Free Churches was more comparable with that of Trade Union leaders. Keir Hardie's hopes for international socialism were shattered when most Labour supporters in both countries showed a more instinctive solidarity with nationalism than with the working class of Europe.

Primitive Methodism and the war

The attitudes of Primitive Methodism to the war have a special significance. With 206,000 members in 1910, it was larger than the United Methodist Church, but less than half the size of the Wesleyan Methodists. (The three bodies united in 1932.) The society of Primitive Methodists was created in 1812 as the result of expulsions by Wesleyans of those who had participated in revivalist camp meetings, which were suspected of religious excesses. Wesleyans, in the early nineteenth century, responded to charges of being subversive, by annual declarations of loyalty to the Crown. The Primitive Methodists' corybantic enthusiasm seemed liable to undermine all the efforts of Wesleyans to achieve recognition as loyal and reliable subjects. Thus Primitive Methodism was a dissenting body twice over. It is not therefore surprising that it produced more political radicals than the other Free Churches. Despite being one of the smaller churches, more Primitive Methodists went to prison for Passive Resistance between 1902 and 1907 than any other Nonconformists. Apart from the Quakers, Primitive Methodism up to 1914 thought itself the most pacifist or peace-loving of all the denominations. Yet by the end of the war it claimed that 150,000 of its men had joined the forces. Therefore the fact that the majority of Primitive Methodists supported the war is obviously of much greater significance than the support given to it by Wesleyans. That such a quintessentially dissenting group, proud of its working class origins, should so easily succumb to the prevailing pressures of the period, reveals the persuasive power which English society can exercise on various types of dissenter.

The career of the Rev. Arthur Thomas Guttery (1862–1920), the Primitive Methodist leader, was dominated by large scale campaigns which he described in grandiloquent language. So he told the Primitive Methodist Conference in June 1914 that he would not accept its Presidency because he would soon be involved in a campaign 'that would involve the changing of the face of rural England'![21] His father, also a Primitive Methodist minister, had once declared to applause: 'I derive my orders, as Paul did, straight from Christ, not from the fat palm of a bishop's hand.' Note here the identification of Nonconformity with St Paul's efforts to establish his right to be an apostle and also the implication that bishops lived lives of sensual ease ('fat palm'). A. T. Guttery was trained for the ministry on the job, not in a college. He was keenly aware that few, if any, Primitive Methodist ministers had achieved a national reputation and set himself to breaking that barrier. In his earlier days, Gladstone was his hero, and he lectured all over the country for the Liberal cause. The 'foe of all privilege' he 'hated landlordism and priestcraft, the drink traffic and the sweater'. He regarded himself as a prophet called by God to denounce abuses and to stir up a healthy discontent. 'I was born to declaim. Declamation is the breath of my nostrils.' Naturally he became a Passive Resister and was fined many times, though others paid his fines. Lloyd George (who wrote the preface to his biography) regarded him as one of the most gripping orators of the day, and the *Times* wrote of his ability to arouse and inflame an audience. But he was also a devoted minister. He declined invitations to stand for Parliament. He was President of the Primitive Methodist Conference 1916–17.[22] But some worried that he was liable to confuse the pulpit with the platform.[23]

In his New Year message for 1914 (printed in the *Primitive Methodist Leader* on 1 January) Guttery celebrated the progress achieved in 1913 with the rhetoric of the platform. The prestige of Islam has been shattered and is now open to 'victorious evangelism' by Christianity. The virtues of free trade are everywhere being recognized, militarism is abashed, science is ceasing to be materialistic. True, there is industrial unrest, but this is better than industrial stagnation. There is a new conscience towards the needy. 'Our audiences grow tired of wild appeals to hate the foreigner or insular pride.'

On Sunday 2 August 1914 Guttery gave a characteristically hyperemotional address in the Winter Gardens, Blackpool. The *Leader* reprinted it on its front page on 6 August under the headline 'The Madness of Europe'. We are being urged to 'wreck our commerce, endanger our Empire, and to abandon all our dreams of social progress that the Slav may conquer the Teuton and Russia may dominate the Continent . . .It is the policy of Bedlam and it is the statecraft of hell.' We must not be deceived by the 'loathsome press' which is used by armament manufacturers to increase their dividends. How could we ally ourselves with Russia 'the most barbarous and selfish of the Great Powers' against Germany that 'great Protestant nation which is nearest to us in blood and faith and all the ideals of human progress?' The duty of the church is plain – brotherhood and peace. We must 'refuse

to share an international infamy', and be neutral. A week later in the
Leader, under the significant headline 'The Duty of the Empire',
Guttery was beginning to employ the same type of rhetoric in support
of the war. Teutonic civilization is preferable to that of the Slav, but
we cannot stand aside when small nationalities are crushed to powder.
The 'defeat of the Kaiser's ambition is the first step to securing the
peace and progress of mankind'. The nation is now united in its duty
to Belgium. The English government strove for peace to the last
moment. We must curb our passions and 'have faith in our imperial
resources'. Fortunately our servicemen are volunteers and Britain is
not 'cursed by the servility of conscription'. We must pray and regain
the faith and, if need be, 'the fanaticism of our Puritan sires', together
with the Ironsides' conviction of God's presence. Autocrats are
doomed by the advance of democracy and socialism. The government
now controls the economy, a responsibility which must never be
returned to private enterprise.

On 3 September he charged Germany with Napoleonism. But
Britain must be 'loyal to the meek and lowly Nazarene'. By 17
September he was 'thrilled' by the British victories: 'the smashing of
Prussian militarism will be the redemption of the German people'.
'Amazing Conversions' a week later was not a celebration of an
evangelistic campaign, but about the ways in which the war was
turning attitudes upside down. A Liberal government promotes war
on the continent. Lloyd George becomes 'an evangelist of war'. Belfast
is peaceful. Party feuds are forgotten. A united nation is resolved to
'smash pan-Germanism in the dust'. Labour, with a few exceptions is
enthusiastic for the war. The churches, especially the Free Churches,
are united in approval. On 8 October Guttery published a rabble-
rousing polemic against the Kaiser entitled 'The Balaam of Berlin'.
'His ideal is that of the swaggering, brutal and lustful super-man who
will tread opposition to powder and sweep the poor and feeble from
his path. His memory is covered in blood . . .' On 22 October he
praised Sir John French for both his military achievements and his
sense of humour. On 5 November he declared that the Kaiser was not
only mad, 'the poor victim of a tainted ancestry', but also a lover of
Romanism and a would-be-prophet for Islam. On 10 December he
replied to those who criticized him for his abrupt change. 'I believed
a world-war was impossible two thousand years after Bethlehem.' But
he never dreamt that 'an imperial lunatic could upset the world by his
madness' and that a great nation would follow him. War is still hateful,
but now he honours 'the daring and devotion of our gallant lads, who
have gone to battle with no lust for blood'. He still believes in 'the

final victory of Christmas over Corsica'.[24] On Christmas Eve, after the bombardment of the north-east coast, Guttery decided that the Kaiser should be tried. If found mad, he should be confined. If not, he should be hung. On 18 March 1915 he called for prohibition in war-time and gleefully quoted Lloyd George on the sapping of the war effort by alcohol. On 25 November he celebrated 'The Glory of our Empire' with its 'sublimely unselfish' care of other peoples. The war had 'forced imperial thinking upon us', he declared.

At a public meeting associated with the 1915 Conference (reported 1 July), Guttery appealed again to all the powerful stored-up emotions surrounding the Protestant and Nonconformist heroes of the sixteenth and seventeenth centuries: 'our fathers suffered at Smithfield . . . and slew the Stuart Kaiser at Naseby and Marston Moor'. At the end of his speech, he shouted like a Primitive Methodist version of Henry V: 'God save England! God save the King'. The audience spontaneously rose to its feet and sang the National Anthem. (This identification of the Kaiser with Charles I, is a remarkable example of the way in which many Nonconformists reconciled their consciences to the support of the war, by interpreting it as a re-run of their struggles in the seventeenth century.) On 9 March 1916 he asserted that God had delivered Britain at Gallipoli and Mons, as the Puritans had been defended by the celestial host at Edge Hill.[25] In other articles in the *Leader* early that year he wrestled with the likelihood of conscription, which if introduced would (he believed) be a moral defeat for the nation whose greatness was founded on the voluntary principle. But by 18 May he had completely capitulated: 'Compulsion is a hateful thing, but the temple of British freedom is not going to fall because we accept the Government verdict as to its immediate necessity.' He attacked those who used the conscience clause to 'screen cowardice', but a week later argued that the clause made conscription just acceptable and criticized the conduct of some tribunals as scandalous. 'To save Belgium is a sacred task, but it must not involve the shooting of Quakers.'

When Scott and his companions were found dead in the Antarctic, Guttery wrote an article 'We Glory in our Dead' in the *Leader* for 20 February 1913. 'All Britain has been thrilled . . . Progress still demands its price . . . sacrifice is imperative if the greater victories are to be won.' England paid tribute to those dead heroes of the South Pole with that interweaving of images from the world of chivalry with those of Christian self-sacrifice which were often employed to describe the deaths of the soldiers in the First World War.[26] So Guttery, as President, in June 1916 conducted a Conference memorial service, for

Primitive Methodists killed in battle. He reassured his congregation that such an unprecedented occasion was completely congruent with the Nonconformist devotion to the cross and Christian teaching about self-sacrifice:

> We need to tread a path that we have never trodden before . . . the way of the Cross, but by another route to that by which our fathers came . . . in this service we see death robbed of all shame and defeat . . . They died, thank God! not because their bodies were wasted with sin, nor enfeebled with self-indulgence; they did not even pay the inevitable price of mortality. They died under oath, willing captives of a great ideal . . . Sacrifice! Sacrament! Cross! I think of a home in Warrington – six sons, four killed, the fifth wounded . . . These boys of ours shall not die in vain . . . We keep them on our rolls of honour. Never let them get dusty or be forgotten! . . . We mourn, but we are proud in our grief. Never before have we thought of the Army as we think of it now. Never before have we had captains and chaplains of the Army with us. Those who have died have consecrated the Army in our thinking. Let us go with them the way of the Cross![27]

We see here the same unthinking patriotism, the same idealization of young soldiers, the same identification of their deaths with the sacrifice of Christ, the same appeal to touching anecdote that characterized the war-time utterances of Bishop Winnington Ingram. In 1918, Guttery, that fierce opponent of priestcraft, travelled with the Anglo-Catholic Bishop Gore to the States. There Guttery promoted the war as a moral crusade and was awarded the honorary degree of Doctor of Divinity. Guttery's nomination as President of the Free Church Council that year was greeted with loud applause. 'I used to be an extremist', he joked, 'Dr Meyer knows how to deal with extremists – move them to the chair.'[28] Those who attended the Conference memorial service in 1918 were told that the 15,000 of their number who had been killed had 'given themselves for England and humanity, and . . . are now assembled as God's happy warriors on the Plains of Peace, clothed in the white robes of immortality'. They died believing the faith they had learnt at Sunday School and expressed by Rupert Brooke before he died.[29]

If the columns of the *Leader* are a reliable guide, the majority of Primitive Methodists found Guttery's patriotic fervour congenial, though a minority disapproved of his more outrageous language, and a small minority dissented from the war altogether. An editorial on 20 August 1914 regretted that there were no Primitive Methodist chaplains, but on 8 October the *Leader* reported that the War Office was now prepared to allow Primitive Methodists to register as a separate religious group. Various writers exhorted them to be more visible in the forces. A correspondent from the Cowley Barracks suggested on 1 October that perhaps Primitive Methodist servicemen should wear a small badge so that they could recognize one another. Regularly ministers and chapel officials celebrated the numbers of their men who were enlisting. On 8 October a 'Roll of Honour' was advertised by the Primitive Methodist Bookroom subtitled 'For King, Country and Humanity'; the form ended with this patriotic jingle:

> Not once or twice in our fair island-story
> The path of duty was the way to glory.

Also advertised was a book entitled *My Friends the French* – yet before August 1914 France represented all that dissenters most detested. A layman wrote an article on 12 November lauding the new alliance with the forces: 'The Territorials are thoroughly welcome at our church. In fact, we are proud to have them.' The Bookroom offered 'British Military Prints' on 10 December as a suitable present for Christmas. On 31 December the first of a series of articles 'Early Methodists as Soldiers' pointed out that whereas few Primitive Methodists had been soldiers in the past (because they had taken the 'Quaker attitude' to war), John Wesley offered the help of Methodists to fight against the papacy. On 25 November 1915, an officiating minister for the forces welcomed the creation of the United Board for chaplains from all the Free Churches. The soldier was not the 'lewd and loose creature we once thought him to be'; he is now our son, our former Sunday School scholar. In the same issue the Bookroom offered for sale *Some Chaplains in Khaki*, which included accounts of Primitive Methodist chaplains.

Many Nonconformists interpreted the war in such a way that it fitted into their understanding of history as a great and irresistible march of the people towards freedom, democracy and the Kingdom of God on earth. So a letter-writer in the *Leader* for 13 August 1914 viewed the outbreak of war as a disappointing set-back to, not a refutation of, the hope of progress towards international peace. War will become progressively more difficult to wage because the working classes will refuse to be pawns of emperors and diplomats; because the increasing resort to arbitration is part of the divine process; because war does not gratify the lust for strife as it once did, now that it is fought with machines. In that issue the Rev. William Younger portrayed the war as 'the representative conflict of autocracy and democracy'. But the German oligarchy will be defeated. 'Out of this unprecedented European war we may hope that a new seriousness will be born, and an opportunity given for the triumph of Leo Tolstoy and Norman Angell, but still more for the advance of the Kingdom of God.' On 10 September he argued that the Prussian military aristocracy regarded God as a kind of Turkish Sultan, heedless of right and wrong. We can rely on the intervention of God on our side because we are fighting for the solemnity of the pledged word on behalf of small nations. 'The great struggle against the Stuarts is an undying inspiration.' In a front page article on 27 August another minister compared the Kaiser with both the Stuarts. As an arbitrary monarch, the Kaiser had committed his people to war without their consent. On 12 November a letter-writer claimed that God had helped the Puritans to save Protestantism; 'our brave fellows at the front' were doing the same. A fortnight later a correspondent pointed out that the Puritans had struck down Charles I without a moment's hesitation. The Kaiser was much worse. 'If the Hohenzollerns were hanged on a gallows high as Haman no eye would pity them.'

Fortunately a minority in the pages of the *Leader* rejected such blood-thirsty patriotism. On 24 September 1914 'Pax' said that he preferred to stay at home because the churches had been turned into adjuncts to recruiting offices and pulpits had become platforms for announcing the latest war news. But there were surprisingly few letters criticizing the regular articles by Guttery. However, on 1 October a letter attacked Guttery for failing to grasp that both the nation and the Primitive Methodist church were divided about the war. Another tartly commented: 'The day of the tribal god is past, save in the pages of some of the religious weeklies.' A letter on 22 October protested against the sale of forms for Rolls of Honour by the Primitive Methodist Bookroom. This was a slur on our conscientious objectors. On 5 November a contributor to the series of letters for and against Rolls of Honour said that it was 'utterly un-Christian' for the church 'to talk so loudly about "honour" and "glory" in connection with a barbarous, bloody murder-dealing war'. The most eloquent and notable protester in these first few months of the war was Victor Murray whose 1500 word letter was published on 10 December. (Murray was a Primitive Methodist undergraduate at Magdalen College Oxford, and a member of the World Student Christian Federation; he was President of Cheshunt College, Cambridge 1945–59.) 'Has the whole church gone mad?' he asked. A year ago we heard sermons on atonement, forgiveness, love; now all this is shelved for national unity. 'The unity of opinion of Church and State is not our glory but our shame.' He had looked in vain for some expressions of doubt and dissent in the *Leader*. We have postponed the hope of 'a better way' and talk instead of an 'interim ethic'. We have surrendered the gospel and thrown in our lot with politicians and diplomats. Which is our primary loyalty – the preservation of the Empire, or the survival of the international fellowship of the church? Can we really draw a parallel between the sacrifice of Christ and the death of soldiers as in the picture 'The Great Sacrifice'?[30] 'Was there no way of helping Belgium other than war?' It is significant that this lengthy, passionate protest received comparatively little support in the *Leader*. Next week three correspondents wrote in. One told Murray that he ought to be in the trenches. Another regarded his letter as an affront to 'our brave men'. We ought to be praying that God would help us as he helped Moses to defeat the Amalekites. Only one correspondent supported him. But in subsequent issues other letters showed that he had given voice to a tradition of dissent which felt it had been submerged.

Another notable dissenter was A. S. Peake. In two agonized articles on 13 and 20 April 1916, he reminded his readers that the conflict was not simply between Christians and Mohammedans, or between Catholics and Protestants, but between Catholic and Catholics, Protestants and Protestants, Orthodox and Orthodox. (Peake's argument was directed against those Christians who tried to evade the scandal of this inter-Christian war by justifying it as a renewal of the Wars of Religion; some Nonconformists portrayed it as a conflict with State religion, some Evangelicals as a conflict with rotten German liberal theology, some Anglo-Catholics as a conflict with Lutheranism.)[31] 'Unity of belief has not availed to withhold the nations from deadly strife.' However, Peake accepted the analysis popular at the time (and given currency by Professor Cramb)[32] that Germany had absorbed the ideas of Nietzsche, Treitschke and von Bernhardi and therefore had chosen Napoleon and Odin instead of Christ. Britain has never taken the power of ideas seriously enough. Recognizing that the pacifists had a powerful case, he nevertheless believed that Britain was engaged in 'international policemanship on a colossal scale'. Pacifists must not act as though they had a monopoly of morality or fearless thought, and he appealed to them to be less pugnacious. The pacifist preacher should show that he respects other views, eschew a controversial manner and show tenderness to those who are bereaved or have 'dear ones' at the front. Visiting preachers should not preach about the war. Sermons supporting the war should be less frequent. It should figure more largely in prayers than in sermons. In his second article he appealed to the churches, especially the Free Churches, to respect the supremacy of conscience. He condemned those who spoke with hatred of the Germans. We must remember how much they have contributed to the world. Though we must fight to liberate the demoniac, we must curb our tongues 'when we are tempted to wild talk of smashing Germany'.[33]

In the *Leader* there was some discussion of conscientious objection, but rather less than one might expect. On 19 November 1914 a letter-writer asserted that he had been addressing meetings up and down the country, but had never met a genuine CO, but only those who objected for selfish reasons. On 30 March 1916 another protested against the failure of the Free Church Council meeting at Bradford to support the COs, and some similar letters appeared in the following weeks. A leader of 18 May argued that the Free Churches ought particularly to stand up for COs, a theme echoed in correspondence in that issue. Stories of the ill-treatment of COs by the authorities reactivated the Nonconformist memories of past persecution by the state. But ironically, those Nonconformists who wholeheartedly supported the war also justified their stance in part by evoking the image of another oppressed and powerless victim, namely Belgium. On 25 May 1916 the *Leader* published a letter defending the rights of the COs signed by an impressive list of church leaders including John Clifford, A. E. Garvie, Scott Holland, the Bishop of Lincoln, the Dean of Worcester, W. E. Orchard, A. S. Peake and P. B. Meyer.

On 8 October 1914, R. F. Wearmouth, a minister and former soldier (in later life a well-known church historian), wrote to say that he had tried to enlist, but had been turned down. The question as to whether clergy should enlist as combatants – a few did – was regularly debated during the war, particularly in the light of the conscription of the French clergy.[34] A local preacher at the Liverpool church where Guttery was minister, argued in a letter of 22 October 1914 that ministers should be allowed to join the forces; they would do more good than chaplains who were set apart. On 1 November 1916 a vicar from the Yorkshire coalfields pleaded in the *Yorkshire Post* for bishops to give permission for clergy to volunteer. He said that when miners and other workers were approached about the National Mission, they retorted that they would not listen until the clergy did their part in the war effort.

Christians desperately wanted to believe that good was coming out of the war, and particularly that it was reviving churchgoing and faith.[35] 'The war has had a bad effect upon atheistic propaganda' wrote a correspondent in the inter-denominational *Christian World* on 26 November 1914. 'While the "Free-thought" crowd is thinning, the churches are filling as they have not been filled for years.' So too we read in the *Leader* for 27 August: 'The war is making men already turn their thoughts Godward . . . Men are driven from frivolity and sport to face realities, and behind everything to realise the great reality.' On 12 November a contributor asked 'Are the Churches Useless in War-Time?' No, he answered, for they care for the needy and the bereaved. Free church soldiers are putting into practice the gospel of self-sacrifice which we have preached. Many also pointed to the way in which the war was drawing the churches together and breaking down old barriers. On 3 September it was reported that 3,000 had attended a united service of Anglicans and Free Churchmen at Stoke. 'The Bishop (Dr Kempthorne) was there; how free, brotherly, genial he was in the ante-room – no side, no pomp, a man first, a Bishop afterwards!' (Note here the characteristic Free Church delight at being noticed by the establishment and a typical assertion of the belief that what matters about a person is a democratic human warmth not the office he holds.) Free Churchmen also rejoiced that the war was promoting the temperance cause. Russia leads the world with prohibition. When will Britain follow its example? asked the leader writer on 29 October.

Free Church chaplains

Most of the regiments in Cromwell's Model Army had their own chaplains, but their descendents were much less well provided for. It was not until 1915 that all Free Churchmen were granted their own chaplains. During the nineteenth century the Free Churches began to gain recognition from the military authorities. In 1827 English Presbyterian chaplains were employed for the first time. (In 1836 the position of Roman Catholic chaplains was regularized.) In the early nineteenth century Wesleyans had to struggle for the right of their soldiers to worship according to their conscience. But in 1881 Wesleyan chaplains began to be paid on the same basis as others. However, the situation was complicated by the fact that many Nonconformists were strongly opposed to providing ministers for these and other state-paid chaplaincies, for example those in workhouses. They were afraid (with some justice) that if they were to accept payment from the state, this compromise of the principle of voluntaryism in religion would lead to a loss of liberty for chaplains. The Rev. O. S. Watkins, a Wesleyan chaplain (who served in both the Boer and the Great Wars), was still campaigning in 1906 for an improvement in the status of Wesleyan chaplains in his book *Soldiers and Preachers Too: Being the Romantic Story of Methodism in the British Army*. The *Methodist Times*, however, on 22 October 1914 was able to congratulate him on being mentioned in Sir John French's despatches.

When in 1914 thousands of Nonconformists joined the colours, there were only Presbyterians and Wesleyan chaplains to minister to them. Lloyd George supported representations from the Free Church Council that chaplains for other denominations should be appointed. This was effected by the creation of the United Board in 1915 which covered Baptists, Congregationalists, Primitive Methodists and United Methodists. The Rev. J. H. Shakespeare, Secretary of the Baptist Union, was its first chairman. Nonconformist servicemen could now also register under their own denominational allegiance without suffering the indignity of having their church dismissed as a 'fancy religion' or being set down as 'C of E'. The new status granted to Free Churchmen in the forces was indicated by the week's visit which the President of the Free Church Council spent with the Grand Fleet in 1918. By Armistice Day, there were 3,475 army chaplains of whom 1,985 were Anglicans, 649 Roman Catholics, 302 Presbyterians, 256 Wesleyans and 251 United Board.[36] In January 1918 Shakespeare complained that a disproportionate number of decorations were being awarded to Anglican chaplains. As a result a supplementary list was issued.[37] Who would have predicted before the war that dissenters would be petitioning for more honours from the military establishment?

It is only in recent years that the heroism, devotion and agonizing perplexities of the first war chaplains have begun to be sympathetically treated after years of habitual scorn.[38] O. S. Watkins, the veteran Wesleyan chaplain, movingly described one aspect of the ministry of the chaplains during the Retreat from Mons:

> We could hold no Services but none the less the chaplains were busy about their Master's business. To them no service was too menial, no task ever came amiss. They washed the swollen, filthy feet of the footsore infantry; the white-haired Bickerstaffe-Drew [the Roman Catholic Chaplain], on bended knees, swabbed up the blood-stained floor of a dressing station; they helped the doctors with the wounded, lent a hand to carry a stretcher, rode ahead to choose bivouac or billets, and then guided the unit to its place of rest. These were the things which brought us close to our men and opened their hearts to us so that we could minister to their spiritual needs. But most precious and most sacred was the service rendered to the dying, and when the end came, the last sad office to the dead.[39]

But the eight books I have discovered written about or by Free Church chaplains, though often poignant and vivid, hardly give any hint of the severe theological and ethical struggles with the experience of war which dominated the writings of such Anglican chaplains as Studdert Kennedy, Tom Pym, Geoffrey Gordon, Oswin Creighton and F. R. Barry.[40] Perhaps other Free Church material will come to light to redress the balance. Perhaps Free Church chaplains agonized in private rather than on paper. Were Free Church chaplains more deferential than some Anglicans to military authority and propaganda? Were they perhaps apprehensive that if they published anything too critical about the war their hard-won opportunity to minister would be jeopardized? Four out of the five Anglican chaplains I have instanced were educated at public school and Oxford or Cambridge, and two were sons of bishops. Did their background give them a degree of ease with the powers-that-be which made them less deferential and therefore enabled them to be more critical towards authority both human and divine? Certainly those Anglican chaplains who were disciples of the conservative evangelical Chaplain-General (Bishop Taylor Smith) were usually unquestioning about the war and believed that their ministry was primarily concerned with individual conversions. But the five Anglican chaplains I have mentioned found the war such a searing experience partly because they refused to confine their ministries to the committed and therefore were forced to ask radical questions as to what the 'gospel' might be for womanizing, drinking soldiers who had no time for organized religion, but who unconsciously seemed to follow an *incognito* Christ in their acts of compassion, and who bore witness to an unacknowledged resurrection by their irrepressible humour. The depth of human suffering forced these chaplains to ask radical questions about the character and purpose of God himself.

O. S. Watkins's book, *With French in France and Flanders* (1915), originally articles in the *Methodist Recorder*, is sober, vivid and mercifully free from jingoism and pietistic moralizing. But there is hardly a sign that the war raised deep questions in his mind and heart. *Some Chaplains in Khaki* (1915) by Frederic C. Spurr is by contrast written in the style of a missionary yarn or of an evangelistic campaign report. Spurr, a Baptist minister who had been a missioner on behalf of the Free Church Council before the war, and became its president in 1923, visited France to write this account of the work of the chaplains of the United Board. He and Shakespeare (who wrote the preface) celebrated the new recognition given to Free Church chaplains and soldiers by the War Office and the military authorities and the fact that the size and importance of the Free Churches at home and abroad was thus being acknowledged at last. Shakespeare characteristically saw the mutual co-operation of Free Church chaplains as a foreshadowing of the united Free Church so dear to his heart. Spurr told a story to indicate how the war was proving the validity of Free Church ministries. A Free Church chaplain, in the absence of a priest, pressed a crucifix to the lips of a dying Roman Catholic soldier and assured him of Christ's absolution. 'What priest of the faith of that dying lad would dare to challenge the validity of his Free Church brother's pronouncement of the Divine Absolution in that supreme moment?' Secondly, Spurr believed that a genuine religious revival was happening at the front and told many conversion stories. 'Ministers and missionaries, deacons and students are carrying the rifle, and as they go preach the unsearchable riches of Christ. On their faces is a settled happiness because in their hearts burns a pure zeal for God.' He tells of a Salvation Army Officer, now a gunner, who 'where the ground is stained and steel tubes spit fire . . . preaches the glorious Gospel'. Trench life is bringing men to God, 'straightening out crooked lives, making better men of them, awakening their souls to higher things'. Hundreds are taking the King's Pledge, though the temptations of gambling, drink, prize fights and impurity are an ever present menace. Hymns evoke poignant memories of home. Many men 'enjoyed' Holy Communion for the first time. Thirdly, he presents the conflict in simple jingoistic terms. British soldiers are brave and full of humour; Germans are cowards and so arouse contempt. The soul of the nation and the empire has been rediscovered. When a soldier who had sung in the *Messiah* and in *Elijah* at home wondered how he could fire on Germans as though they were vermin, he reflected that they were not individuals but representatives of a nation. Vandalized churches and outraged women and children convince the ordinary soldiers that they are indeed engaged in a 'holy war'. *Souls in Khaki* (how significantly disembodied is that image of the soldier), by A. E. Copping (1917) includes a preface from General Bramwell Booth of the Salvation Army in which he declared that many soldiers would return with a new sense of the supernatural. The tone of the book can be gauged from such sub-titles as 'Death-bed rapture' and 'Unselfish Crusaders meet'.[41] There was of course a long, well-established evangelical tradition of exploiting catastrophe to hearten the faithful and to convert the impious.

By contrast a Free Church chaplain who had been at the front for two years told the Free Church Council in 1918 that 'war is not likely to produce revival among our boys'. A regular boxing referee, he spoke with (what the reporter termed) 'daring frankness' about the soldiers' defects, particularly profane swearing. Should we ban cards and place even dominoes on the moral margin? he asked. 'After the war we must candidly revise our judgements about all wholesome pleasures for young people.'[42] Such debates about ethically trivial matters astonished and alienated those at the front. The soldiers themselves were much more aware of the irony, ambiguity, tragedy and farce of the war than churchmen moralizing away at home. A sergeant in Anthony Eden's company wrote home to his mother: 'This is what struck me as being very funny. You hear Whizz! – Bang! – Cuckoo! The birds sing all the time the shells are bursting – it is really astonishing. The nightingales sing when the machine-guns are firing during the night.'[43]

Free Church patriotism

Why were the majority of Free Churchmen, including the majority of the ultra dissenting Primitive Methodists, so easily swept along by the general surge of patriotic fervour? What had happened to their so recent professions of pacific internationalism?

The 'rape of little Belgium' had a particular appeal to Nonconformists and Lloyd George. He often fired Nonconformists' imaginations with memories of having been oppressed by the powerful. They had fought hard for the humble and meek chapels of Wales and succeeded, as war broke out, in putting down the mighty Anglicans from their seat as the established church there. Until 1916 recruitment was on a voluntary basis and this appealed to the Free Church belief in free individual moral choice. When conscription came, many Free Churchmen accepted it only with reluctance, though a few like Nicoll had been advocating it for some time. Clifford strongly opposed it as a betrayal of freedom. A Baptist historian comments: 'Idealism seemed faced with a sad choice: on the one hand, to make ineffectual protest; on the other, to bow to the grim realities of power and conflict. Either way, it spelled the end of that Nonconformist idealism which believed that politics in this world could and should be directed by clear moral choices.'[44] Ironically it was Asquith, brought up as a Congregationalist, who introduced conscription.

Free Church faith concentrated upon the atoning power of the cross, as did the faith and eucharistic language of other traditions. So there was a potent (and dangerous) source of sacrificial imagery available for Christians to use (intertwined with pre-Raphaelite and Tennysonian imagery of chivalry) to idealize the soldiers' deaths and justify the ways of God to men. We should remember the all-pervasive influence of such popular hymns as 'Onward Christian Soldiers',

'Fight the good fight' or this by William Cowper which was a favourite among Nonconformists:

There is a fountain filled with blood
Drawn from Immanuel's veins;
And sinners, plunged beneath that flood,
Lose all their guilty stains.

Hymns like these, when sung at home or at the front in war time, took on a new patriotic meaning. Fr William Doyle, the Irish Jesuit chaplain, killed in 1917, had from his novitiate prayed for a martyr's death for which he prepared by waging what he called a 'relentless war' against his own will. He toughened himself by devising mortifications. On one occasion he made a discipline of razor blades with which he scourged himself until he stood in a pool of blood. He taught his soldiers to unite their sufferings with those of Jesus through the sacrificial rite of the Mass. He believed that 'the God of Battles', though not indifferent to the suffering, was 'scourging the world' through the war.[45] Fr Doyle's use of the imagery of atonement, mortification and martyrdom can be paralleled from the utterances of Christians of other traditions who used this imagery to nerve the nation not only to accept, but also to glorify the slaughter. An old boy of Mill Hill Congregational public school, a son of the manse, wrote from the forces to his parents in 1917: 'I am setting out on a crusade . . . We've been carried up to the Calvary of the world, when it is expedient that a few men should suffer that all the generations to come should be better' – echoing John 18.14.[46] Edmund Gosse, the author of that mordant study of Evangelicalism, *Father and Son* (1907), wrote in the *Edinburgh Review* for October 1914: 'War is the great scavenger of thought. It is the sovereign disinfectant, and its red stream of blood is the Condy's Fluid which cleans out the stagnant pools and clotted channels of the intellect.' This astonishing statement was obviously influenced by neo-Darwinism, passages in Ruskin's writings praising war as a cleansing and revivifying experience,[47] atonement theology, and texts such as Hebrews 9.22 – 'without shedding of blood is no remission' – a text which haunted such diverse figures as Hensley Henson[48] and the hero of H. G. Wells' popular novel, *Mr Britling Sees It Through* (1916). Horatio Bottomley, the editor of *John Bull*, who used the war to feather his own nest, often employed the type of patriotic rhetoric with biblical undertones which proved so popular. Like Guttery, Lloyd George and Winnington Ingram and many others, Bottomley used atonement imagery to sanctify the killing: 'Every hero of this war who has fallen on the field of battle has performed an Act of Greatest Love, so penetrating and intense in its purifying character that I do not hesitate to express my opinion that any and every past sin is automatically wiped out from the record of his life.'[49]

'Nonconformity needs to be told very plainly that its place in English life will be lost if it fails to play its part in this War' wrote Nicoll in 1915.[50] By 1910 the Free Churches believed that they had attained parity in communicant numbers with the Church of England. But what was to be the strategy for the future? They could continue to demand a more and more influential place in the establishment – but even though the establishment was now rendered morally more acceptable by the dominance of the Liberals, the Free Churches would lose their *raison d'etre* as dissenters if they became neo-Anglicans. Or should they try to turn the clock backwards and become sects again, joyfully accepting a dissenting role on the side-lines of national life? Had not Jesus suffered 'without the gate?' 'Let us go forth therefore unto him without the camp, bearing his reproach' (Heb. 13.12–13). But Free Churchmen enjoyed their new-found and hardly-won power too much, they had become too assimilated, for this to be a real option. There were now many Nonconformist laymen with wealth and social position. The socially aspiring among them felt it uncomfortable to belong to chapels some of whose members refused to pay rates, and to be regarded as unpatriotic because some agitated against the Boer War. So when it seemed possible to support the First World War as entirely in accordance with Nonconformist principles and tradition, no wonder that the majority of Free Churchmen felt a sense of relief.

Robertson Nicoll had both supported Passive Resistance and the Boer War. He cultivated the influential in literature and politics – he was particularly close to Joseph Chamberlain and Lloyd George, fellow Nonconformists. As a member of a number of clubs he 'warmed both hands at the fire of life in London'. In 1909 he was knighted. Yet in 1900 he had written that 'if society is to be saved . . . there must be a return to the great Puritan idea of separation from the world'. When war came he was able to claim to be the true patriot for he had defended the Navy Estimates, despite Nonconformist abuse for doing so.[51] So too Winnington Ingram, like other Anglicans, saw the war as the opportunity for the Church of England to vindicate its claim to be the national church. For British Roman Catholics the war was an opportunity to prove that they were neither the 'Italian Mission' nor 'the Irish colony'.[52] German Protestants had been concerned by falling numbers in the pre-war period. Many of them viewed the war as a chance to recover their support among the German people by allying the church with the fight of German culture and faith against barbarism. The war enabled German Roman Catholics to feel integrated with national life.[53] In both countries churchmen rejoiced at the new national unity produced by the war, and therefore often silenced or muted their criticisms for fear of being regarded as divisive in a time of national peril. Sir Arthur Haworth, a Congregationalist, a Manchester cotton merchant and a former Liberal MP was educated at Rugby, and commanded the First Home Battalion of the Cheshire Regiment. He pointed out, when chairman of the Congregationalist May meetings of 1915, that men and women had set aside their quarrels, political rancour had been buried, industrial strife had ceased, duty had replaced the quest for pleasure. Was not all this in accordance with the gospel?[54] He listed his recreations in *Who's Who* as 'hunting, shooting, fishing'.

It was widely asserted by churchmen that the war would stem the tide of secularism and revive religion by recovering the spirit of self-denial and self-sacrifice and by facing people with the ultimate reality of death.[55] The churches, like the politicians, sought to justify the war by prophesying that a new society, cleansed by precious blood, would be created after the war. This war to end war would bring lasting peace. The comradeship forged in the trenches would be expressed in the post-war period by a new reconciliation between classes, sexes and churches. But no religious revival occurred. The unprecedented efforts of the Church of England in the National Mission of Repentance and Hope (1916) or in the Woolwich Crusade (1917) had no appreciable effects on church going.[56] Nor did the 1915 'Come to Church' campaign of the Free Churches, in which 950 local Free Church Councils participated, and which was publicized by millions of coloured stamps and promoted by house-to-house visiting, seem to make any real impact.[57]

Support for the war came naturally to those who regarded evangelism as a type of conquest and to those who saw themselves as engaged in a perpetual warfare against evil at home and abroad. The euphoric optimism of nineteenth-century missionary hymns was the religious equivalent of the spirit of imperialist songs like 'Land of Hope and Glory'. It was not difficult to transpose the language of the Nonconformist crusade and to use it against Germany, particularly when stories of atrocities and church desecration made it possible to identify the Germans as devilish, and the Kaiser, ally of the Sultan, as anti-Christ. The Primitive Methodist Conference in June 1914 had used the language of moral populism to blame 'war-scares' on the large syndicates who used them 'to add to their already swollen dividends'.

The Conference in 1915 laid the blame for the war on Germany in equally populist language:

> This hideous calamity has been forced upon us by the brutal arrogance and lawless ambition of a military caste, and a materialistic philosophy, which would, if triumphant, fling the world back into the most piteous savagery. We have been called to resistance by sacred claims of honour, by the impulse of fidelity to international relations, and by the urgent need of small nations. We support His Majesty's Government in its call to Britain to spare neither blood nor treasure to crush the German conspiracy against the freedom and peace of the world.[58]

Though Free Churchman felt a deep bond with Germany for its contribution to the Protestant heritage, their heroes were Bunyan, Cromwell, Calvin and Wesley rather than Luther, whose support of state religion was anathema to the voluntary principle. In any case, asked the conservatives in all the English churches, was not Germany the mother of liberal attitudes to the Bible, a potent source of modern scepticism?

Another important device used by Nonconformists to reconcile their consciences to the war was to portray it as the latest version of the conflict between Cromwell's godly Roundheads and the one whom Guttery termed 'the Stuart Kaiser'. (Where George V fitted into this scenario is unclear.) Carlyle wrote of the Ironsides in Lecture VI of *Heroes and Hero-worship* (1841): 'No more conclusively genuine set of fighters ever trod the soil of England, or of any other land.' These essays demonstrated that it was possible for heroes to arise from humble beginnings (as Carlyle had done) – a theme dear to Victorian England, Samuel Smiles and aspiring Nonconformists. In *Letters and Speeches of Oliver Cromwell* (1845), Carlyle presented not the absurd, ambitious fanatic portrayed by David Hume, but a sincere religious idealist. The influential Victorian historian S. R. Gardiner portrayed a Cromwell whose ideal was constitutional monarchy, gradual reform and moderate puritanism, thus transforming Cromwell into a liberal Victorian Nonconformist.[59] Roy Strong has pointed out the way in which, until a couple of generations ago, English children understood their history through the images of Victorian historical paintings which popularized British History as a romantic pageant of progressive development. (Nonconformists claimed that they had played a crucial, if rarely recognized, role in this pageant of progress.) So Ford Madox Brown's picture, 'Cromwell on his Farm', hinted at parallels with St Paul's conversion. Augustus Egg's portrait of Cromwell on the eve of the battle of Naseby likened him to Christ in Gethsemane. 'The Death of Oliver Cromwell' by David Wynfield echoed paintings depicting the death of the Virgin.[60]

Robert Horton, the Congregational leader, dedicated *Oliver Cromwell* (1897) to 'The Young Free Churchmen of England' and presented Cromwell as 'the man of the hour for you'. After centuries of odium he was at last coming into his own. You (Horton told his readers) will have to pass through the same odium, misrepresentation and conspiracies, and you will have to wait for recognition for centuries. But 'the dearest liberties and the brightest hopes she [*sc.* England] owes to that sternly-tender workman of God, Oliver Cromwell'.[61] Clifford, brought up among Chartists for whom Cromwell was the great hero and forerunner, regularly invoked Cromwell's example as an inspiration for his many campaigns. The Tercentenary in 1899 was marked by Nonconformist celebrations and by the erection of a statue of Cromwell in Old Palace Yard, Westminster, paid for by Lord Rosebery, imperialist Liberal and former Prime Minister, patron both of Wesleyanism and the turf. There was a considerable hullabaloo over the statue as there was in the 1950s when it was proposed to call a Durham college after Cromwell; so fierce was the opposition that it was called 'Grey College' instead.

In 1900 Walter Begley, an Anglican priest and bibliophile, published a facsimile of *Cromwell's Soldier's Catechism* (by an anonymous author, 1644). In the Preface, Begley wrote about Puritanism in terms which would have appealed to Free Churchmen:

> The Puritan is not a soldier by choice, quite the contrary; he has the strongest aversion to bloody-minded men, and would desire as earnestly as ever Gladstone did to be delivered from blood-guiltiness; but when King Charles I left no other door open, the Puritan went boldly through in the fear of God and for justice as between man and man. But many of these men, nay, most of them, had what we now call the 'Nonconformist conscience', and that had to be dealt with, soothed, satisfied, convinced, justified . . . Like the Maccabees of old, the Puritan warriors of Cromwell's time had the sword in their hand and the praises of God in their mouth.

The influence of Puritanism has been mostly silent and obscure (he wrote), not much chronicled in the court, castle or camp, alien to the famous and powerful, but it has found a home among the humble and unknown. He ended by drawing a parallel between the Boer War and the battles of Cromwell and bade his readers cherish the spirit of the

Ironsides. The actual *Catechism* includes the frightening statement: 'We are not now to look at our enemies as Country-men . . . or fellow-Protestants, but as the enemies of God and our Religion, and siders with Antichrist; and so our eye is not to pitie them, nor our sword to spare them. Jer. 48.10.' That spirit was still active in the First World War.

The two hundred and fiftieth anniversary of Cromwell's death in 1908 was marked by an article in the *Leader* by the Rev. H. J. Taylor (President of the Primitive Methodist Conference, 1922) on 27 August 1908. It 'is most desirable to see the great battles of this age in the light of those Cromwell fought and won'. Today there is also much irreligion. The rich force working people to desecrate the Sabbath by running trains and publishing newspapers on Sundays. Cromwell replaced autocracy with democracy, but the power of the Lords and the brewers remains. We too live in a time when ritualism is rampant: the 'Church of England has ceased to be Protestant, and now carries its Romanism into the common schools at public expense'. We must maintain the protesting spirit to preserve national righteousness and so be 'worthy sons of England's Uncrowned King', the 'farmer of St Ives'. The former leader of the Labour Party, Michael Foot, whose father Isaac Foot was a Liberal MP, a Wesleyan, and an active campaigner against drink and gambling (and who in 1937 founded the Cromwell Association) described the atmosphere of his home during and after the First World War: 'We must fight the good fight and keep the faith. Books were weapons, the most beloved and the sharpest. And there spread out before us were enemies enough for a lifetime: historical figures and their modern counterparts melted into one; brewers, Protectionists, Papists . . . Spanish tyrants and Stuart kings . . . sons of Belial or Beelzebub, normally disguised as West Country Tories . . .'[62]

It was therefore completely congruent with this tradition for the *Baptist Times* on 11 September 1914 to call on all who could to 'join the armies that are fighting for the Kingdom of God as surely as did the Puritans in Cromwell's day'.

Free Church pacifism

No wonder that Free Church Pacifists felt isolated, though there were far more pacifists in the Free Churches than in the Church of England. But because of the Free Church crusading mentality with its accompanying hyper-emotional rhetoric, opinions among Nonconformists were more sharply polarized than in the Church of England. Among Anglican leaders there were those like Archbishop Davidson,

Bishop Gore, William Temple and Peter Green whose support of the war was expressed in a more sober, cautious, questioning style, characteristic more of the Anglican than the Free Church ethos. The best Anglican leaders knew more at first hand about the moral ambiguities and complexities of political power than did most Free Church leaders, whose approach to politics tended to be messianic and utopian.

We look now at the experiences and attitudes of some of the Free Church pacifists. Many of the leading Free Church pacifists were ministers in the Congregational Church. Its polity and tradition encouraged sturdy independence. D. R. Davies, after working as a miner, studied during the First World War for the Congregational ministry at Bradford United College. He was a militant pacifist, a modernist and a supporter of the ILP. (Later he revolted against Nonconformity, pacifism, socialism and liberal theology and in 1941 was ordained as an Anglican priest. He chose as his new mentors Reinhold Niebuhr and A. R. Vidler and he became a well-known popularizer of neo-orthodoxy.) At Bradford he was bitterly resentful that the Principal was so often away recruiting for the army or on propaganda visits to the States. The Old Testament lecturer, much to Davies' fury, used his lectures to indulge in anti-German tirades. When Davies, as a student and later as a minister, preached pacifism with equal vehemence, he became the centre of a maelstrom. This brought him both 'acute misery' and 'exquisite satisfaction'. Only two members of his congregation at Ravensthorpe, in the West Riding, were pacifists; the rest were 'a solid hostile phalanx'.[63] Nathaniel Micklem, also a Congregationalist (Principal of Mansfield College, Oxford 1932–53) came from a very different background. His father was a well-to-do barrister and Liberal MP and Nathaniel was educated at Rugby, New College and Mansfield. He was also President of the Oxford Union. In the middle of the war, the church meeting of the chapel at Withington, Manchester where he was minister, decided that he could only remain if he was silent about his pacifism. He refused to agree and left. 'It took me many years to recover from the wound.' After a time with his parents, he found employment with the YMCA in France.[64]

Leyton Richards was brought up in a lower middle class family. From early days he appeared both in local pulpits and on Liberal Party platforms. After studying at Glasgow University and at Mansfield, he was ordained as a Congregational minister in 1906. He became a founder member of the Fellowship of Reconciliation in December 1914. Though he received some support for his pacifist views from his congregation at Bowdon, some protested and left. Others pleaded with him to moderate his views. A mother came one Saturday to tell him that her son was home on leave. Could he refrain from references to the war on Sunday? When in 1916 he signed a leaflet published by the No-Conscription Fellowship calling for the repeal of conscription, he and other signatories were charged, convicted and fined. Though the church deacons paid his £100 fine, he felt he had to resign because his pacifism was dividing the congregation. Next day he received his call-up papers, but after representations from Sir Arthur Haworth they were withdrawn. Haworth had strongly objected to Richards' pacifism and had left to worship at the local parish church, despite being a staunch Congregationalist. But he was incensed at the implication that Free Church ordination and ministry were less valid than the Anglican – no Anglican priest could be conscripted, even if without pastoral charge. Richards was appointed General Secretary of the FOR. Its office was frequently raided by the police. On one occasion he said to them 'I will save you some trouble by giving you straight away the most subversive literature we have in this office' and handed them the New Testament. On a train journey he met a prominent Free Church minister who told him that he ought to be in a pulpit not in an office. Richards replied 'I thoroughly agree with you, but will you give me a Sunday in yours?'. There was no reply. Very few churches invited him to preach. However, in April 1918 he became a pastor to a Liverpool church, and in 1919 returned to the chapel at Bowdon. When in 1924 he became minister at Carrs Lane, Birmingham, he discovered that only one man out of its 1,200 members had been a conscientious objector during the war. In 1946 he became a Quaker.[65]

C. J. Cadoux, another Congregationalist, had worked in the Admiralty before the war, but reading Tolstoy and re-examining the Gospels moved him to become a pacifist and he became an early member of the FOR. While a lecturer at Mansfield, he frequently incurred the wrath of the Principal (W. B. Selbie) by preaching pacifist sermons, and by appearing at tribunals for the defence and giving the college as his address. In 1918 it seemed likely that clergy would be conscripted. C. H. Dodd, also on the staff, wrote to Cadoux that he was more afraid of the prospect of telling the Principal that he would refuse to be conscripted, than of going to Wormwood Scrubbs.[66] In 1919 Cadoux produced *The Early Christian Attitude to War*, a scholarly defence of pacifism. (Later Cadoux served at Mansfield under Micklem, whose neo-orthodoxy he regarded as a betrayal of Congregationalism. In the Second World War, Cadoux and Dodd modified their absolutism;

Micklem abandoned pacifism altogether.[67]) The preface to Cadoux's book was written by W. E. Orchard, a fellow member of FOR, whose pacifism also owed much to Tolstoy. Ordained as a Presbyterian, in 1914 Orchard became minister at the Congregational King's Weigh House, London, to which he soon drew large congregations with his combination of socialist pacifism and neo-Roman ritual. Partly because he had a magnetic personality and was one of the best preachers in London, partly because the church was in low water when he arrived, Orchard did not have to contend with the hostility and isolation which most pacifist ministers experienced from their congregations. He became a Roman Catholic in 1932 and a priest three years later, but continued as a pacifist for the rest of his life, but his church authorities attempted to limit his pacifist activities during the Second World War.[68]

However, the vast majority of Free Churchmen were opposed to pacifism. Robertson Nicoll condemned it as heretical and immoral. P. T. Forsyth, the Congregational theologian, declared roundly that it was impossible for the Christian living in society to live according to the precepts of the Sermon on the Mount. Pacifism he characterized as 'facile idealism', for it 'preaches love without judgement'. 'It is the climax of a generation of genial and gentle religion with the nerve of the Cross cut.' To adopt neutralism 'is simply to discard morals and trust miracles. It is throwing on God the dirty work you were called to do.' However, Forsyth pleaded for a just treatment of COs whom he termed 'national sectaries'. Originally the Free Churches also had been obliged to claim from the state the right to exist.[69]

The Rev. Frank Kelley remembered how early in 1916 there was uncertainty as to whether ordinands would be conscripted. As a pacifist student at Hartley Primitive Methodist College, he requested a letter of support from the Rev. Dr Edwin Dalton, a former President of Conference, which could be presented, if need be, to a tribunal. Dalton kindly acceded, assured the tribunal of Kelley's high character and that he was motivated by conscience not cowardice, but ended by distancing himself from Kelley's stand: 'He acts for himself and for himself alone.' He signed himself with that deference characteristic of one who felt himself addressing his social superiors: 'I am, Yours very respectfully.' Nevertheless, Kelley found the General Secretary of the Primitive Methodist Church and the superintendent of the circuit to which he went as a student pastor in 1917, both very sympathetic.[70] Arnold Rowntree, the Quaker and Liberal MP for York asked his assistant in 1916 to discover how officials at the Wesleyan headquarters regarded the possibility of clerical exemption from conscription. He was curtly treated. 'We don't want to have anything to do with Mr Rowntree, or with you, or with any of your kind!' He was told that all pacifist Wesleyan ministers had been placed on a black list. (At least one of these subsequently became President of Conference.)[71] A. E. Garvie, Principal of New College, London (who was not a pacifist), contended sharply with those of the Free Church Council executive who had no sympathy with COs and were unwilling to use their influence to prevent ill-treatment. However, in May 1916 the Council was persuaded to agree to demand a new deal for COs and this had some effect.[72] A. S. Peake drafted a lengthy resolution for the Primitive Methodist Conference of June 1916 which passionately defended the rights of conscientious objection, but also pointed out that tens of thousands of their members had followed their conscience and enlisted. This was passed unanimously. Peake was one of the few Christian leaders to understand the position of the absolutists. In 1917, the *Leader* published a series of articles by him entitled 'Who is offended and I burn not?', reprinted as *Prisoners of Hope* (1918). He recalled Jeremiah and the early Christian martyrs who expressed their patriotism by opposing the policies of the state. Stephen Hobhouse, one of the absolutists, wrote to Peake that he had described their position more successfully than even his fellow pacifists could do.[73] In 1916 Clifford told a group of COs that though he supported this war, he had suffered because of his opposition to the Boer War: 'there is no liberty so great and absolutely essential as liberty of conscience'. He also pleaded their cause with Lloyd George.[74]

William Wilson in his Quaker study guide *Christ and War* (1913) included a chapter entitled 'Voices in the Wilderness' which celebrated those few who, despite persecution, bore witness to pacifism during the middle ages and Reformation period. But he shook his head sadly over Luther and Calvin. If Free Church pacifists could not claim to be following the teaching of the mainstream Reformers, they could claim to be in the tradition of Anabaptists and Quakers. Their own forefathers had suffered at the hands of the state for the right to worship according to their own conscience. Dr John Marsh, the Congregational scholar, was brought up as an Anglican, but began to attend a Congregational chapel. He heard there stories of the oppression of the early separatists which no Anglican had ever hinted at.[75] More immediately COs could appear to the example of the Passive Resisters. Walter Ayles of the No-Conscription Fellowship (later a Labour MP) was brought up by his Nonconformist parents on stories of how his forefathers had been evicted from their chapels and homes, had been impoverished and imprisoned. He told his tribunal that as a CO he felt he was following in that tradition.[76]

During the First World War, although an impressive proportion of COs were Quakers, in fact thirty-three per cent of Quakers of military age enlisted. Although Quakers were rightly credited with being the only Christian body which corporately bore witness to pacifism, a higher proportion of the members of such sects as the Christadelphians, Jehovah's Witnesses and Plymouth Brethren refused military service. Through social concern, philanthropy and commercial success, Quaker businessmen now held a secure place within English society. Arnold Rowntree helped to create the Friends' Ambulance Unit, but was also a Liberal MP, an active promoter of Quaker private education and later a close friend of Archbishop Temple. (H. L. Goudge, the Anglican theologian, pointed out in 1915 that wealthy Quaker families did not interpret 'Lay not up for yourselves treasures upon earth' with the same rigour as 'Resist not evil'.[77] Goudge may be accused of waspishness here, but he was genuinely trying to face people with the difficulties of interpreting the New Testament.) Quakers were always in the forefront of peace movements and courageously engaged in relief work among aliens in England during the war, and afterwards in the devastated areas of Europe.[78] Membership of the Society of Friends during the last half century has remained fairly constant and has not suffered the decline common to both the Church of England and the Free Churches. Could this be in part accounted for by the consistent Quaker witness to peace?[79]

3

THE ASSIMILATION OF DISSENT

When at the Diamond Jubilee in 1897 Free Church leaders were relegated to the steps outside, rather than places in St Paul's Cathedral, Nonconformists protested.[1] However, the First World War changed their status in national life. In 1918 J. H. Shakespeare wrote that no longer was Nonconformity always in a backwater and shut out of everything.[2] On 16 November of that year, Free Church patriotism was awarded the highest possible recognition by the attendance of the King and the Queen at the Thanksgiving Service arranged by the Free Church Council, the first time that a reigning monarch had attended a Free Church ceremony. Clifford had too much Chartism in him to be taken entirely off his guard, but he nevertheless rejoiced: 'It was a great and impressive gathering. It is the beginning of a new day in the relations of the State to "Dissent". It is the lifting to a slight extent of the social stigma. Of course, it will not go far, but so far as it goes it is in the direction of greater freedom in religious thought and life, and may be regarded as a movement toward reality. The Free Churches are glad; but they must not forget that their strength is in their inward simplicity and faith.'[3] The final sentence contained an important warning. But how should it be interpreted? A few days later his eighty-second birthday was celebrated by a lunch with toasts from the Prime Minister and Dean Inge. In 1921 he was made a Companion of Honour.

The close identification of Nonconformity with the war effort was contrary to some of its deepest instincts, however much there was a continuum between its stance and earlier aggressive crusades. This identification therefore led to a destructive confusion in its own mind and that of others as to what it really stood for now. The hyper-emotional language adopted by some of its leaders during the war was, no doubt, a way of suppressing deep doubts and moral confusions beneath the surface of their own minds. Certainly the war convinced many of the general public that all the churches were impotent, mere pawns of nationalism, and had nothing distinctive to say, or were too cowardly and subservient to say it. And much of the theology received in theological college, church pew or Sunday School seemed totally inadequate to cope with the experience of the war.

Mr Jackson Page joined up in 1915. He had been a pupil at Shebbear College (a school founded in 1841 by the Bible Christians, a small Methodist group) under a pacifist Headmaster. (He later returned to the school to spend the whole of his teaching life there.) When deciding to enlist he put aside part of his religion as impossible for a soldier. 'Can one ask Jesus Christ to help one fire a machine-gun? No, then, as I did in November 1915, with regret, but with resolution, one must remove J. C. from one's conscious mind and conscience. Now, once you do this, you get on with the war, and you have finished with your religious core for a long time. But *not* with your religious practices: I still said my prayers a year later in the Hindenburg Line, becoming then more efficient and more callous. And one night on a slope before Passchendaele had annihilated the belief held since childhood that God is Love.' Looking back he sees the fate of the chaplains in the war as tragic, in the strictest sense of that word, and believes that despite all that has been written, justice has not yet been done to them. For him the Church of England chaplain of his battalion remains a loved and Christ-like figure. 'I can still see what I saw as I came back wounded on September 26, 1917, the bodies of doctor and padre, mute and still, under the wet ground-sheet.'[4]

But it would be a gross over-simplification to ascribe the decline of institutional religion to the First World War. It had already begun to ebb in the Edwardian period. But the war did powerfully accelerate and intensify pluralism, secularization and the belief in modernity, which have proved to be most potent solvents of allegiance to institutional religion. It is not so much that faith and religious experience have declined in our century, but that fewer and fewer people have found it possible to express their faith and experience through the means which the churches provide.[5] The war created particular difficulties for Nonconformity. But they were not new difficulties, but the old dilemmas rammed home with apocalyptic force.

Free Church decline

Why (asks Daniel Jenkins) did the Nonconformist vision of an 'alternative society' fade so rapidly?[6] The decline of the Free Churches cannot of course be separated from the general decline in religious observance. The membership figures of the mainstream British churches seem to rise or fall together.[7] But though church statistics are notoriously difficult to compare, the allegiance to the Free Churches in England seems to have declined even more seriously between 1910 and 1980 than allegiance to the Church of England. The censuses of 1911 and 1981 show that the population of England has increased from 33,649,000 to 46,363,000 – an increase of 27.4% – so the decline of allegiance in proportion to the population is much greater than the bare figures of allegiance indicate on their own.

	1910	1980	% decline	% decline as a proportion of population
Church of England Easter Day Communicants	2,212,000	1,550,700	29.9	49.1
Methodist Membership	791,961*	467,850	40.9	57.1
Congregational Membership	287,952	151,212†	47.5	61.9
Baptist Membership	266,224	139,930	47.4	61.9

The statistics refer only to England. Sources: Currie, Gilbert and Horsley: *Churches and Churchgoers*; denominational records.

* i.e. Wesleyans, Primitive Methodists, United Methodists.
† 1970 figure: Congregationalists and Presbyterians formed the United Reformed Church in 1972.

What were the factors which made the Free Church decline more severe? In 1896 it seemed plausible for Hugh Price Hughes to claim that dissenters now represented the majority of English committed Christians.[8] But he disregarded the problems created by such success. At least by the end of the war, Nonconformists after decades of struggle against various restrictions, had succeeded in gaining almost complete freedom from religious discrimination. In 1918 they were at last allowed to take divinity degrees in Oxford and Cambridge. In 1920 the Welsh Church was disestablished. What rallying cries were now left? Paradoxically, the struggles of both Nonconformists and humanists against the Anglican monopoly helped to create the relativistic pluralism and privatization which have made the absolutist claims of evangelical religion so difficult to believe.[9] Nonconformists had become junior partners in the establishment, partly through the Liberal Party, partly through the war. Free Church scholars now dined out on Oxbridge high tables and their leaders established personal friendships with bishops through the ecumenical movement. The establishment was modified through the Enabling Act of 1919. This devolved powers from Parliament on to the Church Assembly and created at every level a more decisive role for committed lay people, all of which went some way to meeting criticisms by Nonconformity that the Church of England was dominated by its clergy and its life determined by half-believing or atheistic MPs. (Nonconformist rejection of Parliamentary control of religion did not, however, prevent some Free Churchmen from using Parliament in 1927 and 1928 to defeat the Church of England's proposals for Prayer Book revision.)

In addition, in the post-war period, both Anglicans and Free Churchmen became increasingly aware that Christians were united also by a common sense of weakness in relation to the life of the nation. No wonder that the cries for disestablishment died down. The Liberals had never adopted it as party policy. The Labour Party was uninterested. As early as 1902, R. F. Horton the Congregationalist, had pointed out that the Church of England was developing a seductiveness liable to disarm Dissent. What Laud had failed to achieve by persecution, the Church of England was now achieving by sweetness and light, renewed devotion, and by providing a religion with social rewards. 'Who can question that a large proportion of the Dissenters who attain wealth and social position become Churchmen, or, at any rate attendants at Church?' But if dissent were to disappear, England would be the poorer. Half the best Anglican clergy and parishioners were former dissenters, he believed.[10]

Obviously there was some connection between the fact that both Nonconformity and the Liberals achieved their zenith in the Edwardian era and then declined. Nonconformity had become so identified with the ideology and political activity of the Liberals, that their fortunes were intertwined. In practice this resulted more in the secularization of Nonconformity than in the adoption by the Liberals of Nonconformist principles. The Congregational minister, Silvester Horne, who always looked longingly back to the Commonwealth, tried to combine being both an MP and minister of Whitefields Mission in London, but in 1914 he was contemplating resigning either his seat or his pastorate when the strain of his dual role killed him. C. P. Scott of the *Manchester Guardian* admitted privately in June 1914 that 'the existing Liberal Party is played out . . . if it is to count for anything in the future it must be reconstituted largely on a labour basis'.[11] By 1918 much the same might have been said of Nonconformity. By their support of the war, both the Liberals and the Free Churches had been forced to deny, one by one, almost all their most cherished principles with which they had defined themselves in their own minds, and those of the general public. The war seriously compromised the Free Churches and ruined the Liberal Party. But the war seemed at the time to vindicate Conservative policies and it immensely strengthened the power of organized labour.[12] After 1918, a good deal of Free Church support began to shift to the Labour Party, but there was also some movement to the Conservatives. Though until recently, many Labour politicians had Nonconformist roots, the Free Churches never corporately identified themselves with the Labour party as they had done with the Liberals.

Nonconformity also had become too identified with Victorian culture and morality. This disabled it from responding to post-war society in which Victorian values were increasingly scorned. Lytton Strachey's sardonic treatment of nineteenth-century personalities in *Eminent Victorians* (1918) appealed to those who now regarded Victorianism as out-moded, discredited, stuffy and hypocritical. Recently a poster outside a Victorian Methodist church in Leeds proclaimed 'A modern church in an ancient building'. But the Free Churches were neither modern enough for those who wanted to be 'up to date', nor ancient enough to evoke the historical atmosphere which the English believe to be the appropriate setting for either a drink or a wedding. The rural nostalgia so carefully cultivated by English pubs since the 1920s is an important clue to English attitudes to leisure – and religion became increasingly viewed as but one among many competing ways of occupying leisure time.[13] In 1916 the London Underground Railways produced a poster to remind servicemen of home. It depicted a village green, thatched cottages and an ancient parish church. Beneath was a poem entitled 'A Wish' which began:

Mine be a cot beside the hill . . .[14]

It was this romanticized rural England that Stanley Baldwin celebrated in his addresses about the character of English life during the inter-war years, despite being a former industrialist. The rustic novels of Winifred Holtby and Mary Webb were his favourite reading. As an undergraduate he had considered becoming an Anglican priest. Dreams of rural England were more easily evoked by the Church of England than by the Free Churches.

Sabbatarianism and Teetotalism

Sabbatarianism and teetotalism were two important legacies of Victorian evangelical religion. Until recently, Nonconformists preached them as among the prime demands of Christianity. Both proved difficult to maintain in the post-war era. The new mobility created by cars, charabancs, motor-cycles and bicycles enabled thousands to spend their Sundays enjoying the new passion for the open air. In the 1930s a number of Anglican parishes, particularly in the new housing areas, moved towards the Parish Communion as the main Sunday service. It was usually celebrated at an early hour, around 9 am to encourage fasting Communion. But the growing emphasis on the weekly eucharist as the main obligation made Evensong seem an optional extra, and the regular provision of an 8 am. Communion and the early time of the Parish Communion enabled those Anglicans who wished, to go off for part or the rest of the day. This facilitated the growth among Anglicans of what Nonconformists called with strong disapproval 'the continental Sunday'. However, the time of Free Church Sunday morning worship remained firmly fixed at 10.30 or 11 am. At the turn of the century, in C. H. Dodd's home, his father shaved on Saturday evenings to avoid Sunday work. My mother always cooked the Sunday joint on Saturday. My father, throughout his ministry, set his face firmly against the erosion of the English Sunday. In a pamphlet published in 1922 he traced its origins to the Jewish Sabbath, celebrated the glories of the English Puritan attitude to Sunday, and deplored the war's effects on Sunday observance:

> Why cannot a man go to church on Sunday morning, and having accomplished his religious exercises, then work in the garden in the afternoon or play a game of golf, or go into the country for the rest of the day; or, if a choirboy at a certain cathedral play cricket after service duties are over. To this we answer: There is no reason whatever why we should not do these things – *if* religion is merely a matter of exercise and ritual observance . . . The Hebrews lit the temple lights on the altar at sunset on Sabbath Eve: so the Christian should light the lamp of worship in his own heart and home ere the Sunday dawns. Then it will be devoted to quiet, meditation, prayer, worship, instruction, charity.

(Probably the growth of the (largely Anglican) retreat movement during the last fifty years is, in part, an attempt to compensate for the disappearance of this understanding of Sunday.) In his church magazine for July 1931 my father quoted this 'saying' of Jesus from the Oxyrhynchus papyri: 'Except ye keep a true Sabbath ye shall not see the Father'. D. H. Lawrence in 1928 wrote of his gratitude for his Congregational upbringing.[15] His moving pictures of the Sabbath rest in his novel *The Rainbow* (1915) showed how much he owed to the Nonconformist tradition: 'after church on Sundays the house was really something of a sanctuary, with peace breathing like a strange bird alighted in the rooms'. But Ursula found that she could not bring together the 'Sunday world of absolute truth and living mystery, of walking upon the waters and being blinded by the face of the Lord' with her weekday world (Chapters X and XI). By contrast J. B. Priestley's *English Journey* (1934) contained several Dickensian protests against Sabbatarians on behalf of the common people. Why should Sunday laws be imposed on so many people who disagreed with them? He was angry that young people should be prevented from going to art galleries, plays, concerts and films on a Sunday.[16] One of my uncles (on my mother's side) exemplified the new leisure which in the 1930s was eroding sabbatarianism. We were shocked to learn that he often preferred to use his newly acquired Morris 8 to go on Sunday outings rather than to chapel. I remember when he took me inside a swimming pool in 1945 on a Sunday afternoon, I felt guilty, and was astonished to see swimmers actually enjoying their sinfulness.

The arguments for total abstinence, which were powerful in the nineteenth century, somewhat weakened with the restrictions upon opening hours introduced during the war. These restrictions greatly reduced drunkenness. But the American post-war experiment of prohibition suggested that legislation to ban alcohol could have unexpectedly harmful effects on society. Hensley Henson gave up alcohol as an example when he was Vicar of Barking from 1888 to 1895, as did other Christians working among the poor. But during the war, as Dean of Durham, he poured scorn on calls for total abstinence, enjoying the controversy that resulted, but grew alarmed when brewers used his name in advertisements.[17] Throughout his ministry, my father used the arguments against alcohol familiar in Nonconformist circles: the economic argument – so much more was spent on drink than on education; the moral argument – alcohol produced deterioration in character; the argument against moderate drinkers – they must remember the weaker brother. A survey of the attitudes of Methodists and Anglicans in 1965 showed that only two per cent of Anglicans supported total abstinence against forty-eight per cent of Methodists. Only sixteen per cent of Anglicans disapproved of Sunday sport, compared with fifty-seven per cent of Methodists. Whereas seventy-six per cent of Methodists disapproved of football pools, this was true of only twenty-three per cent of Anglicans.[18] These figures reveal not only the scale of the divergence about these ethical issues between Anglicans and Methodists, but also the degree to which Methodist attitudes to all three issues had become much less absolute and cohesive. Puritan ethics about Sunday, alcohol and gambling could look to the working classes like a middle-class attempt to prohibit their favourite pastimes, and after the First World War, working people grew in political independence and general self-confidence and were much less willing to defer to those whom they once thought of as their betters. It was a remarkable moment when in 1974, the Methodist Conference abandoned its traditional policy of enjoining total abstinence and decided to leave the question to the individual conscience: paradoxically a reversion to the attitude of most nineteenth-century Nonconformists. The decline of sabbatarianism and teetotalism in Nonconformity during the last fifty years is another example of the success of the pressures to make Nonconformity conform.

The chapels and education

The increased use of colleges and universities for the training of Nonconformist ministers exerted another pressure towards conformity with the norms of middle-class English society. In 1886 Beatrice Webb recorded the complaints of a Nonconformist millworker that her minister, being one of the 'new college men', was a snob, and no longer one 'called of God from among the people'.[19] A cutting from the *Leader* of the 1920s referring to my father (trained at Hartley and Manchester University) was obviously a riposte to this type of complaint: 'There are still a few people who have an idea that culture is a drawback to a Primitive Methodist minister . . . some of the finest work being done in our Church today is that of men who have earned University degrees . . . a lingering prejudice which some times manifests itself against Hartley College should for ever cease.' It was also a response to the wounding charges made by Matthew Arnold, Charles Dickens, Mark Rutherford and others that dissent lacked intelligence and culture.[20]

Until the 1930s the chapels, and to a lesser extent the parish churches, exercised an important educational function among adults, as well as among children and young people. An advertisement for a United Methodist Bazaar in 1912 included quotations from Shakespeare and Dr Johnson. Wherever my father was minister, education was a prominent aspect of his work. He strenuously endeavoured to enable his congregations to enter into the great literary, artistic and theological riches of the pre-1914 world in which he was reared. He had almost no interest in the characteristic novels, poetry, films, art or plays of the post-war period. Chapels built in the late Victorian or Edwardian periods usually had at their side an equally large building for adult education, Sunday schools and social activities. Sunday schools were an important source of recruitment. They also gave considerable pastoral and educational responsibility to large numbers of lay people. They kept the churches in touch with many who never became adult members. Sunday schools declined rapidly in the inter-war period, hit heavily by the increased use of Sunday for leisure activities. In 1933 there were 1,297,953 children in Methodist Sunday schools; by 1974 the figure was 332,129.[21] The Primitive Methodist church of Grainger's Lane, Cradley Heath, Staffordshire, where from 1924 to 1932 my father was minister, in 1927 had 600 scholars and 200 adult members on its roll. Sometimes 700 people attended the Sunday evening service. Apart from Sunday worship and Sunday schools (the latter followed by a teachers' prayer meeting), there were four classes for young people on Sunday afternoons; Women's Own meetings on Monday afternoons, with Church Lectures, Band of Hope and Junior Christian Endeavour on Monday evenings; a preaching service on Tuesday evenings; Senior Christian Endeavour and Sunday school teachers' preparation classes on Wednesday evenings; Sisters' Class and Intermediate Christian Endeavour on Thursday evenings; Young People's Educational Association on Friday evenings. Saturdays were free. The circuit steward, introducing the winter's activities for 1924–25 told the one hundred and fifty people present that he was sad to see that some churches 'had resorted to a sort of competition to provide the allurement of the world'.

By contrast, the programme at Grainger's Lane was 'mind-expanding and character-building'. That winter included a series of lectures by my father on 'The Puritan Movement in England', a series of sermons by him on 'Pen Pictures from Hebrew Poetry' and a series of twenty sermons by him for young people on Sunday evenings on two of St Paul's Epistles. An average of sixty young people heard lectures at the Young People's Educational Association on (for example) George Stephenson, Dickens, Tennyson, Samuel Smiles, Bunyan, George Eliot, Robert Raikes, John Wesley, Dante and English Monasticism. (In the summer the young people went for conducted rambles, and the Sunday school enjoyed its annual outing.) Other groups had equally solid fare. In 1924 a visiting preacher lectured for eighty-five minutes on John Knox. In each issue of the 'Quarterly Guide' my father provided a catholic selection of 'Golden Thoughts' from (for example) Tennyson, Browning, Ruskin, Keble, Thomas à Kempis, Newman, Wesley, Wordsworth, Bunyan, George Herbert and Baxter. The young men were promised in their prospectus that through their class they would find 'mutual spiritual improvement'. Their class and that for the young ladies worked steadily through the Bible. Groups also studied more general subjects: League of Nations, Temperance, Gambling, Use and Abuse of Sunday, Christ and Unemployment, Winning by Character. Nothing seems to have been provided about sexuality and little about working life or social issues, apart from drink and gambling. Regular lectures on 'missionary advance' also widened the horizons of the congregation.

Though the intensity and extent of this educational programme was probably exceptional, it was by no means an isolated example. When at the turn of the century, Lang was vicar of Portsea, there were often 300 men at Sunday afternoon lectures. At Clifford's church in London the educational facilities included a chemical laboratory. In 1903 the language, technical, scientific and art classes became part of the Paddington Technical Institute. This was prophetic of what was to come. The 1918 Education Act raised the school leaving age to fourteen. In 1920 State scholarships were created to enable more to go to university. Between 1920 and 1930 the Workers' Educational Association doubled its student numbers. Extra-mural departments began to provide adult education. Ironically, Nonconformist agitations in favour of 'undenominational' teaching ensured that religious education in state schools was taught as solely a matter of biblical knowledge, without any reference to a connection between faith and the life and worship of the churches. Broadcasting (which started under the British Broadcasting Company in 1922) offered talks, discussions and classical music as well as entertainment. Those who wanted adult education no longer needed to look to the chapels to provide it. In any case the increasing pluralism of society made some suspicious of education offered under church auspices. The new educational opportunities took young people to college and university and removed them from the control and ethos of the chapels. Some became Anglicans, others lost their faith.[22] Since the chapels often appealed to the socially mobile and the aspiring, they were agents of educational, class and social change, especially as much Christianity was expressed through middle-class culture. Ministers, who had themselves benefitted from their own experience of education and so were often re-classed in the process, helped to re-class their congregations. Ironically therefore, the chapels helped to destroy the old pattern where it was possible to spend almost every evening and all Sunday under the control of the chapel ethos. By the 1930s there were so many other agencies providing education and social life that the chapels were left more and more to concentrate upon the strictly 'religious' needs of their people. Attendance at class meetings, at one time mandatory in Methodism, had withered. Expulsions for indiscipline, once such a marked feature of Nonconformist life, became a rarity.[23] The chapels were no longer centres of cultural vitality. By the 1930s culture was found outside rather than inside the chapels.

The new leisure

' "Take her away, into the sun," the doctors said' is the opening sentence of D. H. Lawrence's story 'Sun' (1926). The story expressed the new worship of the sun, the new passion for the open air, the new delighted awareness of the body. Priestley described in 1933 what he saw one Sunday in the Yorkshire Dales: before the war 'we used to set out in twos and threes . . . Now they were in gangs of either hikers or bikers, twenty or thirty of them together and all dressed for their respective parts'.[24] The British Youth Hostels Association was created in 1930. William Temple, one of its Vice-Presidents, actively promoted its work, and so quietened some of those who suspected that it would take young people away from the churches. Some clergy encouraged hikers to attend church in shorts; others put on late evening services for ramblers and cyclists. Dick Sheppard optimistically wrote: 'I believe that the path across the moors and over the hills that the hikers are taking is a path that may lead in the end to God.'[25] But some church-goers regarded such attitudes as sentimental concessions to self indulgence. Churches and chapels promoted youth clubs and tried film services in attempts to win and retain the young. Some abandoned afternoon Sunday schools and tried to attract children to worship with their parents at 'family services'. But outside each Youth Hostel was (and is) proclaimed the new faith in youth, pluralism and internationalism which implicitly challenged the credalism, parochialism and middle-aged ethos of the churches: 'This youth hostel is one of many, both in this country and abroad, where young people, regardless of race or creed, may spend the night.' The formation of the YHA was prophetic of the gradual creation of an autonomous youth culture, liberated from adult control, which expressed and deepened the alienation of young people from the churches.

Between the wars, cities expanded as new suburban railways, the spread of car-ownership (there were 200,000 cars in Britain in 1920, nearly two million by 1939) and the gradual replacement of the tram by the bus, enabled people to live further from their place of work. In 1930 the diocese of London launched an appeal for money to build forty-five churches for the new housing areas. The pageant play 'The

Rock' was written by T. S. Eliot in aid of the appeal and performed
in 1934; it included evocations of the new mobile society:

> I journeyed to the suburbs, and there I was told:
> We toil for six days, on the seventh we must motor
> To Hindhead, or Maidenhead . . .
> And the Church does not seem to be wanted
> In country or in suburb . . .
> But all dash to and fro in motor cars,
> Familiar with the roads and settled nowhere.
> Nor does the family even move about together,
> But every son would have his motor cycle,
> And daughters ride away on casual pillions.

In 1931 at Queen's Road Baptist Church Coventry an appeal was
issued for two members of the congregation to act as car parking
stewards. In the 1930s in order to attract the newly mobile and
the growing number of those with paid holidays, Scarborough, for
example, developed a whole new area of the North Bay to provide a
miniature railway, a vast Open Air Theatre and an open-air swimming
pool. Those without paid holidays enjoyed the new opportunities for
day excursions and hiking offered by public transport, cars and
bicycles. A cartoon in *Punch* for 27 June 1928 entitled 'Our Betters'
depicted two women looking through the window at a car being driven
away. 'New car?' asked the visitor. 'No – new cook' replied her
hostess. Most people (except the unemployed) had more spare money
than ever before to spend on pleasure. The appeal of the earnest Gospel
according to Samuel Smiles became less attractive as Victorian values
waned. Due to contraception families were smaller, so parents had
more leisure time. The first holiday camp was built in 1924. By 1932
there were 187 stadiums for the new sport of greyhound racing. Half
the population went to the cinema at least once a week. More and
more cinemas opened on Sundays as well as on weekdays. Penguin
paper-backs appeared for the first time in 1935.

Broadcasting brought a wider world into the home. Its religious
services were used by some as an alternative to public worship. Why
go to hear a local minister when you could sit at home and listen to
Dick Sheppard? A cartoon depicted a lady interviewing a maid. 'Do
you belong to the Church of England?' the lady asked. 'Well, M'm'
(the maid replied) 'My father goes to Chapel, but personally I'm
wireless.' Such privatization was also the logical result of liberal
protestantism. Broadcast football results encouraged betting on the
pools. By 1939 three out of four families owned their own wireless.

So by the 1930s participation in church-based activities had been displaced from its role as one of the major leisure pursuits of the English people.

Secularization and pluralism united with that other powerful solvent of religious allegiance – modernity, to which the Free Churches with their heavily Victorian ethos were particularly vulnerable. Priestley discovered three Englands on his journeys in 1933: the old England of cathedrals, manor houses, inns, squires and parsons; industrial England created in the nineteenth century but now suffering mass unemployment; and a new post-war England influenced by America:

> This is the England of arterial and by-pass roads, of filling stations and factories that look like exhibition buildings, of giant cinemas and dance-halls and cafés, bungalows with tiny garages, cocktail bars, Woolworths, motor-coaches, wireless, hiking, factory girls looking like actresses, greyhound racing and dirt tracks, swimming pools, and everything given away for cigarette coupons.[26]

Priestley might have commented that the first represented the ethos into which the Church of England fitted most naturally; that the second had largely created Victorian Nonconformity; but that this new third England was the one which baffled church and chapel alike. Nearly four million new houses were built between the wars, nearly half of which were in new areas. The Church of England, with its greater financial resources, was able to build large numbers of churches on the new housing estates; the Free Churches were not able to respond to the challenge as systematically or as extensively.

Nonconformity and ecumenism

The ecumenical movement at first appeared to offer a new theological (and therefore social) recognition to Nonconformity, but it turned out to be yet another development which intensified the dilemmas of dissent. In the post-war period, church leaders proposed unprecedented efforts towards unity: for example, in the Lambeth Appeal of 1920 and in the influential book *The Churches at the Cross-Roads* (1918) by J. H. Shakespeare, Secretary of the Baptist Union.[27] The new efforts were partly a response to the accusation that if only the church had been truly catholic it could have prevented the war. In war-time, united action between Anglicans and Free Churchmen (which to a limited degree also included Roman Catholics) proved that co-operation was possible. During the war, Free Church leaders had grown accustomed to being invited to sign appeals and manifestos jointly with the Archbishop of Canterbury in which Roman Catholic leaders also joined on occasion. Ecumenism (particularly when it took the form of federalism) was the ecclesiastical equivalent of that progressive idealism which produced the League of Nations, and was sometimes promoted as such.[28] The few contacts maintained between German and British Christians during the war were now actively increased by both sides in an atmosphere of penitence and hope. Baffled by the failure of war-time evangelistic campaigns, some church leaders concluded that disunity was the major obstacle to evangelism, and increasingly quoted: 'That they all may be one . . . that the world may believe' (John 17.21). The world longed for reconciliation. Only a reconciled church could offer this. Unity would also strengthen the church by rationalizing resources. In industry too, rationalization was being urged as the key to efficient production and successful marketing.[29] The President of the Primitive Methodist Conference, the Rev. James Lockhart, lecturing in Cradley Heath in 1925, said that while politicians could ignore a divided church, a united church would be a power in the land. Again ecumenism with its message of diversity-in-unity fitted in well with the post-war faith that tolerant pluralism could alone bring reconciliation between classes, sexes, creeds, races and nationalities. Had not millions died for a new order? We must keep faith with them. Churchmen pledged themselves to work for a new relationship between churches (and in some cases between all the faiths). So they could look forward with hope, their faith in human progress unaffected by the cataclysm. Thus in 1916 Clifford declared that the war was 'only a stupendous interlude . . . a tragic episode, separable from the main currents of human experience'. The world was still on its 'upward path'. He pointed out that a 'League of Faiths' had been created, for there was truth in all the religions. He emerged from the war with his faith in progress burning ever more brightly. This extract from his address given in September 1919 as the first President of the World Brotherhood Federation[30] was typical of the optimism of many immediately after the war:

> Brotherhood is like the air, universal and inescapable . . . The world is being made 'all clear' for its march. Labour has long been international, peace movements are world-wide, the temperance crusade assails all barriers and will beat them down, the legislators of different countries meet in conference to harmonize laws. Even the churches are developing international relations and preparing for world congresses, and I cannot doubt that this movement for unity will slough off the obsolete accretions of the past and unite

the religions of the world so that humanity shall become one flock under one Shepherd.[31]

But what if ecumenism meant that Free Churchmen had to accept episcopacy, priesthood and sacramentalism? That, many of them felt, would be a complete retrogression; for was not history, under divine guidance, moving away from hierarchy to democracy, away from sacramentalism to spiritual religion? Surely the future lay, not with catholicism, but with protestantism (particularly in its Free Church form)? In fact, ecumenical theology challenged such simple antitheses, so further blurring Free Church identity.

My father's commitment to ecumenism arose from his eirenic temperament which regarded conflict as irrational, was deepened by his devotion to Baxter and the Cambridge Platonists and was undergirded by his progressive understanding of history. Regularly, throughout his life, he gave a lecture 'Time, Tide and God', first composed in the 1920s. When in the mid-1930s he gave this lecture at Kidderminster, the local press reported it enthusiastically in an article of 4,000 words. (The local and national press then still had a readership interested in lengthy reports of sermons and religious events.) 'It was his own conviction that in their own generation they had seen the turn of the spiritual tide which had so long been an ebbing one. They had seen the first beginnings of a tide that, in the providence of God, would move across all the naked and dreary shingles of the world, and reaching perhaps a higher watermark than had ever been known in the world before.' History enabled us to take a long view. The League represented the culmination of a process, a great ideal. A new understanding had developed between religion and science. Biblical criticism had vindicated scripture as 'the certified book of God' a 'progressive revelation' of God's purpose. Christians were now conscious of all that united them. The eastern races were showing a new sympathy towards Jesus. 'Beyond the movement in our tide is God.' It was congruent with all this that in 1929 he enrolled his Cradley Heath church as a corporate member of the League of Nations Union. When he gave Armistice Day addresses (about which, as a pacifist, he felt misgivings) he appealed for support for the League to bring to birth 'a new world'. In 1931 at Brierley Hill, in the context of a parade of the British Legion, Police, Fire Brigade, Royal Engineers, Scouts and Guides, with a regimental band playing 'In Realms of Bliss', and the congregation singing Kipling's 'Recessional' and 'O Valiant Hearts', he preached in the parish church, ending (as he often did on such occasions) with lines from Tennyson's 'Locksley Hall' prophesying 'the Parliament of man, the Federation of the world'. Missionary work was presented as a story of wonderful expansion and illustrated with photographs of native converts with such headings as 'From Cannibalism to Christianity'. A parade in Cradley Heath in the 1920s in aid of funds for the local hospitals ended with a sermon by my father in which he foretold the final slaying of the 'dragon of disease' and after that a 'diseaseless world'.

In 1932, my father moved to minister in Liverpool. As President of the Free Church Centre and later of the Free Church Council, he developed a close friendship and working relationship with the Dean of Liverpool, F. W. Dwelly, an innovatory and romantic genius who could be affectionate, seductive and pastoral, but also difficult and obtuse. Dwelly (Provisional Canon from 1925 and Dean 1931–1955) and Charles Raven (Provisional Canon from 1924 and Chancellor 1931–32) were gripped by a great vision of the Cathedral as a centre for unity where (as Raven wrote) 'all can sink their divisions in the sole adoration of Him in whom there is neither Jew nor Greek'.[32] But how could it be 'the spiritual home of the people of Liverpool' as Raven desired, when its liberal modernism excluded the catholic tradition? And the marked Christocentricity of Raven's language, so expressive of his own experience and so natural at that period, might now seem (to some) both romantic and divisive. Theological liberalism evidently had its own exclusivities. In the inter-war period, Liverpool Cathedral was convincing proof to many (but not all, for it had its critics) that Christianity could be excitingly relevant to the modern world, a great sign of new life and hope comparable with that offered by Coventry Cathedral after the second war. Ironically for an evangelical diocese, Liverpool Cathedral was architecturally the last great fling of Victorian romantic catholicism, and looked exactly the right setting for a splendid High Mass, lit by a myriad of flickering candles, enfolded in clouds of incense and accompanied by the music of Haydn or Schubert. But in fact its style of worship and life represented the broad church liberalism of *Songs of Praise* (1925). Dwelly's understanding of Christianity and the church was liberal, platonic and mystical rather than credal, catholic and sacramental, and this was exactly my father's outlook. Dwelly was less interested in the eucharist and the statutory services than in pioneering, devising and staging colourful dramatic pageants of worship, expressed with original ceremonial and accompanied by fine music. On these occasions the lavishly produced and typographically elaborate service brochures, together with the Wardour Street English which Dwelly wrote so well, presented modernism with that dash of antiquity and nostalgia so beloved by the English in church and on national occasions. When the Dean and Chapter were officially installed in 1931, the event was reported under such headlines as 'Pageantry in New Cathedral: Ceremony of the Middle Ages' and 'Glories of Bygone Ages Revived'. Large crowds flocked to the People's Service at 8.30 pm on Sunday evenings, especially when either Dwelly or Raven was preaching. 'Dwelly would lie flat on one of the great oak tables in a darkened vestry before going in to preach; Raven would pace up and down, almost physically sick, rehearsing the words and gestures like an actor.'[33] Dwelly told a reporter in 1937: 'Many of the problems of the day would be solved if the outlook of artists and scientists could be fused into one creative vision.' Liverpool (he said) contained many differing types of activity: 'all the time at Liverpool Cathedral men are looking for the unities in these various manifestations of life.' Dwelly showed him forms of service which included quotations from Wordsworth, A. N. Whitehead, D. H. Lawrence, Edward Carpenter and T. E. Brown. Recently, Isaac Newton, Florence Nightingale, Robert Burns, W. G. Grace and the Lancashire cricket supporters had all been suitably commemorated.[34]

Dwelly fought for what he regarded as a legitimate measure of independence from the Bishop for the Dean and Chapter; but others felt that Dwelly was trying to tilt the balance of power so far that, if he had his way, the Cathedral would be more independent of the Bishop than any other Cathedral in England. To demonstrate his independence of the Bishop, Dwelly in September 1934 refused to execute the Bishop's Mandate to instal two new Archdeacons. The Archdeacons brought a public case charging Dwelly with 'causing grave scandal'. Though the Chancellor of the diocese stopped the proceedings during the hearing on a technicality, the case (which was reported widely) revealed a tragic breakdown in elementary courtesy and trust between the Dean on the one hand, and the Bishop and his staff on the other. In addition, Dwelly's liturgical and theological liberalism infuriated ecclesiastical conservatives. Bishops struggling to maintain doctrinal and liturgical conformity in the parishes were dismayed by Dwelly's determination to be free from conventional constraints in doctrine and liturgy, though many of the leaders of the Church of England recognized his artistic creativity.

In 1933, Dwelly invited Dr L. P. Jacks, the Unitarian scholar (whose son-in-law was a devoted friend of the Cathedral) to give addresses to students at the non-statutory services on three Sunday evenings. Also that year, the Rev. Laurence Redfern, a local Unitarian minister and Sheriff's Chaplain, preached at a special Assize service on a Sunday morning. Three local clergy chapters protested. At a national level, Lord Hugh Cecil formally charged Dwelly with encouraging 'heretical opinions' about the incarnation. At the York Convocation in June 1934, the bishops debated the matter, and decided to forbid invitations for Unitarians to preach in Anglican pulpits. When Dwelly and Raven (the latter no longer on the Chapter) arranged for a public reading of their apology to Jacks from the Cathedral pulpit, and sent a similar letter to Redfern, other members of the Chapter wrote to the press to protest that the invitations had been issued without their consent, and that Raven had no longer any right to speak on behalf of the Chapter.

As a result of the bishops' ruling, Dwelly decided to refuse to issue invitations to *any* Free Church ministers to participate in services now that he could no longer do so on his own terms. He did not wish them or the Cathedral to be further hurt by controversy or the possibility of legal proceedings. Such invitations (he said) were now a matter for the Bishop. Dwelly felt bitter at what he regarded as an outbreak of ecclesiastical bigotry and a victory for sacerdotalism and credalism over truly 'spiritual' religion. Dwelly's retraction of invitations bewildered and angered some local Free Church leaders who valued what had become customary practice, now thought by Dwelly to be possibly illegal. By insisting on including Unitarians, Dwelly jeopardized the relationships of the Cathedral with Free Churchmen, and enabled law to defeat custom. Further, Dwelly did not grasp that most Free Church leaders declined to be classed with Unitarians, who were excluded from the National Free Church Council. On the incarnation, most Nonconformists were on the side of the bishops, not Dwelly. Nor was Dwelly sensitive to fears of Nonconformists that if they became *too* identified with the Cathedral, they would betray their heritage and alienate their constituencies. One minister, Secretary of the Free Church Centre, wrote to my father pointing out that the 'eel'-like Dwelly had obviously no intention of seceding as the Nonconformist 'martyrs' had done. Dwelly (he thought) was mistaken in believing that Free Church ministers 'craved' certain rights in the Cathedral, for example, the right to celebrate Communion. 'We regard the Cathedral as a Church belonging to a different section of the Church from ourselves, and while we welcome a joint act of worship, and are proud, like other citizens, that Liverpool possesses such a building, we do not advocate that we as Free Churchmen ought to have any rights to the use of the building . . . Dwelly is apparently working to secure for us privileges we do not crave.' However Dwelly met Free Church leaders for a frank discussion in February 1937 which produced a degree of healing. Relations between the Cathedral and the Free Churches were further renewed and deepened by a united service, framed jointly by Dwelly and my father, entitled 'Affirmations', broadcast on 6 June 1937; 161 clergy and ministers and 1,955 representatives of parish and chapel choirs participated. 4,300 people who applied for places had to be refused as the Cathedral, still incomplete, could not accommodate them. 'The Litany of the Ingathering of the Spirit' (the phraseology was characteristic of Dwelly's emphasis on the Spirit) included Cranmer, the Cambridge Platonists, Baxter, Linnaeus, Leibnitz, Wesley, Arnold of Rugby, Hort and Söderblom, but notably omitted (say) Keble and Gore. The service was prefaced by 'Unity in things necessary; Liberty in things doubtful; Charity in all' – a favourite quotation of my father's from Rupertus Meldenius.

The Bishop of Liverpool (Dr David) was present at the service, but only because my father, at Dwelly's urgent request, had written to him to try to persuade him to alter his engagements. Dwelly, whose relationship with Dr David was (as we have seen) very strained, again used my father as an intermediary a few days later. On a train journey, Dwelly pencilled a draft of a further softening-up letter to be sent on behalf of local Free Church leaders to the Bishop expressing their wholehearted approval of the forthcoming service. The draft included the phrase 'The Dean has indeed made it possible for us to show how much we all would like to say we love you'. Though my father followed Dwelly's draft fairly closely, he omitted that particularly personal leaf of Dwelly's olive-branch. How ironic it was, in view of the history of Anglican-Free Church relationships over the centuries, that a Dean needed to use a Nonconformist go-between in order to communicate with his Bishop, in order that both might express publicly a degree of Christian brotherhood for the Free Churches which they found so very difficult to express in their personal relationships with one another.

Arrangements were made for impressions of the service to be gathered from participants, partly for Sir John Reith of the BBC. Seven hundred replies were received. A Methodist minister wrote: 'A simple brotherliness and utter lack of any spirit of condescension; a real bond of unity. On my left was a little deformed Pastor, humble, unordained and almost poor; opposite me was a Salvation Army Officer; behind me was the Bishop. One felt that there had never been anything quite like it since Gentile and Jew first mingled in the Early Church.' A female chorister, a Congregationalist, thought it a 'splendid service', but it did not go far enough: 'a pity that the Roman Catholics and the Jews were not of the company. What a fine thing if it were possible to have a Service embracing all Christian religions.' (It is interesting that she obviously classed the Jewish faith as a Christian religion.)

Even after we moved to Wales in 1937, until war came, Dwelly continued to ask (usually by telegram) for my father's help with special services, notably for those commemorating John Wesley and the Open Bible in 1938. What did the telegram clerk in our sleepy border village of Knighton make of such requests as these? 'Could you work out a commemoration for our Litany on the names of the forty-seven revisers of Authorised Version?'; 'What answer to question Dictionary of National Biography says there were fifty-four revisers when our list is only forty-seven?'; 'Send list 25 hymns you consider most essential for deepening spiritual consciousness and five that will develop sense of just dealing as set out in Micah.' In 1938 Dwelly tried to get the cathedral statutes revised to allow the appointment of my father to some office in the cathedral, but it was not legally possible. Enclosing a letter from the solicitor, Dwelly wrote: 'This post is the unhappiest I've had. All my hopes so carefully builded are dashed . . . I feel I have failed a friend . . . I so badly wanted you.' If the appointment, so ahead of its time, had been made, I wonder how it would have affected the dissenting strain in my father's make-up? But in 1936 in a public lecture he had welcomed the gradual disuse of the terms 'Nonconformist' and 'Dissenter' in favour of the term 'Free Church', and looked forward to the day when a greater freedom within the Church of England would enable the Free Churches to play their part in 'a national framework of religion'.

Liverpool was in those days bitterly divided between a militant and largely Irish Roman Catholicism on one side, and pugnacious Orangemen on the other. Therefore to avoid controversy it was proposed at first to unveil the cenotaph without prayers. In 1937, a few weeks after my father left Liverpool, he was sent a press report that a trustee and local preacher at the church had given thanks publicly for having been delivered from a 'ministry which seemed to lose no opportunity of blessing things priestly and Romish'. When in reply my father rebutted the charges and alluded to his own devotion to the Puritans, the trustee responded by complaining (among other things) about some lectures on monasticism and a sermon on Christmas Day comparing the number present (twenty-six) with the hundreds who attended Midnight Mass. The trustee wrote: 'there was probably more vital religion in those 26 souls than in the 600 priest-ridden crowd, who would forthwith disperse to drink and gamble and swear to their heart's content until the next High Mass . . . The Puritans were never charitable towards Catholics. You must be a new brand . . . Rome is a system of religion as false as Hell, and as cruel, crafty and corrupt, as the traditional Devil, and is not worthy of your charity. I would say "Have no fellowship with the unfruitful works of darkness" . . . You have very much under-estimated Liverpool's strong Protestantism.' That was the voice of the old militant dissent. My father, as he said, represented a new brand.

Times were also changing in the Church of England. By the mid-1930s liberal modernism was in decline, and a catholic type of neo-orthodoxy was gaining ground which emphasized the corporate nature and tradition of the church expressed in the weekly eucharist. Hopes of a relatively easy progress towards Anglican-Free Church union receded. Dwelly and Raven felt increasingly isolated. Though the Free Churches still included many who clung to progressive idealism, some Free Church leaders began to re-assert the reformed faith with a new rigour. Inspired by Barth and the Confessing Church of Germany, they made a stand against liberalism.[35] In the Methodist Union of 1932, on the whole the non-Wesleyan traditions lost out to the Wesleyan; for example, lay celebration which had been such a strong Primitive Methodist principle was now to be regarded as an occasional exception.

Between the wars, religion was edged from being public news and was becoming a matter of one private opinion among others. A *Punch* cartoon of 4 May 1921 showed a middle-class investigator asking 'And what is your religion?' The working-class woman replied, with her arm round her daughter: 'Well, Miss, I'm Church and me 'usband's Chapel; but little Maudie's County Council.' As secularization advanced, religious belief became more diffuse and institutional allegiance weakened. The churches became less sure of their message. In this situation the Church of England which contained several ideological expressions of Christianity, offered a variety of styles of worship, was willing to accept very different levels of commitment, continued to have low boundary walls, and was prepared to accommo-date folk religion, tended to fare better than the Free Churches which were identified in the public mind with puritan ethics and a high level of regular commitment. As the worship of the Church of England was largely derived from a fixed liturgy, it was less liable to become captive to passing ideologies than the Free Churches whose worship depended so largely upon the choice of the individual minister. Reinhold Niebuhr told Temple that it was the Prayer Book rather than episcopacy which had saved the Anglican Communion from rationalism and pelagianism.[36] Ecumenism deprived the Free Churches of their traditional bogies against which they had pitted their strength and defined their function. Sectarian controversy can be a powerful stimulus to recruitment, solidarity and self-definition, particularly when played out in full public view in association with political parties and social issues, as happened during the full tide of the Nonconformist Conscience, and as we know from the melancholy example of Ulster.[37]

Class and religion

Another factor which accelerated the decline of the Free Churches was their increasingly middle-class character. This made Free Church people more mobile socially (and therefore religiously) and made them less content to be confined within the buildings and ethos of the chapels. The relation of class to religion was also changing. The Liberal Party with a firm base in the chapels gave way to the Labour Party based on the unions. Though religious conflicts before the war (and religious differences afterwards) had a class basis, the class conflicts of the post-war era were fought without religious labels.[38] Ironically, in the General Strike of 1926, if any religious leader seemed to be sympathetic to the strikers it was the Archbishop of Canterbury, though this was more by accident than design.[39] People now defined themselves more by class and occupation than by religion. But in the pre-war era it had been common for someone sharing a piece of toast to ask 'Church or Chapel?' – the round end representing the (Gothic) church and the square end representing the chapel. C. H. Dodd, growing up in Wrexham at the turn of the century, remembered the church and chapel communities as almost entirely separate. 'As a matter of course we bought our food from a dissenting grocer, our clothes from a dissenting clothier; we employed a dissenting milkman, carpenter, jobbing gardener, and chimney-sweep. To do otherwise would have been felt as disloyalty.'[40] In 1949 Dodd meditated upon unacknowledged factors which kept the churches apart and asserted that the real divisions between Anglicans and Nonconformists arose not so much from doctrinal differences as from a cleavage in English life going back at least to the Civil War. 'However little we may resemble our Cavalier and Roundhead predecessors, I believe their conflict is in our bones.'[41] W. E. Orchard had written in 1917 that no one could love England without some love for the Church of England, yet he nevertheless asserted that it was 'essentially the Church of "good form" . . . the gentleman's Church . . . snobby, squirish and a bit feudal . . . It has discovered exactly how much religion the Englishman can stand.' (But he added that there was a nobler side to it as well.)[42] In 1902 Robertson Nicoll claimed that 'the process of passing from the unfashionable chapel to the fashionable church is about the meanest and shabbiest business transacted on this earth'.[43]

Dr W. E. Sangster was minister at Westminster Central Hall from 1939 to 1954. His father was a foreman and his mother a former head cook. When he served in the Army in the first war, he was turned away from an Anglican Communion service. *The Methodist Recorder* on 1 October 1959 published his article entitled 'Defending Methodism': 'The "county people" won't notice us, but who minds that? We have Bible authority for believing that God does.' That remark comes straight from the heart of the old class-conscious dissenting tradition. He had a great veneration for Cromwell, yet corresponded with the Queen (now the Queen Mother) and knew Bishop Bell well enough to hug him. It was characteristic of both Sangster and the tradition he represented that he often explained that the Queen Mother came from 'good Scottish Presbyterian stock'. Whereas some Methodists still disapproved of Sunday papers, in 1950 he became a regular contributor to the *Sunday Times*.[44]

Clergy tend to explain denominational differences in theological terms and to avert their eyes from class factors. A local historian by contrast, giving a valuable lay view of religious groups in Kirkstall, Leeds, at the beginning of the century, assesses them largely in terms of their place on the social ladder. At the top of the social table came the parish church, attended and partly financed by the Butler family, owners of the foundry where most Kirkstall inhabitants then worked. For though Kirkstall is only a couple of miles from the city centre, then it was like a self-contained village. As late as 1931 letters were put into pay packets by the Butlers urging workers to vote Tory. The well-to-do Wesleyans came next, hovering on the fringe of the parish church; many voted Tory. The Congregationalists were regarded as the intellectuals. The United Methodists were known for their entertainments and parties. At the bottom of the social league came the Baptists and Primitive Methodists who had few social pretensions and who were concerned above all to save souls: their religion was 'austere, intolerant and in deadly earnest'. The Baptist minister was a Passive Resister. Some of his books were seized when he refused to pay the rates. In Kirkstall today not one of the Nonconformist chapels has survived. There are now only two places of worship: the parish church and the former United Methodist chapel now used by the Roman Catholics.[45] I am reminded of 'The Chapel' by R. S. Thomas in which he describes it now settling deeper into the grass,

But here once on an evening like this,
in the darkness that was about
his hearers, a preacher caught fire
and burned steadily before them
with a strange light, so that they saw
the splendour of the barren mountains
about them and sang their amens
fiercely, narrow but saved
in a way that men are not now.

Cultural assimilation

English society is subtly equipped to neutralize dissent. Aneurin Bevan (brought up as a Welsh Nonconformist) described the experience of a new MP making a fierce maiden speech, fresh with the grievances of his constituents from which he had just come. His opponent, in accordance with Parliamentary tradition, congratulated him on his fine speech and then totally ignored it. 'The stone he thought he had thrown turned out to be a sponge.'[46] But in the last period of Bevan's life, after many years of dissent and rebellion, it was as if he grew tired of throwing stones at the shop window and now wanted to be in the shop behind the counter. He longed for an end to the wilderness, to martyrdom, locusts and wild honey.[47] In the late Victorian and Edwardian periods, Nonconformists began to feel exactly the same, but thereby exposed themselves to a process of assimilation.

The process of assimilation can be well illustrated by looking at the history of Grainger's Lane Primitive Methodist Church, Cradley Heath, in the Black Country, where my father was minister from 1924 to 1932. Its history might be called 'From Nailer's Shop to Tudor Gothic'.[48] Worship began in a nailer's shop in 1821. In 1827 the congregation moved to a room constructed out of two cottages. In 1841 a severely plain oblong chapel was built and enlarged in 1858. In 1860 a tower with a clock was added. The foundation stone was inscribed 'Prepare to meet thy God'. Pigeon racing enthusiasts timed their birds by the clock. Workers rose by its chimes. But in 1888 mining subsidence damaged the fabric. A new building was needed. Six architects were invited to submit plans. The new church, opened in 1906 with St George's flag flying above it, was in neo-Anglican Tudor Gothic, cruciform, with transepts, red granite pillars, clerestory windows and a marble font. Pulpit and organ were not centrally placed as in traditional chapels, but were on either side of the spacious chancel in which the communion table was central. The building was officially designated 'Grainger's Lane Church' and the term 'Chapel' was dropped.[49] The four stained glass windows placed in the church after the war were the work of an artist who had prepared designs for stained glass in the Palace at the Hague and in a memorial chapel near the Vimy Ridge, and had painted a fresco in the House of Lords. At the centenary celebrations in 1927 a former minister said: 'They had summoned the aid of three of the greatest factors in the enlightenment of the world – architecture, music and art.' Another former minister said in a sermon: 'What a far cry it was from a humble meeting place of 1827 to that "palace" of 1927, from eye-sore environment to the challenge of aesthetic windows, from Corybantic frenzy to reverent worship, from crude illiteracy to sanctified scholarship, from an asthmatical harmonium to a magnificent organ.' The style and furnishing of the church revealed the new cultural standards and the new wealth of some Nonconformist lay people. The leaders of Grainger's Lane Church were now proud to be employing an artist whose work had won the approval of the military and the peers, two groups which until the war, had been widely detested by Nonconformists in general, and by Primitive Methodists in particular.

Worship too was changing. Between the wars a more decorous, less heart-on-the-sleeve style of worship gradually replaced the old corybantic tradition, particularly in the suburban chapels. A robed minister and choir suited bourgeois tastes, though the old dissenters regarded them as undemocratic and popish. Wooden crosses began to be placed on communion tables. However, in country chapels, less subject to ministerial, ecumenical and secularizing influences, the minister still wore the traditional preacher's frock coat and older local preachers would choose revivalist choruses from the earlier edition of the hymn book still in use in rural areas. Older members of the congregation would shout an 'Alleluia' or a 'Praise the Lord' from time to time during prayers and sermons. But even in country chapels such interjections had taken on a quasi-liturgical predictability and seemed like the flying of an increasing tattered flag. The young and the middle aged smiled with embarrassment at such old-fashioned ways. In rural areas they still celebrated Communion with a common cup. This too was thought old-fashioned, for the town churches now used trays of individual glasses, indicating a new fastidiousness towards fellow worshippers, a new individualism and a greater respect for the alleged findings of modern science than for either Christian tradition or sacramental symbolism. An advertisement in the *Leader* on 19 November 1914 announced that 2,000 churches had introduced individual cups 'free from infection, for every Member'. It added an extra topical incentive: 'Will you show your Patriotism by sending your order to keep our Workpeople going?' 'Doctors and Public Health Officers pronounce the use of the Common Cup as Liable to convey Infectious Diseases' was still the message from an advertiser in the *Methodist Recorder* on 17 July 1958.

In short, the Free Churches never managed to achieve a resolution of the tensions, satisfactory either to themselves or to anyone else, between conformity and nonconformity, between assent and dissent. Too often they appeared to be ready to succumb to the wrong norms (as they did in the First World War) and to be fighting with over-blown rhetoric for antiquated causes. So the movement which resulted in the creation of the National Free Church Council in 1896, attempted to give Nonconformity a more eirenic and positive image, while at the same time advocating the movement as a way of combining forces to mount more effectively aggressive campaigns against the enemies of dissent. Dr Charles Berry (First President of the National Free Church Council and in 1897 Chairman of the Congregational Union) told the Third Free Church Congress in 1895 that division had been 'truly born of God', but that now God was leading them to a synthesis of what they had learnt separately. 'This is not a Nonconformist Congress whose *raison d'etre* lies in a negative and critical attitude towards the Established Church. This is a FREE CHURCH CONGRESS . . .' Such moderation was hardly calculated to put steam into the boiler. So he added: 'The king that controls Christ puts the truth in chains. The king that patronises Christ makes Christ fashionable, and a fashionable Christ is an ill-representative of the thorn-crowned victim . . '. (We note that he refrained from mentioning the activities of queens – that would have looked like a criticism of Queen Victoria, and most Free Church people were devoted monarchists.) Hugh Price Hughes put it even more bluntly: 'Every established Church in the world was stained with human blood.'[50] A similar tension between the desire to appear eirenic and the need to rally the faithful appeared in Hughes' speech to the First National Council meeting in 1896. They were still proud, he said, of the titles 'Protestant', 'Nonconformist' and 'Dissenter', but these terms were too negative. He preferred the term 'Free evangelical Churchmen'. The 'sacred right of insurrection' must now be used only as a last resort. We have been 'narrow, bigoted and sectarian' he confessed. Federation was politically and ecclesiastically, the key to the future. Yet he offered them this demagogic slogan: 'We are not one in the Pope. We are not one in the Crown. But we are one in Christ.'[51] The individual Free Churches were indeed beginning to lose their sharpness of identity, but since this was in part caused by a growing individualism among their members, this appeal to the nebulous concept of Free Churchmanship as a new focus for corporate loyalty and identity, was bound to have only limited success.

Seventy years later, Christopher Driver, a Congregational layman wrote: 'Dissent, like any other national institution, has its epic heroes, and ours are men like Bunyan, Fox, Carey: men who laid themselves open to the Spirit of God and therefore became able to step outside the social and ecclesiastical environment into which they were born . . . These heroes are part of a myth – in the truest and religious sense of that word – without which the Free Churches would die at the roots and shrivel.'[52] But how could Nonconformists sound convincing when reciting their martyrology to stir the heart and nerve the will from the high tables of Mansfield College Oxford (built in High Church Anglican style by Basil Champneys in 1888) or Wesley House Cambridge (built in genteel neo-Tudor in 1926 opposite Westcott House which produces so many bishops)? But then how does a Labour Minister of the Crown step convincingly from a ministerial Rover to address a miners' gala about the Tolpuddle martyrs? How can a left-wing MP hold office in an 'ecumenical' Cabinet and retain the support of those who believe that power always corrupts? Similarly traditional Anglo-Catholics and conservative Evangelicals (both forms of Anglican dissent with sectarian characteristics) while theoretically hoping to convert the Church of England to their views, often grieve when one of their number, having become a bishop, is 'mellowed' by office. For dissenters of various kinds maintain morale by holding conspiracy theories about those in positions of power. That is why dissenters, if they come to power, are often rather uncertain as to how to exercise it without a betrayal of their dissenting heritage. Ministers in the first Labour Government of 1924 made a stand and refused to wear knee-breeches to visit the Palace but were willing to wear Levée dress, including cock-hat and sword, which the King's Private Secretary kindly suggested could be obtained cheaply from Moss Bros. Ian Ramsey, born in a humble setting, when he became Bishop of Durham in 1966 wore a cloth cap when he travelled to the Palace to do homage. But he was curiously romantic and self-deceiving in his decision to continue to live at Auckland Castle. Henson, brought up in a small house, revelled in the Castle, while Lord William Cecil, Bishop of Exeter, brought up at Hatfield, refused to live in his palace, preferring to live frugally in a much smaller house where rats appeared at tea-time to be fed with crumpets. The most creative and memorable 'dissenter' of the second war period was to be found at the bishop's palace in Chichester. The reality of human life turned out to be too complex and too paradoxical to be accounted for by the simple populist slogans of Nonconformist ideology.

On 10 August 1939 my father broke his holiday to have lunch with Dean Dwelly. During lunch Dwelly was summoned to the phone. When he returned he explained that it was a call from Lambeth asking him to help with the preparation of prayers suitable for war time. Nevertheless, on our family holiday in a remote area of the Welsh coast, we did not seek access to wireless or newspapers. My father had unlimited faith in Chamberlain's capacity to avert war. Yet as we bathed we could see the concrete pill boxes already in place at intervals along the coast. On Friday 1 September we visited Cardigan and heard in a shop that the Germans had invaded Poland. A loudspeaker outside relayed instructions about air-raid and blackout precautions to a silent crowd. We packed up and returned to Radnorshire. On Saturday evening, by the light of candles, my mother and sister sat up making blackout curtains. On Sunday morning a chapel official stayed at home to listen to the Prime Minister's broadcast, then dashed to the chapel, and creeping up the pulpit steps, whispered the news for my father to announce.

A few Sundays later my father preached on 'Whatsoever a man sows that shall he reap'. Being Harvest Festival the chapel was fuller than usual. He blamed the war largely on the Allies' treatment of Germany in the Versailles Treaty and described Hitler as 'the son of Clemenceau'. The sermon incensed some of the congregation and a number of them refused to attend for a considerable time if my father preached. The news of the sermon was all round the village the same day. That night the manse front gate was taken off its hinges and a patriotic cartoon was nailed to it. On the surface my father professed to be indifferent to the protests, but it was noticeable that though he continued throughout the rest of his ministry to speak on pacifism whenever he was specifically invited to do so, he never (as far as I am aware) sought another confrontation of this kind from the pulpit. Meanwhile the village church school which I attended was organizing the production of patriotic posters by the pupils. My painting of a bomber was among those exhibited in a free-standing showcase immediately at the entrance of the chapel. My father's pre-war practice of giving me a weekly sixpence for National Savings continued, but whereas other pupils brought particularly large sums for special occasions like 'Wings for Victory', I was still given my usual sixpence.

For much of the Second World War the Savings Campaigns were directed with great flair by Lord Mackintosh, a keen Methodist. He had learnt from Victorian Nonconformity those virtues of thrift and hard work which took him all the way from a Halifax market stall and the small world of the Methodist New Connexion to being one of the best-known toffee manufacturers in the country and a Deputy Lord Lieutenant for the West Riding. At the end of the war, he was a natural choice to be chairman of the Christian Commando Campaigns. During the war, Margaret Roberts was growing up in a very similar environment in Grantham where her father, a Methodist local preacher, kept a corner shop. In this strictly sabbatarian home with its strenuously serious atmosphere and an ethos which would have won Samuel Smiles' approval, she grasped the necessity for self-reliance and self-improvement, cultivated the virtues of thrift and hard work, and learnt not to be afraid of unpopularity and singularity when standing combatively against the consensus. Before she went up to Oxford in 1943 her father is said to have arranged elocution lessons for her. As Margaret Thatcher she has proclaimed her admiration for Victorian values and preached her convictions with that pedagogic seriousnsss and crusading moral fervour which characterized the Nonconformist tradition. Thus she has brought into contemporary political life, much to the amazement of many of her own party and of the general public, certain aspects of the dissenting heritage which seemed, only a few years ago, to have gone for ever. The fact that some of her sternest critics have been found among the members of the Free Churches is a measure of how far they have moved away from the spirit of Victorian and Edwardian Nonconformity.

PART II

PACIFISTS AND PACIFIERS
BETWEEN THE WARS

4

NEVER AGAIN!

In this chapter we will examine the growth in Britain during the 1920s and 1930s of a revulsion against war and describe some of the efforts to secure peace. Each year, as people gathered round the memorials to those who had died in the 'war to end war', many vowed that never again should lives be sacrificed in warfare. Surely the nations had learnt their lesson and should be able to devise peaceful methods for solving disputes?

In 1919, Miss Elizabeth Wordsworth, the first Principal of Lady Margaret Hall, Oxford, told those celebrating its fortieth anniversary: 'The daughters of Lady Margaret will go out into a world of ferment, all eyes strained forward; all around the talk is of a new world, a new England, a new social order.'[1] At the end of the war, both inside and outside the churches, large numbers of people in Britain passionately hoped that international co-operation would in future prevent war, and continued to believe this until the mid 1930s. It is very difficult for us to think ourselves back into a period when, despite unemployment and social unrest, people could cherish so much hope. After 1945, hopes for a new world were so quickly extinguished by the cold war. However, the hopes of the 1920s were often based upon a corporate and personal inability to digest the experience of war. Soldiers rarely spoke of their deepest experiences, even to their own families. It is no accident that there was a lapse of roughly a decade between the end of the war and the appearance of most of the memoirs from serving men. An individual who experiences a catastrophe often feels only relief after the immediate crisis is over, though nightmares may signal how much turbulence continues repressed in the unconscious. It is only with the passage of time that strength is given to face, relive and understand the catastrophe.

The anti-war literature of the 1920s expressed and deepened the conviction that there must be 'no next-time'. In 1919 and 1920, selections of Wilfred Owen's poems appeared, decisively rejecting the old values enshrined in Horace's dictum 'Dulce et Decorum est pro patria mori'. Siegfried Sassoon's sardonic war poems were published in 1919. Later war literature included Erich Remarque: *All Quiet on the Western Front* (translated into English in 1928 and made into a popular anti-war film in 1930); R. C. Sherriff's play *Journey's End* (1928) which ran to 594 performances; Edmund Blunden: *Undertones of War* (1928); Sassoon: *Memoirs of a Fox-Hunting Man* (1928); *Memoirs of an Infantry Officer* (1930); Robert Graves: *Goodbye to all that* (1929). In 1930 Laurence Housman, the Quaker playwright and pacifist, produced the moving collection *War Letters of Fallen Englishmen*. In the Introduction he wrote:

> The Cenotaph is a silent memorial of those it stands for. These letters are a memorial that speaks, and that speaks truth. And though they speak of willingness and courage, and devotion, poured out with a generosity and a faith that put to shame the feeble efforts we have made since then for the restoration of world-peace, they speak also of disillusion and doubt, and a growing distrust of war as an instrument for bringing to pass any good commensurate with so huge a sacrifice of body and of soul.

C. E. Montague's memoirs, significantly entitled *Disenchantment*, appeared in 1922. He was for many years on the staff of the *Manchester Guardian*. He wrote at the end of chapter VII entitled 'Can't Believe a Word':

> Most of the men had, all their lives, been accepting 'what it says 'ere in the paper' as being presumptively true . . . Now, in the biggest event of their lives, hundreds of thousands of men were able to check for themselves the truth of that workaday Bible. They fought in a battle or raid, and two days after they read, with jeers on their lips, the account of 'the show' in the papers. They felt they had found the Press out . . . So it comes that each of several million ex-soldiers now reads every solemn appeal of a Government, each beautiful speech of a Premier or earnest assurance of a body of employers with that maxim on guard in his mind – 'You can't believe a word you read'.

Michael Roberts (who edited *The Faber Book of Modern Verse* (1936)) wrote in 1934, echoing Owen's famous preface for his war poems:

> 1914 showed the disaster which followed when hundreds of millions of people gave the old responses to the old stimuli. Soldiers, and

later civilians, saw that 'Honour', 'Courage', 'Patriotism', as they understood them, led to cruelty, lying, and blood-lust on a scale so gigantic that the foundations of civilisation were threatened.[2]

Arthur Ponsonby (a Minister in the first two Labour Governments) in 1928 published *Falsehood in War-Time*. This attempted to expose a number of well-known atrocity stories as fabrications of Allied propaganda, so deepening the scepticism of which Montague, Roberts and others wrote, and disabling many British people from believing stories of Nazi atrocities during the 1930s. (The book reached its ninth impression by 1940.)

Hopes for a new world

The League of Nations was much more widely idealized and supported in Britain after the first war than the United Nations after the second war. The League of Nations Union became the most influential peace society. In 1931 it reached a peak of subscriptions – 406,868 – but lost support thereafter; in 1939 only 193,266 subscribed. Each year church newspapers reprinted long extracts from the sermon in Geneva preached prior to the opening of the Assembly. In September 1922, Randall Davidson, Archbishop of Canterbury, reminded the congregation in St Peter's Cathedral, Geneva, of 'the awful, the horrible, the devil-devised barrier of war . . . We have seen with our own eyes, we have heard in our own homes and hospitals, its unspeakable, its illimitable horrors. And deliberately we say that, God helping us, there shall be no "next time".'[3] At home, Armistice Day sermons every year commended the League to the support and prayers of the people. Armistice-tide was for many, not only a remembrance of the dead, but also an annual re-dedication to peace, fired by a burning conviction that all the sacrifice must not have been in vain. Christians sought to influence the character of these annual remembrances towards the themes of internationalism and reconciliation. A letter-writer in the Anglican church weekly the *Guardian* on 26 October 1934 asked whether it was right to sing 'I vow to thee my country' at Armistice Day and League of Nations services, when it included the line 'the love that asks no question'.

In 1935 the Foreign Office approached Eric Gill, the Roman Catholic sculptor and pacifist, to design a panel for the front of the Assembly Hall at the League of Nations building in Geneva. Gill's memorandum explained his design: 'The central panel of the sculpture represents the re-creation of man, which the League of Nations is assisting.' When completed in 1938 (by which time the League was almost totally discredited) the panel included 'Quid est homo, quod memor es ejus?' (Ps. 8.4), 'Ad imaginem Dei creavit illum' (Gen. 1.26) and five opening lines from 'The Wreck of the Deutschland' by Gerard Manley Hopkins.[4] 'The Churches' (claimed the *Guardian* on 3 March 1933) 'are the strongest bulwark of the League in this country.' A collect for the League was included in the Revised Prayer Book of 1928. Lord Robert Cecil, one of the chief architects of the League, the representative to the League of both Conservative and Labour Governments and President of the LNU, had been inspired to devote his life to the League by a sermon in St Paul's Cathedral in 1921, preached by his brother William, Bishop of Exeter, about Britain's responsibility for moral leadership in the world. Robert wrote to his wife: 'I have had a great feeling that I have been "called" to preach the League spirit on public affairs and there seems to be so much in the Bible about that kind of thing.'[5] (Both he and his brother Hugh took leading roles in Anglican affairs.) In 1933, both Archbishops, thirty-five bishops, and leaders of other churches appealed to governments to work through the League and urged Christians to join the LNU (*Guardian*, 8 December 1933). Stand by the 'one existing public barrier against fear and the lawless forces' – the League – appealed the Archbishop of Canterbury (Lang) in a broadcast sermon reported in the *Guardian* on 5 January 1934. Leyton Richards, the pacifist and Congregational minister, timed four summer holidays to enable him to attend the League Assemblies, until the League's failure to respond to the Abyssinian crisis crushed his hopes.

The Locarno Treaties (1925) and the Kellogg Pact (1928) seemed further guarantees of lasting peace. The Encyclical of the 1930 Lambeth Conference confidently thanked God for 'the achievements of the League of Nations and the Kellogg-Briand Pact'. Arthur Henderson, Foreign Secretary in the second Labour Government, President of the World Disarmament Conference 1932–34 and a devoted Methodist, said of the Kellogg Pact in 1931: 'the obligation is absolute and if the Governments which accepted are acting in good faith, it follows that wars of conquest or aggression to gain national ends are things of the past, and force is eliminated as a means of settling international disputes.'[6]

In 1924, the ecumenical Conference on Politics, Economics and Citizenship (COPEC) drew 1,500 delegates to Birmingham under the chairmanship of William Temple, then Bishop of Manchester. Though divided between pacifists and non-pacifists, the Conference united in condemning war as 'contrary to the spirit and teaching of Jesus Christ'; it urged the churches to refuse to support a war waged before, or in defiance of, arbitration.[7] The Lambeth Conference of 1930 in Resolution 25 (which was influenced by COPEC and declarations of international ecumenical conferences of 1928 and 1929) asserted: war 'as a method of settling international disputes is incompatible with the teaching and example of Our Lord Jesus Christ'. Resolution 26 appealed for support for the League, the World Alliance and arbitration.[8] However, these resolutions of COPEC and Lambeth turned out to be more ambiguous than they seemed at the time.

In the early 1930s much Christian hope was focussed on the World Disarmament Conference.[9] In June 1931 a meeting was held in Central Hall, Westminster to voice Christian support for its work which was to begin the following year. Archbishop Temple, eighteen bishops, Lord Robert Cecil, Fr Bede Jarrett OP, Presbyterians, Quakers, Unitarians, and a General from the Salvation Army were on the platform. So many people came that an overflow meeting had to be hurriedly arranged. In December, the Archbishop of Canterbury preached on the theme at St Paul's to a congregation which included the Prime Minister and the ambassadors of several countries, including Germany. The *Guardian* commented: 'there is a growing feeling that the faith of Christians can accomplish much'. Both the Archbishops, Fr Jarrett and the Rev. Leslie Weatherhead (Methodist) addressed a meeting at the Albert Hall in February 1932. In October that year, the Archbishop of Canterbury and leaders of other churches went to see the Prime Minister to impress upon him the strength of Christian support for disarmament.[10]

By contrast Hensley Henson, Bishop of Durham, was in sombre mood when he preached the Cambridge University sermon on 29 October 1933. The post-war dreams of peace and international co-operation had faded (Henson said); instead, nationalism was now supreme, there was a 'ruinous' arms race and even the prospect of war. It reminded him of Browning's lines:

> And is this little all that was to be?
> Where is the gloriously decisive change,
> Metamorphosis the immeasurable,
> Of human clay to divine gold, we looked
> Should, in some poor sort, justify its price?[11]

But the Anglican weekly, the *Guardian*, in a leader on 10 August 1934, still put its trust in collective action through the League. Following Troeltsch it said that,

those who believe in the necessity of sanctions belong to the Church type, while the pacifist conforms to what he describes as the sect type. The Church type means those who recognize that it is the business of Christians to consecrate as much of worldly practice as possible, to Christianize the structure of human society, recognizing the necessity for order and the element of good in the natural world. The sect type on the other hand is apocalyptic. What must be maintained, even if the heavens fall or the world goes up in flames, is the purity of faith, and of the individual conscience. It is significant that the earnest pacifist, when pressed, generally admits that he does not expect that in the world as it is his pacifism will prevent war. The supporter of the League is on the other hand confident that his plan could be successful.

After the Abyssinian crisis however, this kind of faith in the League began to evaporate.

In all these varying ways the churches sought to influence national and world affairs and gave voice to the yearning of the general public for peace.

Pacifists and pacifiers

Martin Ceadel in his invaluable book *Pacifism in Britain 1914–1945* (1980)[12] points out that the term 'pacifist' was used early in this century to signify both those with a deep desire for peace as well as those who believed that war was always morally wrong and who refused to participate in it. The latter understanding of the term 'pacifist' only began to be adopted in the 1930s. Ceadel uses 'pacificist' to describe those who, though not pacifists, regarded the prevention of war as an overriding political priority because it was an irrational, inhumane method of solving international disputes. I shall use the term 'pacifist' in its modern sense. I shall use the term 'pacifier' as equivalent to Ceadel's 'pacificist'. Though pacifists and pacifiers, as groups, often overlapped, each had a distinctive core of belief. Pacifism was essentially a personal, moral and perfectionist faith which was very difficult, perhaps impossible, to translate into political, as distinct from individual, action. Pacifiers on the other hand believed that it was possible to prevent or limit war through political action. At the centre of the pacifiers' faith was 'the liberal belief in a latent harmony of real interests between nations' which could be actualized through international organizations. Left-wing pacifiers (like some pacifists) believed that war was the result of the machinations of such groups as the arms manufacturers, the capitalist press, the officer-class and imperialist politicians: structural change would remove the causes of war. The pacifiers gained ground in the inter-war period because they could both appeal to the horror with which the war was remembered, and to Victorian optimism about human progress and international co-operation which burned brightly until the early thirties. On the other hand, when the League failed to act decisively in the Manchurian crisis of 1931 some of its supporters turned instead to radical pacifism. Most pacifists supported the pacifiers at those points in the inter-war period when it seemed that war could be prevented through international negotiation without the use of force or sanctions.[13]

Five main features of the inter-war period encouraged the increase of both the pacifiers and the pacifists. But by speaking of the 'inter-war period' we immediately impose later perspectives. Looking back, each act of aggression by Hitler led so obviously to the next and then inevitably to the outbreak of war in September 1939. We cannot understand the attitudes of those who lived in that period until we grasp the obvious, though often neglected fact, that what seems inevitable to us was then unknown, or open to cogently differing interpretations at each stage.

First, there was a widespread belief that the Versailles Treaty was unjust and should be revised. In 1919 J. M. Keynes, in *The Economic Consequences of the Peace*, with the authority of a former treasury official, attacked reparations and argued that the Treaty was morally wrong and economically catastrophic. Kingsley Martin (Editor of the *New Statesman* 1931–60) remembers that this book gave 'enormous encouragement to a generation of idealistic undergraduates. Most of us were pacifists of one sort or another, angry with the "wicked old men" who had stumbled into war and, worse still, carried through a peace which mocked the ideal for which so many of our school friends had died.'[14] Because by the mid-1930s there was virtually universal agreement in Britain that the Treaty was discredited and needed revision, it was almost certain that no war would be fought against a Germany seeking to revise the Treaty. So long as Germany acted only to remove what were regarded as legitimate grievances created by the Treaty, there would be protests, but no effective action against her. When Hitler claimed the Rhineland in 1936, Austria and the German-speaking part of Czechoslovakia in 1938, this could be defended as congruent with the principle of self-determination enunciated by President Wilson and enshrined in the Versailles Treaty. It was not until the invasion of Prague in March 1939, that it was demonstrated beyond all possible doubt that Hitler wanted to achieve much more than the inclusion of all Germans in his empire. Both Harold Nicolson's memoir, *Peacemaking 1919* (1933) and Lloyd George's *The Truth*

About the Peace Treaties (1938), coinciding respectively with the accession to power by Hitler and the Munich agreement, nourished Britain scepticism about the Treaty. So up to the end of 1938 or so, most English people wanted to interpret Hitler's moves as attempts to redress legitimate grievances.[15]

In 1932 Archbishop Temple attacked the war guilt clause in a sermon in Geneva before the Disarmament Conference.[16] In 1933 he wrote: 'In the Treaty of Versailles the victorious nations imposed upon the chief vanquished nation an assertion that this nation was the only real culprit . . . It was disastrous because it was bound to create in Germany a festering sore of resentment – as has in fact occurred.' It divided the nations into innocent and guilty, instead of forcing them to ask what was wrong with the civilization which led to the war and what was their own individual share in that wrong.[17] Henson read Keynes and believed that the Allies had been responsible for 'a great crime' – the Treaty had been 'engineered by hatreds' and 'base ambitions'.[18] The opinion of church leaders very largely reflected the newspapers they read. 'Every British newspaper by 1933 was the disciple of the gospel of Keynes and Nicolson.'[19]

Secondly, there was a widespread determination that the horrors of the first war must not be repeated, and a widespread belief that another war would be even more destructive. Kingsley Martin recalls the temper of the times: 'The oath of "Never Again" which we swore at a thousand meetings was not a Labour aberration nor the soft notion of pacifists and pro-Germans. Almost everyone, Conservatives, Liberals and Labour alike, regarded the French notion of keeping Germany permanently as a second-class power as absurd, and agreed that the Versailles Treaty must be revised in Germany's favour.'[20]

The Cambridge Union in 1927 and the Oxford Union in 1931 passed motions in favour of pacifism. But it was the Oxford Union motion 'that this House will, in no circumstances, fight for its King and Country', carried decisively on 9 February 1933, which caught the headlines. It outraged the leader-writers and others who concluded that the younger generation was disloyal to the glorious dead, soft, decadent and communistic. Though the exact motives of those who voted for the motion have been very variously assessed, it was at the very least a rejection of the kind of war which had been fought between 1914 and 1918, as the provocative language of the motion indicated. Both pacifists and pacifiers eagerly seized upon the debate as evidence of widespread and growing support for their causes. Even if the influence upon the dictators of what Churchill in *The Gathering Storm* called that 'ever-shameful resolution' was greatly exaggerated by him and others, there is some evidence that the Oxford motion was contemptuously cited by Germans as proof that young Englishmen would not fight.

It was not only undergraduates who expressed horror at the prospect of another war. On 10 November 1932, Stanley Baldwin (then Lord President of the Council) told the Commons that any town within reach of an aerodrome could be bombed within five minutes of the outbreak of war:

> I think it as well also for the man in the street to realise that there is no power on earth that can protect him from being bombed. Whatever people may tell him, the bomber will always get through . . . The only defence is in offence, which means that you have to kill more women and children more quickly than the enemy if you want to save yourselves.[21]

Thereafter, the phrase 'the bomber will always get through' was constantly quoted by pacifists and pacifiers to support their cause. On 28 November 1934, Churchill predicted to the Commons that if London were heavily bombed, three to four million people would flee the city. In a week or ten days, 30–40,000 people would be killed or maimed. How could the authorities cope with a catastrophe on such a scale?[22] A film produced in 1934 for the commercial cinema circuit, 'Forgotten Men – the War as it Was', began with actual footage from the first war. This was followed by interviews between Sir John Hammerton, the historian, and some of the veterans. An officer who had been wounded spoke with passionate intensity from a wheel-chair about the urgent need to avoid another war which would be even more terrible than the last, because it would inflict mass bombing on civilian populations. In October 1935, Baldwin told the Peace Society: 'We live under the shadow of the last war and its memories still sicken us. We remember what war is, with no glory in it but the heroism of man.'[23] In May 1935, Lloyd George reported to his mistress 'a most extraordinary outburst' by King George V: 'I *will* not have another war. I *will not*. The last war was none of my doing, & if there is another one & we are threatened with being brought in to it, I will go to Trafalgar Square and wave a red flag myself sooner than allow this country to be brought in.'[24] Vaughan Williams, who had served in France, composed an emotional plea for peace and reconciliation, *Dona Nobis Pacem*, first performed in 1936, using the combined resources of the Christian and liberal humanist traditions. 'For my enemy is dead, a man divine as myself is dead' the soloist sings from a poem by Walt Whitman.

However, many at British Legion and other service reunions remembered (as did J. B. Priestley in Chapter 6 of his *English Journey*) the comedy, absurdities and comradeship of the war more vividly than the horrors:

> I stared at the rows of flushed faces in front of me, and thought how queer it was that these chaps from Bradford and Halifax and Keighley, woolcombers' and dyers' labourers, warehousemen and woolsorters, clerks and tram-conductors, should have gone out and helped to destroy for ever the power of the Hapsburgs, closing a gigantic chapter of European history.

George Orwell and Christopher Isherwood said that the young sensed that they had missed a vast experience which had shaped their elders. Philip Toynbee wrote: 'Even in our Anti-War campaigns of the early thirties we were half in love with the horrors we cried out against, and as a boy, I can remember murmuring the name *"Passchendaele"* in an ecstasy of excitement and regret.'[25]

Everywhere the countless war memorials were still new and arresting features to the eye and the imagination. They had not yet merged with their surroundings or become dusty and untended. Throughout the land, in railway stations, public squares, churches, office entrance halls and school chapels, memorials in varying forms proclaimed their messages of pride and sorrow, listed the names (each one somebody's son or father or husband) and pledged an everlasting remembrance. A climbing club erected a bronze tablet to twenty of its members on the summit of Great Gable. In Wetherby parish church, Yorkshire, the plaque quoted Rupert Brooke:

> These laid the world away; poured out the red
> Sweet wine of youth; gave up the years to be . . . ('The Dead')

Beneath a crucifix in the churchyard at Clyro (the village of which Francis Kilvert was once curate) were inscribed lines from the hymn 'O Valiant Hearts':

> Tranquil you lie, your knightly virtue proved,
> Your memory hallowed in the land you loved.

The memorial to the Machine Gun Corps at Hyde Park Corner London topped by a statue of David, sword in hand, quoted belligerently from I Samuel 18.7: 'Saul hath slain his thousands, but David his tens of thousands.' As students at the City of Leeds Training College filed out of their assembly hall, they read on the Roll of Honour stern words from the most popular poem of the war, 'In Flanders Fields' by John McCrae:

> To you from failing hands we throw
> The torch; be yours to hold it high.
> If ye break faith with us who die
> We shall not sleep . . .

At thousands of services on Armistice Day every year the pledge of remembrance was renewed:

> At the going down of the sun and in the morning
> We will remember them.
> (Laurence Binyon: 'For the Fallen')[26]

But whether as an image of horror, or as a trigger for nostalgia or as something more ambivalent and tragi-comic, the landscape of the Great War dominated the twenties and thirties, and indeed still haunts the communal imagination. In 1938 on 5 October, three days after the churches had been crowded by people giving thanks for the deliverance from war by the Munich agreement, the *Times* published an article under the headline 'Soldiers Blinded in War: Cases Still Entering St Dunstan's'. This was the aspect of war kept alive for churchpeople (but for others as well) by the poems of Studdert Kennedy. His Collected Poems published in 1927 as *The Unutterable Beauty* had reached their tenth edition by January 1936. *Lies* (1919) went into eighteen editions by 1937. 'This post-war world is black with lies . . . There's a bad smell about . . . it is like the smell of the Dead', he wrote in the Introduction.[27]

The third feature of the inter-war period which created support for pacifists and pacifiers was a belief in the rationality and reasonableness of human beings, which in the churches was reinforced by liberal theology. The evidence provided by the war that underneath the conscious surface of European civilization there seethed dark irrational forces was largely ignored until the late thirties. So Arthur Ponsonby in 1927 expressed his conviction that 'all disputes between nations are capable of settlement either by diplomatic negotiations or by some form of international arbitration'. When Baldwin demurred, Ponsonby asserted 'We are of the opinion that unprovoked aggression is a war myth'.[28] The liberal *Manchester Guardian* had a clearer understanding of the evil nature and actions of Nazi Germany than some other newspapers, but when confronted by one crisis after another which revealed Nazism in all its heinousness, it counselled tolerance and moderation because war was unthinkable, or because after all the

Versailles Treaty was unjust, or because no nation had a clear conscience. Underlying the general attitude of the British press was 'a fundamental inability to understand the potential depths of Nazi brutality'.[29] Ramsay MacDonald, the Prime Minister (who had been reviled during the war as one of its leading opponents) told the German Ambassador in April 1933 that 'from the very start he had not believed the reports of excesses'. In November MacDonald assured the Ambassador that if Hitler were to visit Britain, he would receive a most friendly reception. One might plead that Hitler had, after all, only just come to power. Yet as late as June 1937, Sir Nevile Henderson informed the guests at a dinner to welcome him as British Ambassador to Berlin, that far too many people had 'an erroneous conception' of Nazism. Otherwise they would lay less emphasis on 'Nazi dictatorship and much more emphasis on the great social experiment which is being tried out in this country'.[30]

In the 1930s liberal theology in Britain was being successfully challenged by Barthianism and neo-orthodoxy in academic circles, but little of this reached either the leadership of the churches or the man in the pew until the events of 1939. Percy Dearmer, editor of the popular hymnbook *Songs of Praise* (1925) explained in 1933 that it was 'for the forward-looking people of every communion'; expressed his dislike of the traditional Advent themes of death, judgment, hell and heaven; believed that 'tears' provided a more acceptable image of atonement than 'the crude insistence on blood' and asserted that modern psychology taught that it was 'dangerous to teach people to say that they were false and full of sin'.[31] Liberal theology neglected or despised the Old Testament as largely primitive, minimized and rationalized evil, and emphasized the immanence of God in creation and human beings more than incarnation, redemption and transcendence. It eliminated or neglected all that was craggy and disturbing in scripture and believed that a rational, analytical approach to scripture produced a core of material, believable by modern scientific man, an approach that Henson found 'spiritually desolating'.[32] The opinions of Bishop Barnes of Birmingham represented the apotheosis of liberal theology. Parthenogenesis could probably explain the Virgin Birth. The Real Presence could be disproved by experiments. The stigmata of St Francis could be accounted for by the saint scratching because he did not wash. Even his son (in his admiring biography) admits that there was 'little poetry in him'. Though Barnes dismissed the 1928 Prayer Book as a series of 'concessions to religious barbarism'[33] it did, in accordance with the pacific sensibilities of the time, bracket the more violent verses of the Psalms and offer an alternative toned-down form for the confession of sin. The report produced after sixteen years in 1938 by the Archbishops' Commission, *Doctrine in the Church of England*, draws this assessment from Leslie Paul:

> One can only surmise that the Report's tepidity arises from, or rather is a part of, the total intellectual inadequacy of the interwar years, in theology as elsewhere. Men lived the progressive dream still, as if there had been no Great War and there would never be another war. Liberal-minded England and America had no idea what they faced in Stalin's Russia and Hitler's Germany. The Commission indeed found it difficult in that meliorating climate to believe in sin or evil at all, except as something a pre-arranged evolution would presently eliminate . . . The Commission had nothing as trenchant to say about sin as William Golding's aphorism – 'man distils evil as a bee distils honey'.
> The perfunctoriness of the report belongs to a theology not yet in crisis. It had not yet felt the blows of Kierkegaard, that one had to have faith with twenty thousand fathoms beneath one, nor had it heard Barth quoting Luther that man has a passion against deity, he cannot abide deity. Brunner seemed unheard and the existentialism of Sartre was yet in the womb of time. Perhaps I put too much on one report – but yet, sixteen years to produce a theology totally without grief![34]

Carl Jung castigates modern man for wishing to attend only to his conscious rational self. Evil, he said, cannot be dismissed simply as *privatio boni*: 'We stand perplexed and stupefied before the phenomenon of Nazism and Bolshevism because we know nothing about man, or at any rate have only a lop-sided and distorted picture of him. . . We stand face to face with the terrible question of evil and do not even know what is before us, let alone what to pit against it.'[35]

Fourthly, there were elements in British society which took a benevolent view of aspects of the dictatorships, and so further softened public opinion already favourable to appeasement and pacifism. 'How often did one hear it said by educated men and women (wrote Henson) "I only wish we had a Hitler or a Mussolini, in this country".'[36] Expressions of admiration for Nazism were at their peak in 1936–37, then gradually declined and ceased altogether with the outbreak of war, except among the tiny minority of explicit pro-Nazis. Many people praised the new Germany as a bulwark against Communism – even C. F. Garbett, Bishop of Winchester, used a form of this argument as late as 1935.[37] Some complained about the shortcomings of democracy and admired authoritarian regimes. A popular series of books appeared in the mid-1930s under the general title of 'If I were Dictator', written by such various figures as Lord Dunsany, Julian Huxley, Dick Sheppard, Vernon Bartlett and James Maxton. Hitler was often commended for reducing unemployment – even the anti-Nazi *Daily Telegraph* on 23 July 1936 compared the Nazi economic achievements with those of Roosevelt. In addition anti-semitic elements at every level of society covertly, and sometimes openly, expressed their complete comprehension as to why Hitler hated the Jews. Yet it is not altogether easy accurately to assess the significance of all the anti-semitic sentiments in Britain at this period. Lord Robert Cecil privately used disparaging and condescending language about the Jews, but when it came to the crunch he was one of the first Englishmen publicly to condemn the Nazi persecution of the Jews.

At the British Legion Annual Conference in June 1935, the Prince of Wales welcomed the forthcoming visit to Germany of British Legion delegates: 'I feel that there could be no more suitable body or organization of men to stretch forth the hand of friendship to the Germans than we ex-servicemen, who fought them and have now forgotten all about it and the Great War.' The delegates were received by Hitler who emphasized the importance of collaboration of ex-soldiers for peace. As they travelled through Germany they assured their hosts at public functions that Britain's war against Germany had been 'a colossal blunder'.[38] Lloyd George visited Hitler in September 1936 and afterwards praised him as 'the greatest living German' and a 'born leader' who had no desire to invade any other country.[39]

In all this we should remember that many British people wanted to assuage their guilt for having described Germans as 'beasts', 'devils' and 'Anti-Christ' during the war. To construe German policies in as favourable a light as possible was (they also thought) the way to avoid the antagonisms which might lead to another, even worse, war.

Fascism was totally alien to the liberal traditions of the Anglican and Free Church clergy. But ultramontane English Roman Catholicism included some (particularly intellectuals) who were openly sympathetic to fascism. Almost all vocal English Roman Catholics supported Franco in the Spanish Civil War. Even at the height of the Second World War, Cardinal Hinsley, Archbishop of Westminster, retained a photograph of Franco on his writing table. On 11 February 1939, the *Tablet* celebrated the tenth anniversary of the Lateran Treaty as 'the recognition of Italian Fascism as a new State form by the Church which, through the centuries, has always sought to make the best of each temporal order'. Pointing out that there had never been a concordat with Communism ('the chief enemy of the Church') and alluding to the 'increasingly uneasy concordat' with Nazism, the leader warned against 'the worship of numerical majorities, and the dangers of democracy without authority'; 'no sane and instructed man would hesitate to prefer Fascism to Communism'. It appealed to Roman Catholics 'not to join or encourage this anti-Fascist crusade' so popular in England. Cardinal Hinsley, whose years in Rome had led him to perceive good as well as evil in Italian fascism, was informed by a concerned correspondent in February 1939 that it was widely believed in England that the Roman Catholic church was pro-fascist. The Belloc tradition encouraged anti-semitism, adulation of the mediterranean countries and held up Western democracy for derision. On the other hand, in 1934 the official Roman Catholic publishers Burns, Oates and Washbourne made available a translation for English readers of *Judaism, Christianity and Germany*, a collection of sermons highly critical of Nazism by Cardinal Faulhaber, Archbishop of Munich. However, by January 1939 Hinsley had publicly condemned Fascism and Nazism and when war came, he emerged as a belligerent patriot, willing even to subdue his passionate opposition to Communism when the Anglo-Soviet pact made the expression of such convictions impolitic.[40] By contrast, in *Must War Come?* (1935) John Eppstein (founder of the Catholic Council for International Relations and one of the chief officers of the LNU) sought to interpret Roman Catholic and papal teaching as supportive of the League, and to prove that peace work was not the monopoly of protestants and socialists. Obviously he felt isolated and defensive as a Roman Catholic in peace work.

Fifthly, the ecumenical movement affected Christian attitudes to peace and war. The movement was given a powerful impetus by the guilt which many Christians keenly felt for having fought one another in the Great War. The movement brought together an increasing number of European (and other) church leaders in conferences from which a new sense of common, trans-national allegiance to Christ and many personal friendships grew. The first post-war and decisive conference between representatives of fourteen nations including Britain, Germany and France was held in October 1919. The post-war vision of the Holy Catholic Church transcending nationality caught the imaginations not only of church leaders, but also of the type of ordinary Christian who longed for peace and was a fervent supporter of the League. Initially the ecumenical movement reinforced the cause of both pacifists and pacifiers in the churches. Many began to regard a possible war between Britain and Germany as a direct conflict between fellow-Christians, a view which was much less evident in 1914 when ecumenism was still in its early infancy. However, by the mid 1930s, the ecumenical movement tended to influence Christians in the opposite direction, for in both the secular and the religious press, alarming stories about the Nazi persecution of the churches appeared regularly, often relayed through ecumenical contacts. So to be strongly opposed to Hitler's Germany became an expression, not a denial, of ecumenism, a sign of Christian solidarity with the true Germany. As early as 1934, the Universal Christian Council for Life and Work meeting in Denmark, sided controversially with the Confessing Church in Germany. The Oxford Conference, meeting under the darkening skies of 1937, boldly took as its theme the function of the church in a totalitarian society. The absence of Pastor Niemöller and other German delegates through imprisonment graphically underlined what was at stake. 'The first duty of the Church, and its greatest service to the world, is that it be in very deed the church', proclaimed the Conference. If war breaks out the fellowship of the church must be maintained above the conflict. The church must continue to worship, preach, teach and minister, whether the state consents or not. Pacifists and non-pacifists must respect their divergent convictions within the common fellowship of the one Body. Charles Raven's eloquent exposition of the pacifist case failed to convert the Conference. But at least pacifism had gained ecumenical recognition as a genuine Christian vocation.[41]

5

CHRISTIAN PACIFISM

Neither pacifism in general, nor Christian pacifism in particular, was a unitary, but rather a multi-faceted, phenomenon. There were those who approved the use of force by the police or by a world state, but disapproved of the use of force by individual nations. Some contended that the use of sanctions by the League was legitimate; others strongly disagreed. Some regarded pacifism as a dogma, an expression of faith: therefore its truth was independent of any actual consequences. Others preached pacifism primarily on pragmatic grounds: pacifism was a rational method of preventing war. Some contended that the aggressor would be shamed by world opinion into ceasing violent activity if confronted by a disarmed or pacifist population. Donald Soper, the Methodist pacifist, wrote in 1933: 'pacifism contains a spiritual force strong enough to repel any invader'. Throughout the inter-war years (as before and since) pacifists were pulled between two opposing strategies. Should they maintain absolute purity by becoming uncompromising sectarians and keep their hands clean by steering clear of politicians? Or should they risk compromising their purity by co-operating with non-pacifist but peace-loving politicians in order to be more politically effective? Many pacifists were socialists of one sort or another and so were committed (unless they were complete individualists) to working with non-pacifist socialists to change the social order, which in any case they contended was a prime cause of war. Some pacifists were anarchic individualists. In 1935 Bertrand Russell observed about first war COs: 'In some men the habit of standing out against the herd had become so ingrained that they could not cooperate with anybody about anything.' Pacifists were often involved in a variety of other dissenting movements and causes.[1] Orwell remarked on the prevalence of 'cranks' in left-wing movements. 'One sometimes gets the impression that the mere words "Socialism" and "Communism" draw towards them with magnetic force every fruit-juice drinker, nudist, sandal-wearer, sex-maniac, Quaker, "Nature Cure" quack, pacifist and feminist in England.'[2]

Two of the tiny minority of Roman Catholic pacifists of the period, W. E. Orchard and Eric Gill, had crucially determinative Nonconformist backgrounds. W. E. Orchard (as we saw in Chapter 2) had exercised a highly individualist ministry at the Congregational King's Weigh House, London before he became a Roman Catholic. Eric Gill's grandfather and great-uncle had been Congregational missionaries. His father was ordained in the Congregational ministry but was forced to resign because he preached against hell; he then transferred to the Countess of Huntingdon's Connexion. Later he was ordained as an Anglican priest. Eric Gill converted to Roman Catholicism in 1913 only to discover that his extremely individual amalgam of catholicism, eroticism, anarchistic communism and pacifism looked more like dissent than orthodoxy to his fellow-Catholics. His war memorial for Leeds University, unveiled in 1923, depicted Christ expelling well-to-do Leeds citizens from the Temple with a text (in Latin) from James 5.1 ('Go to now, ye rich men, weep and howl . . .'). Gill joyfully stirred the ensuing controversy.[3] Thus to imply that the war was caused by the rich was wholly characteristic of populist Nonconformist ideology. In 1931 when Gill was working on the sculpture above the entrance to Broadcasting House, London, his habit of wearing a crimson petticoat-bodice (without breeches) under his smock must have caused consternation among passers-by below. In 1939, just after the outbreak of war, he defended his pacifism by pointing out that British, Irish and American Roman Catholic prelates had taken opposing moral views about the war. 'In any case, it is Catholic teaching that the individual conscience is the final Judge.'[4] When he died in 1940 he was buried with Roman Catholic rites but appropriately enough, the cemetery was situated next to a Baptist chapel.

The first scholarly book in England to investigate thoroughly the origins of Christian pacifism was *The Early Christian Attitude to War* (1919) by C. J. Cadoux, the Congregational academic and pacifist. He argued that though the Christian mind in the early church was in many ways immature, yet the church was pulsating with the vigorous life of its founder, as never since, and was constantly being purified by persecution. Its conscience was keen, and not yet compromised by worldliness. Cadoux granted that the evidence about early attitudes was complex. Slaves and Jews were exempt from military service so a large proportion of the early Christians were ineligible. All recruits needed could be obtained by voluntary methods. So for most early

Christians, military service was not a live option. Jesus rejected violence for himself and for his disciples. It is incorrect to interpret some of Jesus' statements as legitimizing violence. Was his teaching inconsistent with the moral ordering of society? But Jesus was a far more effective reformer of morals than the police. The Christian community grows by the accession of reformed individuals and thus society would be transformed by decreasing the need of violence to restrain evil. (This, we note, was an individualistic view of Christianity congruent with the heroic individualism of the COs in the war rather than with any pacifist programme for political action.) Since Cadoux did not believe that Jesus was expecting an imminent end to history, his teaching could not be relegated to the status of an 'interim-ethic', which he described as 'the last fortress of militarism on Christian soil'.[5] The early Christians took Jesus at his word and normally refused to serve in the forces. But the early purity did not last; eschatological hope faded; standards were relaxed; biblical images of warfare became influential. But the decisive abandonment of the church's pacifism came with the Constantinian period, though the change was accepted only gradually and with an uneasy conscience. Though Cadoux did not attempt to present any detailed implications of pacifism for the modern world, he believed that nothing in modern life invalidated the teaching of Jesus or the witness of the early church. The Christian, now as then, has 'a method more radical and effectual than the use of arms and involving him in a full measure of suffering and self-sacrifice'.[6]

Cadoux's appeal to the authority of the early church was a shrewd move. By demonstrating with meticulous scholarship that Christ's teaching was interpreted as requiring pacifism by the early church, he attempted to reduce the authority of those New Testament passages which were less amenable to a pacifist construction. By treating Christianity as the call to the individual and by appealing to the authority of the pre-Constantinian church he ensured a hearing from fellow Nonconformists who believed that establishment led to worldliness. But by wholly deploring the Constantinian settlement he evaded the issue on which pacifists were (and still are) most vulnerable. Cadoux's position might have been wholly appropriate for first war objectors, but it was wholly inappropriate for the immediate post-war world where people were looking to international political action to bring peace. For Cadoux, pacifism remains the heroic stand by individuals, but it is politically null. We have here another version of the dilemmas of dissent which we examined in the first three chapters.[7]

If Cadoux's book informed the mind, *Conscription and Conscience*

(1922) by John Graham was designed to stir the heart and fire the imagination. It was prefixed by a poem composed by a Chartist leader in prison. Graham, Quaker Principal of Dalton Hall Manchester, chairman of the Friends' Peace Committee, had acted as a chaplain to imprisoned objectors during the war. The preface was written by the socialist pacifist Clifford Allen, chairman of the No-Conscription Fellowship 1914–18 who had served three terms of imprisonment in 1916–17. (Later he supported the National Government and was created a peer in 1932.) Allen's preface is wholly at variance with the main part of the book. Pacifists, he asserted, must be more concerned with the future than with the past. He urged the organization of a widely-based movement in which pacifists joined non-pacifists to oppose conscription. He was surprisingly critical of COs: their struggle was carried on 'far too often in a spirit of half-arrogant pride, not far removed from that militarism they sought to overthrow'. Yet 'we acted as we did because we loved our country'.[8] By contrast Graham wrote with fierce pride in the objectors and with deep revulsion against war: 'War means blind and wholesale death and maiming of innocent men. It means the torture of wounded men lying in the open, bleeding to death through hours of deadly thirst and moaning pain . . . it means desolate homes, poverty, and a fatherless generation growing to manhood . . . In war hatred becomes a duty, love ridiculous . . . The fellowship of mankind, the brotherhood of man under the fatherhood of God is earnestly denied in word and deed.'[9] By systematically collecting and vividly retelling the sufferings of the objectors, he provided an extensive martyrology which inspired the hearts of, and provided a model for, the outlook of the pacifists of the inter-war period comparable to the martyrologies of both the Free Churches and the Labour Party. The dichotomy between Allen and Graham in the book was prophetic of two different interpretations of pacifism which came to the surface in the 1930s when once again war became an imminent possibility. It was conscription which had created the sectarian rigour and heroism of the objectors. When with the end of the war, conscription ceased and optimism about achieving peace through international co-operation ran high, the specifically pacifist vocation was pushed into the background. As Ceadel points out, the leading pacifists of the inter-war era did not adopt their faith until some years after the war, roughly at the time the most famous of the war memoirs appeared. H. R. L. ('Dick') Sheppard became a pacifist in 1927 and Charles Raven in 1930.

The fact that Sheppard and Raven, two key figures in the Christian pacifist movement, were both Anglican priests is significant. Whereas the large majority of the religious participants in pre-war peace movements and of the religiously motivated COs, were Nonconformist or Quakers, in the post-war period a significant number of Anglican clergy participated in groups of pacifiers or pacifists. Before 1914, the approach to war of the comparatively small number of Anglican pacifiers like John Percival (Bishop of Hereford) and Edward Hicks (Bishop of Lincoln) was one expression of their general liberal attitudes to social questions.[10] So the emergence of an Anglican contribution to societies like the LNU as well as to pacifist groups, was a further development and strengthening of the pre-war alliance between liberal Christianity and a progressivist ideology. Anglo-Catholicism with its dissenting attitude towards authority and its anti-erastianism had an influence way beyond its borders. It fitted well into the spirit of post-war rebelliousness against 'the old men' who had led the nation to war. H. D. A. Major, the modernist, observed about the Church of England in 1932: 'She who had been aptly described as the Conservative party at prayer, became, as the result of Gore's influence, at least in the persons of her Anglo-Catholic clergy, the Socialist party at Mass.'[11] Both Raven and Sheppard were inheritors of the pre-war alliance between political and theological liberalism. Sheppard's churchmanship owed a good deal to Anglo-Catholicism though he interpreted it in a very free-wheeling manner. Both were in the broad stream of the mild Christian socialist tradition, with which Anglo-Catholicism constantly interacted.

Charles Raven

Charles Raven (1885–1964) was Dean of Emmanuel College Cambridge when war broke out. Four times he attempted to enlist as a combatant but each time he was turned down on medical grounds. In 1917 he was accepted as a chaplain. In later years he often vividly described how radically his time at the front changed him as a human being and as a priest.[12] During the spiritual agony of his first night in France, and during the nine months that followed, he had a profound experience of the companionship of Christ. He marvelled at the brotherhood and the spirit of self-sacrifice which surrounded and sustained him. Life 'has tested us to the full. Only those who go down into the valley of death will ever know the glory of life's summits.' Those who stayed at home and profiteered and those who watched from afar, consumed with hate, were the true victims rather than the maimed or widowed. 'Those who can live in it may be purified: those who look on are usually defiled.' Just as before the war he had glimpsed the glory of God in a couple in love or in a dingy fish-and-chip shop, so now he saw a dead soldier and the natural world of plants and insects surrounding him, 'ablaze with the Shechinah of God'. Seeing the whole evolutionary struggle as illuminated by the sacrifice of Calvary, and drawing (as so often) on Romans 8, or as here on Ephesians 6, he believed that the war was 'not a conflict between opposing armies but of flesh and blood against the tyranny of blind and impersonal forces . . . Bitterness and enmity are purged away.'[13] Theologically the war confirmed him in his liberal modernism. He looked backwards to the mediaeval church as apostate, but forwards to the post-war period as a new Pentecost after Calvary, a fresh unfolding of the dynamic and unifying activity of the Spirit. War (he wrote) had stripped away sacerdotalism (chaplains had to be friends before they could be priests) and was pressing the church towards a liberal view of the Bible, a rejection of hell and much else which was impossible for the average man to accept.[14]

Towards the end of his life he repeated with approval the view that there are two unique sacraments – the physical universe and the person of Christ. Both disclose the nature of God if they are allowed to illuminate each other.[15] As a boy he had first learnt the meaning of the worship of God in the mountains of the Lake District. He comprehended that God dwells in darkness and that the Son of Man is revealed in darkness, when he spent whole nights alone in the open observing natural life.[16] Though he knew the 'terror of nature'[17] it was all held within (and distanced by?) his Christocentric view of God and history. Many of his decisive religious experiences were expressed in markedly Christocentric forms. As a young man he grew to love the church because it mediated the knowledge of Jesus and could on occasion offer deep experiences of fellowship, but he was always critical of its institutionalism, credalism and legalism. He was convinced that the development of modern science (which he found such an exhilarating story) only became possible when the control of the mediaeval church was broken. Despite his sympathy for Christian socialism and his work for COPEC, ultimately his Christianity was centred upon the personal relationship between Christ and the individual. This view of Christianity gave him strength to stand against the official church. All forms and structures were for him potentially oppressive and restrictive of life. But repeatedly he was torn by the dissenter's dilemma. His great gifts were as an electrifying and prophetic preacher, but he longed for recognition by the official church that (say) a bishopric would have given him. Yet after all he was Regius Professor of Divinity at Cambridge 1932–50, Master of Christ's College 1939–50 and Vice-Chancellor 1947–49. But a bishopric would have cramped the freedom he needed and his wounded, hypersensitive personality would have been tortured by the incessant routine of attending to the structures. Though he felt excluded from the ecclesiastical high table, in 1942, he was nevertheless still able to write to Archbishop Temple as 'My dear William'.

From 1924 onwards, he became convinced that the abolition of war was the supreme issue for mankind. Temperamentally he was ambivalent about conflict. He could not debate in a hostile environment and his natural *metier* was proclamation, synthesis not dialectic, cooperation not competition. Yet his growing isolation in the 1930s created by his pacifism and liberal theology led him to become increasingly polemical and denunciatory. Yet he could react paranoiacally when critics and reviewers were equally forthright. His distrust of psychoanalysis revealed an unwillingness to face the complexity of human motivation.

> Charles believed that the true and indeed the only possible way of interpretation was to see the universe as a single evolutionary process . . . What he seemed never able to entertain was the possibility that the universe could be interpreted in *two* ways . . . Continuity *and* discontinuity, unity *and* duality, the organic *and* the dialectical, progress through evolution *and* progress through resistance to evolution, steady growth *and* radical change, man cooperating with nature *and* man controlling nature; to attempt to hold dualities such as these together through the use of complementary models seemed to Charles . . . a policy of despair. He hardly seemed to realise that a single scheme was always in danger of being identified as ultimate in itself – an idol, even though a moving, expanding idol.[18]

His cosmic vision anticipated that of Teilhard de Chardin, but was open to some of the same criticisms, not least that it minimized the reality and complexity of evil and the inherent capacity of human beings for self-defeat (a characteristic of Raven himself). Raven was the first English pacifist to give a coherent theological basis to pacifism. His individualism, mystical idealism and suspicion of structures made it difficult for him both to tolerate the institutional nature of the church and to translate his ardent pacifism into the inevitable compromises and half-tones of political action. However, in his earlier books, at any rate, his evolutionary approach to history made it more possible for him than for some pacifists, to give a blessing to intermediate steps towards peace which fell short of the pacifist ideal. He became a pacifist in 1930, joined the Fellowship of Reconciliation and in 1932 became its chairman; he was president from 1945 until his death. He was one of the Sponsors of the Peace Pledge Union founded by Dick Sheppard.

Raven's first major study of pacifism, *Is War Obsolete?*, was published in 1935. The title implied the evolutionary view of history which undergirded the whole book. He grants that the evolutionary process, in which there is incessant war between the species, presents the pacifist with agonizing moral perplexities. But each new struggle is a move upwards and onwards. He had experienced war as a speeded-up example of the whole evolutionary process: the bovine rather than the intelligent and sensitive succumbed to shell shock. But war is now an anachronism. Our struggle today should be to sublimate and harness aggressive forces for peace. Raven read church history in evolutionary terms as well. The emancipation of slaves led to a new concept of brotherhood. The emancipation of women opens the way for their ordination. The ecumenical and peace movements move onwards together. One nation after another has renounced the papacy because it stands in the way of progress. So we cannot indulge in easy condemnations of earlier generations for not realizing the incompatibility of Christianity with war. To criticize the church for the Constantinian settlement is to criticize the method of evolution. (Here Raven parts company with Cadoux and others.) So Christians should be able to 'acquiesce in the internationalizing of armed force', even if this falls short of the ideal, because it would be a step in the right direction, 'while advocating and developing another way of reconciliation'.[19]

Raven defines pacifism as a response to the new way of defeating evil opened up by Christ on the cross. 'Martyrdom is the Christian's ultimate obligation.'[20] Pacifism must not be grounded in a revulsion from pain nor be promoted by painting a totally black picture of war. The last war failed to achieve its aims. Another war would plunge civilization into ruin. Nevertheless he felt impelled to justify the support which he and others had given to the war: they had felt a protective compassion towards Belgium; they were seized by a zest for adventure; how could they seek to preserve their own lives when so many of their fellows were going to their deaths?

> If I may be frank, when I listen to some of my peace-loving friends, their arguments arouse an instinctive antagonism: their horror of death, the falsity of their picture of war, their failure to recognize the existence of human beings whose religion glorifies fighting, their inability to resist the appeal to fear and to disgust, as if Satan could ever cast out Satan – these things merely fill me with a vast

admiration for the simple heroism of the lads whom I buried somewhere in France.[21]

Raven here was torn between his interpretation of the cross as the supreme example of pacifist non-resistance and his belief that the evolutionary process disclosed the principle of self-sacrifice and creative struggle which was focussed on Calvary. He now repudiated war morally and theologically. But his pastoral imagination had been unforgettably stirred by the heroism and self-sacrifice which the conflict had drawn from others and from himself, however much the acknowledgment of this might seem to undermine traditional pacifist arguments. Christian pacifists like Raven pointed to the cross as the condemnation of war. Conversely non-pacifist Christians interpreted the cross as the sanction and the inspiration for the self-sacrifice that war involved.

This book contains early examples of his life-long polemic against Karl Barth and Reinhold Niebuhr. German theologians have failed (Raven asserted) to develop the social implications of the gospel – they are a generation or more behind us. Raven presented an immanentist version of Christianity -- the universe manifests deity *within* it. But to him Barth's God was external and transcendent and Barth's Christ an intruder; the Holy Spirit becomes meaningless; man is unable to co-operate with God. He attacked Niebuhr for believing that human collectives are less moral than the individuals which compose them. Raven's experience of the richness of Christian fellowship contradicted this. He criticized American society for its separation of church from state (here again he revealed the Anglican slant of his pacifism). Raven could not accept Niebuhr's distinction between personal and corporate ethics. Yet at the outset he had addressed his book to the individual rather than to the community.

The only examples he provides as to how Christian pacifism could be applied to actual political situations are somewhat confusing. Because he believed in a step-by-step development, he commends Christ and the greatest of his followers for being patient enough to allow men to crawl before they are asked to walk. So side by side with his uncompromising absolutism about pacifism in theory and his frequent denunciations of the two standards of Catholic moral theology, he nevertheless conceded that physical force is sometimes necessary. War between Christians and cultured men is now as out-of-date as duelling, but we cannot simply withdraw troops from Palestine and the North-West Frontier, where force is the only practical restraint.

So though Raven speaks movingly about the way of Christ's cross, the fundamental scheme of thought which determines his judgments is evolutionary – hence his concessions to force in certain circumstances. He attacks individualistic religion, yet does not attempt to work out the political consequences of his pacifist faith in any detail. His theme is: the tide of pacifism is irresistibly moving in: swim with it, harness it, for it is God's tide. But what if Raven's evolutionary theory of history turned out to be mistaken? Because the pacifism of the inter-war period was so often expressed through an evolutionary ideology and grounded in an optimistic estimate of human nature, it was very vulnerable to attack when the evils of Nazism seemed to explode such a view of history and man.

Three other books by Raven reiterate similar themes but with different emphases. (Though two of them were published during and after the second war it seems advisable to discuss them here so that we can have a total conspectus of his thought on pacifism.)

In *War and the Christian* (1938) he acknowledges that the Japanese invasion of China, the war in Abyssinia, the civil war in Spain have all created difficulties for pacifism. But the pacifist movement continues to gather strength. He condemns war more strongly than in the previous book – it is 'organized hate'[22] and it grows more diabolical every year. The Just War theory is based upon the Old Testament (large parts of which Raven regarded as sub-Christian). Augustinian theology, revived by Barth, leads to an acceptance of war: 'The whole ethos of such a faith is one of pessimism, almost of despair . . .'.[23] He grants the strength of the arguments for an international police force, collective security and sanctions, and as an evolutionist accepts that parts of the world are not yet ready for pacifism. Probably but for the wave of anti-militàrism in Britain, British statesmen would have been able to support the League and prevent the tragic destruction of Abyssinia. As in the previous book, he envisaged the possibility that forces might be 'truly hallowed' if an international army took on the characteristics of the police, and so provided 'the protection of the world against its criminal elements, a bulwark of justice, a guarantee of peace'.[24]

Two passages reveal his fundamental optimism about human nature. He accepts that logically that the Christian pacifist would sit still and see his country invaded. But he adds that the pacifist 'does not believe that a thorough-going pacifism would have this result'.[25] He makes clear why he believes this:

Assuming the worst that can be said of Mussolini or Hitler, it remains true that an intelligent psychology will approach them fearlessly and without parade of arms, will strive to understand and discuss their grievances and ambitions and will meet their advances with generosity and 'sweet reasonableness'.[26]

Because God is love, love is the strongest force in the world. We must act on this belief. In any case we do not have any real grounds for disbelieving Hitler and Mussolini's assertions about their desire for peace. (Here we have another example of the tendency of the pacifist to hedge his bets.) Yet, as previously, he still believed in the necessity of troops in India and Palestine. Did Raven believe that Mussolini and Hitler as Europeans, had a moral nature to be appealed to, which was lacking in Indians and Arabs?

The Cross and the Crisis was published in 1940. Its mood was understandably and appropriately more sombre. He places greater emphasis upon the cross: 'it is at Gethsemane that the Church stands at the present moment'[27] On the Cross God adopted a wholly new method of dealing with evil. He grants that the kingdom theology of COPEC underestimated sin. Pacifism involves the casting out of self, 'a crucifying business . . . until men and women individually have been down into hell they are not mature'.[28] Yet in his very evident agony of soul he still believes that when we discover that someone against whom we have sinned loves us still, 'the power of that appeal is . . . irresistible'.[29] This book does not contain a single hint as to how this faith might be embodied in political action.

The Theological Basis of Christian Pacifism (1952) is remarkable in at least three respects. First, after two world wars he can still look back to pre-1914 as somehow normative, as a time when war had seemed an anachronism and the unbelievable happened. Secondly, he frequently deplores the effects of the war upon society and theology and frequently and violently denounces the influence of Barth and Niebuhr. Neo-orthodoxy is characterized by defeatism and stark pessimism about human nature. Centuries of theological distortion indicate our apostasy from the religion of the cross. He bitterly attacks Niebuhr for his description of pacifists as 'soft Utopians'. For Niebuhr 'taking sin seriously means being content to continue in it'.[30] He still smarts from Temple's denunciation of pacifism in 1935 as a heresy. After years of trying to preach pacifism to what he feels were increasingly deaf ears, his anger, near-despair and frustration are very evident. Thirdly, he asserts that the atomic bomb has made nonsense of the Just War principles. He passionately grieves as a scientist over this appalling misuse of science. But his wrath is at its most fierce against those churchmen who justify the use of atomic weapons:

> Yet if we are really prepared under any imaginable circumstances to murder the whole population of a hundred square miles by a single explosion, it becomes difficult to feel that our church-going and prayers, our duty towards our neighbours and our talk about love, service and sacrifice can be anything but cant and hypocrisy. Has all our theology of crisis and of denunciation merely brought us to the point at which because we are fallen sinners we can excuse ourselves for any sin, however monstrous and diabolical?[31]

Though in retrospect, he accounted for the failure of pre-war pacifism to convince the churches and the world because it was too facilely presented, and 'lacked the concrete issue, the definite objective',[32] at no point did he suggest what might now be done politically. In both the later books the attempts to politicize pacifism have dropped away. The first two books were addressed to the general public and the churches. In the second two books he seems to have been speaking almost exclusively to his fellow-pacifists.

There is a wry footnote to be added to Raven's pacifism, an example of the dilemmas which pacifists experienced in war-time. Soon after the outbreak of war, the Royal Ordnance authorities desperately needed a supply of buck-thorn for the charcoal necessary for the manufacture of time-fuses. Raven was chairman of the trustees of Wicken Fen, Cambridgeshire, where buck-thorn was abundant. Raven gave his permission for the Fen to be used to provide this essential weapon of war.

Dick Sheppard

If Raven sought to give Christian pacifism a coherent theological basis, it was Dick Sheppard (1880–1937) who, more than anyone else, gave it popular appeal.[33] Sheppard grew up and was educated in the heart of traditional England. His father was something of a courtier: after being a minor Canon at Windsor, he became Sub-Dean of the Chapels Royal in London, where the family lived in St James's Palace. In 1900, after Marlborough, Dick Sheppard was on the way to the station to take up a commission in the army in South Africa when the horse drawing the cab slipped on the ice. Dick was lamed for life, putting an end to a military career. After Cambridge he went to work at Oxford House, Bethnal Green. Cosmo Gordon Lang, Bishop of Stepney, appointed him as his secretary. So began a deep, constant and life-long friendship. Through his experiences in the East End and under

Lang's influence he decided to be ordained. His remarkable capacity to identify with the poor and needy arose in part from the deep unhappiness of his early years: a wounded healer of those (like himself) wounded by life. In 1914 he became vicar of St Martin-in-the-Fields. But before his induction he decided to spend two months as a chaplain in France. His father had the ear of the King who fiercely opposed the idea. Nonetheless Sheppard went. He returned broken after characteristically wearing himself out tending the sick and dying. In November only eleven people came through the fog to his induction. He described to them the vision he had seen in France.

> I stood on the west steps, and saw what this Church would be to the life of the people. There passed me, into its warm inside, hundreds and hundreds of all sorts of people, going up to the temple of their Lord, with all their difficulties, trials and sorrows. I saw it full of people, dropping in at all hours of the day and night. It was never dark, it was lighted all night and all day, and often and often tired bits of humanity swept in. And I said to them as they passed: 'Where are you going?' And they said only one thing: 'This is our home. This is where we are going to learn of the love of Jesus Christ. This is the Altar of our Lord, where all our peace lies. This is St Martin's.' It was all reverent and full of love and they never pushed me behind a pillar because I was poor. And day by day they told me the dear Lord's Supper was there on His Altar waiting to be given. They spoke to me two words only, one was the word 'home' and the other was 'love'.[34]

Here are so many aspects of Sheppard's character: his determination to be vulnerable through his devotion to Jesus present in the needy and the poor; his desire to create the warm home for others which he had lacked himself; his understanding of the eucharist as the meal in which Jesus expressed his solidarity with the poor and unemployed; his romantic idealism which often led him to under-estimate the importance of the mundane and routine; his tendency to self-dramatization. Reconnoitering the parish before his induction, he spent the night in mufti wandering round the pubs, visiting the hospital and sitting for hours with the down-and-outs on the benches on the Embankment. As dawn broke, he finished his night's work with a cup of coffee and a bun from a stall close to the church. When in 1921 he commissioned Laurence Housman to write a pageant about the life of St Martin, Sheppard characteristically cast himself as the beggar. It was Sheppard who in 1924 at St Martin's conducted the first service to be broadcast in Britain – an expression of his constant longing to reach the masses on or beyond the frontiers of the church. Later in life, when often racked with insomnia and asthma, he would spend part of the night writing letters and cards, sometimes a hundred a day, to friends, passing acquaintances and those in need: 'like candles on a Christmas tree' Rose Macaulay described them.

Sheppard was an actor and a clown. Peter Berger interprets the priest as a clown figure 'who dances through the world, incongruous in the face of the world's seriousness, contradicting all its assumptions – a messenger from another world, in which tears are turned to laughter and the walls of man's imprisonment are breached'. William Hamilton depicts the Christian as 'the sucker, the fall guy, the jester, the fool for Christ, the one who stands before Pilate and is silent, the one who stands before power and power-structures and laughs'.[35] (Raven was another actor but was too vain and self-conscious ever to be a clown.) Sheppard was always ambivalent about power and authority. In 1910–11, staying at Bishopthorpe with the always class-conscious Lang (another actor incapable of being a clown), he offered the butler a game of golf, much to Lang's displeasure. Later that day, carrying the primatial cross in front of the Archbishop in procession through York Minster, Sheppard muttered 'May I play golf with the butler?' No reply. 'If you don't say "Yes" I'm going to take you all round the Minster *and* into the crypt.' After further whispered exchanges, Lang, who correctly believed that Sheppard was quite capable of such a jape, irritated, gave way.[36] Yet Lang was Sheppard's 'constant anchor, offering him a friendship which never wearied and never failed, and an understanding which that tormented soul could find nowhere else'.[37]

Sheppard's gospel was that God in Jesus had revealed himself as vulnerable love. Christianity was about Jesus. Like Raven, he believed that imitating Jesus was the essence of Christian discipleship, whereas non-pacifists explicitly or implicitly denied that we can resolve all questions by asking 'What would Jesus do?'[38] Neither Sheppard nor Raven would allow much authority to the Old Testament. Their theology was too centred upon Jesus and too determined by a progressive understanding of revelation and history for the Old Testament to have much appeal to them. Like Raven too, Sheppard believed that hell was irreconcilable with a loving Father. For Sheppard the message of Christianity was essentially simple, but he constantly deplored that it had been complicated by the formalities and theological technicalities of the institutional church – a view of Christianity which the vast majority of English people share. And for Sheppard the opinions of the man and woman in the street had always a particular authority. In *The Impatience of a Parson* (1927) he proposed that the Lambeth Conference in 1930 should make clear that the church renounced 'all desire to make moral judgments upon men or to excommunicate or anathemize any single person whatever may have been his short-comings'. On the other hand he wanted the church to take an absolute moral stand against war and 'demand' that its members should refuse to kill. The church should demand disestablishment and be prepared to accept disendowment. Episcopacy is expedient but Apostolic Succession is not essential. Christians must be allowed to receive Communion together.[39] Consistent with this programme of theological liberalism was his readiness, unusual at that time, to remarry the divorced and to give Communion to the divorced and remarried. (Conservative churchmen were situationalists about war, absolutists about marriage. Christian pacifists tended to be absolutists about war, but situationalists about divorce.) That in marriage, as elsewhere, there was no virtue in the form without the spirit, was one of Sheppard's cardinal principles. When his own marriage broke down in 1937, he who had always held a romantic view of women, and whose life had been founded upon the conviction that love was unconquerable, believed he could never preach again.

Like Raven, the aggression Sheppard could not (or dare not) express towards the dictators was directed outwards towards the church and inwards towards himself. The pacifist Bishop Barnes found an outlet for his aggression in ridicule and persecution of the Anglo-Catholics in his diocese and in the country at large. 'What does Dr Barnes think is to be gained' (asked the *Guardian* on 24 July 1931) 'by his persistent advertisement of his quarrels with his clergy in the public Press?' Sheppard had been part of the 'ginger group' which, with William Temple as its leader, had launched 'Life and Liberty'. Sheppard preached at Temple's consecration as Bishop of Manchester in 1921: 'He helped us to say our prayers. It was just what we wanted' was Temple's grateful comment.[40] But after a few years' experience of the institutions which Life and Liberty created, Sheppard asked how the movement, which had seemed so full of bright promise, could result in 'that deadly piece of machinery', the Church Assembly, with its nitpicking legalism and ecclesiasticism? 'If only our ecclesiastics were not so often the safe people!', Sheppard lamented. A bishop had written thrillingly about Christianity in his diocesan magazine as 'A Great Adventure' but it turned out to be a request that each parish should raise money for the effective administration of the diocese. However much he loved the Church of England, he came to believe that the churches had so misunderstood Christianity that what they offered was a caricature. 'The Church, however essential, is subsidiary to the adventure of Christian living.' The 'primary allegiance of the individual is directly to Jesus Christ'. 'I can more easily see our Lord sweeping the streets of London than issuing edicts from its cathedral.'[41] Solutions to problems were to be found through intuition, spontaneity, leaps of faith: 'We don't want committees . . . We want in our hearts the faith that moves mountains . . .' This Rousseauistic and naive attitude towards institutions and power was a prominent feature of his pacifism. He would have been overjoyed to see the women of Greenham Common tying teddy-bears and balloons to the wire fence outside the nuclear base – symbols of innocence. 'Be ye therefore wise as serpents, and harmless as doves' said Jesus (Matt. 10.16). Sheppard was a dove who knew nothing about a Christian vocation to be a serpent. He quoted George Lansbury, another soft-hearted man, as having a theory that if only six men of good will, able to speak for the world powers, were dropped on a desert island with no experts 'to sidetrack them, they could settle all our most dangerous international problems in a week'.[42]

Recently, Archbishop Habgood has written about the way in which close contact with the complexity of decisions facing those in power has 'a devastating effect on prophetic certainties. And actually to share responsibility is even more devastating.'[43] But Sheppard had no direct, and very little indirect, experience of being alongside those who exercise great political power. Again, if Sheppard had actually visited Nazi Germany and talked with the victims of persecution, his attitudes might have been very different. He had assisted at Sir Oswald Mosley's wedding in 1920 and Mosley's mother was one of his oldest friends. She invited Sheppard to attend the Olympia meeting of Mosley's British Union of Fascists on 7 June 1934. He went and was appalled by the brutal treatment of protesters; the *Daily Telegraph* published his indictment the following day.

What Henson in 1927 termed Sheppard's 'career of consecrated eccentricity' outraged conventional ecclesiastics. However, almost everyone recognized what Henson (with unusual open-heartedness) described as 'his essential goodness'.[44] His adoption of lay dress, his celebrations of Evening Communion, his readiness to celebrate the Lord's Supper for the undenominational Brotherhood Movement, his ostentatious sitting down in St Paul's Cathedral during the Athanasian Creed when a Canon there: all came under fire, especially from the Anglo-Catholic *Church Times*. Charles Smyth (Dean of Chapel, Corpus Christi College Cambridge 1937–46 and then Rector of St Margaret's, Westminster) in 1937 published a caustic neo-orthodox indictment of what he termed 'Liberal Obscurantism' exemplified particularly by Sheppard. Entitled provocatively 'The Importance of Church Attendance' the essay quoted T. S. Eliot's riposte to the liberal cult of spontaneity: 'The spirit killeth, but the letter giveth life'. Christian theology, Smyth asserted, was not Christocentric but Theocentric. Nor was the teaching of Jesus simple, as liberals claimed. He reproduced an extract from a Cambridge University sermon by Canon Peter Green, the much-loved parish priest in Salford who had given the church a lot of hard knocks in his time.[45] Green said that he found it hard to forgive Sheppard for *The Impatience of a Parson*. Sheppard seemed to think that the best way to show himself broadminded, up-to-date and free from clericalism was to attack the church.[46]

After the publication of *The Impatience of a Parson* in 1927, Sheppard thought that he would never be offered another job (he had resigned from St Martin's because of illness). But he had many friends in high places. After being ordained only nine years he had been made a Chaplain to the King in 1916. In 1927 he was made Companion of Honour. In 1929 he became Dean of Canterbury. His time there was cut short after eighteen months by a recurrence of severe illness. During his subsequent tenure of a Canonry at St Paul's, his experiences of Cathedral life there drove him to even deeper desperation about the church.[47] But nothing broke the friendship with Lang, however much Lang failed to be the liberating Archbishop Sheppard naively had hoped he might be. On 31 October 1937 flowers from Sheppard arrived at Lambeth for Lang's birthday. An hour later a telephone message informed Lang that Sheppard had been found dead at Amen Court. Lang wrote to Wilfred Parker (Bishop of Pretoria 1933–50, an old friend of both Lang and Sheppard): 'How I wish that somehow or other the course of his life had been different and that the dear man had never written these very tiresome and unhelpful books, but simply allowed his unique personality to radiate its influence of love and goodwill.'[48] But that was to want Sheppard to be somebody different. Nothing could have turned Sheppard into a deferential tailor of clothes for the Emperor-ecclesiastic which Lang often appeared to be.

For two days and nights, a hundred thousand people, including street-cleaners, taxi-drivers, waitresses, charwomen and tramps, queued for sometimes an hour or more to file past the coffin in St Martin's. Crowds lined the Embankment and Ludgate Hill as the coffin was taken in procession to St Paul's. Traffic was halted. Police on point duty saluted. Bargees and tugmen stood on deck and removed their hats. 'Never since the King's funeral, and this without pomp or commerce, have I seen anything like it', wrote Vera Brittain's husband.

'A light seems to have gone from the sky' said Dean Matthews in his sermon.[49] He was buried in the cloisters of Canterbury Cathedral and as he wished, with an impish irony, next to Archbishop Davidson, the 'ecclesiastical moderator' with 'the graces of a great referee', whom nevertheless he admired greatly. He had hoped (in vain) that Davidson would have been succeeded by a 'constructive revolutionary'.[50]

'He was the most completely unique person I have ever known or ever shall know' wrote Canon Tom Pym, a former army chaplain, 'I have never met anyone . . . who knowing him did not love him.'[51] 'The love that Dick so lavishly bestowed and, in bestowing, called forth . . . was the nearest approximation to the love of Christ that any of us are likely to see this side of the grave' wrote Dr Alan Don, Lang's chaplain and later Dean of Westminster.[52] In 1936 a man was found dead on the Embankment; his only possession was a letter from Dick Sheppard which he had kept for twenty-five years. Kingsley Martin affirmed: 'His love had an infectious quality. Some people's lives were changed when they discovered that he really cared about them.' But he added: 'This selfless and affectionate quality did not make him a wise politician.'[53] But in the thirties Sheppard was thrust into a political role. Whereas Niebuhr insisted that relations between individuals were not an adequate model for relations between groups and nations, Sheppard continued to insist that they were. When neo-orthodoxy was proclaiming the radical sinfulness of human beings, Sheppard went on believing in their essential and uncomplicated goodness. Pacifism was fortunate to have a theologian of the calibre of Raven and someone so widely loved as Sheppard, but it was disabling in an age of so much blatant evil for the movement to be led by two men who were incapable of receiving what neo-orthodoxy was saying about the sombre and irrational aspects of human life. And Sheppard died too soon after the break-up of his marriage for him to absorb its own particular and painful lessons about the ambiguous complexity of love and relationships.

It was in 1927 in *The Impatience of a Parson* that Sheppard first publicly announced that he was a pacifist, though as a chaplain in the early months of the war he realized that he was urging men to do what he would not do himself. In the book he wrote: 'If war broke out again to-morrow, the Churches would be just where they were in August of 1914'. He urged the churches not to leave peace thinking to outside institutions like COPEC but to 'wage a great campaign to end all war before the rumblings of a fresh war are heard on the horizon . . . simply because Jesus Christ cannot be identified with the bestial brutalities that war produces . . .'[54] When in 1927 he wrote about his conversion to pacifism to Housman, he made it clear that he wished to distance himself from the type of pacifism associated with the majority of the COs. The ordinary soldier who followed his conscience and gave his life was a 'martyr', and in most cases he was 'an infinitely finer type' than the majority of objectors. He disliked those who replaced 'My Country – right or wrong' with the 'very beastly doctrine' of 'My Country – always wrong'.[55] He longed to feel part of the human race too much for him to be attracted to a path of eccentric and lonely individualism – there was nothing of the puritan in his make-up or background. He enjoyed smart restaurants, loved being Dean of Canterbury and died a wealthy man. He was a rebel, but within the upper-class Oxbridge and Anglican (not Nonconformist) tradition. Sheppard did not conceive of pacifism as simply the struggle of individuals against war. Whole societies and nations had to be converted.

Sheppard was particularly associated with two developments in the pacifist movement: the Peace Army and the Peace Pledge Union. In 1915 at a meeting of the Church Socialist League, George Lansbury argued that wars would cease if unarmed men and women would stand between the two fighting lines. In 1931, Maude Royden, a freelance Anglican preacher, pacifist and feminist proposed the creation of a Peace Army for the same purpose. In February 1932, in response to the crisis in Shanghai, Herbert Gray (a Presbyterian minister and former army chaplain who had joined the FOR in 1931), Royden and Sheppard met and decided to appeal for volunteers. They would be sent out to Shanghai, under Sheppard's leadership, to stand between the Japanese and Chinese forces. Eight hundred people responded to the publicity in the press. But the League of Nations refused to transport a Peace Army into the conflict as it had no government support, and in any case Sheppard had another relapse in health. However, even many pacifists, including Housman, thought the whole idea impractical, and so the notion gradually died through inaction.[56]

On 16 October 1934 the press published a letter from Sheppard calling for men to send him a postcard to indicate that they would support the following pledge: 'We renounce war, and never again, directly or indirectly, will we support or sanction another.' By November he had received 50,000 signatures. He had, however, expected half a million. He had discovered, nevertheless, a method of enabling ordinary people to feel that they could actually do something to prevent the world from plunging into war, whereas previously, with the decline of faith in the League of Nations and international action, they had felt impotent and insignificant. From this initiative was founded the Peace Pledge Union in May 1936, launched with an impressive and varied array of thirty-six sponsors, including Leyton Richards, G. H. C. Macgregor, C. J. Cadoux, Fenner Brockway, C. E. M. Joad, Beverley Nichols, A. A. Milne, Stuart Morris, Charles Raven, Donald Soper, George Macleod, George Lansbury, Vera Brittain, Bertrand Russell and Siegfried Sassoon – a remarkably high proportion of the main pacifist leaders. There were two main reasons for the initially rapid growth of the PPU: first, the only membership requirement was the pledge – and the meaning of this was interpreted in a wide variety of ways; second, though the inspiration of the PPU was Christian, it claimed to appeal to all lovers of peace – the 'religious, rational, or broadly humanitarian in conviction'. Its membership reached 87,000 by 1937, but thereafter its rate of expansion slackened significantly, attaining its peak in 1940 when it had some 136,000 members.[57]

The PPU had its fair share of individualists and eccentrics. At the PPU Camp at Swanwick in August 1937 (when Sheppard delighted everyone by his clowning and theatricals) half the members were (or became) vegetarians. So in very English fashion, the vegetarians and meat-eaters formed two cricket teams and played against each other. Sheppard wanted the PPU to be fun as well as all-inclusive. One day he darted into the camp office and quipped (like some character from a novel by Evelyn Waugh): 'I say we're looking up. We have three girls with red toe-nails.'[58] One can hardly imagine one of the old dissenters like John Clifford making such a remark. Nor was Raven capable of such sexual flippancy. In Chapter 2 of *Good News of God* he suddenly lashed out: 'no society that tolerates a practice so aesthetically hideous and sexually obscene as the red-lacquering of finger-nails could possibly be healthy'.

The Peace Ballot (often confused with the Peace Pledge) was organized by the LNU in 1934 under the leadership of Lord Robert Cecil to exert pressure on the government, and to revive the flagging support for the League and the LNU. The fact that eleven and a half million people took the trouble to vote (just over half the number who voted in the General Election of 1935) indicated the widespread longing for peace. But the results also showed how few Christian pacifists there were among the pacifiers. The Ballot was strongly supported by the leaders of the churches and by the Liberal and Labour parties. But the Conservatives were less enthusiastic and some were strongly hostile. The results declared in June 1935 showed that eleven million had voted for Britain to remain a member of the League. Ten and a half million voted for an all-round reduction of armaments.

Nine and a half million voted for an all-round reduction in the numbers of war-planes. Nearly ten and a half million voted for the international prohibition of the manufacture and sale of arms for private profit. Ten million voted for (a) economic, non-military sanctions against an aggressor, but only just over six and a half million for (b) military sanctions. Only 14,121 exercised their right to declare themselves Christian pacifists in answer to (a) and 17,482 in answer to (b). The Archbishop of York and twenty-three bishops had urged people to vote in favour of continued membership of the League and international disarmament, but said that the other questions were on a different level because they involved issues of method. They therefore offered no guidance about them.[59]

In the last years of his life, Sheppard, despite recurrent bouts of ill-health, travelled frenetically all over Britain to speak for the PPU. Between 27 September and 21 October 1937 (he died on 31 October) he spoke at Ely, Wigan, Aberdeen, Sutton Coldfield, Hornsey, Carmarthan, Acton, Coventry, Queen's Hall London, Newcastle, Epsom, Guildford, Saffron Walden and Eastbourne. Vera Brittain met him for the first time when both were speakers at a peace rally in 1936:

> As I perceived all too clearly on that pacifist platform, to follow Dick meant treading the Way of the Cross in modern guise. He pointed to a path which might end, not in crucifixion or a den of lions, but at internment, the concentration camp, and the shooting squad.

She realized through her work for the PPU that 'a beginning could indeed be made, as it had been made in Galilee; not by saints, but by ordinary men and women'. She heard him tell an 'entranced' audience in Manchester:

> Last night I had a dream. In it George Lansbury and I were playing tennis against Hitler and Musso. George had a game leg and I was asthmatic, but we won six-love, six-love.

(The audience may have been 'entranced', but to invite an audience to indulge in such a childish fantasy about the dictators was surely culpable.) 'Not peace at any price, but love at all costs' he would tell crowds which flocked to hear him. For the general public, his message was optimistic, delivered with debonair charm, jokes and smiles. By contrast his own personal life was often grim, as Vera Brittain recalled:

> On the midnight train to Euston I could not rest in the sleeping

compartment next to his because, throughout the night, I could hear him coughing, groaning, and fighting for breath.[60]

Sheppard gave the fullest exposition of his pacifism in his book *We Say 'No'* (1935). This reveals that, as with many pacifists, there was in Sheppard an unresolved tension between preaching pacifism as a faith derived from special beliefs about God, Jesus and human beings, and preaching it as a commonsense practical political programme, which would commend itself to all men of good will. His preface to the fourth impression (October 1936) enabled him to reflect that he had been right to reject the concept of collective security under the League (the policy of many on the left). He had already put it aside because it rested upon the threat or use of force; now he proclaimed its demise: 'Collective security lies dead in the mountains of Ethiopia'.[61] He also remarked that since the first printing, *The Power of Non-Violence* (1935) by Richard Gregg had appeared, cogently outlining (so Sheppard thought) the arguments for and methods of non-violence. Sheppard said that he based the case for Christian pacifism wholly on the words and example of Jesus, but on the same page refuted the charge against pacifism of 'sentimentalism', by pointing out that Bertrand Russell had come to almost the same conclusions through a purely rationalist belief. It was essential if pacifism was to be commended beyond the ranks of believers, for Sheppard to argue that it was commonsense, rational and practical politics, as well as derived from the authority of Jesus. (Christian pacifism may indeed be faithful to the example of Jesus; can one really, as Sheppard did, commend it as 'common sense'?) He rejects military sanctions because they imply that we don't really trust the other nation's profession that it too wants peace. Governments, he believes, will take the risk of disarmament if they are convinced that people want drastic measures to abolish war. It is no use always blaming the other nation; we must meet it half-way. War would not become right even if disarmament did not awaken a response from other countries, or even if the Empire were invaded. But dictatorships rest upon the consent of those they govern: 'Even of the Dictatorships we need not despair.'[62] – a characteristic example of the way that, when the pacifists of the time half confronted a possibly tragic outcome of their policies, they quickly turned on the sunshine again. Yet he also wants to assert absolutes: 'The moral quality of an action doesn't depend upon its results.'[63]

If (Sheppard argues) you reject the massacre of Jericho (Christian pacifists found the Old Testament revoltingly blood-stained) then you must reject modern warfare because bombing leads to the killing of non-combatants. Did not Jesus in effect tell the people to accept the Roman occupation? Jesus was against war, and the Christian must therefore reject it too. He rejects the idea of a world state, pacts like Locarno or an international force under the League because all rest ultimately on the threat of force. Even if we were able to kill Hitler or Stalin that would be the sin of murder. 'The history of the Jews is the supreme epic of non-resistance; their survival the complete and conclusive proof of the futility of force.'[64] Sheppard reminds those who romanticize war of the reality of modern warfare: more deadly weapons, new varieties of poison gas, mass bombing of civilians, chemical warfare. War always corrupts and brutalizes. In another war women would probably be used as pilots. In war-time the national cause takes precedence over truth – Ponsonby had demonstrated that stories of German atrocities were fictions of allied propaganda.

Germany's regime is detestable but it 'is only suffering in a more acute form' from the fear which affects her neighbours. 'The hand within the mailed glove is trembling.'[65] It is very doubtful either that Germany would be able to repeat the war effort of 1914 or that it is planning a war of revenge. But we cannot be so sure of France. Russian armaments are genuinely defensive for Russia does not want war. Japan may sound aggressive but it is to some extent for home consumption. Like other nations, it is consumed by fear. Since modern governments have to plead a just cause, if the victim were unarmed, an aggressor would obviously stand condemned. We are told that there is no defence against aircraft, but disarmament is a defence which has never been tried.

The British Empire must renounce force and only use police against rioters, slave-traders or tribesmen in revolt, with arms as a last resort; but they might use tear gas instead. (Like Raven, Sheppard finds it difficult to apply absolute pacifism to imperial problems.) Instead of spending money on arms, we should use it for missionary work which would be much more effective if the church lived by the Sermon on the Mount. Sheppard also rejects violent revolution. Because he grants that democracy makes pacifism possible and Fascism and Communism do not, he abjures both.

'What does the pledge mean?' he asks. He does not interpret pacifism as total refusal of co-operation with the state as the first war absolutists had done. Those who have signed it have bound themselves not to bear or manufacture arms. But he cannot condemn the man who might not want to bring privation to his family by giving up working in a munitions factory. 'I don't know what I would do myself if I were in his place.'[66] What about the care of the wounded in war-time? Again Sheppard's tender heart causes him perplexities. A pacifist doctor should go to the front as a civilian, but not join the RAMC. A clergyman should not act as a uniformed chaplain but he could accept a role as a civilian pastor to the forces. In that role he should be totally neutral about the war, neither attacking nor approving it. Since next time there is unlikely to be a conscience clause, pacifists must be ready for imprisonment. Pacifists should not support air raid precautions – they lull people into thinking that air raids might not be so bad after all, and create resentment against the supposed enemy. In any case, gas masks, for example, would soon become obsolete as new gases were invented.

He ends by dreaming of a great exciting international crusade for peace. Leaders like George Lansbury should abandon politics with (what he called significantly) its 'inevitable compromises'[67] – forgetting that he had himself allowed some compromises in his interpretation of the pledge. (In fact George Lansbury did accept in retrospect that he had compromised his pacifism by accepting the political responsibility of being leader of the Labour Party. He was forced to resign after Ernest Bevin's famous onslaught on him in October 1935.)[68] Charles Chaplin, Will Rodgers, Gandhi, Einstein, Lloyd George, Smuts, the Archbishop of Canterbury, the Pope – how marvellous it would be if they all joined an international 'Peace Circus'.

What was the character of Sheppard's pacifism revealed in his writings and life? To Sheppard human beings were essentially good and rational when not shackled by political and institutional structures – a view common among idealistic liberals and socialists. He could never come to terms with the empirical church and longed for it to become the ideal church of his dreams, held together only by spontaneous love, beyond the need for law and only requiring the simplest of structures. So he could not grasp that his dreams of peace necessitated the contingencies and compromises involved in institutions, laws and negotiations for his dreams to be actualized. In July 1935 he wrote to Housman: 'Abyssinia and Italy simply beats me. I don't know what we Pacifists ought to be at.'[69] His answer was another rally, to which 7,000 came. In 1936 he addressed a letter to Hitler asking for permission to preach peace in Germany, disregarding the warning of the translator of the letter that if his request were granted, his hearers might be persecuted by the Gestapo.

By identifying God wholly with Jesus, and a Jesus in whom all the tough, hard side was eliminated, he contributed to the further softening of the already soft centre of pacifism, so that pacifists were ill-prepared for the revelations of Nazi evils when these could not any longer be dismissed as exaggerations or fabrications. He, like Raven, by identifying pacifism wholly with liberal ideology and theology, ensured that it would not be listened to by those whose ideology and theology were of a different tradition.

When he did try to translate his pacifism into practical politics he was either optimistically naive (no country really wanted war) or considerably modified his absolutes in difficult cases. He proclaimed the cross as the lot of the pacifist, but often reassured everyone who might be alarmed at such a tough doctrine that probably the cross wouldn't be required after all, for love and non-violence would prevent it from being necessary. He was willing to countenance the use of tear-gas and even arms against tribesmen in revolt, but in a Church Assembly debate on peace in 1937, dismissed any idea of an international force with the naive riposte that a bomb labelled 'With love from Geneva' was no more Christian than one dropped by a dictator.[70] Like Raven he seemed to think that though 'the spirit of warfare and violence remains an integral part of the character of so many Eastern and African races',[71] Europeans (except possibly the French) were now fundamentally pacific. Lang wrote of his death as 'a very timely and kindly act of Providence' and wondered what his future might have been.[72] Some members of the PPU wondered whether he might have modified or abandoned his pacifism in 1939 or 1940 (as many pacifists did) partly because of his privately expressed uncertainties about it.[73] It is possible that if he had lived longer, the combined effects of the defeat of his love and idealism by the breakdown of his marriage and the defeat of his hopes by the events of 1939, would have impelled him to move beyond innocence, while retaining his pacifism in a modified or more toughly based form. Yet it was this innocence, and the suffering that came to him because he was so unprotected, his gaiety and his sense that the pretensions of the powerful are absurd that were, and continue to be, his contribution to the life of church and nation. He warmed his critics then, and he has the capacity to do so still, nearly fifty years after his death.

The character of Christian pacifism

There were five main characteristics of the Christian pacifism of 1930s. Until the approach of war, Christian and humanitarian pacifists often took up similar or identical attitudes, indicating that ideology was often prior to, or at least, the most potent determinant of, the theology of the Christian pacifists.

First, Christian as well as humanitarian pacifists took a generally optimistic view of the goodness and rationality of human beings. Many preached pacifism as a rational faith and believed that it would be spread through a process of education and enlightenment. Many believed that the potential aggressor would be morally dissuaded from attack if confronted by an unarmed people. Donald Soper in 1936 granted that a nation which renounced force might suffer 'crucifixion' but he added reassuringly that the possibility was 'a small one'. If the invasion were conducted by a civilized power, 'I cannot believe that it would involve any loss of life'. Pacifists, like pacifiers, were always eager to think the best of any potential enemy. Soper in June 1938 was reported as saying that there was something of God in everyone, including Hitler and Mussolini. In July 1938, *Peace News* called for concessions to the Sudeten Germans and in August questioned whether Czechoslovakia was really a nation at all.[74] Leslie Weatherhead, Methodist minister and pacifist, said in 1935: 'Britain should ask Italy what territory now British, would help her in her legitimate and obvious desire for extension, and then make her a definite offer of such territory.'[75] Percy Hartill (Archdeacon of Stoke-on-Trent and, from 1939 to 1955, chairman of the Anglican Pacifist Fellowship, founded 1937) was at first very reluctant to credit reports of anti-semitism and the suppression of free speech in Germany.

Christian pacifists were compassionate, tender-hearted progressiv-ists, generally of a socialist outlook, and usually supporters of such liberal causes as feminism, the ordination of women, ecumenism, open communion, contraception and a more tolerant attitude to the divorced. For example, Raven believed that a society dominated by males could not represent the fullness of Christ and would always be dualistic, ascetic and military. Christian pacifists appealed to the authority of the New Testament and the early church to support their belief that the Christian should be a pacifist. On the other hand, they could hardly have claimed that the New Testament and the early church categorically supported some of their other causes. The way that different Christian groups used the Bible is instructive. Those on the right in politics treated parts of the Old Testament seriously – for example, those strands which saw the community as relating to God through kingship, law and national identity. Imperialists identified themselves with God's call to the Jews, as his chosen people, to conquer other peoples militarily, culturally and religiously. Politically conservative Christians interpreted the New Testament as wholly concerned with God's relationship with the individual, and were fond of quoting such texts as 'My kingdom is not of this world' (John 18.36). Bishop Gore and G. W. E. Russell were once earnestly

discussing an industrial dispute at a dinner given by the elder Lord
Halifax. Halifax thought there were issues of much greater importance.
'My dear Gore,' he broke in, 'I cannot think why you are so interested
in a world which you know is all going to be burnt up.'[76] Christians
on the left charged those on the right with wilfully neglecting the Old
Testament prophets and their passionate denunciations of the rich
and social injustice The prophets were attractive models for dissenters
of various types, for until comparatively recently, biblical scholarship
interpreted the prophets as individualists rebelling against the cultic
and social establishment. (More recent scholars depict the prophets
as members of prophetic, cultic groups which attempted to recall the
nation to return to the true tradition.) Christian pacifists generally
evaded the Old Testament by dismissing it as a catena of bloodthirsty
stories and therefore essentially alien to Christianity, which
represented a real progress in religion and ethics. They concentrated
on the New Testament, or at least on aspects of the Gospels and
Epistles, though of course neglected apocalyptic elements like the
book of Revelation. If, as often, they were socialists, they grasped the
importance of the prophets for a proclamation of the political mission
of Christianity. But as pacifists, by concentrating on the New Testament as the basis for their pacifism, they were constantly appealing to
material which, while it has political implications for discipleship, can
easily be read as a-political. Thus the pacifists' neglect of the Old
Testament reinforced their a-political individualism and their propensity, if they sought to be political, to avoid having to wrestle with the
complexities and ambiguities of political power, the nature of law in
community life and the tragic aspects of human existence. To have
faced these would have forced them to question the evolutionary,
optimistic account of human history which dominated their thinking.

Pacifist militancy was directed not towards potential aggressors
but to targets nearer to hand: Barnes' towards Anglo-Catholics,
Sheppard's towards the institutional church, Raven's towards
Niebuhr and Barth. In any international crisis, pacifists almost
invariably blamed Britain and the Versailles Treaty first. Countless
meetings and demonstrations consumed their energy. Pacifists ranged
from elitists, who believed it was inappropriate for the artist to fight,
to Christian pacifists who commended their stand as the way of Jesus;
from anarchists to those willing to support an international police
force or sanctions; from those who believed that pacifism could actually
prevent war to those who viewed it as an individual witness. As the
war clouds grew darker, Christian pacifists were more likely to retain
their faith than those whose pacifism was based on humanitarian

grounds alone. Thus the theological basis of Christian pacifism became more determinative. Its character as an individual witness with few or no political implications was revealed when it became less plausible to argue that pacifism could prevent war and that pacifism would be widely adopted as part of the evolutionary progress of the human race. So just before, and during the war, the explicitly Christian groups like APF and FOR grew in membership, while the more diffusely based PPU lost a good deal of support. The proportion of COs among conscripts also fell steadily during the war itself, probably indicating the decline of the appeal of humanitarian pacifism.[77]

Secondly, the nature of the pacifist faith was, in the last analysis, an act of individual dissent. Christian pacifists reminded one another that all the disciples had fled, leaving Jesus alone to face the cross. The inheritance of the craggy individualism of the first war COs; the fissiparousness of Nonconformity and left-wing movements with which pacifism was interwoven: these and other factors pushed pacifism towards a sectarian outlook. So pacifist and peace societies proliferated, quarrelled within and between themselves and competed to be the authentic pacifist voice. Christian pacifists included many who were at odds with the institutional church. Therefore they were attracted towards a policy of sectarian dissent and were tempted to give only their secondary allegiance to the church. But those who took their membership of the church seriously, and many did, were all the time having to confess their pacifist faith alongside non-pacifist Christians. However much pacifist Christians differed theologically, politically and ideologically from other Christians, the common loyalty to the one God, the one Christ and the one church prevented most Christian pacifists from moving into self-righteous sectarianism. One thinks for example of the long, if sometimes strained friendships between Sheppard and Lang, Raven and Temple.

Percy Hartill declared himself a pacifist in 1934. As Archdeacon and Rector of Stoke-on-Trent from 1935 to 1955, he made a distinctive and much valued contribution to the life of the Lichfield diocese. In both the Church Assembly and the Canterbury Convocation, to which he was elected by his fellow clergy in 1932, he took a prominent role for over twenty years. At the centre of his life was the daily eucharist and the daily offices. In April 1937 he, Sheppard and others, led a deputation to the Archbishop of Canterbury. During the war he was in regular correspondence with both Archbishops on ethical aspects of war policy.[78] Here was a pacifist priest who, unlike either Raven or Sheppard was daily ministering in an ordinary parish, and also unlike them, was very ready to serve in the engine room of the ark of salvation.

Lang and Temple were sometimes exasperated by the Christian pacifists but they (and most of the bishops) constantly strove both to understand them sympathetically and to keep open the lines of communication.

By contrast with Hartill, Canon Stuart Morris resigned his orders soon after the outbreak of war, and left the church because of its attitude to the war. Morris was a well-known and important pacifist. After Sheppard's death he became Chairman of the PPU and from 1939 its General Secretary as well. He had founded the Church of England Peace Fellowship in 1934, a short-lived body, but was an architect of the Anglican Pacifist Fellowship, founded in 1937, and still in existence. He was a member of its executive 1937–39. Barnes had wanted him as Archdeacon of Aston in 1937. His leaving the church may also have been partly caused by the breakdown of his marriage. (Ceadel speculates on the high proportion of pacifists who, at the time of, or after their conversion to, pacifism, experienced marital or other personal difficulties, so probably making them more ready to adopt views which took them to near or outside the pale. In other ways pacifists dissented from traditional morality: both Leslie Weatherhead and Herbert Gray specialized in preaching liberal, progressive solutions to sexual problems.)[79] In 1942 Morris was arrested under the Official Secrets Act for receiving confidential Government documents on how a rebellion by Gandhi would be dealt with. He was convicted and served nine months' imprisonment. Barnes gave evidence on his behalf, and Temple provided a written testimony for the defence. The PPU, on the other hand, disassociated itself from his actions and he was forced to resign as its General Secretary.

Thirdly, neither Christian nor other pacifists worked out an agreed political programme or set of political objectives. Pacifists oscillated between a policy of absolutism and a willingness to co-operate with non-pacifist pacifiers. Lord Allen, the first war absolutist, author of the contentious preface to *Conscription and Conscience*, told the National Peace Congress in 1933 that mankind could not wait until world opinion was transformed. Machinery for international government with police powers must be created. Pacifists must participate in practical affairs.[80] Leyton Richards in 1935 also argued that, in order to establish international peace, 'it may be necessary to accept half a loaf rather than no bread at all'. The creation of an international police force under the League, willing in the last resort, after all other sanctions had failed, to use force, would be 'a striking and significant step towards the realization of a Christian world-order', even though pacifists could not conscientiously enlist in it. He added that, of course, if the world were wholly Christian such a force would not be needed.[81] But many Christian pacifists disagreed. A letter-writer to the *Guardian* on 10 January 1936 attacked sanctions against Italy and blithely asserted: 'Our safety lies not in armaments but in shaking hands all round the world'.[82] Some who rejected an international force supported economic sanctions provided that they did not lead to starvation. But many thought that all sanctions were a form of coercion. In 1934 at a special National Peace Congress service (*Guardian* 29 June) Barnes preached on 'Abhor that which is evil'. He advocated national disarmament however 'dangerous' and a trust in 'a policy of international righteousness'. By the latter he meant: a reversal of the 'injustice' of the Versailles Treaty, the restoration of former German colonies now under British rule and a willingness by Britain to use and abide by international arbitration. He rejected an international force: 'Intrigues to control such a force would be incessant'.

> Just as I distrust the use of force by the League of Nations, so I doubt alike the effectiveness and wisdom of so-called economic sanctions. The use of commercial boycotts or embargoes is a form of warfare . . . It were better to trust to the influence of an appeal based solely on moral principles than to create a situation in which millions are spent on preparations for war.

After the Abyssinian crisis (when sanctions were used for the first and last time), many Christian pacifists became disillusioned with political solutions in general, and the League in particular, as ways to peace.

Fourthly, there was much discussion about non-violence or non-resistance, stimulated greatly by the example of Gandhi. Many pacifists felt that Gandhi had demonstrated before the world that non-violence was an effective political form of action for groups as well as individuals. But some considered that his methods were a form of coercion, which created rather than solved conflict. Support for a policy of non-violence was given a further impetus by the publication of *The Power of Non-Violence* in 1935. Its author, Richard B. Gregg, was an American admirer of Gandhi, to whom he dedicated the book. 'The struggle in India during 1930–33 proves there is power in the method of non-violent resistance which Gandhi advocates and uses.'[83] He also cited examples from other countries. Non-violence works, Gregg believed, because it is a form of 'moral jiu-jitsu' which causes the aggressor to lose his moral balance, arouses his 'more decent and kindly motives' and so leads him to feel morally ashamed, because virtually everyone has a potentiality for goodness, however dim.[84] Gregg supported his theory with an array of psychological and physiological evidence.[85] By contrast, peace imposed by violence only suppresses the conflict. So soldiers who used violence against a non-violent group, would be forced to question the rightness of their own cause and public opinion would force the authorities to change their policy. Non-violence is not coercion for it respects the opponent. Non-violent resistance enables the ordinary person to act for peace. But it requires spiritual training in organized groups.

Gregg's argument found support from those like Sheppard, who also believed that it was inconceivable that soldiers would obey orders to attack unarmed people. (Sheppard had praised Gregg's book in the 1936 edition of *We Say 'No'*.) However, Sheppard and other members of the PPU, began to draw back from Gregg's theories when in 1936 he published a manual of training which recommended meditation, folk-dancing, communal singing, spinning and knitting as forms of group preparation. The whole programme began to look too eastern and cranky and the PPU withdrew it as an official PPU manual in 1937.[86] Belief in non-resistance was nevertheless basic to pacifism. Both Lansbury and Leyton Richards praised the Czechs for their non-resistance to Hitler in 1938 and both compared their sacrifice to that of Christ.[87]

Fifthly, from about 1936, many pacifists placed their political hopes for peace in appeasement. Soper wrote of the Munich agreement: 'I am thoroughly in favour of umbrellas, for I think that they have done more in the last few months than battleships could have done.'[88] Barnes had been one of the few who had attended the reception by the first post-war German ambassador, but disliked Nazism and attacked its anti-semitism. But (like Lord Robert Cecil) he blamed the failure of the Disarmament Conference of 1932–34 on Britain. Barnes blamed Lloyd George for the Versailles Treaty. By the beginning of 1938, however, Barnes gave up criticizing German policies, fearing war above all else, and strongly supported Chamberlain and appeasement. He explained his silence on international affairs at this period by remarkably acknowledging that 'the existence of pacifism would be taken as a sign of weakness by the dictators and lead them to make increasingly extravagant demands'. Though he was thankful for Munich, he knew the cost and had few illusions about Nazi tyranny. Yet he opposed conscription in 1939 and as a eugenist voiced his approval of Nazi 'race hygiene' and its programme of voluntary sterilization. He refused to sponsor an appeal for clergy to act as air-raid wardens, but accepted that they should be approached. At the same time he deplored the 'slovenly inadequacy' of the precautions. As war grew nearer Barnes 'could only watch and pray, helpless and

desolate'. The oscillations in Barnes' attitudes indicated the turmoil
in his own mind, yet also revealed the unresolved tension between his
hatred of Nazism and his determination to think well of German
actions. He was unwilling with one part of his mind to grasp the
likelihood of war, so he distanced himself from air-raid precautions,
yet with another part of his mind he was proposing alternative
precautions which he believed would be more effective.[89]

Hartill wrote in September 1938 that he found it difficult to believe
that even non-pacifists would 'go to war with any enthusiasm in
order to compel three and a half million Germans to remain in
Czechoslovakia' – exactly the type of reductionist language used
by appeasers. He welcomed the Munich agreement and remained
consistently loyal to Chamberlain, even when later, opinion turned
against him. On the other hand he had been consistently distrustful
of Churchill since 1914. 'I'm quite pro-Chamberlain (except as regards
re-armament) . . . the terms Hitler and Chamberlain had agreed were
first put forth in 1920 in the official programme of the Labour Party.'
'Can we trust Hitler?' he asked in his parish magazine, and answered
by quoting part of the following letter from the Rev. A. G. M. Pearce
Higgins, published in the *Daily Telegraph* on 8 October 1938:

> How far can Herr Hitler be trusted to keep his promises? Believing
> as I do that the prayers of the Christian Church have proved the
> decisive factor for peace during these last few weeks, I would answer
> that question by affirming emphatically that Herr Hitler can be
> trusted to keep his promises just so far as Christians all the world
> over are prepared to pray that God's Holy Spirit will direct and
> control his life. I would, and do, rather trust in the power of prayer
> than in all the armaments in the world.

(Higgins' language echoed the attitudes of the Oxford Group movement.) But when Hitler marched into Czechoslovakia in March 1939,
Harthill wrote: 'One cannot even attempt to defend Hitler now'.
Nevertheless in June he argued against regulations in the Church
Assembly designed to secure effective pastoral care in the event of
war, opposed as he was to a 'Measure which rests on the assumption
that God will not give His people the blessing of peace'.[90]

Finally, we come to the views about war and peace expounded by
two pacifist academics.

In September 1938 C. H. Dodd gave an address to the Council of
Christian Pacifist Groups. In it he recognized that the Christian who
refuses military service is 'not doing the ideally right thing', because
he denies his country support while sharing the benefits of citizenship.

'When once war has broken out, there is no way, for the time being, of reconciling the claim of God upon us through the social order with His claim upon us through the Christian order. Both claims we cannot satisfy. Either way we must act with a bad conscience.' But the Christian pacifist 'having contemplated the meaning of Christ for the world . . . is conscious of an inward compulsion which leads him to say "Here I stand, so help me God: I can no other" '.[91] Dodd here notably does not make absolute claims, theological or ethical, for pacifism; he recognizes with more sensitivity than many pacifists the Christian responsibility to the natural social order; he concludes not by commending pacifism as a political solution, but as an act of individual faith wholly determined by theological belief.

G. H. C. Macgregor was Professor of Divinity at Glasgow, President of the Church of Scotland Peace Society, a member of FOR, a sponsor of PPU, and helped George Macleod to found the Iona Community in 1938. He and Raven were close friends. Macgregor's *The New Testament Basis of Pacifism* (1936) was the most scholarly and eirenic presentation of the biblical and ethical basis for Christian pacifism to appear between the wars. Unlike Raven and Sheppard, he genuinely wrestled with the neo-orthodox critique of pacifism. Unlike nearly all other Christian pacifists, he argued the idea of pacifism almost exclusively from theological belief. But like Sheppard, Raven and others, his pacifism rested upon a distinctively Christocentric faith, based entirely on the New Testament interpreted, with the history of the church, in terms of progressive revelation. Pacifists (argued Macgregor in the Preface) are too apt to assume that the ethic of Jesus is pacifist, and even if true, that he intended this to be applied politically. Christian pacifism is to be based not on an absolute repudiation of force, nor on the Sixth Commandment, nor on certain sayings of Jesus. Rather its true foundations are: (1) the love of one's neighbour (2) the faith that each individual is loved by, and of infinite value to, God (3) all the teaching of Jesus must be interpreted by his life and above all by the cross. If these are taken seriously, then war as we know it, violates the Christ's method of meeting evil. He rejects the plea that Jesus expected an imminent end – if we dismiss his teachings about non-resistance on these grounds, what authority have his other ethical teachings? Nor can his sayings be treated as *ad hoc* or hyperbole, for he lived by his own teachings. Nor can they be treated as counsels of perfection, which have to be modified in an imperfect society. Nowhere in the Gospels does it assert that the disciples are to postpone their obedience until everyone obeys. 'Evil can be truly conquered only by the power of truth and goodness and self-sacrificing love.'⁹² Even if (as he grants) there is a stern side to Jesus's and Paul's picture of God, are we permitted to imitate it?

If Law has to precede Gospel (as Temple claims) then Paul's epistles go by the board. Macgregor preaches pacifism as an act of individual dissent based on the teaching and life of Jesus. 'If nations cannot or will not act as Christians should, then Christians cannot conform to what the nation does.'⁹³ Yet he also claims that if the church were publicly to become pacifist, 'the whole world situation would be radically changed'.⁹⁴ What does all this mean politically? It is not the job of the church (for example) to predict the results of an invasion upon a pacifist Britain. We cannot escape suddenly from the consequences of the policies of the last twenty years. The Disarmament Conference is dead and the League has failed to halt war in Abyssinia. We must now risk everything in the belief that God's way would work even if this leads to national martyrdom. We cannot expect a Christian witness from a sub-Christian state. But, for example, the Empire's resources could be made available for needy nations. If the League were to use sanctions and to develop an international police force this could not be directly approved by pacifists, but it would be a step on the right way.

So when Macgregor descends from the pure air of the uplands where he had wrestled with theological questions which Christian pacifists usually evaded, the actual policies he advocates turn out to be mostly those of appeasement, second-hand and unadventurous. The power of the book lies in the clear theological basis which he provides for acts of individual dissent. However, we should remember that both Niebuhr and Temple (as we shall see in Chapter 7) were themselves also very ready to grant the value to church and world of pacifism as an individual Christian vocation. But Macgregor offers virtually no help to the pacifist who feels impelled to incarnate his distinctive theology in political action. Pacifists could not accept the ethics of compromise for themselves, though they could, as unsullied spectators, approve of ethically dubious actions by others. (Here he follows the early thought of Raven and that of Leyton Richards.) Macgregor does not consider that the pacifist who encourages others to do what would be ethically impossible for him, is like the orthodox Jew who is happy for the Gentile to work on the sabbath so he may keep it in obedient tranquillity.

The Relevance of the Impossible (1941) was Macgregor's reply to Niebuhr's critique of pacifism. The title was exactly the wry commendation that Christian pacifism of the period merited. He still defended appeasement. For twenty years before the war, (he wrote)

Christian pacifists had urged a positive policy of reconciliation and reconstruction based on sacrifices by the nations. 'Such a policy, if adopted before the demonic powers of evil had become enthroned in the high places of Europe, would almost certainly have saved the peace.'[95] He cited a statement by Christian pacifists made in September 1938, which blamed the then crisis upon the injustices of the post-war settlement, and our tardiness in meeting grievances e.g. about reparations, colonies and trade. Four months before the war, the Church of Scotland Peace Society quoted this statement and commented: 'This policy still stands . . . If "appeasement" failed it was because such a policy of true peace-making was never tried. "Appeasement" too often demanded sacrifices not from ourselves but from weaker nations. Can we honestly claim that we ourselves have ever offered those great sacrifices for the sake of peace which are demanded by our territorial and economic predominance in the world?'[96] Thus Macgregor identified Christian pacifism with an optimistic interpretation of Nazi political motivation.

In Macgregor's writings we have yet another pacifist attempt to combine a stern call to martyrdom with reassurances that rational political policies could probably deliver us from having to choose it. The call to martyrdom implied a realistic estimate of evil. The hope of avoiding it through appeasement did not. The first could appeal to the New Testament. The second owed more to Victorian optimism.

The coming of war forced most pacifists towards a sectarian interpretation of pacifism as an individual act of dissent, though many still thought Nazi Germany would respond positively to policies of appeasement. No longer could they believe, as many had done in the thirties, that both nations and churches would adopt pacifism. So in spite of unprecedented efforts, Christian pacifism failed (and has continued to fail) to convert the churches. In 1936, for example, the Methodist Conference, despite attempts to commit it corporately to pacifism, publicly recognized that both pacifism and non-pacifism were legitimate expressions of Christian faith. The Church of England included only one declared pacifist among the diocesan bishops – Barnes – and he was too eccentric a personality to be a very persuasive influence for pacifism. Pacifists among English Roman Catholics were an even tinier minority than in the other churches. Eric Gill, co-opted on to the PPU Council in May 1939, was lone and unrepresentative. In 1936 a predominantly Roman Catholic peace society 'Pax' was formed, which officially stopped short of absolute pacifism, but believed that modern warfare was incompatible with the principles of the just war. It defined its aim as 'resistance to modern warfare on

grounds of traditional morality'. By September 1938 it had attracted
about a hundred and fifty members. By April 1942 the numbers rose
to over five hundred, but by the end of the war they had dropped back
to about two hundred and fifty. During the renaissance of the peace
movement of the 1960s its membership grew significantly. Durings
its early years, E. I. Watkin was President. Eric Gill was Chairman
1939–40. It was by no means an exclusively Roman Catholic group
and included Hugh Ross Williamson, then an Anglican and John
Middleton Murry. But Pax ran into conflicts with the Roman Catholic
hierarchy. In June 1939 Cardinal Hinsley ordered Pax to cease
distributing literature outside churches in his archdiocese. Pax
declined his request that all its publications should be submitted for
censorship, pointing out that it was not a specifically Roman Catholic
society. In 1944 Cardinal Griffin told two Roman Catholic priests to
resign their membership – one was W. E. Orchard, the convert from
Congregationalism.[97]

So at the beginning of the war, enrolled Christian pacifists numbered
15,000 at the most – a tiny minority of the total pacifist movement,
itself a small minority of the nation as a whole. Yet as late as November
1937, Donald Soper had claimed that Europe was on the verge of a
pacifist landslide.[98]

6

CAN DICTATORS BE PACIFIED?

In this chapter we will describe the attitudes of those English Christians who sought the pacification of the dictators in the 1930s. The varying reactions of churchmen to the German church struggle, to the persecution of the Jews and to the main international crises of the period will also be outlined.

On 14 November 1940 Hensley Henson attended the service for the burial of Neville Chamberlain's ashes in Westminster Abbey. Two days later Henson wrote: 'I am glad that he is buried there . . . and I think that (though he made a great blunder in his policy of so-called "appeasement") his character was high, his motives generous, and his sacrifice great. Personally I liked and respected him.'[1] Archbishop Lang, unlike Henson, supported appeasement (as did Temple, Bell and other bishops). Lang and Chamberlain were personal friends. In October 1940, failing health forced Chamberlain's resignation as Lord President of the Council. By then his reputation was under a cloud. Lang wrote to him comfortingly on 6 October:

> I have always been a supporter and defender of your policy when you were Prime Minister. I am sure that it was right . . . When the time to meet the challenge of Hitler came, you had made it plain to the whole impartial world that you had done everything possible to keep Europe from war, and to fix the blame for that calamity on the unbridled ambition of Hitler. You enabled the country to enter the war with a clear conscience and a united will.

Chamberlain in reply thanked Lang for his 'generous and affectionate letter' and continued: 'You know how much I value your good opinion, and I have always thought you had pre-eminently that political sense which is notoriously rare among the clergy and civil servants . . . it is a solace to feel that I have no terrible blunder to reproach myself with.'[2] Lang could hardly have relished being compared (however favourably) with civil servants.

Lang was 64 when he was translated from York to Canterbury in 1928.[3] He never fulfilled his early promise despite his notable work for Christian reunion and an influence on public affairs, which, according to Owen Chadwick, has been greatly underestimated. As a curate at Leeds Parish Church, Lang chose to live in a disused pub and then for three years in a condemned house, to identify himself with the poor of the area. As Bishop of Stepney he continued to feel a genuine love and concern for the poor and at that period (and later as Archbishop of York) spoke out passionately on their behalf. But he also developed a romantic detachment, a patrician withdrawal from aspects of ordinary life. He arranged for his clothes and other necessities to be bought for him. His tailor and barber were summoned to his home at Amen Court. After he became Archbishop of York at the age of 44, he never entered a shop again. He decided that he was incapable of filling a fountain pen or dismantling and cleaning a safety razor. He cultivated the role of the judicious statesmen. Despite his regular pronouncements on political issues of the day, he gave increasingly little sign in public that he personally felt affected by the theological and ethical perplexities of the age. For example, he was curiously uninterested when the Lambeth Conference of 1930 (of which he was President) debated the important human and moral issue of birth control and when it decided, amid controversy, to give strictly limited approval to the use of contraception in special cases. Thus he revealed himself far removed from the deep agonies of those, including some Anglican clergy and their wives, who in the 1920s were consulting Marie Stopes about their sexual problems. By contrast, in 1929 William Temple wrote to thank her for a book she had sent and assured her that he was working for a change in the church's attitude to birth control.[4] In his Diocesan Visitation to the Canterbury clergy in 1935, Lang lamented that many features of modern life – cars, wireless and films, for example – had come down like a mist between people and God. (Yet he himself always travelled by car between Lambeth and Canterbury.)

In his days at Portsea Lang enjoyed visiting the Royal Family at Osborne. As Archbishop of York he increasingly sought the company of the nobility and of the wealthy. Lord Robert Cecil and Lang once stayed with a middle-class host in Yorkshire. Cecil tartly commented: 'His Grace of York despised him utterly. But I'm not sure that I did not find the middle class chieftain as pleasant as the middle class Archbishop.'[5] After Lang had given a lunch at Lambeth exclusively for dowager duchesses, Alan Don, his chaplain, remarked that they seemed no different from anyone else. 'That just shows, Alan, how mistaken you can be' replied the Archbishop.[6] He genuinely enjoyed contemplating his 'progress' from a Scottish manse to Lambeth Palace, yet, having arrived, he felt on occasion it was all 'dust and ashes'. (As a teenager he had compiled an imaginary entry for *Who's Who* showing his progress as a Conservative politician to 10 Downing Street and an earldom.) In public he came over as the smoothly eloquent priest acting the part of a great prelate with consummate ease. (His cousin was Matheson Lang, the actor.) But there was sadly little exchange between his public and his private self. If he had allowed some of his private self-doubt and self-accusation to surface and to have disturbed his deceptively self-possessed exterior, he might have been a more convincing figure in public. What might have been, with his early background, a ministry of creative dissent, was suppressed for the sake of a role of public conformity to the norms of English society. He treated his home country of Scotland as a romantic world to which he could escape for his annual retreat, not as a vantage point from which to view church and society in England with a critical eye. His disastrously phrased broadcast at the abdication was the most extreme, but by no means the only, example of the way in which he (like some other bachelors and bishops) developed an unctuous and patronizing paternalism. Henson, who had also travelled a long way, believed that Lang was unable to distinguish between dignity and pomposity. Yet when Michael Ramsey, as Archbishop of York, visited the older clergy of the diocese, in their vicarages the photographs of Lang outnumbered those of Temple. In 1932 Lang gloomily reflected on the decline of his mental energy: 'it is dangerous: it leaves me too dependent on meeting each call as it arises, too content to keep the ship moving somehow without a clear sense of the journey it ought to be taking'. Bishop Bell said Lang had many excellent qualities but no policy. By the 1930s Lang was usually to be found swimming with most of the prevailing currents in church and state. One such current was appeasement.

Appeasement became (and has remained) such a dirty word that it is almost impossible to remember that up to 1939 it had a noble, hopeful ring. To most people of the Christian tradition appeasement seemed the embodiment of the gospel – penitence for past sins by the allies and the offer of reconciliation and forgiveness to the outcast: the equivalent in international affairs of the ecumenical vision of international Christian reconciliation. However deeply most church people disliked Nazism, before war broke out no church leader was likely to feel that it was his Christian duty to call for an armed crusade against it. Church and nation had had their fill of belligerent clergy exhorting others to sacrifice themselves for ideals which now, in retrospect, seemed tarnished or even futile. Many, inside and outside the churches, looked back with shame to the bellicose utterances of some of the clergy during the war. In 1934 the Secular Society gleefully published *Arms and the Clergy 1914–18* (ed. G. Bedborough) with quotations from war-time sermons from over two hundred clergy. The views of Winnington Ingram, Bishop of London, were described in the preface as 'indistinguishable from the language and sentiments of a cannibal chief'.[7]

In the inter-war period Christian leaders often reiterated the message that co-operation rather than competition, arbitration rather than conflict, were to be the guiding principles in international and industrial affairs. This was the basis of the Industrial Christian Fellowship, founded in 1919 with Studdert Kennedy as chief missioner. Like Baldwin, the ICF disliked talk of class conflict, feared that industrial unrest, if unchecked, might lead to civil war, and strove for reconciliation between employers and employees. The ICF worked for the same ideals which had inspired the creation of the League. Support for the League was almost axiomatic among ICF supporters. Just as pacifists and pacifiers believed that there was a latent harmony of interest between the nations which could be actualized by international co-operation, so the ICF believed that the two sides of industry could be reconciled if they perceived their common interest, were aware of the common danger posed by industrial strife, and so became more willing to resort to arbitration.[8] There was a tradition of church leaders offering mediation in industrial disputes, dating back at least to Bishop Fraser's attempt in 1878 to mediate in a strike of Lancashire mill workers. But Anglican leaders, with their overwhelmingly public school and Oxbridge backgrounds, as they looked with eirenic eyes through their palace windows, averted their gaze from the bitterness of class antagonism exemplified by trade union militancy or by the story told by Wilfred Owen in 1917 of a major who refused to travel from the front in a train without special accommodation for officers. 'Aw I decline. I ebsolutely decline, to travel in a coach where there are – haw – *Men!*'[9]

The preference of English Christians for consensus rather than conflict was also evident in the welcome given by many Christians to the formation of the National Government in 1931. Like parents who had been longing for an opportunity to teach their children some long overdue moral lessons, church leaders lectured the nation on such themes as 'bills must be paid'; we have all been spendthrifts and have lived 'beyond our means'; we must all offer sacrifices for the common good.[10] When in the *Guardian* for 29 April 1932 a correspondent drew attention to a church report on under-nourishment in Newcastle, the editor retorted: 'The policy of spending lavishly to help the helpless' had been tried and resulted in an emptying of the Exchequer. In the nation, those who praised the coalition for sinking differences for the national interest and hoped that it would produce strong government, displayed attitudes which were likely to be initially somewhat sympathetic to the new German regime which also seemed determined to put an end to indiscipline, thriftlessness and feeble government. Christian approval of order often leads to the support of punishing attitudes towards those who seem likely to threaten it.

George Bell, Bishop of Chichester from 1929 to 1958, made the name of that lovely cathedral city synonymous with all that is most admirable in the Christian tradition and famous throughout the world. Bell, as diocesan bishop, was chairman of the Council of the theological college. The college, firmly in the Anglo-Catholic tradition, is situated near the Bishop's Palace and the cathedral (whose Dean, A. S. Duncan-Jones, after taking an initially benign view of Hitler, became a fierce opponent of Nazism). During the early and mid-1930s, the *Cicestrian*, the college magazine, presented, in articles by students, the full range of Christian attitudes of the period towards peace and war, Fascism and Nazism. 'Catholicism and War' (Trinity 1933) propounded the tradition of the just war. A reply 'Christianity and War' (Michaelmas 1933) cited the authority of Jesus and Lambeth 1930 for the belief that for the Christian, war is never right. But underlying the article was the optimistic credo of the pacifiers: 'International co-operation cannot fail. No State in this modern economically interdependent world would be foolish enough to clank her arms if she knew that the rest of the world would isolate her immediately, which would mean starvation.'

These views in the *Cicestrian* are in line with those described, as typical of Christian opinion, in previous chapters. But it is startling to discover that the *Cicestrian* published two pro-Nazi and anti-semitic articles as well. 'The Nazi State' (Advent 1933), while sharing some common ground with both pacifists and pacifiers, was much more explicitly pro-Nazi and anti-semitic than they were. The pseudonymous author put the familiar case that the allies, by their humiliating treatment of Germany, at and since Versailles, were responsible for creating the conditions which produced Hitler and Nazism. The writer was particularly hostile to the French, whose occupying troops had brought 'dirt and immorality' to Germany. Britain blindly followed the policies of the French. But then the totalitarian sympathies of the writer emerged. We are apt to be horrified by the ruthlessness of Nazi methods, forgetting that Mussolini's conduct at first provoked an international outcry: 'it took some time for us to see the inestimable benefits which he was bringing to Italy'. No one can criticize the Nazis for cleaning up prostitution, and though state laws on sterilization are 'distasteful', they must come in every country: 'Germany must be praised as a bold pioneer in the cause of the production of a healthier human race'. The Nazi treatment of the Jews is explicable when we recall the association of the Jews with communists and the Versailles Treaty. Jews are not true Germans. They bank much of their money abroad 'so that like rats they can desert a sinking ship'. After all, Jews are also disliked in Britain and America. He replied to criticism of Nazi treatment of the church by remarking that a state church must expect the state to legislate for it. By contrast, Roman Catholics are left alone. While it is hardly Christian to deny Jews entry to the church, it is justifiable if they are enemies of the state. If Parliament has the right to reject the Revised Prayer Book, 'there is presumably no reason why it should not, with equal right, order that no Jew be admitted to a Church of England place of worship'.

A letter in the Lent 1934 issue praised this article, but another contributor declared that it had caused 'much resentment' in the college. It was not the allied treatment of Germany which had created Nazism, but the spirit of Prussianism exemplified by the Kaiser. It was hard to believe that Hitler's intentions were peaceful. There was no excuse for Nazi treatment of Jews: 'Many of us may intensely dislike Jews, but we cannot for that reason deny that they render signal service to whatever country they inhabit.' If the church rejected Jews, it rejected Christ. It was 'scandalous' that a rejection of the Jews should be even suggested in a theological college journal.

The *Cicestrian* for Advent 1936 published an article on 'Fascist Policy' which warmly commended the programme of the British Union of Fascists (led by Oswald Mosley, it included anti-semitism as one of the main planks in its platform). After explaining its proposals for a Corporate State, the writer went on to claim that neither Hitler nor the German people wanted war. Jews control the finances of Britain, use sweated labour and have used their finances to combat the movement. The editor commented that the article 'contains all the worst vices of interfering collectivism . . . and destroys the foundations of English liberty' but made no mention of its blatant anti-semitism. By contrast, immediately following this article there is an account of lectures given to the college Rover Crew about anti-gas precautions which would be needed in the event of war.

Ironically the Principal of Chichester from 1919 to 1932, Canon Herman Leonard Pass, had been brought up as a Jew. He was baptized after graduating at Cambridge. Sadly this excellent Hebraist grew to regard the Hebrew Scriptures with a profound distaste, refused to lecture on them and would gladly have seen them expunged from the services of the church. A deep admirer of Mediterranean Catholic culture, he was never really acclimatized into the Anglican ethos. Nevertheless he had a deep dislike for Italian fascism. For Germans he felt only contempt. From 1935 until his death in 1938, he was a residentiary Canon at Chichester Cathedral and still exercised an influence on some of the students.[11]

While it is clear that these two pro-Nazi and anti-semitic articles in the *Cicestrian* were unrepresentative of general opinion both in the college and among Anglican clergy generally, it is significant that they could be published at all. Anti-semitic attitudes were among the stock responses of many Christians, as among the general population in Britain. It was really only after the holocaust that people realized for the first time to what horrifying actions commonplace anti-semitic attitudes could lead. These two articles and the other opinions cited from the *Cicestrian* also indicate that appeasement attracted a wide variety of supporters, ranging from liberal optimists to explicit fascists. It is probable that the authors of the two articles were influenced by current Roman Catholic attitudes, then favourable to fascism, which would carry some authority in an Anglo-Catholic college. Former staff and students of the period speak of the determinative influence of Bishop Bell upon their attitudes to the German church situation. One also mentions the influence of the Oxford Group movement on the college. Leaders of this movement supported the pro-Nazi 'German Christians'. In 1936 Frank Buchman, leader of the Oxford Group movement, returned from an interview with Nazi leaders, including Heinrich Himmler, and exclaimed: 'I thank Heaven for a man like Adolf Hitler who built a front line of defence against the antichrist of Communism.'[12] The *Cicestrian* in Advent 1938 reprinted a lecture given to the college by a refugee pastor of the Confessing Church (almost certainly Franz Hildebrandt) which vividly depicted the nature of the German church struggle and called for support for the Confessing Church and Martin Niemöller. Both the editor and vice-principal wrote about the deep impression which this visit had created and pledged their active support for the persecuted Christians of Germany.

Another, all too predictable, reaction by Christians to the crises of the 1930s was to seek to exploit them in order to commend Christianity as the only solution. 'The Church's Opportunity – the Sad Condition of Mankind' read a headline above the report of an episcopal pronouncement in the *Guardian* on 27 November 1936. In 1933 a huge, sprawling symposium *Christianity and the Crisis*, was published with many distinguished contributors. Percy Dearmer, the editor, wrote stumblingly in the preface: 'It is in a very real sense true that only Christ can save the world from ruin to-day.'[13] E. A. Burroughs, Bishop of Ripon, who had attained a spurious reputation as a prophet during the war,[14] produced the tired slogan 'man's extremity is God's opportunity' and like many church leaders before and since, thought there were all kinds of signs that people were coming to realize that 'It is Christ or Chaos'.[15] Though in various places in the book there was an awareness that the League was not fulfilling the hopes placed in it in the 1920s, all agreed with E. N. Porter Goff (Secretary of the Christian Organizations Committee of the LNU and later Provost of Portsmouth) that despite its defects it provided the best machinery for international co-operation. And no one was likely to disagree with the Archbishop of Canterbury when he drew attention to the disease of selfish nationalism. John Oliver comments that though it included a few judicious essays it was 'sadly typical of the general disarray in the field of Christian social thought in the early thirties'.[16]

The German Church struggle

If Christians were sometimes tragically ambivalent about the persecution of the Jews in Germany, and often as blind as the rest of the nation to the real nature of Nazism, the German church struggle did more than anything else to awake at least some English Christians to what was happening in Germany. It is important to remember that foreign newspaper correspondents in Germany (unlike Russia) were subject to very few restrictions and the Nazi treatment of the churches and the Jews were reported throughout the world. Tourists, including Jews, could travel with only a few restrictions, and large numbers of British holiday makers visited Nazi Germany.[17] Certainly those who read the Anglican weekly the *Guardian* were well supplied with regular and critical coverage of the conflict between Hitler and church.[18] On 30 June 1933 the *Guardian* declared roundly in a leader that anti-semitism in Germany was inspired not by Christianity but by racialism. In the same issue another leader headed 'The Attack on German Protestantism' began bluntly: 'The Nazi Government has made mincemeat of the constitution of the German church.' On 13 October it asserted that press freedom had ceased in Germany. On 15 June 1934 it wrote: 'Doctrines of race and nation are being inculcated in Germany in a way that is entirely subversive': a person enters the church by baptism not through nationality.

However, a few articles in the *Guardian* by contributors repeated milder forms of some of the arguments in the two pro-Nazi articles from the *Cicestrian*, already cited. On 1 December 1933 'CHM' declared: 'The rebirth of a nation is a wonderful thing to witness and that rebirth has taken place.' But in the following issue this article came under fire in the correspondence columns. Dr B. Iddings Bell, an American Episcopalian priest who had preached at the 1933 Anglo-Catholic Congress, wrote an article 'A Trip to Germany' (12 June 1936). He said that, while allowing for a few who 'disfigure the political landscape', he had not for a long time been among a people 'as happy, as realistic in their thinking, as cool-headed, as well-governed and as well-behaved, as peace-loving and peace-desiring'. Germans generally admitted that the attempt to coerce the church had been a mistake, and this had now been abandoned. However, he regarded the Aryan theory as 'ridiculous' and disliked the treatment of the Jews. On 17 July his optimistic account of Germany was strongly contested by someone who had travelled extensively in Germany.

Oliver Tomkins, Secretary of the British SCM 1935–40 (Bishop of Bristol 1959–75) contributed some incisive and passionate articles to the *Guardian* about the German church struggle. In the issue for 3 January 1936, after a World Student Christian Federation Conference in Berlin, he summed up in Barthian language the essence of the conflict. The conflict (he said) had dominated the minds of the delegates:

> When a church finds itself fighting for life, conscious of the need to assert its own essential nature over against the world, where do we look to find that objective expression of the core of the faith, by which we are prepared to stand, and for which we would sacrifice everything?

A. C. Headlam, Bishop of Gloucester 1923–45, held the influential post of chairman of the Church of England Council on Foreign Relations from 1933 to 1945. Shy, with deep emotions rarely revealed, often unconsciously or deliberately rude, he had little interest in conciliating opponents. 'People think me a hard man, and I suppose I have a rather hard exterior, but really I want affection very much and feel it.'[19] Politically he was on the right and consistently attacked socialism (which he contemptuously described as 'the creed of the

German-Jew'), strikes, the ICF (and later the Welfare State) with vigour and patrician superiority. He was attracted to firm government and assailed any likely to subvert the *status quo*. He regarded liberal political policies as soft-headed and sentimental. It was wholly characteristic of him that he kept the pain and loneliness of his long widowerhood hidden from public view. Headlam's middle-of-the-road churchmanship; his deep commitment to the idea of a national church; his distaste for Barthianism; his aversion to rebels against the established order: all led him to take a benign view of those Christians in Germany who supported Hitler for his strong leadership and for his plan for a united protestant church. Conversely, these views led him to oppose the anti-Nazi Confessing Church as schismatic and infected by Barthianism. In addition. Headlam had a deep horror of Russian Communism. Hitler could be presented as a bulwark against its spread. So, as Henson wrote, Headlam 'to the surprise and regret of his friends, came forward as the pertinacious apologist of the Nazi Government in its treatment of the German Churches, and the singularly ungenerous critic of its victims'.[20]

Headlam, with his long and wide experience of ecumenical affairs was the natural choice as chairman for the Council on Foreign Relations, which covered all areas of inter-church relations outside Britain. The charge against Headlam is not only that he drastically mis-read both the nature of the church struggle and the intentions of the Nazis (many English people were equally blind) but that he obstinately persisted in rejecting carefully documented evidence on the other side supplied by German and English churchmen, which few others in England received in such detail and with such regularity. In 1933 Headlam despatched A. S. Duncan-Jones, Dean of Chichester, on a fact-finding mission to Germany. He returned with a soothing account. He also wrote a letter to the *Times* (7 July) describing his interview with Hitler who assured him that he had no wish to interfere with the internal life of the church. All Hitler wanted was a unified protestant church 'to strengthen the moral forces . . . If the churches would abstain from politics they would have complete freedom in religious matters.' The Dean also reported the view of Dr Müller (whom Hitler forced on the church as Reichsbischof) that all church parties were now co-operating in negotiations for the united church. Unlike Headlam, Duncan-Jones was willing to allow evidence to change his mind. The Dean became such a pugnacious critic of Nazism, that Hitler mentioned him twice in broadcasts as 'one of the enemies of Germany'. Duncan-Jones' book, *The Struggle for Religious*

Freedom in Germany (1938) was widely praised in Britain and in Europe, by Jews as well as Christians.[21]

In 1937 Headlam and the Rev. Dr A. J. Macdonald (a Council member, on whose views of Germany Headlam relied) produced a report which took a benevolent view of Hitler's intentions towards the German Churches and advised the Confessing Church to rejoin the main body. Bishop Bell and Duncan-Jones were aghast and persuaded the Council to reject the report. Nevertheless, Headlam insisted on writing his own preface to a revised version of the report, prepared on much more critical lines by Duncan-Jones. Both in his preface and in his speech on the report at the June session of the Church Assembly, Headlam reiterated his optimistic view of events in Germany. The Archbishop of Canterbury (who in interviews with the German ambassador had strongly condemned the Nazi treatment of the Churches) declared that Headlam's preface had the authority of neither the Council nor the Church of England. Bishop Bell (who had formed very close relationships with leaders of the Confessing Church, including Dietrich Bonhoeffer) protested that Headlam had ignored clear evidence of persecution. However, Bishop Heckel, head of the German Evangelical Church's Foreign Relations Department, wrote to the General Secretary of the Council to express his gratitude for Headlam's preface. When, in January 1938, Bell asked the Upper House of the Canterbury Convocation to voice its deep concern about the sufferings of Christians in Germany, Headlam moved the previous question. The Archbishop responded sharply and Headlam could not even find a seconder. Bell circulated copies of his statement to leaders of the churches in Britain and Europe. On 12 August 1938 the *Church Times* called for Headlam's resignation as Chairman of the Council because his attitudes to German affairs were so much at variance with the weight of Christian opinion. Philip Usher, one of the two assistant secretaries to the Council, and Headlam's former domestic chaplain, warned Headlam that he might be on the point of provoking a schism in the Council.

Headlam, it was true, had been prepared to write to Dr A. Rosenberg, a Nazi Commissioner, refusing an invitation to visit Germany in 1934 and in correspondence with Rosenberg criticized the Nazi treatment of the churches and non-Aryan pastors. But by his letters to the *Times*, by speeches to church gatherings and in other ways, he used his authority as a bishop and Chairman of the Council to commend a favourable view of Nazism to the churches and the general public.[22] For example, the following extraordinary and deplorable pronouncement by Headlam was published in his diocesan magazine for August 1933. It was significantly thought suitable for republication by the anti-semitic and imperialistic journal *The Patriot*.

> We all condemn the folly and violence of the attacks upon the Jews in Germany, and the violence with which the members of the Socialist and Communist parties are being treated, but to both Jews and Socialists some words of warning are necessary. Many Jews were responsible, particularly at the beginning, for the violence of the Russian Communists; many Jews have helped to inspire the violence of the Socialist communities; they are not altogether a pleasant element in German, and in particular in Berlin life. Those of alien nationality who receive the hospitality of other countries ought . . . to become healthy elements in the population.[23]

Here, his initial condemnation of Nazi violence was completely negated by his anti-semitic insinuations which echoed those of the Nazis and their British sympathizers.

During the first war, Headlam had taken a hard-headed line against Germany. In 1931 he publicly announced his refusal to take the chair at meetings organized to discuss disarmament and the Lambeth resolution on peace and war, unless the organizers recognized that he would speak against unilateral disarmament, in support of the supremacy of the British navy and in warning against the spread of Russian Communism. In 1932 he attacked pacifists for not grasping the essential function of armed force in international relations. Yet by 1933 he was complaining that we had not treated Germany fairly. The situation in Germany was not 'deplorable'. Life had become 'more wholesome and healthy' under the Nazis. Certainly things had been done which cannot be excused, yet at least the Germans were seeking to 'win back their self-respect by self-discipline and good order'.

> The nations of Europe seem to be like a lot of schoolboys playing cricket who are angry with one of their number because he has been indulging in body-line bowling. They have lectured him, they have told him what they think of him in no measured language, and they have tied both his hands behind his back. They then tell him that they expect him to go on playing with them . . . is it reasonable to expect him to go on playing under those conditions?

(This prolonged cricketing metaphor, so characteristically Anglican and English, showed how incapable Headlam was of comprehending the real nature of Nazism.) At the Church Assembly in June 1934 he deprecated criticisms of the Nazi treatment of the churches. We would not react favourably if other churches passed resolutions about the Church of England.[24]

On 2 September 1938, in the early stages of the crisis about Czechoslovakia, the *Guardian* published an article of some three thousand words by Headlam entitled 'The German Church'. Headlam asserted that the English newspapers grossly distorted the religious situation in Germany:

> The idea that prevails in this country is that Christianity is being persecuted, and that a crude neo-paganism is being forced on the country by the National-Socialist Party . . . There are some things which give colour to this picture, but they are grossly exaggerated and the picture is not true.

The Confessional Church is a small and decreasing minority. Protests against the imprisonment of Pastor Niemöller irritate the authorities and do harm. The Thuringen 'German Christians' (who were an extreme nationalist group who regarded Hitler as a God-sent saviour) Headlam regarded as entirely orthodox:

> They supported Herr Hitler because he had restored to the German people their belief in God and their belief in themselves . . . What they were opposed to was the theology of Karl Barth . . . The theology of most of those that I met is much more in harmony with the teaching of the Church of England than that of the Confessional Church, which has been influenced by Calvinism and the teaching of Karl Barth.

True, many Nazis are anti-Christian, but 'It is quite untrue to say that National-Socialism is incompatible with Christianity . . . it is a foolish and dangerous thing to say so.' Hitler has never been anti-Christian. But if Hitler is 'irritated' by the opposition of the Confessional Church and the English bishops, 'he might be driven' to act against the church: 'that is why a moderate and intelligent policy is so essential'. It would be as foolish to judge Germany by Rosenberg's 'neo-paganism' as to judge the Church of England by the modernism of Dr Major. The Hitler Youth can be antagonistic to the church, but it all depends on the local leader. 'If the Church were united, there would be very little difficulty.' People in England identify Christianity with democracy, but Germans think that this is a 'foolish form of government'. 'In no real sense is there State persecution of Christianity in Germany.' No pastors or congregations which refrain from political action are interfered with. Headlam concluded with a final Anglican argument designed to clinch the matter: whereas a large section of the

Confessional Church opposed episcopacy, some 'German Christians' favoured the consecration of their bishops by bishops of the Church of England.

The *Guardian* in its leader dissociated itself from Headlam's assessment of the German situation which differed (it said) so markedly from the majority of its other contributors: it was inevitable that Christianity and totalitarianism should be in conflict. On 16 September two letters criticized, one praised Headlam's article. On 23 September three very critical letters were printed, including one from Dorothy Buxton, an authority on the German church struggle, who detailed the history of the Nazi persecution of the church since 1933.[25] On 10 February 1939, it reported that a Berlin firm had published a translation of Headlam's sermon preached in Berlin in June 1938 and an essay on the German church by him. In the preface Georg Wobbermin, Professor of Theology at Berlin, a 'German Christian', wrote of Headlam's high reputation in Germany because of his persistence in counteracting lying propaganda about German religious affairs. He drew particular attention to the article by Headlam in the *Guardian* (cited above) because it disposed of the fairy tales spread by Karl Barth and others. Since the war clear evidence has appeared that the Nazis deliberately attempted to use Headlam as a tool for their propaganda.[26]

In the autumn of 1931, Martin Niemöller, pastor of Dahlem, a suburb of Berlin, broadcast a call for a leader:

> When will he come? Our seeking and willing, our calling and strivings fail to bring him. When he comes, he will come as a present, as a gift of God. Our call for a leader is a crying for compassion.[27]

In 1924 Niemöller had voted for the Nazis. Early in 1933 he preached with enthusiasm for the Nazi programme. But by the end of that year he began to see that the pro-Nazi 'German Christians' were adulterating the faith. He came under the influence of Barth. He became a leader of the Confessing Church. Its basis was the 'Barmen Declaration' (1934) which Barth helped to draft. In 1934 he said in a sermon:

> We have all of us – the whole Church and the whole community – been thrown into the Tempter's sieve and he is shaking and the wind is blowing, and it must now become manifest whether we are wheat or chaff! . . . Satan swings his sieve and Christianity is thrown hither and thither . . .[28]

Niemöller was arrested on 1 July 1937 and subsequently charged with (among other things) rebellion against the state. His arrest dramatically personified and focussed the German church struggle for many British people who had been confused by, or uninterested in, the issues at stake. Nathaniel Micklem, Principal of Mansfield College, Oxford, who took a passionate interest in the struggle, wrote in retrospect: 'Never, I think, since the days of the Reformation have the British been so aware of Continental Christianity' as at the time of Niemöller's trial.[29] But as Keith Robbins points out,[30] it was very difficult for English people to find the correct categories for understanding the struggle. Luther's theology was little known or understood in England. Many Anglicans regarded Lutherans and continental Protestants as marginal ecclesiastically because they lacked bishops in the apostolic succession. Free Churchmen did not approve of state churches, and rather felt a kinship with the German Free Churches which had Anglo-Saxon origins. In the nineteenth century the German Free Churches had been persecuted by the state and the established church. English Baptists could not understand why German Baptists supported Hitler, though in 1937 E. A. Payne, the Baptist leader, explained that the German Baptists believed that Hitler had brought them unprecedented freedom and recognition. Those Anglicans who still regarded the Free Churches as schismatic were unlikely to be sympathetic to the Confessing Church which seemed a breakaway group. (By contrast Bonhoeffer regarded it as the true church and in 1936 provocatively declared: 'Whoever knowingly separates himself from the Confessing Church in Germany separates himself from salvation.')[31]

Headlam played upon Anglican dislike of Barthianism and Calvinism to discredit the Confessing Church. He and others asked why so much agitation should be directed against events in Germany when the raging persecution of the church in the Soviet Union drew so little comment, by comparison, from English church and political leaders. Anglicans and Free Churchmen found it hard to understand why church elections at which 'German Christians' gained a majority should be suspect, not realizing that the elections had been rigged and the opposition stifled. Some English churchmen feared that protests about the treatment of the churches might worsen Anglo-German relations. Nevertheless both the Archbishops, Bell, Henson, Micklem and others openly expressed their indignation.

In addition, Anglicans and Free Churchmen had a very different understanding of the relation of church to state from that of the German Protestants. Anglican and Free Church leaders believed it was their duty to criticize actions of the state where necessary, even (however circumspectly) during wartime. They were used to living in a state where the law was just and impartially administered and had no conception of what it meant to live in a police state. The Lutheran tradition of a clear distinction between the functions of church and state; the pietistic and nationalist character of much German Protestantism; its tendency to be monarchistic, conservative in politics, and suspicious of the Republic of Weimar; the German emphasis on law and order:[32] all led to the virtual absence in the German Protestant tradition of those elements in the English Christian tradition which regard criticism, and even defiance, of the state as a necessary part of Christian discipleship. These elements in English Christianity found classical expression in Nonconformity. They were reinforced by the anti-erastian and dissenting character of much Anglo-Catholicism. The *Official Handbook* of the 1933 Anglo-Catholic Congress included a page of photographs of five priests imprisoned for ritualism in the nineteenth century, headed with terminology, significantly as well as ironically borrowed from Nonconformity 'Lest we forget – Prisoners for Conscience Sake'. The growth of pacifism, during and after the war, also strengthened the number of Christians ready to stand against the state. Anglican and Free church leaders defended the rights of pacifist objectors during the war. By contrast, there was virtually no Christian pacifist tradition in German Christianity.

Hitler and the Nazi leaders were able to rely on the conservative and pietistic character of much German Christianity. Hitler told the Reichstag on 23 March 1933 that by cleansing political and moral life the government was creating 'the conditions for a really deep and inner religious life . . . The national government sees in both Christian denominations the most important factor for the maintenance of our society . . . The rights of the churches will not be curtailed.' No wonder that most churchpeople, like Niemöller, felt enthusiastic for the new regime. When from its very early days in power, the Nazis began to proceed against opposition groups, including critics within the churches, Hitler was able to quieten many Christians by saying on 24 October 1933: 'We have brought the priests out of the party political conflict, and led them back into the Church. And now it is our desire that they should never return to that area for which they were not intended.' Josef Goebbels declared in August 1935: 'For the Churches there is only one solution which will ensure peace: Back into the sacristy. Let the churches serve God; we serve the People.'[33] Both Hitler and Goebbels here were appealing to the traditional distinction of function between church and state in Germany about which Barth wrote in 1939: 'Luther's very dubious teaching on Matt. 28.18, concerning the separation between the kingdom of Christ and all "worldly" spheres, lies like a cloud over the ecclesiastical thinking and action of more or less every course taken by the German Church.'[34]

In Germany, as in Britain in the post-war period, church leaders were conscious of the increase in secularization and the decrease of church allegiance. R. J. C. Gutteridge, an Anglican ordinand who had studied in Germany, wrote 'German Protestantism and the Hitler Regime' which appeared in the Anglican magazine *Theology* in November 1933:

> There can be no real denying that the Hitler regime offers the Protestant Church opportunities that have not been hers hitherto at any period since the War . . . a championing of a 'positive Christianity' in opposition to the 'Marxian' godlessness belongs to the very essence of the new order . . . Hitler himself is manifestly of the conviction that he is called by God . . .

(Many years later Gutteridge was to write a very different assessment of Nazism: *Open thy Mouth for the Dumb!* (1976) – a sombre analysis of the attitudes of the German Evangelical Church towards the Jews.)

The division among English Christians between those favourable or hostile to Nazism in the 1930s cut right across traditional divisions of churchmanship and theology. The Kelham monk, Fr Gabriel Hebert, approved of Barth's assault on liberalism. Hebert's *Liturgy and Society* (1935), in which liberal theology was regarded as 'corrupting'.[35] went through five impressions in nine years and persuaded many Anglicans to adopt liturgical corporatism and to despise liberalism as individualistic. There seems to have been a connection between all this and his qualified approval of Nazi corporatism:

> We may well be cautious about accepting the criticisms of the Nazi régime so commonly made in this country, in the name of the Liberal ideal of individual freedom; for with all its faults, the Nazi state has actualized the unity of the German nation, as the Liberal-democratic régime which preceded it was powerless to do.

Though he went on to say that the object of worship in Germany was 'the magnified corporate ego of the nation' rather than God, he commended 'experiment on communistic lines' and wrote of the 'success' of the 'great national movement' in Germany.[36] Yet Bonhoeffer visiting the monastic orders at Kelham and Mirfield in 1935 learned much about their worship and communal life which he incorporated into the ethos of his seminary at Finkenwalde. High doctrines of the church among some German Protestants, derived partly from Anglo-Catholicism, nerved them to fight for the indepen-

dence of the church. Sir Edwyn Hoskyns, Dean of Corpus Christi
College Cambridge, a former First War chaplain, a translator of Barth,
was a leading neo-orthodox theologian, contemptuous of theological
liberalism, a type of Anglo-Catholic and a Tory. Despite his neo-
orthodoxy, Hoskyns took a favourable view of the 'German Christians'.[37] Other Anglo-Catholics were led to totally different conclusions.
No one could have been more fierce in his opposition to the Mosleyites
and the Munich agreement than the Anglo-Catholic Fr St John Groser,
the East End socialist priest, a rebel against established authority in
both church and state. Headlam was middle-of-the-road in churchmanship and theology. His adviser, Macdonald, was a Conservative
Evangelical. But both were establishment minded and disliked
dissenters from authority. Bell admired Hebert's book and supported
the liturgical movement, but there was an element of the dissenter in
his character. So he consistently supported the Confessing Church.
During the second war he stood almost alone against political and
military policies of the British Government. Of course he was also
fired by a great vision, the *Una Sancta*, a horror of another war and
an innate feeling for the oppressed. Henson was an ex-dissenter, a
Tory individualist, who always felt himself a lone wolf and consistently
upheld the rights of minorities against the power of the majority.
Theologically neither Bell nor Henson were Barthians yet both
vigorously sided with the Confessing Church. Lang was an establishment man but attacked the persecution of Christians and Jews in the
name of civilized and Christian values. The prime determinants of
English churchmen's attitudes to Nazism, Fascism and the church
struggle were therefore not churchmanship, nor theological stance.
The most potent determinants seem to have been: attitudes to dissent
from established authority; political ideology; differing estimates of
the rights of the individual in society; attitudes to the outsider and the
oppressed.

When Niemöller was arrested Bell immediately wrote to the *Times*
(3 July 1937):

> What is his crime? The truth is that he is a preacher of the Gospel
> of God, and that he preaches that Gospel without flinching. I know
> Dr Niemöller. He is a man whom any Christian might well be proud
> to count as a friend. I have never seen a braver Christian nor a man
> in whom the lamp of faith burns more brightly . . . It is a critical
> hour. The question is not only a question of the fate of a particular
> minister, but of the whole attitude of the German State to Christ-
> ianity and to Christian ethics.

Bell also wrote to Rudolf Hess. In February 1938 when the trial began, Bell held an intercession service for him in London and appealed for prayers from the whole church. Micklem remembers seeing a placard outside Poplar Mission Hall, 'Pray for Pastor Niemöller', which explained that his only offence was that he was obeying God rather than men. When he was sentenced Henson called Niemöller the 'freest man in Germany in spite of his confinement in a concentration camp'.[38] The *Guardian* on 1 July said that he was in prison because he was being a true Christian in a totalitarian state. On the other hand a few days before Niemöller's arrest, Headlam had written that pastors, who, contrary to new laws, were publicly interceding for others under threat 'are deliberately irritating the Government, and they cannot complain if as a result of that they are arrested; and it seems to me very foolish on our part to encourage them in these pin pricks. They are exactly what a good Christian clergyman ought not to indulge in.'[39] In the *Times* of 7 July 1937 Macdonald described Niemöller as 'fanatical' about church-state questions. 'We in this country have also to obey police instructions.' Free Churchmen naturally felt an immediate identity with a persecuted pastor. But M. E. Aubrey, General Secretary of the Baptist Union and Moderator of the Free Church Federal Council, while deploring that Christianity was under attack from Nazism, pointed out that there was a grave anomaly in the protests of the Evangelical and Confessing Churches. They do not renounce their special status in the state and are financially dependent upon it, yet demand to be free from state control: a position which 'is completely foreign to our Free Church way of thinking'.[40] In the *Times* for 14 July 1938, Headlam wrote that he had just returned from ten days in Germany. Pastors are free to carry on their work and to preach the Christian faith providing that they do not preach political sermons. 'Pastor Niemöller is in confinement because he has stubbornly and determinedly defied this law.' We should try to understand, not to scold other nations. Two days later Henson replied to Headlam. The church cannot keep silent in the face of the persecution of Christians and Jews by the Nazis. The flood of refugees from Germany cannot be regarded as purely a domestic matter for Germany alone.

English newspapers gave a good deal of alarmed attention to Niemöller's case. The Archbishop of Canterbury joined world church leaders in a declaration of protest against Niemöller's detention and forcibly reiterated this to the departing Ambassador, Ribbentrop. Robbins points out the unacknowledged conflict between Bell and his critics: 'Bell attempted to deny that Niemöller might be described as an agitator against the State by saying that the truth was that he was an unflinching preacher of the Gospel. But it is, of course, both logically and empirically possible to be both a preacher and an agitator against the State.'[41]

On 7 February 1938 the trial opened in secret. Duncan-Jones and Dr W. G. Moore, a Congregational layman, who had arrived as observers were refused admission. As Niemöller was led into court a guard whispered to him from Proverbs: 'The name of the Lord is a strong tower: the righteous runneth into it and is safe.' His defence council recounted Niemöller's war-service as a U-boat commander, his service in the anti-Republican *Freikorps* in 1920 and how he had supported the Nazis in 1924 and 1933. Even one of Goering's sisters appeared and witnessed to his patriotism. Niemöller admitted that he found Jews uncongenial, but God had revealed himself in a Jew. He pleaded that his oath to the Kaiser had pledged him to oppose anything which might shame the Fatherland. But his primary allegiance was to the Word of God. Niemöller was virtually acquitted. Hitler was furious, rearrested him and sent him to Sachsenhausen as his 'personal prisoner'. There, and later in Dachau, he spent eight years, beginning with three years solitary confinement when often the only sounds he heard were prisoners being tortured. 'Uncle George gives his love to you' his wife would tell him when she visited him bringing a message from Bell, representing the ecumenical movement he had once disdained. Fear of international opinion almost certainly saved him from execution. But Niemöller remained in many ways a conservative figure until after the war. In 1933 he had sent Hitler a telegram congratulating him on withdrawing Germany from the League of Nations. In September 1939 he astonished world opinion by offering as a reserve officer, to serve his country 'in any capacity'. He explained to Bell six years later: 'we had a people and a mother country that we loved.' A victory by Hitler would destroy the soul of Germany. An Allied victory would crush Germany. Both horrified him.[42] Bonhoeffer, who had moved towards pacifism, supported Niemöller's offer of service in September 1939, and that month volunteered as a chaplain, but was turned down because he had no record of military service.

It is important (as J. S. Conway argued in *The Nazi Persecution of the Churches*) to demythologize the church struggle and present its leaders without idealization. During and after the war, Christians often presented over-simplified accounts of the struggle entirely from the side of the Confessing Church, in order to promote Christianity as the only bulwark against totalitarianism, and so underplayed the fact that the struggle was between Christians, as much as against

Nazism. It has been painfully difficult for Christians in general, and those in Germany in particular, to accept how deep and prolonged was the compromise of most Christians in Germany with Nazism. Barthians too have had an interest in promoting an over-simplified picture in order to prove that neo-orthodoxy is the only guarantee of true discipleship. But, as we have seen, there were some neo-orthodox whose corporatism and authoritarianism led to a sympathy with totalitarianism. The liberal values (represented, for example, by Bell in England and to some extent by Otto Dibelius in Germany)[43] though despised by many neo-orthodox, deeply influenced the resistance to Nazism. Peter Berger grants that neo-orthodoxy may have been the ideology of the resistance for the Confessing Church. But historically both theological liberalism and orthodoxy have been used to defend the *status quo*: 'no particular theological position guarantees social or political clear-sightedness'. Jerusalem always has need of Athens.[44] Barth himself saw things differently, as he made clear during a visit to Britain in 1937 in an article in the Free Church *British Weekly* (22 April 1937). That 'freedom of conscience' and 'freedom of the Church' are approved of in Britain is well known in Germany, but either it makes no impression on the Nazis or they do not comprehend it:

> And the Confessional Church is not thereby helped, because the fight is not about the freedom, but about the necessary bondage, of the conscience; and not about the freedom, but about the substance of the Church, i.e. about the preservation, rediscovery and authentication of the true Christian faith.[45]

Yet, a year before, Barth had berated the Confessing Church for its silence about the persecution of the Jews, the treatment of political opponents and the suppression of press freedom.[46]

Bell reached his convictions from a different theological tradition which valued the natural world sacramentally because it had been hallowed by the incarnation. He enthusiastically promoted modern art and drama in the life of the church. In an article for Christmas 1929 he quoted Ecclesiasticus 38: working men 'maintain the fabric of the world, and in the handiwork of their craft is their prayer'. The church should 'blow a trumpet' for education, health, science, art and now for a National Theatre. 'She should also blow a trumpet for Peace and for Justice . . . she should not be afraid, when need is, of denouncing authority in the wrong, and even opposing all her moral forces, in defence of her ideal and her trust, to the princes of the world.' He quoted Milton ('I cannot praise a fugitive and cloistered virtue') and commented: 'Nor, least of all on Christmas Day, can I praise a fugitive and cloistered Church.'[47] This article might be regarded as the charter for Bell's astonishingly wide-ranging ministry. For the rest of his life he strove painstakingly and unwearyingly to discover, at first hand wherever possible, what was happening in Germany and to keep the world, the ecumenical movement, the Church of England and the British and other governments fully informed. At the Stockholm ecumenical Conference of Life and Work in 1925, Bell had had a major share in the drafting of the final message which proclaimed a commitment to Christian internationalism and the universal character of the church. The Conference (the message said) also considered the relation of the individual conscience to the state. After 1933, Bell constantly strove to give a voice to those suffering in Germany, though his efforts to persuade the ecumenical movement to side unequivocally with the Confessing Church were not always successful. So in the year 1934, for example, he chaired the Fanö Conference on Life and Work (which expressed grave anxiety about the suppression of freedom in Germany and conveyed sympathy to all Christians there, especially those of the Confessing Church). He discussed these matters with the Swedish Archbishop. He visited Confessing Church leaders in Germany. He carefully briefed the leaders of Life and Work on the German situation and appealed to them to make representations to their respective German Embassies. He had an interview at the German Embassy in London and persuaded Archbishop Lang to meet the German Ambassador. Hitler's envoy Ribbentrop visited Bell in November. Bell gave him a detailed inventory of acts of coercion against the church. At the end of the previous year Bell's friendship with Bonhoeffer began, so crucial to them both. At the beginning of September 1939 Bell wrote:

> My dear Dietrich,
> You know how deeply I feel for you and yours in this melancholy time. May God comfort and guide you. I think often of our talk in the summer. May He keep you. Let us pray together by reading the Beatitudes. *Pax Dei quae superat omnia nos custodiat.*
> Yours affectionately,
George[48]

It was to Bell that Bonhoeffer sent his last message before his execution on 9 April 1945.

Meanwhile the Rev. Dr A. J. Macdonald, Rector of St Dunstan-in-the-West and Headlam's adviser on the German situation, continued to purvey his totally different accounts of what was happening in Germany. Just as Ribbentrop was instructed to cultivate Headlam, so a Nazi agent, Friedrich von der Ropp, began to cultivate Macdonald. Ropp was the founder in 1936 of the Anglo-German Brotherhood designed to propagate the Nazi view of the church conflict. Macdonald was the Vice-Chairman of the English branch which seemed to the unsuspecting to be innocently trying to forge bonds between German and English churchpeople.[49] In 1936 Macdonald contributed an article 'Why I believe in Hitler' to a German symposium. In March 1938, the *Nineteenth Century and After* published his article 'Church and State in Germany'. This was based, he said, both on visits and a close study of documents over a number of years. There appeared 'to be ground for a more hopeful view of the whole situation'. He was glad to see on a visit that Nazis in uniform were devoutly worshipping in church. If pastors confine themselves to the proclamation of the gospel the authorities do not interfere: 'the value of a conciliatory attitude and the avoidance of a defiant attitude appears to reap a reward – freedom to do the work of a Christian pastor, evangelist and minister'. But the pastors of the Confessional Church are 'forthright, uncompromising'. Niemöller reminded him of an officer of the British Navy: 'His theological views are clear-cut and simple . . . Yet he has the martyr spirit, and honestly believes that he is engaged in a cause as vital as that upheld by Martin Luther.' Among the 'German Christians' he found pastors whose views on the Old Testament were like those of Modern Churchmen or Liberal Evangelicals, yet otherwise orthodox. The church parties have no desire for conciliation and wish to continue a fight 'no longer of moral significance'. He met Herr Kerrl (the government Minister for Ecclesiastical Affairs) who believed that Hitler had been sent by God. Christians, Kerrl thought, wanted to hear about Christ not about the Old Testament. Jews had purveyed destructive ideas through eighteenth-century liberalism and Marxism. Independence for the church would produce a state within a state. Kerrl (wrote Macdonald) was 'a robust and kindly personality, a man doing his best in a difficult situation'. Macdonald had long interviews at the Foreign Office, Propaganda Ministry, Hitler Youth headquarters and at the offices of the Nazi charitable Winter Help organization:

The personnel in every case impressed me as a fine body of bright, honest young men, trying to do their duty. They resembled the best type of Boy Scout master and Scout assistant commissioners in this country. At each of these ministries the idea was prevalent that the Confessional Church minority, like the Roman Church, was not backing up the Government's efforts to restore prosperity to the German people. At the Hitler Jugend office . . . I received the impression that any intelligent and tactful pastor should be able to cooperate with these bright, open-hearted young men.

The Jews

Headlam, in his lengthy article in the *Guardian* of September 1938, already referred to, notably omitted any reference to the persecution of the Jews or the sufferings of Christians of Jewish blood. By contrast, as early as 30 March 1933, the *Baptist Times* saw clearly what was happening to Jews: 'Nothing but evil can come of the Hitlerite policy in stirring the passions of the people against the Jewish race . . . We hope that the entire Christian Church will unite in protest against these outrages.'[50] In June 1933 a large protest meeting at the Queen's Hall London was addressed by the Archbishop of Canterbury, whose resolution deploring the German treatment of the Jews was seconded by Dr Scott Lidgett, the Methodist, and unanimously approved. Lord Reading expressed the gratitude of the Jewish community. The Archbishop renewed his protests in the Church Assembly in November 1935. Bell moved a resolution expressing sympathy with the Jews in Germany, and Henson and Lord Hugh Cecil supported this in strong speeches. Late in 1938 on behalf of the Church of England, the Archbishop of York, the Bishops of Chichester, Bradford and Bristol, the Deans of St Paul's and Chichester, George Lansbury, other clergy and lay people addressed a letter to the Chairman of the Jewish Board of Deputies expressing their concern about anti-semitism in Britain: 'anti-Semitism remains wicked folly . . . We are all children of the one father.'[51] In November 1935, when Henson spoke with such power in the Church Assembly against the persecution of the Jews in Germany, his speech was received with an ovation, and praised by many newspapers the next day. But when he arrived back at Auckland Castle he found a heap of hostile letters. He was startled to discover so much anti-semitism in Britain. On 4 February 1936 the *Times* published a long, fierce letter from Henson condemning any British participation in the 550th anniversary of Heidelberg University because of its dismissal of Jewish professors and lecturers. If British academics were to attend it 'could not but be understood everywhere as a public and deliberate condonation of the intolerance which has emptied the German universities of many of their most eminent teachers, and which is filling Europe with victims of cynical and heartless oppression'.

In 1937 Lord Londonderry, a leading apologist for the Nazis and a former Secretary for Air, was inaugurated as Mayor of Durham. He took Ribbentrop, the German Ambassador, to the Cathedral for the service. Henson's suffragen, Geoffrey Gordon, a notable first war chaplain, pointedly preached on freedom and human rights. Londonderry, who was also Chancellor of Durham University, helped to persuade the University to send representatives to the University of Göttingen for its bicentenary celebrations. Henson was visitor to Durham and regarded Göttingen as 'a Jew-baiting university'. Henson wrote to the Vice-Chancellor of Durham to say that if the University were to be represented, he would have to make known publicly his total disapproval. Henson sent Londonderry a copy of this letter with a warning that if the decision were not reversed, he would refuse to take part in the celebrations of the Durham University centenary. The University bowed to Henson's pressure. No wonder that when, in July 1938, Henson spoke to 3,000 Jews in Leeds they gave him a standing ovation. This ex-dissenter who always felt an outsider and who had been deeply wounded by life, was the natural champion of the Jews. 'He stood with head erect among the ostriches.'[52]

W. R. Matthews, Dean of St Paul's, had close relations with Jewish scholars in England, but like many others, was slow to recognize fully what was happening to Jews in Germany. On the brink of war he was involved in helping individual Jews to escape from Germany. Deeply concerned about anti-semitism, he became associated with a scheme to found a powerful Anglo-Jewish society. Preparing to speak at a lunch for possible supporters, he decided to make a random survey of opinion in shops, trains and so on. The result astounded him: 'out of between twenty-five and thirty-five separate opinions, not one was in favour of the Jews and three or four, so far from being shocked by Hitler's anti-semitic acts, were heartily in favaour of them'.[53] In 1942 the Council of Christians and Jews was created, strongly supported by William Temple, leaders of other churches and the Chief Rabbi. Temple was at the centre of efforts to help persecuted Jews. On 23 March 1943 in a speech in the Lords he passionately denounced the systematic slaughter of Jews by Germany: 'We stand at the bar of history, of humanity, and of God'.

In 1945 Niemöller revisited Dachau and saw the crematorium for the first time. He stood profoundly shocked in front of the notice: 'Here in the years 1933 to 1945, 238,756 persons were incinerated.' He felt deeply guilty looking back that he and the Confessing Church had been almost wholly concerned with the sufferings of the church and of the baptized Jews; they had failed to perceive that Christ was also suffering in others who were outside the church:

If we had then recognised that in the communists who were

thrown into concentration camps, the Lord Jesus Christ himself lay imprisoned and looked for our love and help, if we had seen that at the beginning of the persecution of the Jews it was the Lord Christ in the person of the least of our human brethren who was being persecuted and beaten and killed, if we had stood by him and identified ourselves with him, I do not know whether God would not then have stood by us and whether the whole thing would not then have had to take a different course.

He also wrote: 'We acted as if we had only to sustain the Church. Afterwards from the experience of those bygone years, we learned we had a responsibility for the whole nation.'[54] Though there were a few courageous Christian protests at some points in the horrifying story and a few individual Christians who gave help to the Jews at great cost to themselves, most German Protestants and Catholics remained silent both about the sufferings of the Jews and about the fact of anti-semitism itself. It was only after the war that Christians in general began slowly to realize how much anti-semitism was inextricably interwoven with the history of the whole Christian church from very early days. Rolf Hochhuth's play *The Representative* (1963) indicts the papacy and Roman Catholicism for its failure to stand for the Jews. But the indictment applies to some extent to all the churches, and not only in Germany.

In 1933, Bishop Bell began his work for Jewish Christians in Germany. Other Jews were being helped by world Jewry, but this group had no one to whom they could turn. Bell immediately sought support from the International Missionary Council, other ecumenical bodies and the leaders of the Anglican and Free Churches. The Chief Rabbi commented on Bell's Speech to the Church Assembly on 20 November 1935: 'Your words will come as a ray of hope to hundreds of thousands whose annihilation seems to have been decided upon by the Nazi rulers.' However, the results of financial appeals in 1933 and 1936 were meagre. In 1937 Bell lamented the general lack of English interest in the plight of Jewish Christians: 'There have been individual Christians who have been generous. But the Churches as a whole are silent and, it seems, unconcerned.' Nevertheless through Bell's efforts expressed in the 'Church of England Committee for non-Aryan Christians' a number of refugees and some pastors were able to escape and found a home in England. It was not until 1939 that English Christians began to wake up to their responsibilities. But by that time the refugee problem had grown so much that it could not be met by voluntary organizations alone.[55]

What Bell's work meant to German Jewish Christians can be focussed in the remarkable story of Werner Simonson told in his autobiography, *The Last Judgement* (1969). Simonson was born near Berlin in 1889 of Jewish Christian parents. After fighting for a short time in the First World War he was captured and spent five years as a prisoner of war. When released he resumed his legal training. In 1925 he was appointed a judge. But in 1933 during the first pogrom, local Nazi leaders discovered that all Simonson's four grandparents were Jewish. That was the end of his career as a judge. Publishers refused to handle his writings. Friends shunned him. In 1938 he had a breakdown. A woman asked Simonson's Aryan wife why he did not commit suicide to make life easier. Hitherto he had regarded religion as a philosophy of life. In despair he went to a church and heard a pastor preach that only when people reach the abyss can they find their way to God. Through the sermon God spoke to him and seemed to promise a new life. But as persecution increased, his life was hemmed in by ever greater restrictions. One of his colleagues, an active member of the Confessing Church, was sent to a concentration camp and died. The Simonsons now dreaded every time the door bell rang. Their young son Jürgen, who is now an Anglican priest, was persecuted at school. In November 1938, Simonson only escaped arrest because his new address had not been registered. His wife urged him to flee. Through a personal contact with someone in the British foreign service, he offered himself for church work in England. After much harrassment he obtained a passport. Leaving his wife and son behind (temporarily as he thought) he set out with two suitcases and ten marks. On the train he wrote a poem which included this verse (translated):

> Silently I fold my hands in prayer for you, my Germany,
> as I see for the last time those German trees.
> I pray that you will survive these dreadful times:
> I want to see you free again, my Germany.

He arrived in England in March 1939. He was put in touch with the Bishop of Chichester's committee. But because of his age and poor English he failed to get employment. He appealed direct to Bell:

> Dr Bell had been seeing other refugees, who were in as great need as I was, and he listened to them all sympathetically. As I entered the room he greeted me like a friend. His huge warm blue eyes reflected his love and inner peace and I felt a personal contact which made me lose all my fear and nervousness.

As a result of the interview, in October 1939 he began training for the ministry at Cheshunt Congregational College, Cambridge. But on Whit Sunday 1940 he was taken off by police and interned on the Isle of Man with many other German nationals. The Nazis had told him he was not a German. Now he was interned because he was. Depressed, he heard God say: 'You are a citizen of God's kingdom; it is not confined to any nation or race; it is open to all who will enter in. This citizenship no one can take away from you wherever you are.' Bell came to see him when he twice visited the camp. In November, Bell secured his release. Simonson resumed his training at Cambridge, this time at Ridley Hall, the Anglican college. At Michaelmas 1942 he was ordained by the Bishop of London (Geoffrey Fisher) in St Paul's Cathedral to serve in the parish of Christ Church, Fulham. Afterwards press photographers crowded round him. 'German Judge to be curate in London' was the headline in the *Evening Star*. Simonson wrote: 'It was an act of faith and courage when the Church admitted me – a German – into its ministry without asking what the public reaction might be.'

Hitler scornfully described the reactions of the democracies to the Jewish refugees in a speech on 30 January 1939: 'It is a shameful spectacle to see how the whole democratic world is oozing sympathy for the poor tormented Jewish people, but remains hard-hearted and obdurate when it comes to helping them . . .' 'Refugees Get Jobs – Britons Get Dole' was one headline in the British press, which pointed out that there were almost two million unemployed already. The British Government was deeply concerned that a sizeable Jewish influx into Palestine, then under British mandate, would disturb the already tense relations between Jews and Arabs there. Yet the British public was in a position to know what happened to Jews who did not escape from Germany. For example, in 1936 Victor Gollancz published *The Yellow Spot* (with a weighty introduction from Hensley Henson) which documented the persecution and killing. On 7 January 1939 the *News Chronicle* on its front page carried a large photograph of shaven-headed Jews in Sachsenhausen concentration camp, and on 15 June published an article by a former Jewish prisoner, now a refugee in England, starkly describing the degradation and brutality. Early in 1939 advertisements in the press for the Lord Baldwin Fund for Refugees (sponsored by all the churches and the Jewish community) appealed: 'Before It Is Too Late: Get Them Out'; it went on: 'Homeless, Hated, Hopeless – 600,000 doomed to a living death in Germany unless you rescue them soon. Christians as well as Jews, many of them children . . .' It was not until October 1939 that it became politically advantageous for the British Government, by then anxious to promote the war as a moral crusade, to publish in a White Paper details of what had been happening in the concentration camps. By then there was little risk of any of the persecuted escaping to Britain.[56]

Abyssinia

When we examine the attitudes of English churchmen to the main international crises of the 1930s it is evident that virtually all were appeasers. Yet it is also important to remember that the vast majority of Christian pacifiers would have agreed with the *Church Times*, which after calling for a proscription of Mosley's blackshirts on 15 June 1934, a week later declared: 'Fascism is alien to the traditions of this country'.

The Italian aggression in Abyssinia was condemned by the Archbishop of Canterbury in the Lords on 25 October 1935. Lang, like many others, recognized that this was the crucial test for the League. At the Church Congress he asked: 'how can we fail to be indignant . . . when we see a Great European Power which has signed the Covenant of the League of Nations and the Pact of Paris treating these solemn obligations with cynical contempt and launching a fierce attack on a fellow member of the League?' He believed that other members, of the League should restrain the aggression by whatever means were necessary, including sanctions. But surely (he said) we also have to recognize the need for Italy to expand and have fuller access to raw materials. Temple also supported sanctions.[57] Lang sponsored a British Ambulance Service unit to accompany the Abyssinian troops and gave it his blessing before it departed.

The hearty support for the war by many Italian bishops and the suggestion that they viewed the war as an opportunity to convert heretics, hardly endeared them to English Protestants. The Pope's unwillingness to condemn Mussolini also drew highly critical comment.[58] Cardinal Hinsley, rattled by these damaging accusations, made things much worse by a sermon in October 1935 which even his adulatory biographer John (later Cardinal) Heenan termed a 'blunder'.[59] Hinsley granted that 'Indignation has no bounds when we see that Africa, that ill-used Continent of practically unarmed people, is made the focus and playground of scientific slaughter'. He denied on the authority of the Vatican that the bells of St Peter's had been rung for a war rally. But he continued:

Well, what can the Pope do to prevent this or any other war? He is a helpless old man with a small police force to guard himself, to guard the priceless art and archaeological treasures of the Vatican, and to protect his diminutive State . . .

If the Pope were to excommunicate the Italians he would make war against the Vatican State inevitable and create a fierce outbreak of anti-clericalism. Before the League pronounced, the Pope could not 'in decency' have stigmatized either side as 'wrongdoers' and would have been criticized if he had done so. Naturally the newspapers had a field day. 'Hinsley Calls Pope Helpless Old Man' was one headline. On 18 October the *Church Times* plunged in the knife with relish, glad to be able to be triumphantly scornful about Roman Catholicism and the papacy, which its Anglo-Catholic readers both admired and feared:

> Here, indeed, is the nemesis of temporal power – Christ's Viceregent on earth, a timid old man fearful of his life and his treasure, terrorized into silence by wickedness in high places! . . . We deeply regret the silence of His Holiness, and the regret is intensified now that the reason for the silence has been explained.

The *Times* also carried some very critical letters. The Vatican was displeased. Hinsley took a long time to recover from this debacle which occurred only six months after his enthronement.[60]

Leslie Weatherhead proposed a conference between Britain and Italy about Italy's need for expansion and suggested that Britain should offer territory to Italy for this end. Was not Italy only following the methods which had created the British Empire? Britain was a successful but unconvicted burglar. 'Let us cease talking about sanctions, armed or economic.' But in August 1937 he changed his mind and was apprehensive lest Britain should recognize the conquest.[61]

Henson in a letter to the *Times* for 30 August 1935 argued that here at last was an act of aggression which could be stopped: Britain as a member of the League, as a guarantor of Abyssinian independence and as a Mediterranean power must interfere in the cause of justice and international good faith. Henson's consistent opposition to appeasement enabled him to externalize and focus his violently aggressive nature in a righteous crusade against the dictators. An element in his character took grim satisfaction in events which confirmed his pessimistic view of modern civilization. His whole personality was mobilized by disaster; he found despair more congenial than hope. Often at times of crisis he would quote as sources for his transcendent faith such texts as: 'he endured, as seeing him who is invisible' (Heb. 11.27); 'Clouds and darkness are round about him'

(Ps. 97); 'The Lord is King, be the people never so impatient' (Ps. 99); 'I see that all things come to an end: but thy commandment is exceedingly broad' (Ps. 119). Horrified by the success of the Italian invasion, strongly critical (like both Archbishops) of the Hoare-Laval pact and contemptuous of those who urged the end of sanctions against Italy, in July 1936 Henson published what Chadwick calls the 'angriest' book he ever wrote: *Abyssinia: Reflections of an Onlooker*. Abyssinia, the 'last home of African freedom', a Christian state which Haile Selassie had sought to civilize, had been 'brutally stamped out'. He compared Mussolini's 'criminal ambition' with that of Ahab for Naboth's vineyard and his 'craft and violence' with those displayed by the Borgias. The Italians had waged war with 'cynical brutality', using poison gas and bombing Red Cross stations. Yet Italy and Abyssinia were both members of the League. Italy had pledged itself to respect Abyssinia's integrity and signed the agreement prohibiting the use of poison gas. Initially Britain had taken a bold lead, then subsided into ineffectiveness. Sanctions had turned out to be futile. The League 'has certainly been discredited and defeated, probably destroyed' by Mussolini's 'cynical realism' and by lack of effective action. The Papacy, to which Christians had begun to look with a new respect, had failed to join fifty nations in condemning the aggression. 'In face of treaties broken, oppression flagrant, barbarous cruelties inflicted, the Pope kept silence, or prated helplessly of peace to men who were sharpening their weapons for war.' The outlook was now 'extremely dark'. A probably fatal blow had been given to collective security. Another war, on an even greater scale than the last, now seemed almost certain. 'The nations in the grip of a malign fate are expecting its outbreak, as a ship driven by the tempest towards a rocky coast awaits its approaching and inevitable destruction.' Henson's booklet appeared just after the British government ended sanctions. He sent it to every member of Parliament. But it was largely ignored.

When Britain recognized the conquest, Henson protested strongly in the *Times* (21 April 1938) and in a debate in the Lords (18 May). In the debate, Lang uneasily defended appeasement as the only way to stop the armaments race, but emotionally recognized the bitter humiliation of impotence. Henson delivered a biting speech condemning the surrender to Italy as shameful. He characterized Lord Halifax's speech at Geneva defending the Government's policy as 'the cold sophistry of a cynical opportunism' and as 'the funeral oration' of the League. Halifax retorted that Henson's claim that one could not believe the word of either Hitler or Mussolini, hardly helped the cause of peace. In June 1938, at the Canterbury Convocation, Lang criticized those who spoke as if war was inevitable; such language made war more likely.[62]

The Spanish Civil War

The Spanish Civil War began in July 1936. The *Left Review* addressed its readers: 'It is clear to many of us throughout the whole world that now, as certainly never before, we are determined or compelled to take sides.' But the British government adopted a policy of non-intervention. At first, the literary left celebrated the war in rhetoric ironically reminiscent of first war poets like Rupert Brooke, but as the complexity of the issues began to dawn, doubts grew. W. H. Auden's departure for Spain in January 1937 merited the headlines in the *Daily Worker* 'Famous Poet to Drive Ambulance in Spain'[63] but to his own surprise the experience of the war led him gradually back to Christian faith. The coming to power of the Nazis in one of 'the most highly educated countries in Europe' made it impossible for him to believe any longer that 'the values of liberal humanism were self-evident'. Then he went to Barcelona and found all the churches closed and not a priest in sight.

> To my astonishment, this discovery left me profoundly shocked and disturbed. The feeling was far too intense to be the result of a more liberal dislike of intolerance, the notion that it is wrong to stop people from doing what they like, even if it is something silly like going to church. I could not escape acknowledging that, however I had consciously ignored and rejected the Church for sixteen years, the existence of churches and what went on in them had all the time been very important to me.[64]

For D. R. Davies, the left wing pacifist and ex-Congregational minister, the Spanish Civil war coincided with his reading of Reinhold Niebuhr's destructive analysis of Marxism. In 1937 Davies set out with a party for Spain which included Hewlett Johnson, Dean of Canterbury. The war brought Davies, like Auden to a personal crisis:

> Little did I realize that my experiences in Spain would be the end of the faith by which, in different forms, I had lived since I left the ministry in 1928. The humanist, self-sufficient hope of inevitable progress was rapidly disintegrating . . . On my journey to Spain I possessed a dying faith. On my return I brought back a corpse . . . I passed through an experience in which I felt the magnitude of human frustration, pain and defeat . . . A whole lifetime's optimism was disintegrating . . . War is the greatest symbol of the inescapable

impotence and contradiction of humanity . . . It was in Spain that
I began to be aware of the ultimate implications of the loss of
Christian faith . . . I went to Spain a politician, merely, I returned
a theologian . . . What I mean is that the realization of an inner,
personal need, beyond the power of social action to satisfy, displaced
politics as the *supreme* issue in human existence.[65]

By contrast most Anglican leaders remained detached. Lang said
that 'sparks from the conflagration in Spain should be kept away from
the explosive material lying about in Europe.' We should be neutral.
There are no clear issues. Both sides have been guilty of savage
cruelty.[66] Allison Peers, an Anglican layman, Professor of Spanish at
Liverpool who had held a visiting professorship at Madrid, also argued
for neutrality in an article in the *Guardian* on 6 November 1936, but
contrasted sadly and bitterly the attitudes of the two sides towards
church and religion. His book, *The Spanish Tragedy* (1936), has been
described as the most widely-read and prescient book on the civil
war. In January 1937, Duncan-Jones, Francis Underhill (Dean of
Rochester), the Rev. Henry Carter (a Methodist pacifist), the Rev.
Philip Usher and others, including a Quaker, visited Spain in January
1937 at the invitation of the Republican government and so only
visited the area under its control. The group concluded that the
Republicans were anti-church and anti-clerical rather than anti-God.
But all Roman Catholic churches were closed or secularized. The
church had come to be regarded as an instrument of the powerful to
keep the mass of the people ignorant and poor. Republican leaders
hoped that a good number of the churches would reopen. Neither
Fascism nor Communism would be congenial to the majority of the
Spaniards.[67]

On the opposite side a group was formed, to co-operate with Roman
Catholics, to combat 'the Red menace' in Spain. It included C. A.
Alington (Dean of Durham), J. K. Mozley (Canon of St Paul's), J.
E. Rattenbury and H. B. Workman (both Methodist ministers),
N. P. Williams (the Oxford theologian), the Bishop of Brechin and
the Bishop of Glasgow and Galloway. The English bishops were
unrepresented. The *Guardian* expressed the widespread conviction in
the Anglican and Free Churches that strong feelings against the church
predated the war. They were not simply to be blamed on Communists.
We should remember the power of the Spanish Inquisition. The
church must accept its share of blame for the state of the nation.[68] As
we saw earlier, most English Roman Catholics supported Franco,
though Eric Gill supported the Republicans. He joined a few other

Roman Catholics in writing to Cardinal Hinsley to protest against the bombing of open towns by Franco's forces. Needless to say they received a dusty answer. In March 1939 Hinsley wrote to Franco as 'the great defender of the true Spain'.[69]

C. F. Garbett, Bishop of Winchester, was one of the few Anglican leaders to get involved in the controversies. On 29 April 1937 in the Lords he launched an emotionally charged attack on the bombing of Guernica by Franco's forces. In a sermon on 2 May he declared: 'It was a cruel, deliberate, cold-blooded act against the laws of God and against every law of civilisation and of man'. J. A. Spender rebuked him in the *Times* of 5 May for not condemning the Republican forces for their massacre of the people of Oviedo. It was, C. H. Smyth (Garbett's biographer) loftily observed, 'the last occasion on which Garbett allowed his heart to run away with his head'.[70]

Austria

In the early stages of the Austrian crisis, Lang spoke during a Foreign Policy debate in the Lords on 16 February 1938. Like many supporters of the League, he was being driven to the conclusion that it could not fulfil all the purposes for which it had been designed. Defections by Germany, Italy and Japan had altered its character. It now looked like one set of alliances against another. Many states were now ready to risk war for purposes far removed from their vital interests. Sanctions had not proved effective. But the League could still be a focus for world opinion, however incomplete, and could be still a source of conciliation and arbitration. If the League were fully used in these ways, sanctions could be enforced against aggressors. After Hitler's annexation of Austria on 13 March, Lang on 29 March again spoke in the Lords. He supported the Government's policy of appeasement. It had proved impossible to bring in the League. The annexation had shocked the world, but the Versailles Treaty had long been regarded as 'vindictive and arbitrary, and could not possibly be permanent'. The union of Germany and Austria was 'inevitable'. Though the manner in which it was accomplished was 'reprehensible' it might bring some stability to Europe. 'Is it wholly unreasonable and merely quixotic to think that Herr Hitler, having now achieved the one great ambition of his life, may be less disposed to embark on other adventures?' Lord Strabolgi, Opposition Chief Whip, was shocked and 'bitterly disappointed' by the Archbishop's failure to condemn his annexation. The next day the *Daily Mirror* proclaimed: 'Primate Backs Hitler' and Lang regretted omitting certain qualifying sentences from his speech.[71]

Munich

In the nine months following the Anschluss, appeasement flourished. The Munich agreement of September 1938 was its climax, but also the beginning of its end.

On 25 February 1938 the *Church Times*, more favourable to appeasement than the *Guardian*, produced a representative statement of the case for a 'rearrangement in Central Europe'. It brushed aside Eden's resignation which it attributed to a now discredited faith in the League and collective security. 'The Christian's first concern in the world, as it is to-day, is the preservation of peace.' Chamberlain may fail in his efforts, but he is obeying the biblical injunction: 'Agree with thine adversary quickly, while thou art in the way with him.'

> But it is quite certain that Nazi Germany will steadily pursue the ambition of including all the German-speaking peoples of Central Europe – with the possible exception of German Switzerland – in the Reich. We confess that this seems to us a reasonable ambition. We are convinced that it is inevitable. And would not the independence and commercial prosperity of Czecho-Slovakia be better assured if it lost its discontented German minority? There must be rearrangement in Central Europe. The Christian must favourably consider any way that may secure the rearrangement without the slaughter and destruction of war . . . We are, above all other things, opposed to war.

On 2 June the *Times* published a letter from Dean Matthews which advocated a plebiscite among the Sudeten Germans; had we not fought the last war for the principle of self-determination? (Matthews, and many other liberal Christians, seemed to have no inkling that totalitarian regimes rig plebiscites and elections to produce the desired results.)

On 16 September, as Chamberlain met Hitler in Berchtesgaden, the *Times* printed a poem by John Masefield, Poet Laureate:

NEVILLE CHAMBERLAIN
As Priam to Achilles for his Son,
So you, into the night, divinely led,
To ask that young men's bodies, not yet dead,
Be given from the battle not begun.

Few could have withheld their 'Amen' to such a prayer. But when it became clear that Chamberlain was willing to give Hitler what he wanted, Mass Observation discovered that two-thirds of people questioned thought that Chamberlain should have defied Hitler. In the sample women were much more ready to support Chamberlain. Chamberlain flew to meet Hitler at Godesberg on 22 September and again to Munich on the 29th. War seemed imminent. ARP services were mobilized on the 25th. Cellars and basements were requisitioned for shelters. Barrage balloons appeared over London. Thirty-eight million gas masks were distributed to regional centres. Evacuation plans were hastily created. Some rushed to get married or to make their wills. Some hoarded foodstuffs and petrol. Louis MacNeice began writing his 'Autumn Journal' in August:

> The heavy panic that cramps the lungs and presses
>   The collar down the spine.
> And when we go out into Piccadilly Circus
>   They are selling and buying the late
> Special editions snatched and read abruptly
>   Beneath the electric signs as crude as Fate.
> And the individual, powerless, has to exert the
>   Powers of will and choice
> And choose between enormous evils, either
>   Of which depends on somebody else's voice . . .
> And at this hour of the day it is no good saying
>   'Take away this cup';
> Having helped to fill it ourselves it is only logic
>   That now we should drink it up.

MacNeice who had always been the least political of the poets of the period vividly and movingly depicts the way that public events were invading private and individual life. Against his will and all his instincts he was being sucked into the maelstrom:

> Hitler yells on the wireless,
>   The night is damp and still
> And I hear dull blows on wood outside my window;
>   They are cutting down the trees on Primrose Hill.
> The wood is white like the roast flesh of chicken,
>   Each tree falling like a closing fan;
> No more looking at the view from seats beneath the branches,
>   Everything is going to plan;
> They want the crest of this hill for anti-aircraft,
>   The guns will take the view . . .
> And we who have been brought up to think of 'Gallant Belgium'
>   As so much blague
> Are now preparing again to essay good through evil
>   For the sake of Prague.

The reactions of English church people during the crisis and to the Munich agreement were those of the general population – church people took their opinions from the same newspapers as everyone else, though probably most Christians were less ready to go to war than other people. Headlam remarked in a bathetic letter in the *Times* of 20 July: 'I have just been at a Scouts service, at which we were bidden to be courteous. I venture to think that it would be wise to be courteous even to dictators . . .' The *Guardian* for 23 September reported a sermon by the vicar of Leeds, Canon W. Thompson Elliott: the church in Germany was the only effective opposition to Nazism. But there must be 'compromise for alleviation' in our relations with Germany, as the Prime Minister was demonstrating by applying Christian principles to the crisis.

At the height of the crisis, prayer for peace was intense. For some days there was continuous intercession at Westminster Abbey. On 27 September Chamberlain mobilized the fleet; he told the Empire in a broadcast:

> How horrible, fantastic and incredible it is, that we should be digging trenches and trying on gas masks here because of a quarrel in a far-away country between people of whom we know nothing . . . However much we may sympathise with a small nation confronted by a big and powerful neighbour, we cannot in all circumstances undertake to involve the whole British Empire in war simply on her account. If we have to fight, it must be on larger issues than that.[72]

(Had Chamberlain forgotten that the image of small defenceless Belgium raped by a powerful neighbour had been persistently employed to evoke British chivalric compassion during the Great War?) On the same day the *Times* published a letter from Bishop Bell which made no mention of the Nazi persecutions or policies of aggrandisement, though he did say in passing 'I am no friend of Nazi methods'. He pleaded the case for appeasement, based on the injustice wrought at Versailles:

> In the last 19 years grievous mistakes have been made by us, and expectations on which the defeated had a right to rely have not been fulfilled. There is a nemesis in these things . . . Even a defeat in negotiation now, if we should be defeated, however humiliating, would be better than a war.

That Bell, who knew as few others, of the loathsomeness of Nazism, should use such language indicates how deeply the horror of another war had gripped the national imagination and sapped its will. Two of

Bell's brothers had been killed in action within a few days of one another in 1918. He had also lost many of his former Oxford pupils. Temple said a few days before the Munich agreement: 'There is a strong moral case for avoiding the outbreak of war even at great cost – even at great moral cost.' The modification of the Czech frontier must, however, be made only in the context of a new order for Europe.[73]

On 28 September a letter from General Sir Frederick Maurice, President of the British Legion, appeared in the *Times*, explaining the offer by the Legion to the Prime Minister of a group of ex-servicemen to supervise the orderly transfer of Czech territory. The Legion had just been entertaining eight hundred German ex-servicemen and had discovered that they were as desirous of peace as the British. General Maurice, grandson of F. D. Maurice, had been Haig's Director of Military Operations. In 1918 he hit the headlines when in a moral, but naively conceived, stand he denounced as inaccurate, statements in the Commons made by Lloyd George and Bonar Law. During the inter-war period he was a leading member of the ICF and shared its belief in consensus politics. He personally visited Hitler to offer the use of ten thousand ex-servicemen. Hitler refused, but in error some embarked at Tilbury.[74]

After the Munich agreement was announced, the vast majority of church people joined in the general euphoria. On 1 October the *Times* entitled its leader 'A New Dawn' and printed a letter from Mervyn Haigh, Bishop of Coventry: people have a 'profound sense of deliverance, gratitude and joy' which should be expressed by gifts to the Czech government for 'their self-sacrificing action'. The Archbishop of Canterbury declared Sunday 2 October a Day of Thanksgiving. Crowds queued in the rain to get into churches and chapels. The Archbishop of Westminster decreed that the *Te Deum* should be sung after all principal Masses. Lang, after consultation with other church leaders issued a statement:

> We cannot, we dare not, doubt that this sudden uplifting of the cloud which for the last weeks has darkened and oppressed our life is an answer to the great volume of prayer which with a most impressive unity and reality has been rising to God.

The efforts of the Prime Minister and other statesmen at Munich must be included in our gratitude. We remember 'with sympathy' the 'self-restraint' and the 'very hard sacrifices' of the Czechs. After looking into 'the abyss of war' and discerning its 'horror', we have been given a breathing space in which to root out the causes of war. In a broadcast

Lang again stressed the agreement as God's answer to fervent prayer. 'The League must be revived.' The Dean of Westminster also saw the deliverance as God's answer to the prayer which had been poured out for eighteen days and nights in the Abbey. The Bishops of Birmingham and Exeter, the Deans of York and Durham, echoed these sentiments.[75] Wilson Carlile, head of the Church Army, in a letter in the *Times* on 3 October wrote: 'Thank God for the Miracle of Munich; a prophet of the olive leaf has been raised up.' The congregation of St George's German Lutheran Church in London wrote to Chamberlain to express their gratitude.

The history of the Baptist church at Queen's Road Coventry, an important community dating back to the seventeenth century, provides some unexpected oscillations of attitudes by Christians to public issues during the twentieth century. It gave very active support to Passive Resistance between 1902 and 1911, invoking the example of John Bunyan. A number of Nonconformists in Coventry went to prison rather than pay rates. But the congregation accepted the First World War with some enthusiasm and little dissent. Four stained glass windows on themes from *Pilgrim's Progress* were placed in the church as a war memorial to the twenty-one men who died on active service. So Bunyan was invoked by both defiers and supporters of the state. But during the 1930s, partly under the influence of a pacifist minister, church meetings regularly passed pacific resolutions against armaments and war and for arbitration and the League. On Sunday 2 October 1938 the church was packed for a 'Peace Thanksgiving Service'. During the second war the congregation produced over forty Conscientious Objectors, twice the number of those in the forces.[76]

On 4 October 1938 William Temple, in a sermon at the Church Congress in Bristol said that they were 'assembled on the morrow of a great deliverance':

They gave thanks to Almighty God that He had removed the immediate menace of war with all its horrors, not only of destruction, and slaughter and suffering, but of ill-will, suspicion, and the suppression of truth. Most sincerely they acknowledged with gratitude the initiative, courage, and perseverance of the Prime Minister, to whom, under the hand of God, we owed the deliverance in which we rejoiced, but they remembered also that, even if the settlement now made was in its own terms just and reasonable, it had been imposed upon a State friendly to ourselves with a harsh suddenness that must involve bitterness of heart and widespread suffering of an intense kind.

The settlement at Munich could only be tolerable morally, if the Versailles settlement was 'at best mistaken' – and we carried a share of responsibility for that mistake and for others since.[77] So once again Christian guilt about Versailles was used to provide an alibi for Hitler.

A month after Munich, at the London Diocesan Conference, Bishop Winnington Ingram rebuked those who were beginning to turn against the man who had saved them. 'A desperate situation had to be met by desperate remedies', he explained. No Christian could justify the post-war treatment of Germany. He had evidently forgotten that, in an Advent sermon in 1918, he had declaimed that God wanted Britain to 'punish' Germany 'for the greatest crime committed in the world for a thousand years'.[78] Or was his assertion now that it was 'the Christian thing' to take the hand so repeatedly held out by Germany, an unconscious desire to atone for the jingoism of his first war utterances, so frequently held up to moral obloquy during the 1930s? Winnington Ingram always loved to swim heartily with the prevailing emotional tide. At the Conference it was announced that W. H. Elliott's 'League of Prayer for Peace' now had half a million members.[79] (Elliott, vicar of St Michael's Chester Square, London, was a popular broadcaster and columnist for the *Sunday Pictorial*. By the outbreak of war five and a half million had joined the League. How did the coming of war affect their faith in prayer? When 'Munich' became a term of abuse, did people remember how Lang and others had claimed it an answer to their prayers?)

W. R. Inge, formerly Dean of St Paul's, thought that we had been 'on the brink of a criminally foolish war' and all for the sake of 'a ramshackle republic, not twenty years old' and so hailed the agreement with enthusiasm.[80] On 30 September the *Church Times* rejoiced. True, there are still difficulties to be overcome, but there is no doubt that Mussolini is as eager for peace as Chamberlain and Daladier.

> The nation, and indeed, the whole world have good reason to be grateful for the Prime Minister's courage, energy and persistence. He has given a new meaning to the term *Realpolitik*. He has accepted facts as they are and men as they are. He has been unaffected by sentimentality . . . no man in history has fought so strenuously to prevent war . . . as the news of the reprieve spread throughout the world there was everywhere a fervent 'Thank God for Neville Chamberlain!'

A week later it returned to the subject. 'Mr Chamberlain has done what the common people, British, French, German and Italian wanted done. He has saved them from the horrors of war.' It made common cause with an unlikely ally – James Maxton, of the ILP who had praised the Prime Minister for saving 'the common people of the world' from a repetition of the last war which destroyed the lives of ten million men and 'achieved none of the objects for which it was fought'.

> From the beginning we have considered the international crisis from the point of view of the Christian realist. We have been guided by two convictions. The first is that a modern war, with its ghastly scientific contraptions for destruction and slaughter . . . would be the most awful misfortune that could happen to humanity. Our second conviction is that evil is not to be destroyed by evil.

Nazism is 'brutal and ruthless' but it cannot be destroyed by bombs. Czechoslovakia has been dismembered. The ambitions of *Mein Kampf* have been brought nearer to realization by the Munich agreement. 'But let it also be remembered that the Versailles Czecho-Slovakia should never have been created. It was an artificial State certain sooner or later to break into pieces.' The Czechs have behaved with 'splendid self-control'. They have earned the sympathy and gratitude of the world. But had there been a war 'radical territorial changes' would have resulted and 'millions of lives would have been lost for little or nothing'. The 'creation of a Greater Germany was inevitable'. There has been 'a step forward to general appeasement' in which Mussolini played the part of 'peacemaker'. It will mean that more people will be brought under Nazi rule, that more Jews will be persecuted. 'All that can be done is to pray that Pharaoh's heart will become less hard.' Rearmament must alas continue. 'Peace is secured, at least for a time.' We must pray that 'our trespasses may be forgiven as we forgive them who trespass against us'.

People were moved to create memorials to a new type of victory. Mr Bernard Docker gave £1000 for to endow a 'Neville Chamberlain bed' for the new Westminster Hospital. Someone in Blackpool offered to build twelve houses for ex-servicemen free of rent.

But a minority of churchpeople were uneasy. Leslie Weatherhead, though still a pacifier, asked his congregation 'Do you feel just a little as though you had made friends with a burglar?'[81] Temple, a month after his welcome for the settlement, said that Britain was right to press forward with rearmament.[82] The *Guardian*, less favourable to appeasement than the *Church Times*, on 30 September declared that although war might have been averted, it still had to be prepared for. A week later it produced an uneasy apologia for the agreement, which it said was nothing more than 'a pious aspiration'.

In the Lang correspondence for the summer of 1938 there are many letters between the Home Office and Lambeth about war preparations. The Home Secretary in August wrote to the bishops reminding them that he had appealed for a million ARP volunteers in April. He suggested that Sunday 2 October might be a suitable Sunday for clergy to press the appeal from the pulpits 'if they felt inclined'. (That Sunday turned out to be the day on which churches were crowded with people giving thanks for the Munich agreement.) In the midst of the crisis, on 21 September, E. G. Selwyn, Dean of Winchester, Editor of *Essays Catholic and Critical* (1926) and of the periodical *Theology* (1920–33), wrote to Lang pleading for him to call the nation to fast and pray. This might fittingly be combined with the observation of Armistice Day, All Saints Day or Advent. Could that day be proclaimed by the King as a Day of Humiliation or by the episcopate as a day or days of fasting?

> Whatever may be the issue of the present crisis and whatever view of it men hold, there seems to me to be a wide-spread sense of humiliation to me and shame at the steady deterioration of public affairs, and the continued abandonment of openly professed principles and ideals, which we have seen during the last few years.[83]

A few churchpeople protested against the Munich settlement as a great moral betrayal. Lloyd George praised Hitler fulsomely in 1936. But on 26 October 1938 he addressed a luncheon at the City Temple on 'The Free Churches and the World Situation'. He launched into an emotional attack on the Free Churches for their failure to denounce the Munich agreement. Why had they failed to speak out? It was because the 'metal' of Nonconformity had been 'corroded very largely by the patronage of the ecclesiastical and official hierarchy'. (Lloyd George knew how to wound Nonconformists where it hurt most.) The Rev. Henry Carter (Chairman of the Methodist Peace Fellowship) deplored this 'ferocious and irresponsible speech' and called on Free Churchmen 'over against this vengeful utterance' to work with rulers of any State 'to lessen tension and to build peace and social justice'. Sir Henry Lunn, a Methodist ecumenist, resigned from the the the Liberal Party. But J. Chuter Ede, a Unitarian (like Chamberlain) and a Labour MP (Home Secretary in the 1945 Labour Government) wrote to Lloyd George to thank him: 'One has been asking one's self for weeks what would Joseph Parker and John Clifford have said . . . If totalitarianism is tolerable, nonconformity is indefensible.'[84]

Henson instinctively distrusted the agreement: 'Peace is welcome but may be disgraceful' he confided to his diary. But he failed to attend the debate in the Lords because probably (as Chadwick surmises) he was uncertain, for once, as to what he should say. In church he prayed for peace but refused to include special thanksgiving for the settlement. On 7 October the *Guardian* included Henson's lapidary comment among its catena of sermon quotations:

> The Ethiopian does not change his colour, nor does the leopard change his spots. Self-deception is easy, and hope grows quickly in the soil of desire. Britain must make itself efficient against the day of trial, which may be postponed for the time being but which will surely come in time.

Duncan-Jones offered a less gnomic assessment: 'If we are to present the gospel to this generation we cannot pretend that it is a gospel that teaches people to sacrifice their friends that they themselves may be safe and sound.' He sent a telegram to both Archbishops: 'Earnestly looking to your Grace swiftly to voice the conscience of England in protest against most shameful betrayal in English history.' Temple soothingly replied 'Very likely you are right, though I do not think so.' The Sudeten Germans were suffering 'really bad oppression'.[85]

The most blistering attack on the settlement from within the churches came from a letter by Fr St John Groser in the *Guardian* for 7 October. Groser was an Anglo-Catholic socialist trained in the Mirfield tradition of political dissent, perhaps the greatest of East End priests of the period. He had been a questioning army chaplain in the first war. He had also been awarded the MC. He passionately believed in the duty of the church to stand up to the state. He was beaten with police truncheons in the General Strike, had preached against the Means Test in St Paul's and in 1939 organized rent strikes against grasping landlords who neglected their property. A passionate opponent of fascism, he had been horrified when Mosley's blackshirts paraded in the East End. He told a conference in Geneva in 1933 that Christians must identify themselves with those who suffered from the social system: 'I must be one of the victims'.[86] His letter in the *Guardian* blazed with righteous anger:

> Blackmail has succeeded. The threat of force has triumphed. . . . That Mr Chamberlain should talk of 'peace with honour' when he has surrendered to this blackmail, torn up Article 10 of the League Covenant without reference to Geneva, and sacrificed the Czechoslovaks in order, as he says, to prevent a world war, is bad enough; but that the Archbishop of Canterbury should say that this is the answer to our prayers – while Czechoslovakia mourns – and even praise Hitler and ask for a day of thanksgiving is beyond endurance.

He has paid no regard to the tremendous wave of disquiet among all sections of the people in this country at the cumulative German demands and the consciousness of the dishonour involved in our Government's curt insistence of Czechoslovakia's acceptance. He has dismissed Czechoslovakia's self-sacrifice and our honour in a single sentence.

The church had once again surrendered to the values of the world. We should have been called to repentance not to thanksgiving. The *Guardian* commented at the end of the letter: 'The matter is not so simple. Our correspondent seems to be as unable to see both sides as are the emotional people who have thrown up their caps with undiluted joy.' For several weeks afterwards the correspondence columns were full of angry letters on both sides of the argument. Groser and others in the Socialist Christian League printed fifteen thousand copies of a manifesto which reiterated the message of the letter.

MacNeice provided the appropriate comment:

> But once again
>> The crisis is put off and things look better
> And we feel negotiation is not vain –
>> Save my skin and damn my conscience. . . .
> And here we are – just as before – safe in our skins;
>> Glory to God for Munich.
> And stocks go up and wrecks
>> Are salved and politicians' reputations
> Go up like Jack-on-the-Beanstalk; only the Czechs
>> Go down and without fighting.

On 2 October Chamberlain wrote to Lang to thank him for his 'moving letter' about the Munich agreement. Chamberlain continued: 'I am sure that some day the Czechs will see that what we did was to save them for a happier future. And I sincerely believe that we have at last opened the way to that general appeasement which alone can save the world from chaos.'[87] However, in private, Chamberlain was less sure whether he had secured peace with Hitler.[88] Lang again showed himself Chamberlain's disciple when he wrote to his old friend Bishop Wilfred Parker on 4 November, aware of the growing doubts being voiced about the wisdom and morality of the Munich settlement:

I always ask myself at what stage and in what way would it have been possible to 'stand up to Hitler' as people say. I have no patience with those who think it would have been well to play the game of calling his bluff at an earlier stage. As I have repeatedly said that is like gambling with millions of human lives. But the main thing is that at the very last minute and certainly by Chamberlain's own vigorous and courageous initiative, we have been delivered from the unspeakable horrors of a modern war and I cannot think that this has been done at any substantial sacrifice of justice.[89]

No Christian leader wanted to be accused of crusading for the sacrifice of more young men after what happened between 1914 and 1918. It was primarily Lang's horror of war which led him to support appeasement. The Great War had started with expectations that it would all be over by Christmas but had lasted four long terrible years. And in the end, was it worth it? Convictions like these enabled the pacifiers to believe that the sacrifice of the Czechs had been for the good of the whole world. Lang saw Chamberlain and Halifax frequently. In this and other utterances he showed that he had little but pietistic colouring to add to the views of the politicians he trusted. In a New Year broadcast for 1939 he granted that the outlook was now more sombre, but still looked back to September 1938 with its 'imperishable memory' of how 'the awful prospect of another war stood before our eyes and then suddenly vanished' (did he have in mind the miraculous deliverance of Jerusalem described in II Kings 19?). Nevertheless our civilization is under judgment and there are many signs of a return to the Dark Ages.[90]

It was a layman, not the Archbishop, who went to the heart of the matter and gave memorable voice to Christian penitence and questioning. T. S. Eliot looked back from March 1939:

I believe that there must be many persons who, like myself, were deeply shaken by the events of September 1938, in a way from which one does not recover; persons to whom that month brought a profounder realisation of a general plight. It was not a disturbance of the understanding: the events themselves were not surprising. Nor, as became increasingly evident, was our distress due merely to disagreement with the policy and behaviour of the moment. The feeling which was new and unexpected was a feeling of humiliation, which seemed to demand an act of personal contrition, of humility, repentance and amendment; what had happened was something in which one was deeply implicated and responsible. It was not, I repeat, a criticism of the government, but a doubt of the validity of a civilisation. We could not match conviction with conviction, we had no ideas with which we could either meet or oppose the ideas opposed to us. Was our society, which had always been so assured of its superiority and rectitude, so confident of its unexamined premisses, assembled round anything more permanent than a congeries of banks, insurance companies and industries, and had it any beliefs more essential than a belief in compound interest and the maintenance of dividends?[91]

These themes were taken up by many during the 1939–45 war as liberal Christianity retreated and dogmatic Christianity was promoted as the only belief strong enough to stand up to totalitarianism. As Eliot himself remarked just before the above passage: 'The term "democracy" . . . does not contain enough positive content to stand alone against the forces that you dislike.'

Later there were many who wanted to make acts of contrition. F. R. Barry, a liberal theologian who greatly influenced the clergy, was a Canon of Westminster in 1938. (Later he became Bishop of Southwell.) He wrote thirty years after Munich:

> To confront the powers of destruction with 'goodwill' is like trying to quench a volcano by smiling at it . . . I think it must now be honestly admitted that Christians, and liberals in general, must take some share of responsibility for helping to bring about what they were trying, with the best possible motives, to avert . . . Right up to Munich I was myself a pacifist, as indeed most of the chaplains probably were. In the first war, while I was in uniform, I had been tormented all the time by doubts about its moral justification. Now I used to vow that if war did break out, I would use the Abbey pulpit to disseminate 'disloyal' and anti-war sentiments; and I must admit with shame that after Munich I shared in the popular hysteria. Only slowly and painfully did I realise the wickedness of Nazism and Fascism and the moral duty of saving the western world from being enslaved to their obscene dominion. Intensely though I shrank from it and dreaded it, yet when war came I had no moral doubts.[92]

In 1938 Ulrich Simon, a German refugee of Jewish parentage (now Professor Emeritus of Christian Literature at King's College, London) was preparing for the Anglican priesthood at Lincoln Theological College. His Anglo-Catholic confessor told him not to take political events so seriously; they were 'crowding out the real object of life, the knowledge and love of God'. Then came Munich.

> God so it was said, had come to our aid. On the Sunday following the news the Dean of Lincoln preached at a solemn thanksgiving service. He held the congregation spellbound by ascribing the turn of events to God's wonderful providence. I ran out of my stall and feeling sick to the point of convulsion I gazed at the great west

facade of the cathedral. The facade, in all its magnificence, is a sham, for it is not integral to the nave behind it. I saw in it the empty gesture of false prophecy.[93]

The closing words of Louis MacNeice's 'Autumn Journal', written at the end of 1938, convey the conviction of many by that time, that war was now inevitable:

> To-night we sleep
> On the banks of Rubicon – the die is cast;
> There will be time to audit
> The accounts later, there will be sunlight later
> And the equation will come out at last.

Keith Robbins reflects about the significance of Munich:

> . . . the only great lesson of Munich, the most difficult to learn, is that there are no great lessons . . . There is a telling irony in the fact that, for many of Chamberlain's followers, the lessons of the First World War led straight to Munich, and for many of Chamberlain's critics, the lesson of Munich led straight to Suez.

To argue that Britain should have gone to war in the summer of 1938 is to presuppose not only a Britain of a different character but a Hitler with a different policy. He was sure he could obtain what he wanted by a threat of force. And he was right. But we should remember that almost any conceivable non-Nazi German government would have demanded a revision of the frontiers of 1919, including those of Czechoslovakia, and might well also have threatened or have used force to achieve these ends. In retrospect it looks as if 'Munich was the necessary purgatory through which Englishmen had to pass before the nation could emerge united in 1939'.[94]

On 15 March 1939 the Germans annexed the Czech provinces of Bohemia and Moravia. Hitler spent the night in Prague. Munich, Chamberlain had told the British people, was the final settlement. Now on 15 March he speculated that the end of Czechoslovakia 'may or may not have been inevitable'. Conservatives began to rumble with discontent. A. J. P. Taylor argues that the Conservatives had never been comfortable with appeasement and that it was 'in spirit and origin a Left-wing cause' promoted by leaders with a Nonconformist background – Neville Chamberlain was a Unitarian; Sir John Simon the son of a Congregational minister; Sir Samuel Hoare had a Quaker background. But Lord Halifax was an Anglo-Catholic, and for this and other reasons was, Taylor asserts, 'an in-and-out member of the appeasement group'. On 17 March Chamberlain changed his tone. His prepared speech for the Birmingham Conservatives included the statement that no one 'could possibly have saved Czechoslovakia from destruction' but he added an improvisation at the last minute: 'Any attempt to dominate the world by force was one which the Democracies must resist'.[95] Most English people welcomed the new firm tone. Lang spoke in the Foreign Affairs debate on 20 March. He began with Munich. He had (he said) consistently failed to obtain from the critics any indication as to what they would have done. It was a choice of the lesser evil. But he struck a new note of penitence:

> I quite admit that it was not one which ought to have been hailed as a triumph. There was too much sacrifice demanded of that gallant people . . . brute force played far too large a part in the ultimate Agreement.

He went on to speak about the invasion of Prague (and faithfully followed Chamberlain's change of policy):

> . . . surely a challenge has been flung at all that we look upon as the basis of civilised order among nations . . . there has been this complete proof that good faith and the honour of pledged words cannot be trusted. Moreover, there is an end to all the confidence upon which the future must be built . . . some answer must be given to this challenge, and that the only answer that avails is an answer given in the only terms which the German rulers appear to understand. That is to say, that against their claim that might is right there must be the massing of might on the side of right.

It is 'hateful' to be contemplating massing force when twenty years ago we learnt so much about 'the folly and futility of war' but 'there are some things that are more sacred even than peace'. We must be ready to co-operate even with Russia. He still hoped that Christendom would be given a voice and that the Pope might be willing to give leadership to world Christian opinion.[96]

The *Church Times* was also repentant in its leader of 17 March. It drew a significant parallel between Hitler and Napoleon: during the first war the British had often compared the Kaiser with Napoleon. 'The rape of Czecho-Slovakia is the most important and the most menacing event that has happened since the end of the Great War.' In defending the Munich agreement it had been convinced that Mr Chamberlain had chosen the lesser of two evils and saved the world from war. It expected, as a result of the agreement, that Czechoslovakia would become more politically and economically dependent on

Germany. 'It did not occur to us that . . . German troops would within a few months be in occupation of Prague.' Hitler 'marched into Prague as the would-be master of Europe, as Napoleon marched into Vienna a hundred and forty years ago'. Napoleon marched in after a military victory; Hitler has conquered 'at the mere threat of death and destruction'. It was glad that the Prime Minister had not abandoned appeasement, but 'it will be sheer madness to attach the smallest importance to any pledge that Herr Hitler may find it convenient to make'. There is no reason to despair. The Easter faith, if it could quicken the nation 'might inspire a general determination to be ready for the limit of individual sacrifice for the common good'. Eden's proposal for a National Government is welcome. It seems the will of God that Britain should be the defender of Christian civilization. So the nation 'must turn from the pin-table to the prayer-desk'.

But in May, Lang, speaking to the Canterbury Convocation, could not believe that, when so many people the world over longed for peace, 'anything so wrong, so hideous and so futile as a great war could be thrust upon the world'.[97] Matthews, of St Paul's, appealed in the *Times* (27 April) to the Pope, the Archbishop of Canterbury and other Christian leaders to lay aside conventional caution and to act for peace. 'Let us hear the Word of God before the killing begins.'

The Lambeth correspondence of the period indicates that church and state were in almost daily correspondence as to how the church should conduct its life if war came. By early January the London diocese had drawn up detailed plans for the care of the wounded and dying in air raids – a certain number of clergy in each deanery must be trained in first aid. Suggestions were made about the care of artistic treasures if war came. In February the Church of Scotland and the Scottish bishops asked for copies, when ready, of the Archbishop's instructions in the event of war. On 20 March Temple wrote to ask when these would be available; clergy were pestering him almost daily. That month a group under the Bishop of Southwark prepared instructions to be circulated to bishops as 'Private and Confidential'. The instructions stated that the spiritual ministrations of the clergy would be even more needed in war-time. Clergy must be given opportunity by the civil and military authorities to carry out their work. The bishops were to prepare lists of clergy between 28 and 38 who were suitable as chaplains to the forces. All clergy should undergo ARP training. Church buildings could be used in emergencies as first-aid posts, shelters and dormitories for the homeless. On 28 April the Bishop of Guildford asked whether petrol would be available in war-time for bishops and others who have to be mobile? On 18 July the

Archdeacon of Middlesex wrote to tell Lambeth how many steel hats and respirators would be needed for the clergy of the Church of England and other denominations.

In May Dr Don, chaplain at Lambeth, requested a meeting with the Minister of Labour to discuss on behalf of the Archbishop the Government's attitudes to conscientious objectors and the conscription of clergy. Clergy were exempt, he reminded the Minister, in the last war. The Archbishop hoped that absolutist COs would be able to do forms of national service compatible with their conscience, because in the last war they were prepared to go to prison rather than do anything which might be construed as war work. Don's memorandum about the meeting of 8 June recorded that clergy would be exempt and that 'official policy aims at treating genuine conscientious objectors with much greater fairness and consideration than was the case during the last war'. The bishops' meeting of 28 June asked the Ecclesiastical Commissioners to reconsider their dismissal of a typist who had declined to obey ARP instructions. The bishops were informed on 20 July that servicemen had only to announce their wish to go to Communion to ensure that breakfast was kept for them. On 4 September the Bishop of Birmingham asked that the fee for Special Licences for Weddings should be reduced from £2.12s. 6d. to 10 shillings for serving men, as happened in the last war. The Archbishop's chaplain wrote to all bishops on 7 September to inform them that the Michaelmas and Advent ordinations could go ahead; the decision about whether ordinands would be exempt from conscription would be made later.[98]

All this feverish correspondence went to and fro in private, but in public the bishops, like everyone else, hoped against hope that war would not come. William Temple speaking to the York Convocation in May, said that they met 'under the shadow of a constant menace'. We have to prepare ourselves to meet an emergency which we hope will never arise, but also carry on as though no danger threatened. People ask whether the church has any guidance to offer. It has, but not in 'the area of political contrivance'. For example, it would be 'ridiculous' for the church to advocate that all colonies should be placed under international control, as has been suggested. The basic political problem is how 'to contrive ways in which selfish nations may live together in peace. The Church has no means of designing such a contrivance.' It can point to general principles and urge obedience to international law and commend arbitration. 'But its chief message to us all to-day must be the declaration that we stand together under the judgement of Almighty God for the neglect of His law.' So 'repent, forgive, pray'. Above all the church must be 'the household of the Lord, super-national and one despite all the divisions and enmities of men'. In May, Temple preached at the annual military service in York Minster and defended the increase in the armed forces.[99] Evidently Temple, who in the past had been lavish in offering specific political solutions for international questions, now thought that the time for them had passed.

There was another reason for the widespread support given to appeasement by English Christians, in addition to those already suggested: the trust, respect, even veneration, of many Christians for Lord Halifax – Lord Privy Seal 1935–37, Lord President of the Council 1937–38, Foreign Secretary 1938–40. Clement Attlee in a marvellously pungent phrase described Halifax as 'all hunting and holy communion'.[100] The Christian public thought him a humble and devout believer *par excellence*, genuinely striving to relate his Christianity to the conduct of foreign affairs. Surely, he was the one who, by his noble virtues and intuitive skill, would understand and moderate the wild men of Germany and Italy as he had promoted reconciliation (they believed) as Viceroy of India. In July 1939, at the Canterbury Diocesan Conference, Lang praised a recent speech by Halifax and commented: it 'had united the whole nation. Its reception had been a tribute to the confidence of all parties in his spirit, his motives, his calmness, his steadiness of judgement.' People (Lang said) were deeply thankful that such a man should be Foreign Secretary at such a time. The same month the *Liverpool Diocesan Review* said that the churches could do very little in the crisis. But it was sure that Lord Halifax did not put his sincerely held Christian faith aside when he entered the Foreign Office.[101] On 23 August 1940, the *Guardian* reviewed a collection of speeches under the headline 'The Christian Tradition in Foreign Policy'.

However, Halifax's background did not provide him with any categories by which he could judge Hitler and the Nazis. Arriving for his first meeting with Hitler, Halifax for a moment mistook him for the footman, until the German Foreign Minister urgently muttered 'Der Führer, Der Führer'. Later Halifax lunched with Goering, the man who had established concentration camps. Goering was dressed in a green leather jerkin complete with a dagger in a red sheath. Halifax wondered how many people he had killed, but his depravity seemed to escape him. He was (he noted) apart from his reputation as a butcher, 'frankly attractive: like a great schoolboy . . . producing on me a composite impression of film-star, gangster, great landowner interested in his property, Prime Minister, party-manager, head

gamekeeper at Chatsworth'. Halifax was clearly out of his depth as he
fumbled with one analogy after another. Nothing in his upbringing
had equipped him to fathom the wickedness of these men. They were
bad but also slightly comical. They might almost have been curiosities
employed on his estates, rough and violent indeed, but their danger-
ousness distanced by the disdain Halifax felt for their vulgarity.

What attracted him to religion – he was an extremely devout Anglo-
Catholic – was its offer of detachment from the mundane world. His
biographer describes Halifax's reactions to the Munich agreement:

> The belief in a Divine control over the affairs of the world led him
> to think that human beings could only move the course of events a
> little in certain directions, so that while prepared to do this, he was
> not ready to step in and stem the flood: and his profound belief in
> a future life made the disasters of this world seem by contrast
> transient and insubstantial. Thus armoured he could envisage
> human afflictions with an almost unearthly calm, and face war,
> when it came, with complete inner tranquility. . . .[102]

Was it not a liability to have as Foreign Secretary one whose background had given him no comprehension of the demonic; one whose
calm reasonableness disabled him from understanding the irrational
in human life (despite his experience of communal violence in India);
one who had little difficulty in shutting his eyes to unpleasant realities;
one whose style of faith led to a certain detachment from, and a fatalism
about, human affairs?. His aptitude for conciliation and religious
idealism, which had borne some fruit in India, proved largely ineffective when confronted with Hitler and Mussolini.

Did it matter what bishops and church leaders said and did? Owen
Chadwick has demonstrated that at least the Nazi leaders took the
opinions of the English bishops seriously and thought it important to
be in close touch with those who were most influential. Goering in his
memoirs (admittedly written when he was awaiting execution) wrote
of his meetings with Lang – 'a man with special influence in England
. . . He was a very clever man, who combined the roles of prince of
the Church and statesman. My visits to him reinforced my impression
of the importance of the Church of England . . .' The German
Embassy regularly reported back to Berlin the speeches of bishops in
the Lords and the Convocations, their letters to the *Times*, even their
diocesan pastorals.[103] Rosenberg corresponded with Headlam. Hess
wrote a four page letter in reply to Bell's protest about Niemöller's
arrest. In 1934 the German Embassy reported to Berlin that the Nazi
treatment of the churches was 'the main bone of contention in German-

British relations' and that this was alienating circles otherwise likely to be sympathetic to Germany.[104] 'Why do your bishops, M.P.'s and press interfere in my German church' complained Hitler to the British Ambassador in 1938.[105]

Finally, we should note revealing parallels between Christian attitudes to authoritarian regimes in the 1930s and today. Those who, since the second war, have appealed constantly to the failure of appeasement to pacify Hitler have adopted hard-line attitudes towards Soviet Russia. Yet the same group has often commended a policy of appeasement as the best method of inducing change in the regimes of South Africa and Rhodesia. By contrast, Christians of the centre and left have often appealed for a dialogue with Russia and pleaded for sensitivity to its massive casualties in the second war and its fears of encirclement since. But the same group has regularly attacked a policy of appeasement towards racialist regimes. In October 1965, Rhodesia seemed on the verge of declaring its independence unilaterally. The Archbishop of Canterbury, Michael Ramsey, responded that if the British Government thought it practicable to use force to protect the rights of the majority of the people, Christians should agree with such an action, just as it had been necessary in 1939 to use force to fulfil Britain's obligations towards Poland. For this statement he was congratulated by Liberal and Labour MPs but it caused an uproar among Conservatives and traditional church people. Those Christians who have urged the churches in South Africa to stand up against the authorities have often pointed out the failure of Christians in Germany to oppose Hitler's treatment of the churches and the Jews. In the 1930s ecumenists were often reluctant to side unequivocally with the Confessing Church believing that it was vital to keep doors open towards other Christians in Germany. So ecumenists in the World Council of Churches have often been reluctant to criticize persecution in Eastern Europe too publicly lest this might endanger the safety of its church leaders and prevent them from attending ecumenical conferences.

Thus the attempts to pacify the dictators during the 1930s continue to be a paradigm against which Christian (and other) political policies are still regularly tested.

PART III

ENGLISH CHRISTIANITY
AND THE SECOND WORLD WAR

7

THE RETREAT FROM LIBERAL OPTIMISM

C. E. M. Joad was the main visiting speaker for the 'King and Country' motion at the Oxford Union on 9 February 1933. (During the war he became well-known as a member of the BBC 'Brain's Trust'.) Joad's brilliant and emotive speech advocating total disarmament and Gandhi-style non-violence did much to sway the audience to vote by 275 to 153 that it would 'in no circumstances fight for its King and Country'. Martin Ceadel describes Joad as 'a puckish and lightweight amalgam' of Bertrand Russell and H. G. Wells. A libertarian progressivist and a sensual hedonist, Joad believed that of all evils, physical pain was by far the worst. In 1932 he formed the 'Federation of Progressive Societies and Individuals', with Wells' blessing, to promote the rational solution of human problems by the activities of an enlightened intellectual elite. Kingsley Martin, a friend of Joad's, described its ethos: 'They met together in Summer Schools to assert their rights as ramblers, to climb mountains, to demand easier divorce and the reform of the homosexual and abortion laws. They included nudist and other nature cults and they demanded the right to libel people they didn't like.'[1] Joad supported sanctions during the Abbyssinian crisis, but as his hopes of international action died, he returned to more orthodox pacifism. In 1940 he renounced pacifism altogether.

Liberal optimism dominated the intellectual *Zeitgeist* until the late 1930s, though some were highly critical of it – for example P. T. Forsyth, G. K. Chesterton, Evelyn Waugh, T. S. Eliot, C. H. Smyth and Graham Greene. Joad's renunciation of pacifism was part of a general shift among many intellectuals from progressivism towards a more sombre view of the human condition. Having spent years shocking the conservatives with his hedonistic liberalism, Joad now turned with equally iconoclastic vigour to shock the progressives.

During 1938 he was working on *A Guide to Modern Wickedness*, published in May 1939. He could no longer believe that evil could be removed by psychoanalysis and socialism. He breakfasted with a friend who insisted on reading a passage from Jeremiah to him, because it described the human plight in the modern world so forcibly. Scarcely had the reading concluded when two Jews arrived from Germany to plead the cause of German Jewry. To Joad it seemed a parable of the contemporary world. Why did young Germans treat Jews so fiendishly when so many of them had enjoyed the benefits of being educated according to modern theories?

He confessed to attending various parish churches. The services were ill-conducted and ill-attended, the sermons were either incomprehensible or trivial. Why then did church attendance exhilarate him? Why should he feel the need for religion? Was it because, as a life-long pacifist, he had always been a dissenter at odds with his environment? The church service created a deeply satisfying bond with his fellowmen, comparable to the sense of community he had enjoyed at George V's Jubilee celebrations. 'The sonorous beauty of the Psalms, the solemnity of the prayers, even the familiar banality of the hymns which, like holy relics, had attained through long usage a certain polished dignity – all these moved me not by their content, but by their associations. Their significance lay in the past; in their ability to twitch the threads which stretch back from the individual into his ancestral being.'[2] But he noted that his friends who accompanied him, typical of the modern generation, had no idea as to how to use their prayer books and took violent exception to the repeated liturgical references to human sinfulness.

Nazism he judged to be a substitute for religion, for man was a religious being. Yet Christianity was theologically and institutionally bankrupt and had nothing effective to say about war. Though he believed that the threatened war should not be fought, he would no longer simply stand aside from the needs of the community as he had done as a young man, even though he would not fight. He now realized that the late Victorian and Edwardian periods in which he had grown up were untypical. 'To take a survey of the contemporary world is to launch out upon an ocean of human misery.'[3]

In *God and Evil* (1942) Joad explained that it was the rise of Nazism which had turned his mind in the direction of religion. Many of his generation now believed that evil had to be accepted as 'a real and possibly incorrigible factor in the world and, therefore, in man's nature'.[4] He could not accept traditional Christian doctrines, but he now accepted belief in God as reasonable. He pitied the clergy because churches were so empty and the clergy themselves so often confused, yet felt a sense of awe and admiration for them. In *The Recovery of*

Belief (1952) he explained why he had now accepted the Christian faith. In an autobiographical chapter 'The Significance of Evil' he described how he had come to endorse wholeheartedly the account of man expressed in the General Confessions of the Prayer Book. He revealed that for some time he had been a communicant Anglican and ended with this tribute:

> I am grateful, more grateful than I can say, to the Church of England and more particularly to its country churches, and to the men who, in spite of every discouragement, persist in teaching there the Christian religion as the Church understands it. Without them, I should not, I think, have come to Christianity.

Before we go on to describe other examples of the rejection of liberal optimism, it is important to be clear that we are here outlining a shift of opinion among the intelligentsia – theologians, some churchmen and writers; that is the people whose lives are affected by ideology. But of course most English people are pragmatic rather than ideological. David Martin has pointed out how inapplicable is the Marxist analysis of religion to England. It is the middle class not the working class which is addicted to political and religious opiates. 'The English working class remains one of the most unrevolutionary and one of the most irreligious in the world.'[5] If the prospect of war induced a mood of *angst* among intellectuals, the mass of the people were relieved, fatalistic, stoical or just plain fearful. Ordinary English people were more likely to regard the continental dictators as ridiculous rather than demonic. 'Half a Mo' Hitler. Let's Have Our Holidays First' was the jaunty message on printed placards tied to the luggage racks of family cars setting out for the summer break of 1939. Just as children had sung ribald songs about Mussolini during the Abyssinian crisis, so throughout the war, in children's comics, skipping rhymes and in comedy programmes like 'ITMA', the dictators were presented not as demons or Anti-Christs but as ridiculously pretentious foreign clowns.

Moreover, though intellectuals paraded their loss of faith in progress, the general political climate in Britain became more optimistic from about 1942 as victory became more certain. Indeed some official documentaries as well as many popular films encouraged support for the war by portraying it as a fight for a better Britain. Intellectuals who through the common war-effort, enjoyed becoming part of the one nation, shared the widespread hope that the collectivist mobilization of the national life which had been successful in war-time would be applied to post-war problems. Theologically William Temple abandoned some features of his liberalism, but in the Malvern Conference of 1941 and in *Christianity and Social Order* (1942) he continued to proclaim much the same liberal social hope he had expressed in the COPEC Conference of 1924, though with some modifications. Nevertheless, the retreat from liberal optimism among the intelligentsia was of importance for the nation as a whole, because it enabled an influential group of people to support the war wholeheartedly as a fight against evil. This is one reason why the second war has never been regarded as 'futile' and 'unnecessary' – terms which were used about the first war in the 1920s and 1930s and have been common currency since. In 1984 it seemed right, even invigorating, to celebrate the fortieth anniversary of D Day. In the inter-war years no one wanted to celebrate the Somme or Passchendaele. The ideological basis of the British war effort between 1939 and 1945 has proved remarkably durable.

Literary pessimism

Samuel Hynes in *The Auden Generation: Literature and Politics in England in the 1930s* (1976) charted the rise and fall of faith in political action among the writers of the period. As early as 1930, Evelyn Waugh, in Chapter 8 of *Vile Bodies*, evoked a sense of human helplessness, faced with the certainty of another war, which is only in part to be accounted for by Waugh's Catholic belief in original sin. (Others wrote of the way in which modern society had to get used to being in a constant state of crisis so different from the supposed security and stability of pre-1914 England.) In Waugh's novel, Fr Rothschild casually remarked on the coming war. The Prime Minister replied '*What war?* . . . No one has said anything to me about a war . . . What do they want a war for, anyway?' The priest replied:

> Wars don't start nowadays because people want them. We long for peace, and fill our newspapers with conferences about disarmament and arbitration, but there is a radical instability in our whole world order, and soon we shall all be walking into the jaws of destruction again, protesting our pacific intentions.

In George Orwell's novel *Keep the Aspidistra Flying* (1936) Gordon Comstock in Chapter 1 remarks: 'Our civilization is dying. It *must* be dying. But it isn't going to die in its bed. Presently the aeroplanes are coming. Zoom – whizz – crash! The whole western world going up in a roar of high explosives.' In Orwell's *Coming Up for Air* published in June 1939, the sense of doom and coming cataclysm is all pervading. George Bowling, an insurance inspector revisits his home town where as a child he had known the stable, changeless world of pre-1914. He remembers fishing in a quiet pool 'before the radio, before aeroplanes, before Hitler'. But as he travels, visions of the coming war obtrude: 'Christ! how can the bombers miss us when they come? We're just one great big bull's-eye. And no warning, probably . . . If I was Hitler I'd send my bombers across in the middle of a disarmament conference . . . Houses going up into the air, bloomers soaked with blood, canary singing on above the corpses.' 1941 was already booked, he believed, for the war to begin. He knew from the first war that war was like an enormous machine from which there was no escape, against which there could be no resistance. 'Ordinary chaps that I meet everywhere . . . have got a feeling that the world's gone wrong. They can feel things cracking and collapsing under their feet.' He ruminated about the coming war: 'there's no way out. It's just something that's got to happen.'

Orwell who had fought on the Republican side in Spain, afterwards denounced the communists for having exploited the struggle for their own ends. After the announcement of the Nazi-Soviet pact in August 1939, he renounced his anti-militarism and quasi-pacifism and discovered he was patriotic after all. When war broke out he tried to enlist in the army. Having been repeatedly rejected on medical grounds, he enthusiastically joined the Home Guard and worked for the BBC. At last he had found a 'People's War' in which he could identify himself with common humanity in a common cause. Having loathed imperialism, he now found himself supervising broadcasts to India which attempted to stimulate the Indian war effort by inducing a love for British culture. One more dissenter had rejoined the fold, though he still hoped for a revolution and quaintly believed that the Home Guard should develop into a quasi-revolutionary People's Army.

In his essay 'Inside the Whale' (1940) he judged that what united the characteristically modern writers was a 'pessimism of outlook'. The following year, in 'Wells, Hitler and the World State', he derided the rationalistic optimism of Wells (upon which a whole generation had nourished their visions of the future). Wells 'was, and still is, quite incapable of understanding that nationalism, religious bigotry and feudal loyalty are far more powerful forces than what he would describe as sanity. Creatures out of the Dark Ages have come marching into the present . . . Wells is too sane to understand the modern world.'

When Orwell died in 1950 his will directed that he should be 'buried (not cremated) according to the rites of the Church of England'.

Through the intervention of David Astor, the newspaper magnate, he was buried in the churchyard of All Saints Sutton Courtenay. Astor owned an estate nearby. Though Orwell had no connection with the church, the manner of his funeral and the direction to be buried, not cremated, revealed Orwell's love of traditional England and its liturgical traditions.[6] All this, together with the fact that he owed his place of burial to a newspaper magnate and landowner, indicated the ambiguity of Orwell's left-wing dissent.

There were other literary dissenters from British society whose hopes for a clean revolution had been blighted in Spain, and who in 1938–39 wrote what Hynes calls a literature of preparation. In March 1938, the month in which Hitler annexed Austria, Bernard Spencer published his poem 'Waiting' which drew an analogy between waiting for the results of an operation upon a friend and the public waiting 'until the guns begin'. To Stephen Spender, W. H. Auden, Christopher Isherwood and Rex Warner, who in 1938 wrote three political parables, liberalism seemed utterly helpless before the onward movement of the fascist tide. In December 1938, the sage of liberal humanism, E. M. Forster, asserted: 'In 1938-9 the more despair a man can take on board without sinking the more completely he is alive.'[7]

Auden who had shared Marxist hopes for a new world and had believed in the capacity of literature to help this forward, wrote in his poem 'In Memory of W. B. Yeats', published in April 1939, that 'poetry makes nothing happen', but

> it survives,
> A way of happening, a mouth . . .
> In the nightmare of the dark
> All the dogs of Europe bark,
> And the living nations wait,
> Each sequestered in its hate . . .

Auden remarked just before the war: 'the English intellectuals who now cry to Heaven against the evil incarnated in Hitler have no Heaven to cry to; they have nothing to offer and their protests echo in empty space.' In 1941 he reviewed the first volume of Reinhold Niebuhr's *The Nature and Destiny of Man*: 'it has taken Hitler to show us that liberalism is not self-supporting.'[8] His poem 'September 1, 1939' looked back at the 1930s with a detachment, in part aided by his self-chosen exile in the States:

> I sit in one of the dives
> On Fifty-Second Street

> Uncertain and afraid
> As the clever hopes expire
> Of a low dishonest decade . . .

So the hopes of pacifism, the Popular Front and revolution were now dismissed as 'clever'. The decade has been 'dishonest' because it evaded the reality of evil:

> Accurate scholarship can
> Unearth the whole offence
> From Luther until now
> That has driven a culture mad,
> Find out what occurred at Linz,
> What huge imago made
> A psychopathic god:
> I and the public know
> What all schoolchildren learn,
> Those to whom evil is done
> Do evil in return.

He went on:

> All I have is a voice
> To undo the folded lie,
> The romantic lie in the brain
> Of the sensual man-in-the-street
> And the lie of Authority
> Whose buildings grope the sky;
> There is no such thing as the State
> And no one exists alone;
> Hunger allows no choice
> To the citizen or the police;
> We must love one another or die.

It was, as Hynes remarks, a startling message from the political poet of the 1930s. In 1940 he began to practice his rediscovered Christian faith as an Anglican again.

In the Preface to *After Strange Gods* (1934) T. S. Eliot characterized Western society as 'worm-eaten with Liberalism'. Eliot's pessimism about society and his detachment from humanity were deepened by the breakdown of his marriage. *The Waste Land* (1922) was read as a soured assessment of the post-war world. But it was also his autobiography:

> These fragments I have shored against my ruins . . .

The Munich agreement confirmed his belief that Western civilization was worthless and immoral. The war itself, however, evoked from him a new sense of identification with the national community. He took on the arduous duties of a fire-watcher and wrote about this obliquely in 'Little Gidding'. Early in 1940 he even wrote an overtly patriotic poem 'Defence of the Islands' to accompany an exhibition of British war photographs in New York. But he continued to insist that Britain needed a conversion from paganism.

David Gascoyne in his poem 'Farewell Chorus', dated New Year's Day 1940, accepted Auden's thesis about the 1930s:

And so! the long black pullman is at last departing, now,
After those undermining years of angry waiting and cold tea . . .
And so let's take a last look round, and say Farewell to all
Events that gave the last decade, which this New Year
Brings to its close, a special pathos . . .
To the delusive peace of those disintegrating years
Through which burst uncontrollably into our view
Successive and increasingly premonitory flares,
Explosions of the dangerous truth beneath, which no
Steel-plated self-deception could for long withstand . . .
. . . Years through which none the less
The coaxing of complacency and sleep could still persuade
Kind-hearted Christians of the permanence of Peace,
Increase of common-sense and civic virtue . . .
. . . Beyond despair
May we take wiser leave of you, knowing disasters' cause.

During the inter-war period three theologians led a Christian assault upon liberal optimism: Karl Barth, E. C. Hoskyns and Reinhold Niebuhr.

Karl Barth

On 4 December 1931, F. R. Barry, then vicar of the University Church, Oxford, wrote in the *Guardian* about 'The Menace of Brunner' and the disastrous effects of Barthian theology which isolated religion from the ordinary goodness of ordinary people by its 'exaggerated other-worldiness'. Other ex-chaplains, such as Charles Raven, Dick Sheppard, Tubby Clayton and Studdert Kennedy, like Barry, never forgot how much they had grown to love and admire the virtues of the ordinary soldiers, with whom they had shared so much during the war. And of course Anglicanism itself, by its very nature and history, was unlikely to be hospitable to Barth's theology. According to A. M.

Ramsey, very few Anglicans were interested in Barth's theology as such. But many 'underwent a theological and religious "shock" '. So directly, or through the 'somewhat diluting medium' of Brunner, Barth began to have an effect on English theology.[9] The decisive moment for Barth was that day in early August 1914 when ninety-three intellectuals, including almost all his most venerated theological teachers, had publicly proclaimed their support for the Kaiser's war policy. To Barth this showed that nineteenth-century theology had no future. Barth's commentary, *The Epistle to the Romans* (1921) was published in an English translation by Edwyn Hoskyns in 1933. It provided a direct challenge to every basic assumption of the liberal English theological tradition:

> In Jesus, God becomes veritably a secret: He is made known as the Unknown, speaking in eternal silence; He protects himself from every intimate companionship and from all the impertinence of religion . . . In Jesus the communication of God begins with a rebuff, with the exposure of a vast chasm, with the clear revelation of a great stumbling-block . . There are no human avenues of approach, no 'way of salvation'; to faith there is no ladder which must be first scaled.[10]

> Grace is not grace, if he that receives it is not under judgement.[11]

> How vast a gulf separates the nineteenth century conquering-hero attitude to religion from that disgust of men at themselves, which is the characteristic mark of true religion![12]

> Whenever men claim to be able to see the Kingdom of God as a growing organism, or – to describe it more suitably – as a growing building, what they see is not the Kingdom of God, but the Tower of Babel.[13]

> The knowledge of God directs us to God; it does not direct us to some human position or to some human course of action either in time of war or in time of peace. A Church which knows its business well will, it is true, with a strong hand keep itself free from militarism; but it will also with a friendly gesture rebuff the attentions of pacifism.[14]

Over against liberal theologians who had interpreted eschatology as a future which could be realized on earth, Barth and his followers preached that the new day had dawned in the death and resurrection of Christ and certainly could not be brought about by human achievement.

Shortly before the war, Nathaniel Micklem, Bernard Manning and John Whale addressed a manifesto to Congregational Ministers. Designed to recall them to the purity of the Reformed faith, it revealed the influence of continental theology:

> The world, it is clear, is in a condition to justify almost any amount of lamentation and warning. We can read the Bible today with new eyes; the cries of the oppressed saints in the Psalms, the threatening of the prophets, the dooms foretold against all that is high and lifted up, come home to us with a new vividness and reality . . . In the chaos and fear of the present situation the Church exists to declare the righteousness and the proffered grace of God.[15]

Barth's *A Letter to Great Britain from Switzerland* (1941) was written at the invitation of A. R. Vidler and J. H. Oldham. Christians, Barth said, are in a very different situation from that during the first war. This war is not 'a necessary evil'. It is a 'righteous war, which God does not simply allow, but which He commands us to wage'. In the present crisis the arguments of Christian Pacifism have no power to convince. The mistakes of the Allies made the war possible but not necessary.

> The enterprise of Adolf Hitler, with all its clatter and fireworks, and all its cunning and dynamic energy, is the enterprise of an evil spirit, which is apparently allowed its freedom for a time in order to test our faith in the resurrection of Jesus Christ . . .[16]

The war is to be fought not to defend 'western civilization', 'the liberty of the individual' or 'social justice' – concepts which an atheist, Buddhist or Hindu might support – but 'unequivocally in the name of Jesus Christ'. Arguments based on Natural Law led to Munich. The war will not automatically extend the Kingdom of Christ, which will come without our assistance. There is no need to busy ourselves with plans for a new order for the post-war period. We cannot shape the future. Barth's transcendental theology was totally at variance with such characteristic British publications as George Bell's *Christianity and World Order* (1940) which among other things fervently welcomed the Pope's Five Peace Points, and William Temple's *Christianity and Social Order* (1942) which offered specific political suggestions for post-war reconstruction and made considerable use of Natural Law. Both were Penguin Specials.

Sir Edwyn Hoskyns

A. M. Ramsey remembered E. C. Hoskyns' lectures at Cambridge in the 1920s as 'an exciting experience'. They were novel and provocative because they clashed with 'the general ethos of religious culture' of their hearers. 'What was strange and foreign was the idea that the Kingdom of God meant the breaking-in of the divine righteousness in a particular history in such wise that moral idealism was itself under judgement.' In *Essays Catholic and Critical*,[17] Hoskyns began by asserting that 'What think ye of the Church?' is the same question as 'What think ye of the Christ?', only differently formulated: a direct challenge to the liberal protestant placing of the church in a lower category to that of Jesus. Hoskyns ended *The Riddle of the New Testament* (1931): 'neither the Jesus of history nor the primitive church fits into the characteristic nexus of modern popular humanitarian or humanistic ideas'. Ramsey writes that, though Hoskyns was neither a disciple of Barth's nor interested in his dogmatic theology, what Hoskyns chiefly derived from Barth was '*eloquence, language*. He caught something of Barth's tone of speech and mode of expression: incisive, passionate, paradoxical.'[18] In 1936 Hoskyns addressed an Open Letter to Barth: 'For us, as for you in Central Europe, the subject-matter of the Bible is difficult, strange and foreign. Yet in our aloofness we know that its relevance lies in its strangeness . . .'[19]

Hoskyns' sermons preached in Corpus Christi College Chapel, Cambridge during the 1920s and 1930s were a prolonged onslaught on the dominant liberalism of English theology and thought. He said in a series on 'Eschatology', preached 1926–27:

> The Lady Margaret Professor of Divinity recently defined the immediate task of Christian theology to be the re-expression of Christian faith in terms of evolution. I would venture to suggest that the task of the Christian theologian is rather to preserve the Christian doctrine of God from the corrupting influence of the dogma of evolution, at least as that doctrine is popularly understood.

In reply to those who expressed dissatisfaction that the New Testament offered so little clear guidance about the moral problems which concern us, Hoskyns ringingly affirmed:

> These problems are all ethically secondary problems to a Christian. The one fundamental moral problem is what we should still possess if the whole of our world were destroyed to-morrow, and we stood naked before God. The eschatological belief crudely and ruthlessly sweeps away all our little moral busynesses, strips us naked of

wordly possessions and worldly entanglements, and asks what survives the catastrophe.

(The adjectives 'ruthless', as applied to God, and 'naked' and 'little', as applied to man, were characteristic of Hoskyns' aggressiveness as he sought to re-establish a belief in the sovereignty of God and the sinfulness of man.) A series on 'Sin' preached 1927–28 began:

> When a Christian man declares that the four-times repeated response in the Litany of the English Church – 'Have mercy upon us miserable sinners' – has no meaning for him, he proclaims in public, either that he has as yet no understanding of the Christian religion, or that has apostasised from it.

At the end of that series he condemned efforts 'to bring the Church into greater harmony with the modern world' for that would subject it to passing fashions: 'the Church remains the one hope of salvation, reformed or unreformed' because it proclaims 'truths' which 'exist on a plane distinct from other truths or half-truths'. On Armistice Day 1934 he took as his text the passage from Hebrews 9 so often quoted by preachers and writers during the first war: 'apart from shedding of blood there is no remission of sin'. He refused to apologize for the war: this country 'was called upon to face a great issue . . . in terms of right and wrong'. Britain was 'compelled to fight'. We commemorate a victory, and we are bound to be grateful for it.

> Are we to say that it was all a ghastly mistake? Are we to say that there was no issue and that human life was merely thrown away? This is surely to play with the real world, and if we play with history here, shall we not be driven to play with it all along the line, until we become purely frivolous?[20]

His sermon on 'The Soldiers' was part of a series on those who surrounded Jesus in his passion:

> We shall never, of course, understand how the themes of war and of the profession of a soldier are handled in the Bible unless we become once again critical of the modern fear of the word 'destruction'. We are obsessed by the desire to preserve anything that men have made and done. No doubt this must be a dominant human interest, and it too has great significance. But there is an arrogance behind it, and somewhere or other we must be reminded that our works are not permanent or eternal . . . No, sin must be destroyed, and of this destruction the soldier is the parable; he

reminds us that all is not well with us; and because this is so, we stand trembling before him. There is here, of course, no idealizing of war, not even of the profession of a soldier. War is a far more terrible thing to the Christian than it is to the ordinary pacifist; for it is the place where human pride receives its most obvious blow, and where sin becomes most clearly evident.[21]

Here Hoskyns, who had been a first war chaplain, reacts to war in a strikingly and challengingly different way from so many of the well-known ex-chaplains like Sheppard, Studdert Kennedy, Barry and Raven whose war experiences moved them to liberalism and pacifism (or quasi-pacifism). For them the lay theology of Donald Hankey[22] was a determinative guide to the necessary reform of the church and theology after the war, whereas Hoskyns disliked Hankey's Christian humanism. He wrote with characteristic defiance of modernizing liberalism: 'I long to sacrifice an ox, and sprinkle its blood over the battalion, especially over the C.O.'[23] For Hoskyns, liberal humanism was to be fought as an enemy not courted as an ally.

Yet Hoskyns, despite his reiteration of the theme of the sinfulness of man and despite the influence of Barth upon him, remained blind to the evils of Nazism. Indeed his authoritarian tone, his *schadenfreude*, his loathing of liberalism, his refusal to identify Christianity with social democracy and his patrician Toryism seem to have made him sympathetic to a movement which promised strong government and a crusade against 'wetness'. His friend, the German theologian Gerhard Kittel, had joined the Nazi party in 1933. Hoskyns hoped to arrange the publication in England of Kittel's lecture on the Jews given in Germany in 1933. This blamed the decadence of Germany on Jewish influence and advocated a form of racial separation and a distinct Jewish Christian Church. Barth was among those who protested at the lecture. Richard Gutteridge, whose hopeful account of the Nazi revolution in *Theology* in November 1933 Hoskyns had supervised and approved, prepared a translation of the Kittel lecture with a friend. But Kittel was unwilling to allow its distribution in England. Hoskyns persuaded the University of Cambridge to invite Kittel to give two lectures in Cambridge in October 1937. Kittel delivered the lectures wearing his Nazi badge of membership, which disgusted many. But by then Hoskyns was dead. Gordon Wakefield believes that while Hoskyns never realized the evils of Nazism, there is no doubt where he would have stood in 1939.[24] That may be true. Nevertheless, that the leading exponent of neo-orthodoxy in England should have been so blind to the nature of Nazism, damages very considerably the argument that because neo-orthodoxy proclaimed the sovereignty of God and the sinfulness of man, it was the only theology capable of unmasking and withstanding totalitarianism.

Reinhold Niebuhr

More influential in Britain than either Barth or Hoskyns were the writings of Reinhold Niebuhr. Niebuhr's theology was rooted in what he learnt from his parish ministry in Detroit between 1915 and 1928. It was his experience of the car industry there rather than the distant war in Europe, which underminded his youthful optimism. He witnessed a sharp and bitter power conflict between employers and unions. His mild moralistic idealism seemed irrelevant. He wrote in *Leaves from the Notebook of a Tamed Cynic* (1929):

> If a minister wants to be a man among men he need only to stop creating devotion to abstract ideals which every one accepts in theory and denies in practice, and to agonize about their validity and practicability in the social issues which he and others face in our present civilization. That immediately gives his ministry a touch of reality and potency . . .

By 1923 he realized that the black and white categories with which the war had been fought were an illusion: 'If the moral pretensions of the heroes were bogus, the iniquity of the villains was not as malicious as it once appeared.' It was totally inadequate to reduce Christianity to winning individuals to Christ. Christians needed to face the specific and complex issues of modern society.[25]

Like Barth, Niebuhr believed that all forms of religion could be idolatrous. But he parted company with Barth on many other issues. Niebuhr asserted that there are moral principles evident to man apart from those known through relevation. The image of God is not destroyed in sinful man. 'Karl Barth's belief that the moral life of man would possess no valid principles of guidance, if the Ten Commandments had not introduced such principles by revelation, is as absurd as it is unscriptural.' Barth protested against the use of human analogies when speaking about God, yet inevitably used them. He also criticized Barth for his attempt to dissuade British Christians from trying to formulate answers to post-war problems. He accused Barth's theology of having initially weakened forces opposed to Hitler, by inducing a spirit of pessimism and by making it more difficult for Christians to accept the inevitable relativity of political decisions.[26]

Over against the optimistic view of man espoused by liberal theology and derived from the Enlightenment, the French Revolution and the nineteenth century, Niebuhr emphasized the sinfulness of man, his capacity for self-deception and his fatal attraction to illusions:

> There has been little suggestion in modern culture of the demonic force in human life, of the peril in which all achievements of life and civilization constantly stand because the evil impulses in men may be compounded in collective actions until they reach diabolical proportions; or of the dark and turgid impulses, imbedded in the unconscious of the individual and defying and mocking his conscious control and his rational moral pretensions.[27]

Both Marxism and Freudianism (Niebuhr believed) understood the demonic and tragic aspects of human life better than evolutionary optimism. The crucifixion demonstrated that 'sin is so much a part of existence that sinlessness cannot maintain itself in it'.[28] It is part of the function of Christianity to deflate moral pretensions and to keep before the human race the sharp and disturbing polarities of human existence: man is suspended between glory and wretchedness, between freedom and limitation.

He believed in the need to fight Nazism, but exposed the moral ambiguities of the Allied cause and the terrible dangers of falling into self-righteousness. All wars are between sinners:

> 'If any man stand, let him take heed lest he fall' is a warning which is as relevant to bishops, professors, artists, saints and holy men as to capitalists, dictators and all men of power.[29]

It is only when we measure ourselves against Christ, and therefore despair, that there can be hope. Prophetic Christianity inspires us both to seek the impossible and to recognize that being sinners, all our efforts will fall short and therefore we need grace and forgiveness. The personal encounter with God humbles and enables. But God also provides 'common grace':

> the Church must recognize that there are sensitive secular elements within modern nations, who though they deny the reality of a divine judgement, are nevertheless frequently more aware of the perils of national pride than many members of the Church.[30]

A hidden Christ operates in history. Therefore there is always the possibility that those who do not know the historical revelation may be more repentant than those who do.[31]

Niebuhr was not really a pessimist. He genuinely hoped that human beings could deal constructively with their problems if they relied on grace and forsook illusions, however incomplete their achievements might be. Niebuhr's characteristic balance between realism and hope can be exemplified in the often-quoted dictum: 'Man's capacity for justice makes democracy possible; but man's inclination to injustice makes democracy necessary.'[32] On the one hand 'the dream of perpetual peace and brotherhood for human society is one which will never be fully realised'. Yet the existence of the vision 'is the measure of man's rebellion against the fate which binds the collective life to the world of nature from which his soul recoils'. But meanwhile man 'must content himself with a more modest goal. His concern for some centuries to come is not the creation of an ideal society in which there will be uncoerced and perfect peace and justice, but a society in which there will be enough justice, and in which coercion will be sufficiently non-violent to prevent his common enterprise from issuing in complete disaster.'[33] 'The city of God is no enemy of the land of promise. The hope of it makes tolerable the inevitable disappointments in every land of promise.'[34]

In 1943 Niebuhr described how a group of British pilots refused to receive Communion because of their moral revulsion against their military tasks. He believed that they acted in this way because they had no understanding of justification by faith.[35] For Niebuhr it was this doctrine which enables human beings to live among the moral ambiguities of ordinary life:

> If we live and act in faith, the imperfections of our momentary achievements are transmuted and become a part of God's perfection. There must be forgiveness in the attitude of God toward us; for our acts are not merely imperfect, in the sense that they only approximate to their ideal possibility, but there is always a positive element of evil in them. One thinks, for instance, of the degree to which national egotism and self-interest was one of the driving motives of the nations, prompting them to do their duty.[36]

In his theology, the Last Judgment also had an important ethical function. 'The final enigma of history is therefore not how the righteous will gain victory over the unrighteous, but how the evil in every good and the unrighteousness of the righteous is to be overcome.'[37] The completion of history and all final solutions are to be found beyond history. But here and now, every solution is partial and creates a new problem in its turn. History requires a Last Judgment if there is to be any ethical meaning to existence, in which good and evil are inextricably intermingled.

As a Detroit pastor he became involved in industrial conflicts. In *Moral Man and Immoral Society* (1932) Niebuhr argued that Christians must take power seriously. The existence of power leads to conflict. We cannot expect groups to behave as altruistically as individuals. Influenced by Marxism, he contended that a purely individualistic ethic cannot lead to practical political policies. Justice, not love, is the ethical norm for social action. In political action, coercion has an inevitable role. The liberal ideal of a universal brotherhood among the nations, subject only to the law of Christ, is unrealistic and sentimental. Yet liberal protestants, in spite of the war, are still convinced that the kingdom of God is gradually approaching and that the conversion of individuals will solve social problems. He was critical of the League for not using various forms of force to discipline recalcitrant nations. 'The very essence of politics is the achievement of justice through equilibria of power.'[38] In a sermon published in 1946 he wrote:

> A few hardy optimists imagine that the end of the Second World War represents the end of our troubles; and that the world is now firmly set upon the path of peace. Yet it does not require a very profound survey of the available historical resources to realize that our day of trouble is not over; that in fact this generation of mankind is destined to live in a tragic era between two ages, 'one dead, the other powerless to be born'. The age of absolute national sovereignty is over; but the age of international order under political instruments, powerful enough to regulate the relations of nations and to compose their competing desires, is not yet born.[39]

Thus Niebuhr constantly maintained that Utopian hope, whether Christian or Marxist, was an illusion because it neglected the sinfulness of man and the reality of power conflicts.

For some years Niebuhr was Chairman of the American Fellowship of Reconciliation, though he does not seem to have been an absolute pacifist. But he broke with pacifism in 1932 and became its sharpest and most influential critic. In *Moral Man and Immoral Society* he describes society as being in a perpetual state of war. But pacifists preach the illusion that force can be eliminated. Pacifists should note the power exercised by unions and organize themselves similarly to influence the policies of governments. Niebuhr admired Gandhi but pointed out that non-violent resistance was a form of coercion which had to be prepared to sacrifice moral purity for the sake of political effectiveness. The 'absolutism and perfectionism' of Jesus' ethic 'has nothing to say about the relativities of politics and economics, nor of the necessary balances of power which exist and must exist in even the most intimate social relationships'.[40]

In March 1932 the Niebuhr brothers, Richard and Reinhold,

engaged in a public debate in the *Christian Century* about the Japanese invasion of Manchuria. Richard entitled his article 'The Grace of Doing Nothing'. Resolutions and letters to congressmen achieve little or nothing. But there was a theological way of understanding our resultant feeling of powerlessness. Our inactivity could be turned into a positive demonstration of an eschatological faith in the capacity of God to bring good out of the mundane process. It could express itself also in the creation of cells of repentant Christians within each nation, transcending national and class divisions and preparing for the future. Reinhold Niebuhr in 'Must We Do Nothing?' regarded his brother's article as essentially a prayer for the coming of the kingdom rather than as a political programme. He admitted that Richard's position was closer to the gospel than his own, but argued that we cannot construct an adequate social ethic from a pure love ethic, though the latter is necessary to preserve the former from falling into the relativities of expediency. Something has to be attempted politically by checking violence through a balance of power, whatever the moral ambiguities involved.[41]

Reinhold Niebuhr's most sustained and influential critique of pacifism was set forth in his essay 'Why the Christian Church is not Pacifist' in *Christianity and Power Politics* (1940). Christianity is not a new law, the law of love. Christ is the true norm, but we are crucifiers of Christ. Christianity offers Christ as the 'impossible possibility' but we cannot attain to the full measure of Christ. Hence the need for forgiveness and justification. There is no simple way, as pacifists believe, out of the sinfulness of human history. As an individual vocation which makes no claim to be politically effective, Christian pacifism is a valuable witness, not a heresy. But most modern Christian pacifism is heretical because it is based upon a belief in the goodness of man and upon a conviction that perfect love is guaranteed a victory over the world – the latter a perversion of the meaning of the cross.

> If we believe that if Britain had only been fortunate enough to have produced 30 per cent instead of 2 per cent of conscientious objectors to military service, Hitler's heart would have been softened and he would not have dared to attack Poland, we hold a faith which no historic reality justifies.[42]

There is no real distinction between modern Christian and secular pacifists such as Bertrand Russell and Aldous Huxley: all believe that man is essentially good and in no sense a tragic creature. Christian pacifists make Jesus into their symbol of their faith in man. However, the ethic of Jesus is certainly absolute and uncompromising. So, for example, Christians cannot justify their involvement in the relativities of politics by adducing the story of how Jesus drove the money-changers from the temple with a whip. The ethic of Jesus is not immediately applicable to the task of securing justice in a sinful world.

Pacifists argue that the ethic of Jesus is one of non-violent resistance, provided that it does not involve the destruction of life and property. But there is no scriptural justification for such a view. In fact Jesus enjoins non-resistance. Niebuhr ridicules Richard Gregg's advocacy of non-violence as the best method for defeating a foe and criticizes him for implying that Jesus ended his life on the cross because he had not completely mastered the technique of non-violence and therefore was inferior to Gandhi.

The crucial question is whether the grace of Christ can so heal a human heart that it is capable of fulfilling the law of love, or whether the gospel is 'primarily the assurance of divine mercy for a persistent sinfulness which man never overcomes completely'. The New Testament does not view history as a gradual ascent to the kingdom, as do modern pacifists, but rather as moving to a climax of judgment.

The Christian should regard wars as conflicts between sinners. It was the self-righteousness of the victors which imposed the war-guilt clause. A balance of power is inferior to the harmony of love, but it is a basic condition for the existence of justice. We cannot identify Christianity absolutely with democracy, but unless it is preferable to tyranny, moral judgment is meaningless. Sentimental illusions about the evil character of Nazism, combined with ignoble motives for tolerating Nazi aggression, allowed Nazi tyranny to reach its present proportions.

Nevertheless Niebuhr ends his essay with an expression of genuine gratitude that the church has now learned to protect its pacifists and to appreciate their witness:

> We quite understand this scruple and we respect it. It proceeds from the conviction that the true end of man is brotherhood, and that love is the law of life. We who allow ourselves to become engaged in war need this testimony of the absolutist against us, lest we accept the warfare of the world as normative, lest we become callous to the horror of war, and lest we forget the ambiguity of our own actions and motives and the risk we run of achieving no permanent good from this momentary anarchy in which we are involved.[43]

But pacifists would be more effective witnesses against us if they were not corrupted by self-righteousness, did not accuse us of apostasy, and if they were less certain of their claim to possess 'an alternative for the conflicts and tensions from which and through which the world must rescue a precarious justice'.

In 1937 and 1938 Niebuhr attacked American re-armament. But after Munich he came to believe that even world war was preferable to the extension of Nazi tyranny. In 1940 in 'The War and American Churches' (also published in *Christianity and Power Politics*) he scathingly criticized the American churches for clinging on to American neutrality and for suppressing the full story of Japanese aggression in China and German tyranny in Europe for fear of arousing a war spirit. 'The idea that it is possible to find a vantage point of guiltlessness from which to operate against the world is not a Christian idea but a modern rationalistic one.' Nevertheless he refused to regard the second war as a 'holy war' – there were too many moral ambiguities in the Allied cause. These views led him to advocate a moderate policy towards Germany after the war.

Niebuhr's critique put Christian pacifists on the defensive. It was Niebuhr who, particularly after his 1940 essay, set the agenda. In Chapter 5 we outlined G. H. C. Macgregor's response to Niebuhr in his book *The Relevance of the Impossible* (1941). Macgregor's title was derived from the heading to Chapter IV of Niebuhr's *An Interpretation of Christian Ethics*, 'The Relevance of an Impossible Ethical Ideal'. Leyton Richards in *Christian Pacifism After Two World Wars* (1948) still regarded Niebuhr as the most important critic of pacifism, and quoted him frequently.

Three criticisms of Niebuhr's position are relevant here.

First, Jesus is given an exalted religious and ethical status as the one who lived out the impossibility. But at various points Niebuhr implies that Jesus was only able to do God's will perfectly because he kept himself clear of the ambiguities of power.

> The final majesty, the ultimate freedom, and the perfect disinterestedness of the divine love can have a counterpart in history only in a life which ends tragically, because it refuses to participate in the claims and counterclaims of historical existence . . . It is impossible to symbolize the divine goodness in history in any other way than by complete powerlessness, or rather by a consistent refusal to use power in the rivalries of history.[44]

It is seldom that the limitations of Jesus have been more candidly expressed. For Christianity has been widely understood from New Testament times as the imitation of Christ. But Niebuhr's view of Jesus makes him less immediately useful as a guide to ethical decisions than someone (like Niebuhr?) who was seeking answers to ethical problems while immersed in the ambiguities of power. Or to put it another way: Niebuhr's *real politik* can appear so far removed from the style and attitude of Jesus that it is often difficult to construct any connection with Jesus at all. To this, followers of Niebuhr would reply that it is a fundamental error to conceive of Christian discipleship as a straightforward imitation of Jesus, and that Niebuhr's outlook does arise from the specifically Christian understanding of God, human nature, sin, judgment, forgiveness and justification. The absolutely uncompromising love of Jesus is relevant precisely because it transcends and judges our inevitable compromises.

Second, can the clear distinction which Niebuhr makes between ethics appropriate to groups and those for individuals be sustained either morally or in experience? Does Niebuhr expect too little from groups? Does Niebuhr place too pessimistic a limit upon the capacity of groups and individuals for creative acts of forgiveness and atonement? Haddon Willmer asks:

> does Niebuhr do more than exhort us to realism about ourselves and to hope in God who is beyond understanding? For him, was praxis prior to theory in the sense that man must live through what he cannot explain and so cannot fully control or predict? . . . Is there more openness to morality in the texture of society, more room for manoeuvre, than Niebuhr allowed in principle?[45]

Third, Niebuhr has been criticized because he made sweepingly polemical, and sometimes inadequately supported, generalizations about such subjects as liberal theology, Christian pacifism and the 'biblical view' of this or that. Such generalizations, it is said, do violence to the complex and variegated nature of the targets he chose to attack.[46]

When in March 1979 the BBC broadcast a tribute to Niebuhr, Vernon Sproxton was able to demonstrate that Niebuhr's social ethics had had an extraordinary influence, not least on men of affairs, including some not specifically connected with the churches: American trade union leaders, Jimmy Carter, Adlai Stevenson, Denis Healey, Tony Benn and R. A. Butler, for example. In the broadcast, Richard Crossman said that *Moral Man and Immoral Society* was one of the books which changed his life and A. R. Vidler declared that in the long run Niebuhr had made more difference to his thinking than any other theologian. On another occasion he made a similar point, saying that Niebuhr's thinking had some affinities with the theology of crisis and biblical theology, but that he also stood apart: 'he got under my skin more than any of the other critics of theological liberalism'. Vidler said that he had always been concerned about the social implications of Christianity, but that it was Niebuhr who had convicted him of having made 'the mistake of taking those implications to be idealistic, utopian and perfectionist'. Niebuhr demonstrated that there were important Christian resources (of which hitherto he had been unaware) which illuminated social conflicts and problems.[47]

Secular despair or Christian hope?

Vidler's book *God's Judgment on Europe* (1940) exemplified Niebuhr's influence. He claimed that national propaganda was now trying to convince us that right was only on one side. But the Versailles Treaty had imposed crippling terms on Germany. What then was the meaning of the war? For some years we had no clear sense of national purpose, no ideology. Most modern people are utopians, but those who could read the signs of the times had already lost their faith in liberalism and were turning, either to more realistic secular beliefs, or to a rediscovery of Christian belief. Evil cannot simply be ascribed to ignorance or illiberal governments. The goal and meaning of history lies beyond history.

> In the modern period the Church's function as the bearer and interpreter of God's judgment has been lost sight of. Men have supposed that the Church should be an agency of mercy, of brotherhood and peace, and they have not known that mercy presupposes judgment . . . In this perspective then the meaning of the war is that it is God's judgment . . . on the apostacy of Christendom.[48]

The war is not a conflict between a Christian and a pagan society, but between two societies, both secular, but to differing degrees. We must attempt the Christianization of our machine dominated society, but eschew utopian hopes of achieving it.

In this war no completely rational course of action was open to Christians:

> Some Christians may be called actively to participate in the war as ministers of the wrath of God, though this is a hard saying, and who can hear it? Others, however, believe that they may be only ministers of His mercy by serving in non-combatant capacities. Neither line of action can be defended as perfectly consistent . . .

He went on to quote D. H. Lawrence's vision of judgment, with evident satisfaction:

Let the leaves perish, but let the tree stand, living and bare. For the tree, the living organism of the soul of Europe, is good, only the external forms and growths are bad . . . There are unrevealed buds which can come forward into another epoch of civilization, if only we can shed this dead form . . .[49]

It may be that the church will live on as a faithful remnant. It may be that 'we shall have to die with the dying Churches in sure and certain hope of the resurrection. How God will renew the life of His Church, we cannot tell.'[50] He explained in the Preface that his prognostications about the future of European civilization, which had at one time seemed morbidly gloomy, now in 1940 appeared to have been vindicated by events.

This book, and his *Secular Despair and Christian Faith* (1941), showed the influence not only of Niebuhr, but also of Niebuhr's British disciple D. R. Davies, as Vidler confirms in his autobiography. P. T. Forsyth and Hans Ehrenberg, a German refugee pastor, were also potent influences on him at this time. It was to Ehrenberg that Vidler dedicated *Christ's Strange Work* (1944), a still eloquent study of the role of Law in Christianity. Vidler also tells how, after the war, now under the influence of F. D. Maurice, he came to the conclusion that Niebuhr and Davies had led him to make the sinfulness of man rather than the grace of God the basis of theology. Vidler's Cambridge University mission addresses *Good News for Mankind* (1947), inspired by Maurice, so impressed Charles Raven, who had deplored Vidler's previous views, that he suggested that he should be a candidate for a vacant Cambridge Professorship.[51]

Niebuhr also had a considerable impact upon W. H. Auden. In America Auden reviewed Niebuhr's *Christianity and Power Politics* for the *Nation* on 4 June 1941 and the first volume of *The Nature and Destiny of Man* for the *New Republic* on 2 June 1941. Auden told Ursula Niebuhr that, like her husband, he was an Augustinian not a Thomist. Richard Hoggart has described a number of poems by Auden of this period as being like versified paragraphs from *Nature and Destiny*.[52] Auden dedicated the poem 'Nones' to Reinhold and Ursula Niebuhr.

Professor Ronald Preston, in the broadcast already cited, related how Niebuhr gave enormous encouragement to those like himself who, in the end, felt there was no escape from the obligation to resist Hitler. He told of a friend, killed on the beaches of Dunkirk, who had taken *Beyond Tragedy* with him. Niebuhr's book had been his great standby in his role as a 'reluctant crusader'.

Niebuhr also influenced Temple.[53] Temple propagated a mild social radicalism derived from the Christian Social Union, from his incarnational, immanentist and sacramental theology, from a philosophical idealism always questing for synthesis, from an evolutionary optimism, and from an experience of life curiously untroubled by conflict or tragedy. Temple (commented Dorothy Emmet) was 'never seriously puzzled'.[54] One of the themes of COPEC, which Temple chaired in 1924, was that there was a common interest in which all members of society could share and which could be discovered and appealed to without too much difficulty. However, the growing crises of the 1930s, both international and economic, and his increasing contact with Niebuhr and with continental theologians, led to a shift in Temple's theological position. This was evident from Temple's introduction to the Report *Doctrine in the Church of England* (1938). The Report had been in gestation for fourteen years. During that period the centre of theology had shifted from incarnation to redemption:

> A theology of the Incarnation tends to be a Christo-centric metaphysic . . . A theology of Redemption . . . tends rather to sound the prophetic note; it is more ready to admit that much in this evil world is irrational and strictly unintelligible . . . If the security of the nineteenth century, already shattered in Europe, finally crumbles away in our country, we shall be pressed more and more towards a theology of Redemption. In this we shall be coming closer to the New Testament. We have been learning how impotent man is to save himself, how deep and pervasive is that corruption which theologians call Original Sin . . . If we began our work again to-day, its perspectives would be different.

In *Theology* for October 1939 Temple described how he and his contemporaries grew up in a stable world in which the acceptance of Christian ethics and a belief in automatic progress were axiomatic. His own theological writings had attempted to offer a Christo-centric metaphysic to an intellectual frame of mind already spiritual and theistic. Now all this had changed:

> The world of to-day is one of which no Christian map can be made . . . We cannot come to the men of to-day saying: 'You will find that all your experience fits together in a harmonious system if you will only look at it in the illumination of the Gospel. . . . Our task with this world is not to explain it but to convert it. Its need can be met, not by the discovery of its own immanent principle in signal

manifestation through Jesus Christ, but only by the shattering impact upon its own self-sufficiency and arrogance of the Son of God crucified, risen and ascended, pouring forth that explosive and disruptive energy which is the Holy Ghost.

(The adjectives 'shattering' and 'explosive' and the description of the world as arrogant, were characteristic of the triumphalist stridency of neo-orthodoxy.) 'We shall not try to "make sense" of everything; we shall openly proclaim that most things as they are have no sense in them at all.' Is there a Natural Order as Catholic tradition asserts? Or is there only 'Natural Disorder' as continental Protestants believe? For once the serenely confident Temple seems to have been shaken. But he ends with the belief that 'One day theology will take up again its larger and serener task and offer to a new Christendom its Christian map of life' – but that day is distant. For the time being we have to try to 'light beacons in the darkness rather than to illuminate the world'. In 1942 he explained to Dorothy Emmet that he had come to see that the world is not a rational whole like a picture. Rather we are engaged in a drama, the meaning of which is only disclosed at the final curtain, i.e. eschatologically.[55] Nevertheless by background and temperament he was never likely to develop into a theologian of crisis and *angst*.

In 1941 Temple presided over the Malvern Conference on the life of the church and the order of society. Unlike COPEC it was an entirely Anglican affair. It was dominated by the Christendom Group with its sociology based on Natural Law. In his opening address Temple asserted that it was Niebuhr rather than Maritain who grappled with the real issues of the day, because Niebuhr's mind was possessed by the all-pervasiveness of human sin. Dorothy Sayers painted a sombre picture. It is possible (she said) that 'we may have to go down to the deepest bottom of the pit – the point where all faith – literally *all* faith is lost; when words and deeds become completely meaningless'. D. M. Mackinnon delivered a characteristically agonized and apocalyptic polemic against war, the establishment of the church, liberal theology and glib talk of post-war reconstruction.

The coming of Christ in the earliest Gospel is portrayed as tragic, and catastrophic . . . We argue to ourselves that the world cannot be such a bad place after all if it could provide a setting and more than a setting for the Incarnation. Such an argument is, of course, a blasphemous piece of impertinence . . . We must, I believe, seek to create in every Church . . . a centre where is realized a spiritual tension that is well-nigh intolerable; the embrace of that suffering, which a vision of our predicament as citizens in an apostate society, for whose apostacy we are in part responsible, will bring, is our surest safeguard.

John Middleton Murry, the eccentric pacifist layman, whose book *The Betrayal of Christ by the Churches* (1940) was widely read, ended his address: 'The Church fails in leadership, because it shows no sign of having known despair; no evidence of having been *terrified* by its own impotence.'[56] However other contributors, notably W. G. Peck, Sir Richard Acland and Kenneth Ingram, in their proposals for a new collectivist society, showed that left-wing political optimism was still vigorously active.

Temple's attitudes to war and pacifism (to be examined in Chapter 9) also showed the influence of Niebuhr. But his *Christianity and Social Order* (1942), a personal follow-up to the Malvern Conference, indicated that in domestic politics he was still broadly thinking along the lines of COPEC, if in a rather more cautious manner. In his preparation of the book he had sought the advice of R. H. Tawney and Maynard Keynes. Its sale of 139,000 copies as a Penguin Special was a sign both of Temple's own drawing power and of the desire of many, including Christians, to participate in the debate about a new style of society for the post-war period. Though Temple included a section on original sin, the book gave little indication that he had heeded Niebuhr's warnings about the danger of devising political programmes without taking into account conflicts between power groups in society and the tragically self-defeating character of human nature. So on the one hand he wrote that the church should 'stand aside' from industrial disputes: 'It is very seldom that Christianity offers a solution of practical problems.' But then he added with unbelievable naivety that what Christianity can do 'is to lift the parties to a level of thought and feeling at which the problem disappears'.[57] Maurice Reckitt commenting in 1954 on the very little real influence Temple had left behind in social and political questions, remarked that Temple believed that society was redeemable and assumed that the Church of England was the natural basis for such a redemption.[58] Alan Suggate (in *Theology*, November 1981) suggests that Temple's 'Platonic cast of mind, leavened by a Hegelian propensity for synthesis and optimism' made him unable to respond adequately to the dialectical theology of Niebuhr, which had been forged by an engagement with the harsh realities of industrial life and with Marxism; a world far removed from COPEC and Bishopthorpe. Temple's favourite term 'middle axioms' indicated his consensual approach to social problems.

Nevertheless, largely under the influence of Niebuhr, in the late 1930s and during the war, Temple drew a clear distinction between the ethic of love appropriate for individuals and the ethic of justice appropriate for groups and nations. Gospel presupposes Law.

In June 1940 the pilgrimage of D. R. Davies (earlier stages of which have been outlined in previous chapters) led him to St Deiniol's Library, Hawarden where Vidler was the Warden. Davies had returned to the Congregational ministry in October 1939, but soon realized that he needed a liturgical church. The first night of his stay at Hawarden he sat up late reading the *Book of Common Prayer* for the first time. He was then fifty. He found it 'more exciting at that first reading than any novel'. In October he returned to train for the Anglican priesthood. He was thrilled by the Thirty-Nine Articles, especially Articles IX and XI on original sin and justification by faith. Vidler told Temple that he was sure that he had never ordained anyone who believed more wholeheartedly in the Articles than Davies.[59] The General Confession in the Prayer Book so excited Davies that he wrote a book about it, with the significant and evocative title *Down Peacock's Feathers* (1942). The Confession had a universal application:

> It is equally true of every German, from Hitler downwards, of every Italian, from Mussolini downwards, and of every Briton, from Mr. Winston Churchill down to the most insignificant John Smith. The General Confession is the place where all extremes meet. In it Stalin rubs shoulders with the Pope, and President Roosevelt meets with Hitler.[60]

After the collapse of his socialist utopianism in Spain, Davies had fallen into complete despair. He tried to drown himself. But in his sense of 'utter nakedness and worthlessness' he came face to face with God. His new birth from despair to hope was partly effected by reading everything by Niebuhr he could lay his hands on. 'I can never be sufficiently grateful to Reinhold Niebuhr for what his books did for me. He fitted together the elements of my last ten years' experience . . . I came to see, not only the meaning of my own experience, but the meaning of European politics and indeed of European history.'[61] Davies wrote a guide to Niebuhr's thought: *Reinhold Niebuhr: Prophet from America* (1945). Davies became well-known through his book *On to Orthodoxy* (1939). He became what Vidler (with some exaggeration) called 'a British counterpart' of Niebuhr. Vidler read this book with excitement, and it still seemed to him, a quarter of a century later, 'a powerful piece of writing'. Even at his first reading, however, Davies' bold generalizations aroused Vidler's suspicions as well as fascinated him. Vidler came to have 'increased misgivings about his preoccupation with original sin'.[62]

In *On to Orthodoxy* Davies sketched his pilgrimage and the utter despair at the futility of all he had previously laboured for as a pacifist and socialist. He berated Christian liberalism for a false estimate of human nature expressed in the belief in inevitable progress; for its banishment of the other-worldly element in the Christian ethic; for its denial of the uniqueness of Christianity; and for its secularization of life and religion. The 'logical end of Adolph Harnack and his social gospel is Adolf Hitler and his Nazism'.[63] 'Hitlerism is the final consequence of the gospel of Humanism.'[64] Hitler cannot be simply explained in terms of Allied selfishness and stupidity. On the last page he defined his new faith: 'man is radically evil'; 'he is cursed by a fatal contradiction which ordains that the power by which he advances in civilisation nullifies and destroys his progress'; 'if left to his own resources, man is doomed to destruction and History is fated to disintegrate'. History finds its fulfilment beyond death, because all history is under the will of God who has come into history in Christ, who will come again in final judgment. The supreme task of the church is to preach the grace of God and bring men to repentance.

The title of another of Davies' books *Secular Illusion or Christian Realism?* (1942) is as characteristic of the period as that of *The Good Pagan's Failure* (1939) by Rosalind Murray, wife of Arnold Toynbee. She argued that the good pagan is more liable to be knocked off course by the new evil barbarism than the Christian. Against these barbaric forces the Good Pagan is helpless.

It is interesting to trace the impact of this many-pronged onslaught on liberalism upon the writings of F. R. Barry (Bishop of Southwell 1941–1963), whose books were so popular with the clergy. Earlier we noted his attacks on Barth and Brunner in 1931. He had made his name with *The Relevance of Christianity* (1931). His optimism about the world which was expressed in this book and in his support for appeasement was replaced, when war came, by a new sombre outlook typified by the title of the book which he wrote between Dunkirk and the Battle of Britain, *Faith in Dark Ages* (1940). Barry now felt closer to Niebuhr than to any other contemporary theologian and quoted from him frequently. 'He shared with Niebuhr an awareness of man's essential tragedy, coupled with a warm appreciation of man's cultural achievements.' Barry became convinced, like Niebuhr, that the neglect of the doctrine of original sin had been extremely damaging.[65] In his book *Church and Leadership* (1945), like others, he proclaimed that the liberal era was now past. But he saw God's hand too evidently in the human achievements of the last three hundred years to be able to use easy slogans like 'the bankruptcy of humanism'. Despite his rejection of the old liberalism for underrating evil and indulging in rationalistic optimism, he perceived the dangers of the new biblical theology which he thought too much akin to the old fundamentalism which located all truth exclusively in the scriptures. Like other war-time church leaders he was convinced that the intellectual initiative had now passed to Christianity which was out-thinking its competitors.

In *Living by Faith* (1983) Stuart Blanch, the former Archbishop of York, related how he and his wife had their lives permanently altered by their reading in war-time of *Midnight Hour* (1942) by 'Nicodemus'. This was the *nom de plume* of Melville Chaning-Pearce, an Anglican layman. On the title page was a quotation from Kierkegaard: 'There comes a midnight hour when all men must unmask.' Fr Keble Talbot CR (Superior of the Community of the Resurrection 1922–40) among others thought it one of the most impressive religious documents of the century. C. F. Garbett, Archbishop of York, wrote that no book for a long time had so moved him. But Temple was more sceptical about it. Faber, its publishers, seeing it selling so well, decided that the name 'Nicodemus' would ensure success for a book of essays by him. Faber published these under the title *Renascence* in 1943.[66]

Midnight Hour was a journal written in 1941 about an intense personal crisis brought about by the war. The author described his experiences of 1940 as like (quoting Barth) 'a hand shaking the foundations of all that is and will be'.[67] He believed that his inner agony of soul mirrored the agony of the world.

> This conception of some latent, ineluctable evil at the core, not only of the human heart, but also at the core of all creation, at the core of Nature, of our Art and our wisdom, at the core of all natural loveliness and glory, of the beauty of youth and womanhood and at the heart of human heroism, devouring its dark path of corruption and death like a maggot in an apple, is a horrifying vision . . . which probes the Christian creed to its own core.[68]

What he called our 'emasculate Christianity' of course proclaimed a very different account of the world, but real Christianity was committed to original sin. He recounted his experience of a personal hell:

> I am lost; I am damned; I am dead; only Thou, O Christ, can quicken these dead bones. I am a crawling mass of corruption; every thought, every act, every wish, every willing of mine is corrupt – I

can do no good thing. Even this contrition, this horror of myself is rotten with sin and self-will.[69]

The book created a controversy. On 29 October 1941 *The Christian News-Letter* published an extract which included such passages as: 'I believe that they who ally themselves with the Church of England ally themselves with death and go down in spirit to a grave of the spirit.' In his Postscript to *Midnight Hour* 'Nicodemus' asserted that he had been told at the last minute that he was unfit for ordination because he had been identified as the author of the extract in *The Christian News-Letter*. Correspondence in the Temple Papers at Lambeth makes it clear that this was not the reason for the refusal of ordination. That a book which contained so much despair and self-loathing could have been so popular among so many leading Christians, exemplifies the degree to which the masochistic denunciation of human sinfulness had become a stock reaction among Christians, especially in the early stages of the war. Ronald Gregor Smith, commending *Midnight Hour* in *The Christian News-Letter* for 21 October 1942 attacked proposals for saving modern society as 'nugatory, for they are made without that sense of crisis, of doom and disintegration, which alone is able to impart an elemental urgency into the whole situation . . . the call to despair is the call of real hope'.

Certainly the report of the Archbishops' Commission on Evangelism, *Towards the Conversion of England* (1945), took it for granted that a triumph of orthodox Christianity over humanism had taken place. The conservative evangelical Bishop of Rochester (Christopher Chavasse), who chaired the Commission, had a large hand in the writing of the report. Despite its modishly tentative title it was prefixed by a stern quotation from Temple: 'Our problem is to envisage the task of the Church in a largely alien world.' It asked why there had been such a wholesale drift from religion among a people who had showed such self-sacrifice and endurance during the war and in a nation in which humane values had flourished. The first answer given was contained in the polemical sub-heading 'Humanism The Age-Long Lie': 'it is hard to understand why men still persist in being deluded by its specious and thread-bare creed'.[70] It condemned much modern literature and art as 'a corrupter of youth'.[71] But humanism had been exposed: 'The trust in human progress (evidenced in the last war by the high hopes we entertained of a better social order) has been pulverised by the brutal logic of events.'[72] The *Guardian* (17 August 1945) was critical of the report, not least for its wholesale condemnation of humanism. 'Christian Humanism is the antidote to secularist

Humanism . . . Human nature is potentially divine, and those will realize this who strive to be true to the best in themselves. Thus will they ascend through Nature to God.' So much for Barth, Hoskyns, Niebuhr and D. R. Davies! The *Guardian's* comment was representative of the continuing optimism of many British Christians about man, which increased as the war went on. This optimism was demonstrated in 1945, when influenced by the Temple tradition, many Christians placed their hopes in the Labour Party.

The German experience and English theology

English theologians and writers may have felt that the retreat from liberal optimism was sufficiently widespread to convince outsiders that a revolution in thought had taken place. But some of the German pastors who came to England as refugees thought English theology was worm-eaten by liberalism.

Hans Ehrenberg, a Jewish Christian, a Confessing pastor and Assistant Professor of Philosophy at Heidelberg, spent November 1938 to March 1939 in Sachsenhausen concentration camp. In April 1939 he fled to England. He stayed with Bell at Chichester and with Vidler at Hawarden. In his *Autobiography of a German Pastor* (1943) he described how very different was the background from which he came, to that of his English readers.

> Your religion has not been interfered with. The religion of us Christians in Germany has been shaped in the crucible of revolutionary persecution: a thing which you cannot understand because you have not experienced it. Some of us, too, have faced the Beast from the Abyss; we have been in hell and come out again. We bear the scars and the wounds of the conflict on our minds and on our bodies.[73]

He asked his readers to examine their Christianity. 'Several features of your church life in England disturb me, just as others overwhelm me, and I begin to fear for the future of your Christian religion.'[74] In a section addressed to Niemöller, he asked why there was so little point in his telling British people about the concentration camp where for four months he had helped to carry out the corpses:

> Some won't believe it; others stop their ears; others, again, are just morally outraged. And why do the folks here react in this way? Because they always want to believe the best of people and absolutely refuse to have anything to do with the fight against the Devil. For

(and this is really at the bottom of their refusal) they don't want to
begin with the struggle within themselves.[75]

How was it that the British honoured Niemöller, yet repudiated Barth?
In a section addressed to Barth, he ruminated on the English love for
understatement – perhaps the Englishman is afraid to commit himself
too far because he is something of a sceptic. By contrast, Germans
preferred to overstate in order to tempt others to take an opposing
point of view. He contrasted Barth's theology with that in Britain
which regarded natural theology so highly, disliked doctrine and
translated Christianity into a support for civilization and and post-war
reconstruction. 'Our fight, Barth, is not against Hitler, but against
Satan, against the Powers of Darkness. Our struggle is not for religious
freedom, but for the Truth.'[76]

Another German refugee pastor, Franz Hildebrandt, forthrightly
challenged English liberal theology. His blunt, uncompromising but
good tempered and witty book *This is the Message* (1944) was a reply
to Charles Raven's taut, bitter book *Good News of God* (1943). Raven
in his preface contended that Anglican priests had reacted to the first
war by posing as 'medicine men' using the 'cheap methods' publicized
in *Tell England* (1922) – Ernest Raymond's best selling novel about
an Anglo-Catholic chaplain. Raven asserted that Anglicans were
reacting to the second war by adopting equally 'pathological' theology
from the continent. Raven's preface also contained a lamentable
paragraph full of self-pity, bewailing his own present lack of 'official
status, benefice or other position in the ecclesiastical world'.

Raven reflected on his own discovery of Christ in the most unlikely
and unecclesiastical of circumstances. He recalled being under fire
when he was a chaplain in 1917: 'it was surely the power of Christ'
that led a private soldier 'to throw his body between me and the shell-
bursts'. He quoted immanentist texts at the neo-orthodox: 'Raise the
stone and thou shalt find Me' and 'The Kingdom of Heaven is inside
you'. To those Christians who constantly proclaimed that scientific
humanism had failed, he retorted that they should consider the
influence of such scientists as Julian Huxley, J. D. Bernal or C. H.
Waddington. A conversation in any mess, canteen or railway carriage
would reveal that ordinary people had immense confidence in modern
science.

He dismissed D. R. Davies, *Theology* (editor A. R. Vidler) and the
SCM. Their message,

> has much of the paradox and eloquence of Reinhold Niebuhr but
> little of his real passion and sincerity: it is affected, priggish,

arrogant, contemptuous of what it does not take the trouble to understand, and apparently incapable of seeing much beyond its own glibly enunciated formulae; its claims when tested amount to little but ill-digested borrowings from Kierkegaard and Barth, and its assets boil down to a few clichés, 'vertical or horizontal', 'irruptions into history', 'not victory in this world, but vindication at the last day', which sound nice but mean nothing, and to an extensive vocabulary of abuse applied to all who have laboured for critical scholarship, for historical research, for philosophical theology and for a reasonable faith.[77]

He wrote with bitter contempt not only of the 'gospels of depravity' as exemplifed by the writings of C. S. Lewis, but also vindictively about friends who having been elevated to high ecclesiastical office, terminated their relationship with him. The propagators of continental theology had been brought up in an atmosphere of 'acute hostility to any scientific or progressive thought'.[78] He was mordant too about the church. A good lodge of Oddfellows was more like the early church than many ecclesiastical gatherings. He looked back to the movement the 'Way of Renewal' which he organized in the 1920s and of how 'they' had taken the work from him and 'killed the baby'.[79] Instead of the Logos theology of the Greek Apologists and a cosmic doctrine of the Spirit, we have been offered Christ as the alien intruder.

> If all that Christianity offers is a myth of a dying god, and membership in a supernatural church, and participation in a magical sacrament, then, on that showing, we have fallen away from the Gospel into the perversion which the fifth century made of it, and Christianity, which, as I believe, in its original form owed nothing to the mystery religions, has become a somewhat refined Mithraism.[80]

Yet, mixed up with all this angry and bitter polemic are moving, lyrical accounts of Raven's experiences as a chaplain in the first war and a dramatic, personal confession which ironically might have been written by one of the 'theologians of despair' of whom he was so contemptuous:

> In the past four years – since friends and work and hopes went to smash in the cataclysm of war – there has hardly been a single night during which I have not spent at least an hour, generally between 3 and 4 a.m., in hell. That is no figure of speech, if hell means a consciousness of total estrangement from God, of utter dereliction, in which one's eyes are open to the vast selfishness and hurtfulness of one's life . . . Night after night, facing the fact of evil, I was quite

unable to see any sign of deliverance from it – until at last . . . came the knowledge that thus to be aware of it, thus to be tormented by it, was in itself a proof of release from it.[81]

Franz Hildebrandt had been a close collaborator with Bonhoeffer in the Confessing Church. Of Jewish origin, he fled to England in 1937 after Niemöller, to whom he was an assistant, had been arrested. In 1939 Hildebrandt took charge of the Lutheran church in Cambridge. Raven became closely associated with him, both through Christ's College of which Raven was Master and in which Hildebrandt was a doctoral student, and through the Divinity Faculty of which both were members. On occasion they shared the same public platforms. A close friendship developed between these two men of such strikingly differing outlooks and backgrounds. Hildebrandt was due to preach at Christ's on Whitsunday 1940 but had been put in detention as an alien. Raven secured his release for two hours so Hildebrandt could deliver his sermon. Raven presided at his wedding in 1943. But despite all this, after Hildebrandt's book *This is the Message* was published in 1944, tragically Raven felt he had been deeply wounded by a friend and the relationship cooled and eventually became virtually extinct.

Hildebrandt's book was in the form of letters which began 'My dear Charles' and ended 'Yours ever Franz'. Raven disliked the use of his Christian name in the subtitle 'A Continental Reply to Charles Raven' which he described with a lofty chauvinism ill-becoming an internationalist, as a 'failure to appreciate the nuances of English manners'.[82] Like Ehrenberg, Hildebrandt was conscious of writing from a very different background. Raven believed passionately that God was to be found in the world around him. Hildebrandt had found God by standing against the world. Hildebrandt wrote that the very people in Germany who, like Raven, had complained that the church was pre-scientific and its liturgy archaic were the first to proclaim Hitler as a new revelation from God. Those whose theology corresponded to that of the Modern Churchman's Union turned out to be almost invariably supporters of the Nazis. He, like other continental theologians, was deeply concerned about what they regarded as the lack of a biblical basis for English theology. He teased Raven for his reliance on theology derived from his work as a naturalist, by remarking that his much-loved kitten would inevitably grow up into a big fat cat which would kill Raven's birds. 'I believe that our position is fundamentally different from Adam in the Garden; living after the Fall, we have lost the immediacy between creation and creator and the direct understanding of plant and animal'.[83] He poured scorn on

Percy Dearmer's liberal hymns in *Songs of Praise* which praised Plato and Socrates and proclaimed Christ as 'the crown of every creed'.[84] He much preferred Wesley's hymns and the Thirty-nine Articles. There is 'an unmistakable demarcation line between the church and the world which we have neither right nor power to change or to ignore'.[85] Hildebrandt had no time for 'Christianity and . . .' Had not the 'German Christians' erred by adding to revelation in such a manner? He quoted Luther 'we know not of God except through Christ, and we know not of Christ except through the Holy Spirit'.[86] Raven had contended that Christ was known wherever men and women are loving and in all movements toward true brotherhood. Hildebrandt replied: 'I am not convinced . . . that we would be wise in adding the League of Nations and the Friendly Societies to the glorious company of the Apostles and the noble army of martyrs.'[87]

Hildebrandt's biblicist approach to theology was exemplified by the three and a quarter pages of biblical references with which the book concluded. For Hildebrandt, God is known, not by appeals to nature and mystical experience, but only through his revealed word. All is by grace which comes from without to sinners, who do not have that freedom to walk with God that Raven posited. Whereas Raven wanted to jettison some early Christian doctrines as pre-scientific, Hildebrandt had found that Anti-Christ and the devil were a reality in the modern world: 'The Continent has encountered the enemy in such a form that the experience inevitably expressed itself in apocalyptic terms and coloured our whole theological language.'[88] 'You have your scientists, I have my Nazis to consider . . .'[89] he told Raven.

In 1948 Hildebrandt wrote to Raven. He said he had realized when Raven's deep hurt became evident that 'confessions' in the German tradition were not wanted in England. He added sadly 'That one could ever act as a bridge-builder, that another point of view but that of the Cambridge tradition could even find a hearing in the university, was a hope, which I have once had, but have buried long since.'[90]

Another liberal theologian who fought back was James Parkes, writing under the *nom de plume* 'John Hadham'. Parkes at Oxford had been a member both of the SCM and the LNU. In 1922 he went to train for the Anglican priesthood at Ripon Hall Oxford, the home of liberal modernism. Later he worked first for the SCM and then for the International Student Service based in Geneva. In his autobiography *Voyage of Discoveries* (1969) he accused Barthianism of killing the social and political endeavours of students by its 'evil influence'. He began to study the Jewish question in 1929 but was unprepared for his discovery of what he called 'the most crippling sin of historic Christianity', namely anti-semitism.

Good God (1940), his first book written under his *nom de plume* (adopted to avoid confusion with his authorship of controversial books on Judaism), was the first Penguin Special on religion. It sold 100,000 copies in a few months. It also converted Sir Richard Acland to Christianity. *God in a World at War* (1940), also a Penguin Special, sold 75,000 copies. Parkes drew upon his deep knowledge of Judaism to make a powerful point against the neo-orthodox. 'Christian theologians have the moral courage of wood-lice' he declared. Whereas Jewish rabbis had retained their optimism about God's action in the world through two thousand years of tragic exile, Christian theologians 'abandon all interest in this world at the slightest reverse'.[91] He proudly asserted his continuing belief in progress though he recognized that he was living in the last stages of a civilization. He derided Vidler's *God's Judgment on Europe* for analysing everybody's faults except those of the church. Though we were not fighting for the England of 1939, nor for the various Empires and certainly not for the churches, we were fighting on the side of God. Neither the Treaty of Versailles nor the League could be blamed: 'The whole positive responsibility does lie with the National-Socialist leadership in Germany, and nowhere else.'[92] Germany's greatest tragedy was Luther and the Lutheran church's preaching of a private religion and a docile obedience to both God and state. The 'loathsome' influence of continental theology led to a view of God outside the world as judge. But God was in fact fighting with his back to the wall for the souls and bodies of men. Meanwhile the institutional churches are dead: 'behind their imposing facades, their vast budgets, their huge nominal memberships, there is nothing, nothing but dry bones, and words, words, words'.[93] Nor should pacifists believe that cultivating potatoes was an adequate witness. Their present security would not win for them that respect that the sufferings of their predecessors earned in the first war.

Parkes' view of Judaism as a necessarily continuing part of God's revelation and his alienation from the church because of its anti-semitic history, its fossilized liturgy and its anti-liberal theology had turned him into an angry cross-bencher. After a curacy in 1925–28 he never held another post in the Church of England. However he had the firm backing of Temple and Bell when in 1935 he decided to devote himself full-time to research and writing about Jewish-Christian relationships, financed by the Marks Trust. For this pioneering work he won world-wide renown. In 1935 when he revisited Geneva, the

Nazis attempted to assassinate him, an indication that they regarded him as an opponent of considerable importance and influence.

How does neo-orthodoxy appear in retrospect? When the 1938 Report of the Doctrine Commission was republished in 1982, G. W. H. Lampe, the Regius Professor of Divinity at Cambridge, and a noted liberal theologian, wrote an introduction to it. He lamented that the Report, which had raised important questions which were still unanswered, had been ignored or forgotten,

> as neo-orthodoxy swept over the churches of Europe, answering the strident assertions of Nazi irrationalism with its almost equally strident and unfounded assertion of the 'revealed Word of God', while the Church of England clergy often took advantage of the stress of national emergency, and the comforting belief that orthodoxy was being vindicated, to get on with the job and leave the intractable problems raised by the Report to the theological experts . . .

(In 1944 Lampe was awarded the MC for his notable work as a chaplain.)

In theory, neo-orthodoxy preached the sovereignty of God, the crucified Christ, man judged, broken and healed by the word of God. In practice it could come over as a strident triumphalism which gave the preacher the satisfaction of being a powerful and prophetic denunciator speaking directly for God. It called for people to surrender themselves humbly to God but sometimes with such an arrogant, threatening and bull-dozing manner that it sounded as though it was the personal security of the preacher not the honour of God which was at stake. In its desire to commend Christianity and the scriptures as the only sources of truth, and the church as the only ark of salvation, neo-orthodoxy tended to denigrate everything outside its own stock-ades. So theology turned from being a response to truth, in all its complex ambiguity, into a form of propaganda. Fortunately Niebuhr himself never adopted either biblicist or ecclesiological exclusivism and readily recognized the ambiguity of religion and the operation of common grace.

Peter Berger defines neo-orthodoxy as 'the reaffirmation of the objective authority of a religious tradition after a period during which that authority had been relativized and weakened'. But, as he argues, its 'objectivity' is spurious: 'neo-orthodoxy asserts that its faith is given; the critique of neo-orthodoxy must assert that, on the contrary, this faith is found by certain individuals as a result of empirically available efforts'. The 'Word' does not exist in a transcendent and unconditioned realm, but both originates and is received in specific sociological contexts which relativize it. We have seen earlier in this chapter that literary figures arrived at some of the same conclusions as the neo-orthodox but from a starting point which owed nothing to scripture but everything to the same pressures of the growing international crisis which the neo-orthodox experienced. Berger compares the neo-orthodox experience to that of a hierophany, and comments that it is 'by its very nature . . a state of intoxication with the divine. In such a state, one is prone to say things that, later on, must be put differently.' But though neo-orthodoxy contained some vital correctives, it was short-lived as a movement because it acted as though the liberal critique proceeded from a culpably sinful attitude of mind and heart. Berger believes that subsequent history had demonstrated that neo-orthodoxy was 'not the end but an interruption of the development of liberal theology'.[94]

In the first war, clergy, feeling uncertain of their role and anxious to be seen to be contributing to the national effort, often adopted a bellicose patriotism which degraded biblical images of sacrifice by applying them with naive romanticism to the slaughter at the front. In the second war, some clergy compensated for their many years' experience of feeling increasingly marginal to national life by adopting a denunciatory theology which made them feel powerful and effective. What effect it had on people in the pew is of course another matter. Lay and clerical Christianity in England have long flowed in separate channels, and lay people had long since developed the capacity to survive the latest clerical fashions. To people in the pew or in the street, Christian pacifists were regarded as more faithful to Jesus than the churches, but pacifism was regarded as a high, but wholly impractical, ideal of no relevance to the real world. There was a job to be done, not with the high-flown romantic patriotism of the first war but with a deep sense of common purpose, with endurance and with humour. Niebuhrian realism, by contrast with pacifism and liberal optimism, made sense in a world of brute force, but on the way seemed to have lost touch with the gentle Jesus at the heart of much English Christianity. But there was a whole strand of English Christianity which had never been particularly Jesus-centred. By the second war, the Ten Commandments, placed at the beginning of the Communion service in the *Book of Common Prayer*, were beginning to be replaced by the milder Summary of the Law or the Kyries, as allowed by the 1928 Prayer Book. But the Commandments were still inscribed on boards near the altar in many churches. For many they summed up what Christianity was all about. They were still used in churches and schools as part of Christian teaching, thus instilling a notion of religion as centrally concerned with duties, responsibilities and moral law. Only in a minority of parishes at this time was the Eucharist the main service of Sunday, so the staple worship for many was Mattins and Evensong, which unlike the Communion service, contained a large Old Testament element, in the form of psalms and lessons.

So both Christian pacifism and the theology of crisis passed most laypeople by and they did their duty – as servicemen, air-raid wardens or members of the Home Guard. Women like men served in the forces and worked in the factories, but also brewed countless cups of tea for the bombed out, the frightened and the exhausted. This is what they called 'practical Christianity'. Ordinary men and women joked and wept their way through the war, and knowing nothing of the theology of despair, hoped ardently for a better society when it was all over. A war-time cartoon depicted a German airman descending by parachute from his shot-down plane. Over the fields ran a farmer with a pitchfork. After him ran his wife with a cup of tea. That at any rate is how the British wanted to see themselves in the Second World War. Fanaticism was to be combatted, not with an alternative dogmatic ideology, nor with quite un-English *angst*, but with sceptical humour. But then the British never experienced at first hand either Auschwitz or Hiroshima; nor did they experience the rigours of a German occupation.

8

A VERY DIFFERENT KIND OF WAR

In 1935 a modernistic doll's house attracted attention at a building exhibition. Its white walls, metal framed windows, flat roof and open-air swimming pool seemed a confident assertion of faith in the modern age. The booklet accompanying it hymned the young generation 'who are unhampered . . . by old conventions of drawing rooms, calling hours, formal manners or privacy'. It was (it added with chilling casualness) 'a generation bred in one war and living its little time of sunshine to the full before the next one'.[1]

When war was declared on 3 September 1939 few were really taken by surprise as most people had been in 1914. After the Munich crisis every home received a booklet *The Protection of Your Home Against Air Raids*. In a broadcast on 23 January 1939 Chamberlain commended *The National Service Handbook* then being delivered to every home, which gave details about the armed services and Civil Defence. The next evening the National Service campaign was launched by Sir John Anderson (Home Secretary) at the Albert Hall. It was a sign of the new mood in the nation that Herbert Morrison, Labour leader of the London County Council, also spoke. The meeting concluded with the singing of Blake's 'Jerusalem'. During the winter of 1938–39, all over the country volunteers crowded into centres for training in Civil Defence. One volunteer remembers training at the village school. The coloured charts showing the effects of mustard gas, contrasted strangely with the pictures on the wall of 'The Light of the World' and the child lying down with the lion and the lamb. In May 1939, men of 20 and 21 became liable for call-up for military training. On 12 May the *Guardian*, the Anglican weekly, published a photograph showing clergy learning to wear and fit gas masks. After the invasion of Prague in March, people had begun to say 'when war comes' rather than 'if war comes'.

The preparation of the churches

The 1939 files of the then Bishop of Ripon (Geoffrey Lunt) show how readily he and the clergy responded to the confidential instructions from Lambeth and the Home Office to prepare for the eventuality of war. In May 1939 the bishop asked his clergy to inform him whether they were being trained in ARP, whether they would be willing to become chaplains, what plans were in hand in rural areas for receiving evacuees. The style of the replies evokes the period. Most were hand written (there were then fewer typewriters in vicarages). Many were obsequious. Quite frequently they began 'My Lord Bishop' and concluded with some such phrase as 'I am your Lordship's obedient servant' – a far cry from the familiar style of address which clergy use today. The replies showed that a large number of clergy had already trained in first aid and as air raid wardens during the previous winter. One village rectory had been offered as a Dressing and Clearing Station, 'being the only house with hot and cold water supply'. A parish hall in Leeds had already been turned into a gas proof First Aid station. A rural incumbent had agreed with the police to ring the Mission Bell in the event of an air raid. The vicar of Kirkby Malzeard, near Ripon, had been a special constable for several years and so was in charge of a reception centre prepared to receive one hundred and twenty children, three teachers and eighty-four others. The enclosed cyclostyled sheet revealed careful planning:

> When notice of evacuation is received, a member of the local committee will pilot the party to the Mechanics' Institute. The Mothers' Union will arrange for hot tea and food to be served . . . Members of the Nursing Division will attend. Billetting Officers and districts have been appointed as follows . . .

Clergy with large country houses in their parishes expected that they would become hospitals or hostels which would need their ministry. A priest in inner-city Leeds wondered whether his church, being vulnerable to air attack, would have to be closed if war came. Those who had been servicemen or chaplains hoped their experience would be used. One priest, ready to become a chaplain, commented: 'I notice that practically all the effective leaders in the Church of England are men who have had military experience in the World War' – an appropriate opinion to express to a bishop who had been a first war chaplain. Another Leeds incumbent took a very different line:

> . . . having served in the ranks in the last war I know exactly what the Tommies think of a man who has not the complete conviction

that he is doing the right thing. As I believe that the next war will be several degrees nearer hell than the last one I cannot see how we bring God into it at all. That means I shall have no useful message for the troops and so would not be of any use as a Chaplain.

The vicar of Studley, near Fountains Abbey, was caring for a settlement of mostly Roman Catholic refugees from Germany and Austria. 'The sufferings of some of these refugees have been very great.' One of the Leeds clergy believed that whereas in the previous war soldiers had been the most important section of the population, next time it would be the 'common people'. In September 1938 the people would have never accepted a war, now they were prepared to stand against aggression. The vicar of a remote hamlet in Swaledale had found the ARP training 'revolting' but trusted that the diplomacy of the Pope and others would 'preserve humanity from the chaos, barbarism and bolshevism which a European conflagration would cause'. A country priest apologizing for his late reply explained that the maid had put the letter in her pocket and forgotten to post it. When war came, those clergy who had received ARP training were issued with arm bands with a white cross to enable them to minister in the streets unhindered during an air raid.

During the summer of 1939 readers of the *Guardian* learned that prayers for use during times and rumours of war had been published by SPCK, that the Archbishop of Canterbury had welcomed provisions for conscientious objection and that Bishop Hensley Henson thought that there were two roots of pacifism: 'a misunderstanding of Christ's teaching and an unbalanced humanitarian sentimentalism'. By contrast, Bishop Barnes, the only pacifist on the bench, said: 'drawing the sword would in actual practice mean dropping poison gas and high explosive bombs on women and children to destroy the enemy's morale'.[2] The *Daily Express*, from after Munich until about a month before the war, ran messages across its front pages assuring its readers that there would be no war. But on 25 August the *Guardian* said in a leader: 'From day to day we know not whether we and all the rest of Europe have still before us twenty-four hours of this so-called peace.' The former Dean of St Paul's, W. R. Inge, on 22 August suspected that 'Jewish influence' was 'being used against an understanding with Germany'. (Inge combined radical modernism in theology with right-wing political views; he disliked the Old Testament as barbarous and unChristian – 'Our Anglican service-books are clogged with Judaism'.)[3] Inge's son Richard, a curate at Horsforth, Leeds, joined the RAF in 1940 as a combatant, despite the Bishop of Ripon's attempts to dissuade him. He was killed in 1941. A priest's stall at St Margaret's Horsforth commemorates him. Henson, who had retired from Durham to Suffolk in January, wrote in his journal for 24 August that Hitlerism's 'persecution of the Jews, its repudiation of Christianity, its perfidy and violences are conclusive. We can make no terms with it.' But the next day he added 'What can I say to these young soldiers which is fitting, helpful, and definitely Christian? The conventional patriotic tub-thumping is out of the question. We have got past that phase. As Nurse Cavell said, "Patriotism is not enough." '4

Up to 25 August there was no daily news bulletin on the BBC until 6 pm. Now extra bulletins were broadcast and programmes were interrupted for urgent announcements. On 1 September Germany invaded Poland; the ARP was mobilized; the blackout began. That day the *Guardian* reported that stained glass at Canterbury Cathedral was being removed. It also included the headline 'Anglo-Catholic Youth: Their Duty in War', and described the impressive response to the call of the Archbishop of Canterbury and Free Church leaders to prayer. Dean Matthews of St Paul's commented: 'At such a time as this one realises that England still believes in God.'

Meanwhile the Archbishop of Canterbury stayed on in his house in Scotland until the last moment. A. C. Don, his chaplain, an even more fervent supporter of appeasement than Lang, felt frustrated as he strove to keep in touch. It had been the same in September 1938 when Lang did not return to London until 28 September (the day before Chamberlain's final flight to Munich) and Don had to keep phoning and sending telegrams. Then Don commented in his diary that Randall Davidson (Archbishop 1903–28) would have been in London for the previous three weeks holding urgent consultations. Don lamented Lang's detachment and complexity: 'about six different people rolled together in one very complex personality'. By February 1939 Lang had got into the habit of referring to the 'so-called crisis' of the previous September. On 4 August 1939 Lang, far from well, went on holiday for two months. He got into his car in a trance, unconscious of the presence of his staff assembled to say farewell: yet in the meantime (thought Don) the world might go up in smoke. Lang refused to return until on 30 August he believed that war was virtually certain. When on 6 September the sirens sounded, Don went to Lang's bedroom to take him to the shelter in the crypt. There he sat at a distance from the others, wearing his purple cassock over his pyjamas.5 What a contrast with the young idealistic curate who in Leeds had chosen to live in slum property to identify himself with the poor.

The outbreak of war

On Sunday morning 3 September, church congregations were smaller
than usual. Many stayed at home to listen to Chamberlain's broadcast.
Never before had Britain learned that it was at war through the
wireless. In many churches arrangements had been made to convey
the news to the officiating minister. William Temple, preaching at
York Minster, broke off his sermon when he heard the news from a
verger, and called the congregation to prayer. In some areas the wail
of sirens followed the broadcast. Some clergy abruptly ended the
service; others led their congregations in prayer and in the singing of
such hymns as 'O God our help in ages past'. At Chichester Cathedral,
Duncan-Jones, the belligerent Dean, announced the news in 'booming
tones'. An ordinand at the theological college remembered the 'extraordinary' contrast when Bishop Bell 'quite on his own, walked from
his throne and for a few minutes reminded the congregation that
they were to be Christians, to have pity on their enemies, to have
compassion, and throughout the war to have forgiveness in their
hearts'.[6] On his way home from church, Henson learned the news
and, observing an air-raid trench being dug, took a spade and joined
in the work. That afternoon an ordinand read the Book of Revelation.
For the first time is made sense. In the evening, congregations were
large, though some churches could not be used as they were not yet
blacked out. (Blacking out the many large vicarages also proved a
problem; one had fifty-three windows.)

Cambridge had been a centre for German Jewish refugees since
1937. The refugees included Pastor Franz Hildebrandt. Up to the
war, a late Sunday evening service according to the Lutheran rite had
been regularly held for them at Holy Trinity Church. In the week
before the war Hildebrandt, realizing that it would not be possible to
black out the church in time for their usual Sunday service, called
on Max Warren the vicar (later General Secretary of the Church
Missionary Society). Together they devised a joint service for both
the German and the English congregations to be held at an earlier hour
in both languages. That such a service could be held on the first
Sunday of the war represented a pledge that the anti-German hysteria
of the first war would not be repeated. When in 1940 many of the
German congregation were interned, they sent a telegram to Warren:
'Christ is our peace who hath made both one.'[7]

That was the church at its best. The previous day, Saturday, Sir
Kenneth Clark, Director of the National Gallery, experienced the
church at its worst. Having completed the removal of the pictures to

safety, he took his staff in the early evening to St Paul's for quiet reflection. As they entered the Cathedral the vergers shouted 'All out'. It was closing time. In vain Clark protested that the country was virtually at war and that within hours the Cathedral might be destroyed.[8]

The new total powers assumed by the government immediately began to affect everyone. A priest staying in a Harrogate hotel, awaiting his induction to a parish in Leeds, was given six hours to move when the hotel was requisitioned. His furniture was in store and the removal firm could not transport it as its vans were being used for war service.

In the first days of September stations were crowded with schoolchildren clutching luggage and gas masks. Many had never been on a journey before. In four days the railways alone transported 1,300,000 evacuees. By December many had returned home as the expected bombing had not begun. But the threat of invasion in the summer of 1940 and the flying bombs in 1944 produced fresh exoduses. Eric Treacy (Bishop of Wakefield 1967–76) in 1939 was vicar of St Mary's Edge Hill, Liverpool, a tough area. He wrote in the popular magazine *Tit-Bits* on 28 October 1939 that the evacuation was bringing together 'the inhabitants of two different worlds'. He tried to explain the one to the other. In the poorer areas of cities, as many as six to eight children often lived with their parents in a four-roomed house. Diet was usually deficient; fresh milk, eggs, butter and salads were almost unknown. Many houses had neither lavatory nor bathroom. The children, used to the bustle of city life, would find rural life uneventful.[9] An advertisement for ACME wringers pictured a black suited rector surrounded by dancing children, and was headed 'Can *that* be the Rectory?' It continued: 'You can't accommodate twenty small evacuees without telling the world it's washing day . . .' In their turn those evacuated to rural areas had often to cope with well-water, earth closets and oil lamps. A survey in 1944 discovered that nearly one third of 3,500 villages had no piped water.[10] A woman doctor from Northallerton, which had received children from Leeds and Gateshead, reported that the chief topic of conversation on market day was the best method of delousing. Large houses were suddenly invaded. In one village the doctor's house took twenty five evacuees and the rectory a dozen. At Bishopthorpe, York, a dozen evacuees were accommodated; the Women's Institute made jam in the old kitchen; the drawing-room was used for ARP lectures, whist drives and dances; the Home Guard used the walled garden for a rifle range and the fire service practised in the grounds. School children occupied the Palace at Chichester. The Bells moved to a vacant vicarage in Brighton and shared the house with six evacuees. The choir schools of Canterbury and St Paul's suddenly appeared in Cornwall and remote village parishes enjoyed choral evensong on weekdays. Vera Brittain, the pacifist and writer, visiting Oxford, was told that babies' nappies had been seen hanging out in Tom Quad. When she visited evacuees from the East End housed temporarily in an Oxford cinema, she, like many other middle and upper class people, had her eyes opened. She vowed that there must be a strenuous effort to reduce the gap between rich and poor. The 'West End' must really know and care how the 'East End' lives, she wrote in 1940.[11]

At the beginning of the war, the Archbishop of Canterbury and other church leaders stressed that Britain had no quarrel with the German people, only with their rulers. Cardinal Hinsley explained that however much as individuals we might be disposed to turn 'our own cheek to the smiter', we could not 'stand idly by and allow our neighbour to be enslaved or ruthlessly done to death'. The Chief Rabbi said that the Nazis were determined to 'ruin' the House of Israel. No one would respond more wholeheartedly to the call of King and country than British Jews, for Britain remained 'the bulwark of liberty, justice and humanity'. The Quaker publication *The Friend* warned against temptations to lower ideals. 'We remember "the war to end all war" in 1914, and are naturally distrustful of the present-day slogans on the same line.'[12] On 8 September the *Church Times* resoundingly declared that Britain was not fighting for Danzig or Poland but 'for the independence of nations, the liberties of mankind, vital ideals of the Christian religion, a good life'. Hitler had misunderstood Christian statesmanship and persuaded himself that Britain 'would never tire of turning the other cheek'. The Principal of Chichester, Canon C. S. Gillett, wrote in the Michaelmas *Cicestrian* that no national issue had ever been 'defined more sharply'. We must show ourselves loyal citizens, but also citizens of the one church, loyalty to which was 'infinitely more important' than national allegiance. He welcomed conscription: 'Overworked priests will no longer be presented with white feathers by young ladies and old gentlemen in a high state of excitement . . .' The National Peace Council, founded in 1904 (president the Bishop of Chelmsford, H. A. Wilson) welcomed the distinction being drawn between the Germans and the Nazi regime; we should make it clear that we were willing to negotiate a peace. The *Guardian* which reported this on 22 September, in the same issue attacked the Germans for indiscriminate bombing and reminded its readers of the Convocation resolutions of 1916–17 against reprisals.

Between January and August 1939 the monthly, *Theology*, under its new editor, A. R. Vidler, had printed a number of letters about the ethics of war. Vidler's October editorial was characteristically Niebuhrian. 'Our own propaganda no less than the German, the utterances of our national leaders no less than of theirs, seek to induce in us the belief that the issues are perfectly simply and easily intelligible.' True, 'the forcible overthrow of Nazi principles is a moral duty which is laid upon this country'. But our conscience is not clear. We cannot blame the war wholly on Hitler. French policy in the 1920s was also to blame. Moreover, even 'the noblest human purposes' are 'shot through with sin'. We deserve God's judgment. The clergy must 'stand within the nation, but as representatives of a society which transcends the nation'. The government has assumed totalitarian powers; will it ever let them go? (Vidler has always enjoyed being provocative.)

Dr Lowther Clarke, editorial secretary of SPCK (the publishers of *Theology*), wrote to Vidler in June 1940 to tell him that this editorial had agitated the literature committee: 'we cannot permit anything to be published which can be interpreted as anti-British propaganda or as tending to weaken the national will for victory.' He warned Vidler that as a result of this editorial, *Theology* was being watched by the government. Though Lowther Clarke soon calmed down and supported Vidler as Editor, Vidler later discovered that it was one member of the committee who had started the agitation and had proposed that they should seek a new Editor: 'it was Dr X, who during the 1930s had shown a compromising sympathy for the Nazi movement and was no doubt anxious by an excess of patriotism to cause that to be forgotten', Vidler writes in his autobiography.[13] SPCK has recently confirmed the correctness of Vidler's inference. 'Dr X' was none other than Dr A. J. Macdonald, the former apologist for Nazism, Headlam's right-hand man on the Council for Foreign Relations. (Macdonald's views were described in Chapter 6.)[14]

Bishop Bell in an article in the *Fortnightly Review* for November 1939 asked 'What is the function of the Church in war-time?' He answered (echoing the Oxford Conference of 1937) that 'it is the function of the Church at all costs to remain the Church'. As Archbishop's chaplain at Lambeth during the first war he remembered that because the church lacked an ecumenical dimension, the church in each nation became more nationalistic. But church and state have different functions: 'when all the resources of the State are concentrated, for example, on winning a war, the Church is not part of those resources. It stands for something different from these. It

possesses an authority independent of the State.' The church 'is not
the State's spiritual auxiliary'. The church must interpret the moral
law, which like the gospel, is 'both super-national and supernatural',
but humbly for the church has a share in the guilt. It must witness to
the moral law 'whether that is favourable or unfavourable to its
country'.

> It must not hesitate, if occasion arises, to condemn the infliction of
> reprisals, or the bombing of civilian populations, by the military
> forces of its own nation. It should set itself against the propaganda
> of lies and hatred.

No earthly war can be described as a 'crusade'. The church's 'supreme
concern is not the victory of the national cause . . . Its supreme
concern is the doing of the Will of God, whoever wins, and the
declaring of the Mercy of God to all men and nations.' The local
church must preach the gospel, 'witness to the universal fellowship'
and 'keep the fellowship of prayers unbroken'.[15] This noble utterance
was the basis of all Bell's ministry both to Britain and the world, both
during and after the war. It owed something to the example of
Archbishop Davidson to whom he had been chaplain and whose
biography he wrote.

In September 1939 the vocation of pacifists and conscientious
objectors was publicly recognized by church and state to a degree
which would have been inconceivable in 1914. Even in the Roman
Catholic Church, the most hostile to pacifism of all the Christian
communities in Britain, there was a sprinkling of pacifist clergy and
laity. Vera Brittain, a close associate of Dick Sheppard's in the Peace
Pledge Union, asked on 3 September 1939 why the world had gone
back to war when she and her friends had worked so hard for peace
for twenty years? They had learned from 1914 to 1918 that 'only the
Kingdom of Heaven within us has power to overcome the brute forces
of evil'. Yet, unlike most pacifists of the previous war, she was ready
to acknowledge this time that Germany had been 'captured by a
doctrine of cruelty and vengeance'. The pacifist vision of a warless
world had been shattered; but they must keep England's 'courage and
idealism' alive. At least this time conscientious objectors were treated
with 'comparative tolerance'. But why had the peace movement failed?
'We assumed that the keen enthusiasm of an energetic minority
signified a desire for peace on the part of the whole nation.' In St Paul's
she saw the Christ of the crucifix 'gazing down in compassionate grief
upon the sunlit ruins' of the high altar. It reminded her of a visit to
Amiens Cathedral in 1921, still boarded up after the shelling. She

could feel 'only an everlasting sorrow, and a passionate pity which I still have not learned how best to use or express'. She was moved too by the heroism of the British people under the bombing, for there was nothing superior or sectarian about her pacifism. During the Battle of Britain, when the nation's fate hung in the balance, she expressed her admiration for the British judicial system, and for the tolerance surrounding the speakers at Tower Hill and Hyde Park. But like many others that year, it was the beauty of the English countryside which moved her most.[16]

The poetry of war

The 'comparative tolerance' with which pacifists were treated, to which Vera Brittain referred, was one of several signs that Britain had grown up since 1918. The sober realism of the best of second war poetry was another. Sadly, few of the leaders of the churches were interested in this poetry or indeed in the art and literature of the whole post-1918 period. Bell was an exception. He commissioned T. S. Eliot and others to write drama for the church. He was equally keen to draw upon the talents of painters and sculptors.[17] By contrast Temple's literary reading virtually ended with the Victorians. Weatherhead disliked modern music, poetry and art. In his second war writings he quoted Browning, Tennyson, Studdert Kennedy, Stevenson, Henley and Whittier. Ronald Selby Wright, the 'Radio Padre', illustrated his talks almost entirely with literature popular in the first war. When Lang broadcast his New Year Message in 1942 he offered to the nation some lines from Browning's 'Rabbi ben Ezra'. Lunt, Bishop of Ripon, in his diocesan message for Remembrancetide 1939, quoted anachronistically from the most popular poem of the first war – 'In Flanders Fields' by John McCrae.

The best second war poetry was in a decidedly lower emotional key than that of the first war. The emotional force of the poetry of Wilfred Owen and Siegfried Sassoon derived partly from the psychological impact of trench warfare, partly from being a revolt against the simple-minded patriotism of poets like Rupert Brooke, and churchmen like Bishop Winnington Ingram. The *Times Literary Supplement* for 30 December 1939 exhorted poets 'to sound the trumpet call' against the 'monstrous threat to belief and freedom'. But the most mature poets, like the most mature churchmen, were sensitive to the ambiguities of human motivation and therefore refused to subvert their perceptions and suppress their doubts. Both sought to sustain the integrity of the individual, so that it would not be destroyed by the forces of collectivist propaganda. C. Day Lewis, son of a country vicar, though a Communist in the thirties, had been too ready to see both sides and too committed to the vocation of the individual, ever to be a single-hearted revolutionary. He spent the first year of the war in a Devon village translating Virgil's *Georgics*: a sign of his withdrawal from politics and a reaffirmation of his commitment to the traditional values of rural England.[18] In 'The Stand-To' he gratefully honoured his solidarity with his companions in the Home Guard. The second war poets rejected the histrionic and spoke instead laconically, nonchalantly and with matter-of-fact realism. The war was not a crusade but a necessary evil. In 'Where are the War Poets?' Day Lewis wrote:

> . . we who lived by honest dreams
> Defend the bad against the worse.

Alun Lewis wrote in 'All Day It Has Rained. . .':

> And we stretched out, unbuttoning our braces,
> Smoking a Woodbine, darning dirty socks,
> Reading the Sunday papers – I saw a fox. . .

Henson was distressed in 1940 by the 'half-cynical boredom' and lack of 'patriotism' among the troops; they were simply acquiescing 'in an absurd and unwelcome necessity'.[19] Anne Ridler in 'Now as Then' evoked memories of armies setting out for France under Edward or Henry, when

> Poets cried 'God will grant to us the victory'.

But she drew back from a straight analogy:

> War is not simple; in more or less degree
> All are guilty, though some will suffer unjustly.
> Can we say Mass to dedicate our bombs? . . .
> Yet since of two evils our victory would be the less,
> And coming soon, leave some strength for peace,
> Like Minot and the rest, groping we pray:
> 'Lord turn us again, confer on us victory.'

By contrast in 1940 Dorothy Sayers, in 'The English War', and Sassoon, in 'The Silent Service', wrote straightforward patriotic poetry. Edith Sitwell and F. T. Prince drew upon passion imagery but did not identify Christ on the cross with the national cause, as was common in the first war.[20]

The most outstanding poet of the war was Keith Douglas, killed in Normandy on 9 June 1944. He juxtaposed detachment, commitment and realism in a type of poetry foreign to Henson's generation bred on Browning. Ted Hughes wrote in his preface to Douglas' *Selected Poems* (1965): 'war was his ideal subject: the burning away of all human pretensions in the ray cast by death'. In 1943 Douglas explained his outlook, which he believed to be widely representative of opinion among soldiers and civilians on both sides of the conflict:

> To be sentimental or emotional now is dangerous to oneself and to others. To trust anyone or to admit any hope of a better world is criminally foolish, as foolish as it is to stop working for it. It sounds silly to say work without hope, but it can be done; it's only a form of insurance; it doesn't mean work hopelessly.[21]

Douglas wrote in 'How to Kill' (1943):

> Now in my dial of glass appears
> the soldier who is going to die.
> He smiles, and moves about in ways
> his mother knows, habits of his.
> The wires touch his face: I cry
> NOW. Death, like a familiar, hears
>
> and look, has made a man of dust
> of a man of flesh.

Douglas evoked that intermingling of detached callousness and compassionate tenderness which characterizes the experience of war.

> How then can I live among this gentle
> obsolescent breed of heroes, and not weep?

he asked in 'Sportsmen'.

Much of the best of second war poetry was 'a form of insurance', as Douglas put it. It was a defence against another bitter disillusionment like that after the first war. Between 1914 and 1918 both politicians and churchmen used unrealistic hopes of a new world after the war as a way of promoting the war effort and justifying the slaughter. But not all second war writers took out insurances against disillusionment. Stephen Spender, the Communist, rejoiced that human values were being affirmed by the greatly increased interest in the arts and by hopes for a new post-war society. He enjoyed getting 'to know the workers' as he ran educational groups for the Fire Service of which he was a member.[22] After the war he lost his Communist faith and contributed to the symposium by disillusioned ex-Communists, *The God that Failed* (introduction by R. H. S. Crossman, 1950).

The blackout encouraged reading. In paper backs was printed the exhortation: 'Leave this book at a Post Office when you have read it, so that men and women in the services may enjoy it too.'[23]

The people's war

The mood of Britain in September 1939 was very different from that in August 1914, said William Temple, Archbishop of York, in a broadcast on 3 October 1939. Then, despite a sense of moral duty towards Belgium, people were bewildered and divided about the causes of the war. Now 'there is no such feeling'. For months 'the public mind has been habituated to the thought that war might become an evident duty'. We were very much less divided than in 1914. The nation felt compelled to take up what was 'a hateful duty' but without excitement and with 'a profound sadness'. Britain was united and dedicated to its task: 'to check aggression, and to bring to an end the perpetual insecurity and menace which hangs over Europe, spoiling the life of millions, as a result of the Nazi tyranny in Europe'.[24] In 1940 'John Hadham' (James Parkes) pointed out the one desire of the older generation after the first war was to return to the 'comfortable stability of the world before 1914'. Now few people of any age 'want to get back to the depressing insecurity of 1938'.[25]

In the first war conscription was not introduced until January 1916. In 1939 conscription began six months before war broke out. (Equally, food rationing was not introduced in the first war until 1918 and even then it was rather haphazard. In the second, food rationing began in January 1940.) In January 1940, Temple voiced the view of most people that the first war system of voluntary recruitment was 'both wasteful and unfair', but he did feel that it was a loss that each person no longer had to take responsibility for his own decision.[26]

Few needed convincing that Nazism was evil, and conscription meant that the war did not need to be promoted with that jingoism so common in the recruiting drives of the first war. In the second war there were no equivalents in nation or church of Horatio Bottomley and Winnington Ingram, though Sir Robert (later Lord) Vansittart and Cardinal Hinsley viewed the conflict in black-and-white terms. During the first war, Archbishop Davidson and other churchmen expressed some criticims of government policies. But no bishop in the first war came out into public and sustained conflict with key government policies as did Bell during the second. In the first war there was something stagey and unconvincing about suddenly portraying the King's cousin, the Kaiser, as the 'Berlin Butcher'. But from the mid-1930s Hitler's rantings and his brutal conquests were to be seen in the newsreels at any cinema in Britain. The Kaiser could be dismissed as an anachronistic despot. But Hitler was all too obviously a product of the twentieth century.

Since the second war, opinions of some historians about both the Kaiser and Hitler have shifted. New research about the Kaiser is said to reveal a personality like that portrayed by the Allies in the first war – unstable, manic and sadistic.[27] A. J. P. Taylor has controversially revised his understanding of Hitler whom he at first regarded as 'a demon of fantastic genius who carefully and deliberately planned every step towards war'. He now considers Hitler to have been a supreme opportunist who had no clear cut plans.[28] Bereft of the category of the demonic, modern man does not know how to make a judgment about Hitler and Nazism. When Hitler planned the extermination of the Jews and began an essentially unwinnable war against Russia, was he mad or evil? If he is judged to be mad, is this a way of evading the challenge of the mystery of evil? And what of the guards in the concentration camps who spent the day killing Jews and then returned to play with their children and to listen to Mozart? Fania Fénelon in *The Musicians of Auschwitz* (1979) tells the macabre story of Josef Kramer, the commandant of Auschwitz who loved music so deeply that he formed a camp orchestra of which she was a member. So the gassings at Auschwitz (at times 24,000 a day) were accompanied by the music of Beethoven. Buchenwald was constructed near Weimar with Goethe's favourite oak-tree as the focal point of the camp.

Most of the leaders in church and state in 1939 had experienced the first war. Precedents and warnings about 'what happened last time' were stored in memories as well as in filing cabinets. So when forms of prayer were drafted for use in the Church of England in September 1939, the main architects were Lang, who had been Archbishop of York in the first war, and F. B. Macnutt who had edited a famous collection of essays by chaplains, *The Church in the Furnace* (1917). When Temple collected his addresses in *Thoughts in War-Time* (1940) he added as an Appendix 'War, This War and the Sermon on the Mount' by B. H. Streeter. This had been originally one of the *Papers for War-Time* edited by Temple 1915–16. Temple's letter to the *Daily Telegraph* of 4 December 1939 calling for a statement of war aims, began by recalling Lord Landsdowne's famous letter of 29 November 1917 in the same paper. Lang, remembering the obloquy with which pacifists were regarded by substantial sections of the public during the first war, in May 1939 took steps to secure the right of conscientious objection. In a broadcast of 27 August 1939 Temple honoured the pacifist vocation as a call from God, though he thought it was a mistake to regard it as a vocation for all Christians.[29] In October 1939 an eirenic collection of prayers for war-time, *Per Christum Vinces*, was published. It was a revised version of a first war collection edited by Ethel M. Barton who had been on the staff of *The Challenge*, the periodical of which Temple then was editor. Leslie Weatherhead in *Thinking Aloud in War-Time* published in December 1939, quoted against pacifism a passage from *The Faith and the War* (edited by F. J. Foakes Jackson 1916). He warned his readers against anti-German hysteria by quoting examples from the first war when even a German hymn tune could scandalize a congregation. In July 1939 Winnington Ingram, aged 81, at last retired from being Bishop of London, to everyone's relief. He had learned nothing from the scandal which his war-time utterances had given to the inter-war generation. His *A Second Day of God* (1940) was as naive and jingoistic as his *A Day of God* (1914). A. C. Don quoted in his Diary for 13 July 1939, a speaker at that day's farewell to the bishop who had called him 'the Peter Pan' of the bench. Less indulgently, John Kent describes him as 'a prime example of a new soft-centred conception of episcopacy'.[30]

First war precedents were on the whole helpful. In one case they were disastrous. Allied stories of German atrocities in the first war, some fabrications of propaganda, boomeranged with terrible effects during the second war. Arthur Ponsonby's *Falsehood in War Time* (1928) convinced large sections of the public that atrocity stories are almost always to be disbelieved.[31] (Ponsonby in the Lords debate on Abyssinia, on 23 October 1935 deplored Lang's condemnation of the Italian invasion.) According to Walter Laqueur (*The Terrible Secret*, 1980), by 1942 the Foreign Office, the State Department, the Red Cross and the Vatican knew about the Nazi extermination camps. Hugh Trevor-Roper, who early on saw documented, if fragmentary evidence, reviewed Laqueur's book in the *Listener* (1 January 1981). He wrote:

> Between the reception of evidence and belief in its conclusion there is a great psychological gulf; and in wartime, when so much is uncertain – when hatred breeds passion and passion is exploited by propaganda – it is prudent to suspend judgement. I recall that I suspended my own judgement and only gradually, many months later, drew from that dreadful evidence the conclusion which it entailed.

In August 1944 Alexander Werth, the BBC correspondent behind the Soviet lines, sent a detailed report about a German extermination camp. The BBC refused to use it, regarding it as propaganda. In December 1939 Weatherhead told his readers that one of the most famous first war atrocity stories had been fabricated. But he was prepared to treat as unimpeachable evidence the stories of tortures in the German concentration camps derived from the Government White Paper of October 1939 and to use such brutalities as an argument against pacifism. But believing in the cruelty of concentration camps was much easier than believing that Jews were being systematically exterminated. It was only when the camps were liberated and films began to be shown in cinemas that the public, seeing, did at last believe.

The first war opened a painfully deep gulf between those at home and those at the front. But from September 1939 everyone was in the front line. Vera Brittain wrote in 1940 that in the first war, England's 'ordeal was mainly vicarious': there was 'the anguish of detached suspense' as relatives waited daily for news of their fighting men who lived 'some far-off unimaginable existence of which only the few women who went abroad as nurses and canteen workers had the remotest conception'.[32] (Brittain had served as a nurse; her fiancé was killed in action.) In the second war, parish clergy were not so vulnerable to the charge, often levelled against them between 1914 and 1918, that they exhorted others to a sacrifice that they themselves declined. Clergy, like everyone else, suffered the bombing. They ministered in the shelters, took their turn as ARP wardens and some joined the Home Guard. Bishops moved out of their palaces or into one section of them, and lost most of their servants. In 1940 Garbett, then Bishop of Winchester, released his chauffeur for war service. At the age of 65 he learned to drive and tirelessly visited heavily bombed areas of his diocese like Southampton. The Bishop of Ripon in his diocesan letter for May 1940 announced with relief that he was moving out of his Victorian palace into a smaller house. The palace became a Barnardo's home for eighty girls. It was (he wrote) no longer either financially possible or morally justifiable to live in a palace with over twenty bedrooms and eighty-four acres of ground, which required six indoor and three outdoor staff. As Garbett entered York Minster to be enthroned as Archbishop of York on 11 June 1942 he whispered to Barry, Bishop of Southwell, on the steps, 'Just had time to make the beds'.

Another important difference between the two wars was that many who had been vocal dissenters during the first war, became wholehearted supporters of the second. Ramsay MacDonald, the leader of the Labour Party at the beginning of the first war, was one of its leading opponents. Between the wars the Labour Party contained a considerable number of pacifists and pacifiers. But in May 1940, the

Labour Party under Attlee joined Churchill in a coalition. J. B. Priestley (who in 1940 became almost as much a symbol of Britain as Churchill) on 7 July said in one of his broadcasts that he was 'heartened and inspired' to see Winston Churchill and Ernest Bevin representing the two halves of Britain, sitting side by side on the front bench, a symbol of the new national unity.[33] The pacifiers had been deflated by the failure of appeasement. Though there were considerably more conscientious objectors in the second war than in the first, they were better treated, so their dissent was marginalized. Certain of those who had been notable dissenters in the first war, like Herbert Morrison, C. E. M. Joad, Bertrand Russell and Kingsley Martin, now supported the war effort.

The case of Kingsley Martin, editor of the *New Statesman*, is particularly instructive. His father was a Congregational minister, whose whole life exemplified the dissenting belief in the primacy of the individual conscience. In the first war Kingsley Martin was a CO and served as a stretcher-bearer with the Friends' Ambulance Unit. On 22 June 1940 he told his readers that Britain must never surrender to Nazism. He headed his leader 'If not – ': a quotation from Daniel 3.17–18: 'our God whom we serve is able to deliver us from the burning, fiery furnace . . . But if not, be it known unto thee, O king, that we will not serve thy god . . .' This declaration was a remarkable moment in the history of English political and religious dissent. Significantly, the text was one that he remembered his father using for a sermon. He explained in his autobiography: 'I found that my own Dissenting past had ceased to be an obstacle to accepting the war; on the contrary, I had turned into something like a Covenanter.' (The seventeenth century once again exercised an influence on the dissenting tradition.) Putting aside his life-long hostility to Churchill he recognized him as the only possible leader. Martin discovered that he was after all 'a patriot', though civilization might not survive and Britain might not win the war:

> We never imagined, as so many people did in 1914, that this was a war to end war, or that any good result could come from it. We were just forced into it by Nazi Germany; there was no alternative.[34]

The character of the actual fighting in the second war was also very different. The bloody impasse of trench warfare bonded the opposing armies into a sense of mutual plight, but isolated them from patriots at home. By contrast with this largely static warfare, in the second war, both German conquest and Allied liberation were effected by sweeps across vast areas of territory, exhilarating for both the servicemen and those at home on the winning side. Between 1914 and 1918 very few people in Britain were affected by the occasional German sea and air attacks. But in the second war, 'There was no barrier between soldier and civilian and no psychological trauma to be healed after the war was over, accordingly no flood of revelation ten years later. The Second War did not reproduce the morbid states of the First, because the load was shared.'[35] In trench warfare you could see the enemy, smell his cooking, and during lulls, shout across the trenches and even sing hymns and carols together.[36] Much of the fighting in the second war was conducted at a distance by technology which required more ancillary services and fewer engaged in face-to-face combat. In any case, Churchill and other Western leaders were haunted by memories of the Somme and Passchendaele. They were determined to avoid the huge casualties of the first war, so for example they delayed the opening of the second front and hoped to cripple Germany by mass bombing, instead of making a frontal assault in 1942/3. Whereas during the first war 745,000 British servicemen died, in the second war, service casualties were 300,000. A glance at any war memorial listing the names of both wars confirms the contrast.

The first war began with excitement, but disillusionment grew both during the war and after it was over. The second war began without high emotion but with a deep conviction of the justice of the cause which deepened as the war proceeded. Forty years later this conviction still remains unshaken, except for absolute pacifists. So whereas the reputation of the English churches has suffered ever since as a result of their support of the 1914–18 war, their standing was on the whole enhanced by their conduct during the second war. In 1918, even a month before the Armistice, there was no expectation of a speedy Allied victory. From about 1942/3, by contrast, it was pretty clear that an Allied victory was only a matter of time. So by February 1944, the *Guardian* was publishing a series of articles entitled 'When it is over' and a Midland Bank advertisement in the issue of 14 April was headed 'Business Enterprise After the War'. Yet just as Remembrance Day still draws upon rituals almost entirely devised in 1919, so the first war continues to haunt and scarify the communal memory in Britain, whereas the second war is on the whole looked back to with nostalgia. One thinks of poems like 'The Great War' by Vernon Scannell, 'MCMXIV' by Philip Larkin and 'Six Young Men' by Ted Hughes, all published between 1957 and 1964. The subject of all three is the First World War, which ended before their authors were born.

The victory of 1945 was very different from that of 1918. After 1918 it was possible for a decade or more to cling to the belief that lasting peace had been secured. The second war concluded with the revelations of the death camps and the dropping of the atomic bombs. The unwillingness of the West to share the secrets of the bomb with the Russians and the West's alarm about communist machinations in eastern Europe were causing deep rifts in the alliance by September 1945. It was less than a year after victory in Europe, that Churchill in a speech at Fulton on 5 March 1946 sombrely declared: 'An iron curtain has descended across the Continent.' Three popular novels, *Animal Farm* (1945) (whose publication was delayed for a year by fears it would offend the Russians), *Nineteen Eighty-Four* (1949), both by George Orwell, and *Lord of the Flies* (1954) by William Golding, violently and decisively repudiated the Rousseauistic tradition which had nourished left-wing utopianism since the French Revolution. After six years of Labour rule, the socialist politician R. H. S. Crossman wrote in *New Fabian Essays* (1952): 'The evolutionary and the revolutionary philosophies of progress have both proved false. Judging by the facts, there is far more to be said for the Christian doctrine of original sin than for Rousseau's fantasy of the noble savage, or Marx's vision of the classless society.'[37] His indebtedness to Niebuhr here is obvious.

In the inter-war period no one pilloried George V or British political leaders for having held friendly meetings with the Kaiser before 1914. But after September 1939 no British politician wanted to be dubbed an appeaser, or have it recalled that he once warmly shook hands with Hitler. In the *Guardian* of 14 March 1941 Dean Cranage of Norwich questioned that journal's description of the Munich agreement as 'infamy' the week before, argued the case for the incorporation of the Sudeten Germans and asked what Chamberlain should have done. But he was spitting into the wind as protests published on 21 March showed. So though the period after the second war was characterized by foreboding rather than by any conviction that the war had brought a lasting peace, none but pacifists regarded it as pointless. 'Despite all the killing and destruction that accompanied it, the Second World War was a good war' is the (over-sanguine) concluding sentence of A. J. P. Taylor's book *The Second World War* (1976). Elsewhere he has written:

> In the second world war the British people came of age. This was a people's war. Not only were their needs considered. They themselves wanted to win . . . No English soldier who rode with the tanks into liberated Belgium or saw the German murder camps at

Dachau or Buchenwald could doubt that the war had been a noble crusade.

But it was not 'a profound spiritual experience' as the first war had been, but was fought prosaically, without doubt and disenchantment.[38] So convinced has Britain become that the second war was its 'finest hour' that it sometimes acts as if it has had no significant experience or history since 1945.[39]

9

WAR-TIME MINISTRIES

Ecumenism in war time

In the first war ecumenism was still in its infancy. After the war, the non-Roman churches, shocked by the war and their failure to witness to the universality of Christianity, created various ecumenical fellowships and organizations. By the mid-1930s many believed that some of these strands ought to be drawn together into a World Council of Churches. In May 1938 the Provisional Committee of the WCC held its first meeting. But it was not until 1948 that a World Assembly could be held formally to constitute it. During the war, the embryonic WCC in Geneva maintained relationships with Christians in Germany, most of the European churches and with those of the United States. It also did notable work among refugees and prisoners of war. Some Christians hoped that the WCC would speak out about the war. William Temple, in a letter in May 1940 to the General Secretary (Visser't Hooft), disagreed; it would be difficult, almost impossible for Christians to meet again after the war under its auspices if it had taken sides in the conflict, he argued.[1] During the first war there were few if any signs of German resistance to the Kaiser's policies, visible to world opinion. But from at least the arrest of Niemöller in 1937, the resistance of some Christians to Hitler became known throughout the world. Thereafter, not all Germans could be regarded as Nazis.

During the second war the existence of broadcasting enabled Christians in different countries to maintain their relationships throughout the years of bitter divisions and conflicts. The Religious Broadcasting Department of the BBC, under James Welch, supported by leading British churchmen and by Visser't Hooft, was determined to demonstrate the universality of Christianity. Temple's broadcasts on war issues were carried by the European and World Services. Beginning with Christmastide 1941, services were broadcast to

Germany. In 1942 the appointment of Francis House (who had worked for Visser't Hooft) to take charge of overseas, and particularly German, religious broadcasting led to an increase of transmissions to Christians in Europe. Weekly German services began, conducted mainly by refugee pastors. Each Christmas during the war Bishop Bell broadcast a special message to Christians in Germany.[2] Such broadcasts were a marvellous sustenance for Christians suffering from isolation and persecution. In 1942, Eivind Berggrav, Bishop of Oslo, was arrested and confined under guard in a forest cabin. One day the woman who brought him milk managed to whisper: 'My husband listened to London yesterday evening, and he heard the Archbishop of Canterbury pray for you.' Berggrav no longer felt alone but part of a great ecumenical fellowship.[3] In January 1942, an English officer in Dachau told Niemöller, a fellow prisoner, that he had listened on his secret radio to a service of intercession for him on his fiftieth birthday. The Archbishop of Canterbury had conducted the service and Bishop Bell had preached.[4]

The Ministry of Information included a 'Religions Division'. Various churches and the Jewish faith were represented on its staff. The assiduous and ambitious R. R. Williams (Bishop of Leicester 1953–78) soon became its Director. As well as arranging broadcasts to Europe he edited a regular bulletin, *The Spiritual Issues of the War* which provided a stream of information about the churches in Europe. Williams who came originally from a Brethren background (a fact he usually concealed) had worked his way up from commercial school to Cambridge. At the MOI he joined the Home Guard and took his turn at sentry duty in clerical collar and uniform with a rifle at the ready. Later in *Who's Who* he was able to celebrate his rise from private to officer.[5] In a sermon (reprinted in the *Guardian* of 8 January 1943) he portrayed with characteristic pugnacity but in exaggerated colours the resistance of the European, including the German, churches to Nazism. The Religions Division was always in danger of becoming an adjunct to government propaganda, a trap which Welch and his colleagues more successfully avoided.[6] Christian leaders were exhilarated that they could be both patriotic and ecumenical. No longer was the church to be apologized for; it was living, contemporary evidence of the power of the gospel. 'These are very great days for the Christian church' declared Nathaniel Micklem in one of his broadcasts 'Christian News and Commentary' (regularly reprinted by the *Guardian*). 'In Czechoslovakia a Roman Catholic dean and a Protestant pastor and his wife faced the Gestapo firing squad together.'[7] This new solidarity experienced by European Catholics and Protestants bore fruit in the post-war period. When at the Second Vatican Council (1962–65) ecumenism was particularly supported by the Dutch, French and German bishops, someone commented that the 'hand of Hitler' was very evident. At home too the 'super-national' character of the church became more visible than ever before. At a Religion and Life week in Hull in 1943 the speakers included a French pastor, a German emigré, a Chinese Christian and a Russian Orthodox. However, since those heady days it has become clear that Christian resistance to Hitler in Europe was much more patchy and equivocal than the ardent ecumenists of war-time Britain believed.[8]

The war also greatly stimulated ecumenical co-operation within Britain. One result of the Oxford Conference of 1937 was the creation of two ecumenical groups of non-Roman Christians which in 1942 developed into the British Council of Churches. In the dark days of 1940 these two groups, encouraged by Temple, planned a series of Religion and Life weeks. The first was held at Bristol in September 1940. In May 1943 Temple told the Convocation of Canterbury that the public was ready to pay attention to the Christian message if only it was proclaimed by the churches united together.[9] Bishop Barry believed that the success of these weeks showed that though few were willing to come to church, many would attend meetings on neutral ground. So in 1944, for example, Temple spoke on successive days to 2,000 people at the Swansea Guildhall and to 2,000 at Bournemouth Pavilion and to another 1,000 at an overflow meeting. But how ecumenical ought these occasions to be? Anglo-Catholics and other strict churchmen disapproved strongly when Unitarians and Jews were involved. In the first week of the war, J. H. Oldham, architect of the Oxford Conference, approached the Archbishops and other church leaders. The result was the launching of the influential *Christian News-Letter*, edited by Oldham, which fortnightly for the next ten years published a highly intelligent commentary on questions of the day. It cut right across denominational boundaries.

The churches are always tempted to try to use catastrophes to strengthen their position in society. In the 1914–18 war the Roman Catholic church in Britain, conscious of centuries of anti-Catholic feeling, and aware that its Irish and Italian connections branded it a foreign community with external loyalties, sought to prove its patriotism beyond any doubt. So it gave more wholehearted and uncritical support to the war-effort than either the Church of England or the Free Churches. It is illuminating to compare the contributions of the various churches to *King Albert's Book*, a tribute to Belgium, edited by Hall Caine and published at Christmas 1914. The Archbishop of

Canterbury wrote in general terms about 'the ennobling fidelity . . . of a little land'. Dr John Clifford, the Baptist leader, conscious of the need to defend a scorned tradition, compared King Albert to Oliver Cromwell. Cardinal Bourne used the opportunity to beat the Roman Catholic drum: when Roman Catholics were banished from Oxford and Cambridge in 1561, they found refuge in Louvain; in Belgium so many British had seen 'for the first time in action the living practice of the Catholic Faith'; Belgian priests had helped to gather the plentiful harvest from the second spring of Roman Catholicism in England.

When the second war broke out, Cardinal Hinsley of Westminster was determined that British Roman Catholics should again be seen to be patriotic. It was essential to destroy the suspicion that Roman Catholics were pro-fascist. So J. C. Heenan, in his biography of Hinsley published in 1944, began by emphasizing Hinsley's opposition to Fascist and Nazi tyranny. Like a defensive Nonconformist writing the biography of a Free Church leader, for twelve pages he quoted from newspapers ranging from the *Daily Herald* to the *Baptist Times* to demonstrate the nation's high regard for Hinsley. In order to understand this, we have to remember that Roman Catholics were isolated from the mainstream of English life, largely because they were proud to emphasize their dissent from English consensual religion. Archbishop Lang returning from a function to Lambeth in the Cardinal's car in July 1939, thought it would not be discreet to invite him into the Palace, despite their friendship.[10] Roman Catholics often isolated themselves by behaving imperialistically. At the beginning of the war Heenan visited school children from his parish who had been evacuated to Norfolk. After he had said Mass there, the headmaster wrote in the parish magazine: 'Thus our Lord came back to Ingham for the first time since the so-called Reformation.' Not surprisingly Christians in the village felt affronted.[11]

On 10 December 1939 Cardinal Hinsley broadcast an address entitled 'The Sword of the Spirit', which was as fiercely anti-Russian as anti-Nazi. He appealed, not as might have been expected for the defence of Catholicism, but for 'our civilisation . . . nourished and made by our Christian faith'. *The Bond of Peace* (1941) in which this appears was prefixed by a statement by a Cardinal O'Connell: 'Because Hitler controverts the laws of God, of nature, of the individual and of all civilised and cultured states, he is doomed to perdition . . .' In his Foreword, Hinsley tried to present the Pope and the German hierarchy as being as unequivocally anti-Nazi as himself. Thus Hinsley, a blunt Yorkshireman, was eager to give voice to an unqualified and belligerent patriotism which Lang, Temple and Bell were all attempting studiously to avoid. No wonder that Churchill said: 'There are only two men I trust to speak to the nation on the aims of this country at war: they are Cardinal Hinsley and myself.'[12]

As a result of Hinsley's broadcast, a group of Roman Catholics, including the lay historian Christopher Dawson, met with Hinsley and created 'The Sword of the Spirit' movement which was launched in August 1940.[13] Dawson defined its aims in very broad terms: 'it is vital that all the positive intellectual and spiritual forces of Western culture should come together in defence of their common values . . .' Like many people in Britain at that time Hinsley was haunted by the fall of France, and in his address inaugurating the Sword, he blamed it on 'duty neglected, easy living, lack of loyalty, disunion'.[14] On 7 August Hinsley explained the movement to his bishops: 'After the collapse in France, it seemed urgently necessary to show that we in this country were loyal . . . I had reason to fear propaganda against British Catholics if steps were not taken to forestall it.'[15] Hinsley was right. The *Church Times* for example, whose editor had been disgusted by the Roman Catholic acclamation of Franco as a Christian hero, after the fall of France regularly reiterated its charge that the Vatican and some French Catholics were pro-fascist and pro-Pétain.[16] The Ministry of Information was so impressed by the patriotic value of the Sword literature that it printed six of the pamphlets itself.

Two meetings organized by the Sword at the Stoll Opera House, Kingsway on 10–11 May 1941 were packed despite heavy air raids. The Cardinal presided at the first, the Archbishop of Canterbury at the second. On 10 May Hinsley said that the meeting demonstrated the fundamental unity of all in the task of defending the liberty of mankind. The *Church Times* on 16 May for once rejoiced: 'a remarkable demonstration of a united Christian front, leading Churchmen and Nonconformists sitting at the same platform with Jesuit Fathers and a Cardinal in all the glory of his crimson'. Both meetings passed the same resolution urging Commonwealth governments to accept the Ten Peace Points set out in a letter to the *Times* on 21 December 1940 signed by the two Archbishops, Cardinal Hinsley and the Moderator of the Free Church Federal Council. In five points Pope Pius XII had proclaimed the right of nations to independence, and urged progressive disarmament and international arbitration. The signatories added 'five standards' from the Oxford Conference of 1937[17] as a basis for economic policy: '(1) Extreme inequality in wealth and possessions should be abolished; (2) Every child, regardless of race or class, should have equal opportunities of education . . .; (3) The family as a social unit must be safeguarded; (4) The sense of a Divine vocation must be restored to man's daily work; (5) The resources of the earth should be used as God's gifts to the whole human race . . .' (These standards were an early expression of that war-time social consensus which was largely maintained by post-war governments until Mrs Thatcher radically challenged it.)

However, this united Christian front, made possible by the collapse of France and by the threat of German invasion, soon began to fall apart. Hinsley had not convinced many of his own flock. Hardly any of his bishops attended the Stoll meetings. The Archbishop of Cardiff told Hinsley that clergy and laity had been scandalized by instances of common prayer between Catholics and Protestants. Lang was lukewarm about the movement, despite or because of Bell's enthusiasm. Some Free Churchmen were suspicious. Ultra-protestants were outraged. Hinsley was reprimanded by the Vatican. In August 1941 at the first AGM of the Sword, non-Roman Catholics were allowed to become only 'associates', the executive was confined to Roman Catholics and the organization was brought under the control of the hierarchy. The *Church Times* on 15 August published a bitter leader headed 'Not Excalibur': 'an unexpected cold douche' had been thrown over hopes of Christian co-operation. What might have been 'a national Excalibur' had been turned into a 'weapon of exclusively Roman Catholic piety and propaganda'. Bishop Bell and officials of the Sword in letters to the *Church Times* of 22 August tried to pick up what pieces they could. In September 1941 Hinsley received the opinion of his two theologians about the status of the movement in the eyes of the Holy See. They had come to an extraordinary conclusion: 'there is only one way in which non-Catholics can be admitted to full membership of the Sword of the Spirit and that is to exclude all public religious activity, Catholic as well as non-Catholic, from the Movement'.[18] After months of negotiation in which Bell played a leading part, it was resolved in January 1942 that the Sword, and Religion and Life could at least work in parallel. But even that limited degree of co-operation was not always easy.

The death of Hinsley in 1943 and his replacement by Cardinal Griffin finally snuffed out the high hopes which had been initially raised. Nevertheless a precedent had been set. Communication had been established between Roman Catholics and other Christians. Just after the end of the war, Nathaniel Micklem, the Congregational theologian, in one of his broadcasts paid a warm tribute to the Vatican's relief work and to the international character of the Roman Catholic church. Despite disappointments, groups organizing the Sword, and

Religion and Life weeks had co-operated. In Europe Christians had drawn together in a manner not seen since the Reformation.[19]

The formation of the British Council of Churches in 1942 inaugurated a new era of co-operation between the Anglican and Free Churches. Temple, in his enthronement sermon in April 1942, described the new world fellowship of Christians as 'the great new fact of our era'.[20] Whereas the National Mission in the first war had been a wholly Anglican affair, the Religion and Life weeks were fully ecumenical. However, when Neville Gorton became Bishop of Coventry in 1943 and enthusiastically took up the idea of creating a Chapel of Unity for the new Cathedral, the *Church Times* on 2 April 1943 was predictably horrified: 'their Cathedral is to be the scene of a Pan-Protestant tattoo'.

The presence of German refugees and German and Italian prisoners of war provided another ecumenical opportunity. But anyone who held out a hand of friendship had to contend with 'Vansittartism'. Sir Robert (later Lord) Vansittart, the Government's Chief Diplomatic Adviser, in a series of broadcasts towards the end of 1940, argued that the Germans had always been brutal warmongers. Though the MOI was undecided whether to promote Vansittartism, it sometimes gave the impression that all things German were abhorrent. Temple taught a very different attitude. In the autumn of 1939 he said that we should not try to usurp the office of judge. 'We dare not come into the presence of the Holy God pointing out to Him that some others of His children are even worse than we are. We all stand before the judgement-seat of God . . .' When we pray we wish to find our enemies kneeling beside us.[21] In 1942 he asserted that Germany should be re-educated, not corporately punished by a harsh settlement. It was by no means the only aggressor in European history. 'A nation must not be personified. It consisted of a multitude of individuals.'[22] In 1944 Garbett told the York Convocation that the Christian must set his face against 'wholesale and indiscriminate vengeance on the German people'. But those guilty of atrocities must be punished. After the war we must renew relationships with the German churches.[23] In November 1940 Vera Brittain visited St Paul's and saw the bomb-shattered altar. She was given a booklet of prayers. She was relieved and moved to discover that it expressed penitence for Britain's sins and that it included the petition, 'From bitterness and vindictiveness against our enemies, from persecution or suspicion of refugees and aliens: Good Lord deliver us'.[24]

When war broke out, Bell immediately wrote a letter of comfort to all refugee pastors. He founded the German Christian Fellowship which throughout the war held monthly services in London in German and English. When, in May 1940 and the following months, almost all aliens were interned, Bell was outraged that known anti-Nazis had been included. In July he visited them in the Isle of Man and at Huyton. Pastor Hildebrandt, one of those interned, remembered: 'who would have time for a few thousand refugees, when the fate of England and the West was in the balance? Who would speak and act for them, these virtually stateless people? Who else but the Bishop of Chichester?' When Bell arrived in Douglas he was rendered almost speechless by the sight of so many of his friends in captivity. At Huyton (Dean Dwelly wrote to Mrs Bell) 'He was seated, like Jesus, just "hearing them and asking them questions" – as humble as that.' On 6 August Bell continued his protests in the Lords, pointing out that a hundred and fifty of the internees in Douglas alone had been in German concentration camps. Lang and Temple supported his efforts, but he was accused of being pro-Nazi, and the *Church Times* was dismissive. The campaign by Bell, the Quakers and others led to a considerable number of internees being released in the next few months. On 18 May 1941 Bell broadcast on 'German and Austrian Refugees: how they can help us'. He gathered released pastors in London and told them that they would be given opportunities to preach about the Confessing Church. In 1942 he helped to create an institute for training German laypeople for Christian service in Germany after the war.[25]

By the end of the war, 400,000 German prisoners of war were held in Britain.[26] In 1944 Bell asked a Swedish pastor, Birger Forell to minister to them. He was assisted by Dr Herbert Hartwell (formerly Hirschwald) who had been a member of Niemöller's congregation. With Bell's assistance he and his family had escaped by the last train from Berlin in 1939. Under Micklem he trained for the Congregational ministry. Forell and Hartwell worked in association with a Committee which included the Quakers, YMCA and Red Cross. When a War Office official assumed that Forell would follow 'the Vansittart line', Forell replied: 'I will treat everyone as if he were my own son'. At Comrie Camp, Perthshire which had been defiantly Nazi, on 11 November 1945, 2,850 of the 3,000 POWs stood on the parade ground for the two minutes' silence as a sign that they had accepted a declaration of penitence drawn up by a German Jewish refugee, now a British army sergeant. Contact with the British population was at first forbidden, partly to avoid attacks on the POWs. At that period a Quaker lady of over eighty living in Shropshire, deliberately stood at her window each Sunday as the prisoners marched to Mass. Every week the men looked out for her smiling face.

The Rev. Charles Cranfield, then a Methodist army chaplain, also ministered in the camps. In 1946 through the British Council of Churches he invited local congregations to welcome prisoners to worship, the only opportunity then open for fraternization. Soon German voices were heard in churches, chapels and meeting houses and relationships began to form. The Bishops of Sheffield, Lichfield and Chichester all argued in the Lords on 11 July for a more civilized treatment of POWs. By contrast, the Apostolic Delegate, Monsignor Godfrey, was unresponsive when Forell approached him in 1946. One Roman Catholic monastery was prepared to loan a harmonium to a camp only on condition that it was not used by Protestants. But many local Roman Catholic priests and laypeople were more welcoming, and a Roman Catholic laywoman formed a Prisoners-of-War Assistance Society. At Christmas 1946 for the first time, German prisoners sat down to a meal with British families. At Peterborough, 2,000 POWs packed the cathedral and heard the bishop end his sermon with 'Wir heissen Euch hoffen' (We bid you hope). Mansfield College, Bell and others provided books for a special camp for theological students. Jürgen Moltmann, the German theologian, was converted to Christianity during his time as a POW, part of it spent in Britain: 'the experience of misery and forsakenness and daily humiliation gradually built up into an experience of God'.[27]

The last prisoners did not return home until August 1948. After his return a Bavarian Lutheran pastor wrote in English to a Baptist minister who had befriended him. He described how, as he sailed from Britain, he recalled 'all the kindliness I found in your country and promised within myself never to forget how much your very Christian fellowship did to alleviate all the unavoidable hardships of captivity, blessing all my British friends and their country'. Bishop Hunter treasured to the end of his days a Christmas crib set made by POWs who had shared in a Christmas Eve service in Sheffield Cathedral in 1946 at which Bishop Dibelius of Berlin had preached.[28]

In the Orkneys, Italian POWs were employed building concrete causeways to seal the eastern approaches to Scapa Flow. In 1943 they converted two Nissen huts into a chapel at Lambholm. Its concrete altar is flanked by two painted windows of St Francis and St Catherine of Siena. The chapel also includes frescoes, six candelabra and an iron sanctuary screen all wrought by the prisoners. When they left in 1945 the Lord Lieutenant promised that the chapel would be cherished. Members of three different Communions serve on a committee which keeps it in repair. An outdoor calvary was erected in 1961 as a sign of the friendship which had grown up between Orkney and the architect's home town of Moena in Italy. His concrete statue of St George slaying the dragon still stands in the camp square – a symbol of the prisoners' victory over defeat and loneliness.[29]

The ethics of warfare

In June 1940, the month of Dunkirk, a good pious, churchgoing laundress remarked to the Dean of King's College London: 'Well, we have only *God* to care for us now. We must just *forget our Christianity* and get on with the war.'[30] Most English people thought the same. Temple did not. Of all the leaders of the churches it was he, as Archbishop of York 1929–42 and as Archbishop of Canterbury 1942–44, who developed the most comprehensive theological attitude to the ethics of warfare. In this he was greatly influenced by Niebuhr.

Archbishop Lang by contrast had nothing original left to say. He was too identified with appeasement. Almost 75 when war broke out, he was old and tired. He represented an earlier age. He had been Archbishop of York in the first war. As Vicar of Portsea he had witnessed the Kaiser and Edward VII kneeling by Queen Victoria's coffin. His reputation never recovered from his calamitous broadcast at the time of Edward VIII's abdication, when his unctuous moralizing seemed to many like kicking a man when he was already bruised enough. His insensitive and patronizing reference in the same broadcast to George VI's stammer incensed the King's speech therapist. It also increased the King's nervousness about public speaking.[31] By 1939 Lang had become an embarrassment. James Welch, Director of Religious Broadcasting, regarded Lang's broadcast at the outbreak of war as trivial and disastrous, and he and his department felt alarmed at the prospect of his broadcast for the Day of Prayer in September 1940. They devoutly wished that protocol would allow them to invite someone else.[32] Lang announced his resignation to the Convocations on 21 January 1942. Once again his instinct for self-dramatization and his longing for human sympathy led him into another catastrophic utterance:

> You can realise what it means for any man who for long years has been in the very centre of great affairs of Church and State to contemplate a sudden withdrawal to some obscure place in the circumference, and to face the restraints and inconveniences of very slender means.

This was an extraordinary remark to make for one who was being

granted a peerage and a 'grace and favour' house from the King at
Kew. Lang's annual pension of £1,500 was four times the stipend of
many incumbents. Average male earnings in July 1940 were £4.10s
(£234 a year). Agricultural workers from November 1941 received a
minimum of £3 a week – their wages had averaged only 34s.7d in
1938. No wonder the *Daily Mirror* on 22 January, reporting the size
of his pension, quoted: 'Blessed are the meek, for they shall inherit
the earth.' Lang's chaplain realized how important it was to conceal
the fact that Lang had also received a gift of £15,000 from an American
millionaire.[33]

When, at the age of 60, Temple went to Canterbury he was at the
height of his powers and influence. Bernard Shaw commented: 'To a
man of my generation an Archbishop of Temple's enlightenment was
a realized impossibility.' No Archbishop had ever been enthroned
with a greater welcome or higher expectations. William Paton, the
Presbyterian and ecumenical leader, told Temple that he was accepted
as a spokesman of the whole church in a new way by Nonconformists
and even by the Church of Scotland. Paton addressed him 'My dear
William'. Whoever wrote to Lang as 'My dear Cosmo'? When Temple
was still at York, he told Lang: 'I have done something you will never
do!' Lang stiffened. 'I have stood in a queue for a bus outside Lambeth
Palace!'[34]

Edward Carpenter provides a shrewd assessment:

> William Temple was a larger-than-life person, prodigal in his gifts,
> lavish in his generosity, wide in his interests, abundant in his energy,
> holy in his dedication . . . Indeed it is Temple's very wholeness,
> the clarity of his vision, and his preoccupation with ideas (maybe a
> legacy of his early idealism) which make it difficult to come to grips
> with him. The astonishing thing, however, is that this philosopher
> and theologian . . . ended up by 'registering' with ordinary people
> in the sense that he became the embodiment of a vision – the vision
> of a caring Church which believed that social justice mattered.[35]

In 1944 Henson described Temple as 'a very remarkable man'. 'I have
a real affection for him, though a deepening distrust of his wisdom . . .'
Henson disliked his socialist sympathies, criticized him for speaking
too much and for being 'deeply affected by the compromising habit
of Lambeth'. To Henson, Temple's death in 1944 was 'almost tragic'.
But he had died (Henson believed) when the stream of opinion
flowed strongly with him and had escaped its inevitable ebb. His
enthronement sermon had over-emphasized the importance of
ecumenism and the COPEC/Malvern tradition, while neglecting the

deeper problems facing Christianity itself.[36] But many were devastated by his sudden death. On the other hand Churchill seems to have been relieved, even pleased.[37]

The absence of tragedy and conflict in Temple's life has been often remarked upon. Once he and Bishop Gore were walking together after a meeting which had to be adjourned because Gore had lost his temper. Gore, gloomy and miserable, lamented: 'It is a terrible thing to have a bad temper.' But seeing Temple's beaming smile he burst out: 'But it is not so bad as having a good temper.'[38] Temple's idealist cast of mind drew him to the comparatively untroubled Jesus of the Fourth Gospel rather than to the Jesus of St Mark who wrestled in Gethsemane and died crying that God had forsaken him. 'Temple does not disturb and shake your mind, baffle and bewilder you, at once repel and draw you, as the greatest theologians do' comments Vidler.[39] Perhaps church and nation would have gained more if Temple had been a chaplain in the trenches rather than devoted his energies to Life and Liberty. In the late 1930s Temple began to be more aware of the irrationality of human experience, but it did not really disturb the serenity of his faith. Rooted in the pre-1914 world, he remained largely unconscious of the crucial challenges to faith of secularization, pluralism and modernity. Gore, on the other hand, said that the only difficult Christian doctrine was that God is love, and that the whole of his life had been a struggle to believe it. Gore also realized that the majority of people had been forced to fight the organized resistance of the well-to-do to improve their position. Temple, by contrast, talked too easily about fellowship and reconciliation in national life. But he became more realistic about international relations in the mid-1930s. It was congruent with Temple's optimism that he did not believe that man could do evil for its own sake. It is also significant that he was uninterested in psychological thinkers such as Freud, Jung and Adler.

Just after the war, Micklem paid particular tribute to Temple who had enabled British Christians to grasp that 'justice is the foundation of love, and that justice must be *enforced*'.[40] Temple's distinction between ethics appropriate to the individual and those appropriate to social relationships owed much to Niebuhr. In the *Christian News-Letter* of 29 December 1943 Temple explained: 'Christian charity manifests itself in the temporal order as a supranatural discernment of, and adhesion to, *justice* in relation to the equilibrium of power. It is precisely fellowship or human love, with which too often Christian charity is mistakenly equated, that is *not* seriously relevant in that sphere.' Broadcasting on 27 August 1939, he asserted that no 'positive good' could be done by force: 'But evil can be checked and held back by force . . .' In November he wrote that, in an order which had departed from the rule of God, ethically we had to move from the absolute to the relative realm: 'there is no way that I can see in which we could redemptively suffer so as to change the heart of Germany and deliver Poles and Czechs'. The kingdom of God could not be advanced by war, but fighting could prevent Christian civilization from being destroyed:

> . . . it is our duty to do as citizens in support of the State things which it would be inappropriate to do as Churchmen in support of the Church and its cause. The soldiers are therefore quite right when they say that war is not Christianity, but they would be quite wrong if they went on to say that therefore Christians ought not to fight. The duty to fight is a civic duty which, if the cause is good, Christianity accepts and approves, but it is not a duty which has its origin in Christianity as such.

For Temple, Christian action in a fallen world inevitably involved compromise and the abandonment of ethical absolutism.[41] But the important distinctions which Temple made were too new and too subtle for most of the general public to grasp. His tutor at Oxford had warned him that he must not suppose he had solved a problem by finding a formula.

Temple's attitude to pacifism was similar to that of Niebuhr. In 1933 he wrote that though pacifism was an error, it was an invaluable counterbalance to uncritical nationalism.[42] In 1935 he created a storm by declaring that pacifism was 'heretical' – in a further statement he modified this to 'heretical in tendency'. Pacifism was Marcionite. But the New Testament does not abolish the Old. It was Manichaean holding that 'the material cannot be completely subordinated to the spiritual'. It was Pelagian regarding 'man as capable by the action of his own will of living by love only'. The law of love was not appropriate for unconverted or semi-converted nations. Charles Raven vehemently protested. It was Temple who was 'heretical' and who had committed 'an act of apostasy'. Temple replied that to call 'nations to act by love only, when justice is still insecure' would produce no actual result. Until the world was converted and war abolished, international relations must aim at justice not love.[43] Raven to the end of his life smarted from (in effect) being charged with heresy by his old friend. Temple, in his broadcast of August 1939, stated that for some, pacifism was 'a special vocation to bear this witness to the unity of all God's family and to the sovereignty of love'. That autumn, he likened the pacifist witness to the challenge to worldliness by the monastic vocation. But not all are called to be monks or nuns.

I have been urged to receive the evil of the Nazi régime into my own soul as a redemptive sacrifice, instead of resisting it. But no one has told me how I can do this. The actual effect of our all turning pacifists would probably be the continued obliteration of the Polish and Czech States, and the avoidance of any diminution of our own material wealth.

The 'notion that physiological life is absolutely sacred is Hindu or Buddhist, not Christian'.[44] In 1943 he edited a Penguin Special *Is Christ Divided?* It included a joint chapter by Temple and Raven in which they agreed that compromise between the pacifist and non-pacifist interpretations of Christianity was 'impossible'. But there was a common loyalty to Christ which bridged, if it did not annihilate, the gulf.

On 1 September 1939 the Germans horrified world opinion by bombing Warsaw. Chamberlain at the beginning of the war assured the Commons that the Government would never deliberately attack civilians to terrorize them. But by July 1940 Churchill had become convinced that only heavy bombing could defeat Hitler. In 1940/1, bombing was about the only aggressive act against Germany which was open to Britain. When the German blitz on Britain began in September 1940, Britain had been bombing German towns for five months. In February 1942 Bomber Command was directed to destroy the manufacturing capacity and morale of the German population by 'area bombing'. But British propaganda continued to proclaim two contradictory messages: that only military targets were being bombed, but that also the civilian population of Germany was being punished by heavy casualties. The policy of obliteration bombing was well known to, and popular with, many of the British population. So on 21 October 1943 the *Daily Telegraph* boasted that 'Hamburg has had the equivalent of at least 60 "Coventrys" '. In that month Sir Archibald Sinclair, Secretary for Air, explained to the Chief of the Air Staff that the Government had to proclaim that its policy was only to bomb military targets in order to quieten the Archbishop of Canterbury and other religious leaders 'whose moral condemnation of the bombing offensive might disturb the morale of Bomber Command crews'. Nor could it then be admitted (as was known from a survey of August 1941) that British bombing was wildly inaccurate, and that therefore the concept of strategic bombing was largely a fiction.[45]

It is difficult to understand why, throughout the war, Temple trusted Government assurances about its bombing policy. These assurances had a long history. At the Bishops' meeting on 28 June 1939 the Archbishop of Canterbury disclosed that he had corresponded with the Secretary for Air, Sir Kingsley Wood. The Minister stated that the Government accepted the declaration of the League of Nations in 1928: 'The intentional bombing of civilian populations is illegal.' At a meeting between the Archbishops and the Anglican Pacifist Fellowship at Lambeth on 11 June 1940, Temple told the pacifists forthrightly that if bombing of open towns were adopted as national policy, he would probably feel there was no longer anything worth fighting for. On 28 October 1941 Percy Hartill, Chairman of APF, wrote to Lang to protest that Churchill had adopted the very policy condemned at Lambeth. Lang was annoyed to be offered advice about the conduct of the war from those who objected to it in any shape or form, but with Temple's help drafted a conciliatory reply asserting that there had been no change in Government policy. But throughout the war, protests continued to arrive regularly at Lambeth. In 1942 letters critical of bombing policy appeared in the *Guardian* on 12 and 19 June. On 26 June, Paul Gliddon, Secretary of APF, quoted the assurance about bombing policy given at Lambeth. (The APF published a report of the meeting, as a leaflet, with the agreement of the Archbishops. The assurance about bombing policy was attributed to both Archbishops and slightly toned down.) Temple obtained another assurance from the Secretary for Air, Sinclair, on 17 July 1943, that it was 'no part of our policy wantonly to destroy cities – regardless of military objectives'. When Temple wrote on 4 November to a critic 'I do not think there has been any attack upon a centre which is not a military objective', the critic received this assurance with incredulity. On 7 April 1944 Temple wrote to another correspondent that bombing was confined to hindering the manufacture of munitions, but significantly added: 'this is more effectively done by the total dislocation of the whole community engaged in the work than by attack upon the factories themselves, which can be repaired with astonishing rapidity'.[46] Thus Temple had gradually shifted his ground since his declaration to APF in 1940. One of his basic convictions was expressed in a letter of 9 August 1943: 'The one thing that is certainly wrong is to fight ineffectively.'[47]

On the other hand, Temple set his face against blatant reprisals. On 9 July 1944 the *Sunday Express* published an article by D. R. Davies headed 'It is Time for Reprisals!'. Temple of course knew Davies very well. He had ordained him and written a Foreword to Davies' book *Secular Illusion or Christian Realism?* (1942). Davies argued that for every English person killed by flying bombs, ten Germans should be killed. Then flying bombs would cease. On 4 August he asked Temple why reprisals were worse than our own wholesale bombing. Germans need to experience judgment before they would repent. Temple replied that Britain regarded residential quarters in Germany in which war work was in progress as legitimate targets. Every area of Berlin probably contained a factory or two 'but I don't think Bomber Command cares whether it does or not. The object is to break up the whole organised life on which war activities depend.' But a policy of reprisals would only create more bitterness. As belligerents we would make bad judges. Flying bombs were no worse morally than the British bombing. 'I think it is right to say in general – "If you use gas, so shall we" . . . But to say "If you deliberately kill one innocent person we will kill ten – or even one" – seems to me precisely wrong.'[48]

In the air raid on Coventry on the night of 14 November 1940, 554 people were killed, 865 seriously hurt, 9 churches including the cathedral were destroyed, 2 hospitals and 21 factories were badly damaged. The Bishop of Coventry was Mervyn Haigh who had succeeded Bell as chaplain at Lambeth in 1924. At the mass funeral five days later, Haigh courageously spoke of the power of forgiveness. But sections of the press clamoured for reprisals. To the dismay of the *Church Times* and others, on 11 December, Haigh declared:

If the British Government were to decide that this form of attack will be used against German cities, if it continues to be used against ours, it might well be morally justified in coming to that conclusion . . . Nor do I believe that a nation need be morally degraded even by doing horrible things of a new kind in a war which it believes itself morally right in waging, so long as it does them utterly against its will, only so long as others do them against itself, and only if and as long as it seems necessary to do them in order to avert serious risks of defeat.

He took it for granted that the Government would give warning of its intention to retaliate in such circumstances.[49] (Temple believed the attack on Coventry to be a justifiable act of war.[50])

But on the morning after the raid, the Cathedral stonemason took two charred beams from the fallen roof, tied them in the form of a cross and planted it in a mound of rubble. On Christmas Day, Provost R. T. Howard, said in a broadcast service from the ruins: 'we are trying, hard as it may be, to banish all thoughts of revenge'. A group began to learn German so that after the war they could communicate with their ex-enemies. In January 1941, at the request of the Provost, the stonemason built an altar which still stands in the ruins. He set up the charred cross behind it, and carved 'Father Forgive' above the altar. The Provost explained that it did not mean 'Father Forgive Them': for no one is innocent. Thus began that notable ministry of reconciliation which Coventry cathedral has exercised among the nations of the world, and particularly to the German people.[51]

Throughout the war Bishop Bell was the most persistent and pugnacious critic within the churches, not only of Allied bombing policy but also of other aspects of Allied strategy towards Germany. His attitudes were derived from the principles of the Just War tradition and from Archbishop Davidson's application of them to the first war, when Bell was his chaplain.[52] In a letter to the *Times* of 17 April 1941 he appealed for an agreement between Britain and Germany to outlaw night bombing. Supported by advice from B. H. Liddell Hart, the leading military strategist, he regularly questioned Government assurances that only military targets were being bombed. In July 1943 he asked Temple to obtain a statement from the Government about their policy. But Temple refused because he did not share Bell's anxiety. In his *Diocesan Gazette* for September 1943 Bell condemned the growing spirit of vengeance and ruthlessness in Government and other quarters: 'To bomb cities as cities, deliberately to attack civilians, quite irrespective of whether or not they are actively contributing to the war effort is a wrong deed, whether done by the Nazis or by ourselves.' As a result of this statement, Duncan-Jones, Dean of Chichester asked Bell to withdraw from preaching at a Battle of Britain service in the cathedral. Bell agreed without demur, but it deepened his growing sense of isolation in church and nation.[53] However, support came from a surprising quarter – Bishop Headlam of Gloucester whose benign views of Nazism in the 1930s had so dismayed Bell. Headlam, in his diocesan magazine for December 1943 and in a letter to Temple of 1 January 1944, asserted that the massive bombing of Germany was not as militarily valuable as was being claimed and attacked it as 'very largely a war against civilians'.[54]

On 9 February 1944 Bell opened a major debate in the Lords on obliteration bombing. Beforehand Lord Woolton, a member of the Cabinet (later Conservative Party Chairman), told Bell that he and others hoped that he would not make the speech he knew he was going to make. He nevertheless added: 'But I also want to tell you that there isn't a soul who doesn't know that the only reason why you make it, is because you believe it is your duty to make it as a Christian priest.'[55] Bell began by recalling his opposition to Nazism since 1933. He reminded the peers that the Government at the beginning of the war, drew a clear distinction between military and non-military objectives, based on international law. But this had been abandoned. 'There must be a fair balance between the means employed and the purpose achieved. To obliterate a whole town because certain portions contain military and industrial establishments is to reject the balance.' The policy of obliteration was not 'a justifiable act of war'. Both the Prime Minister and Air-Marshal Harris had made it clear that it was the Government's intention to destroy Germany, city by city. Almost certainly, Dresden,[56] Augsburg, Munich and other towns with a great cultural heritage were on its list. This policy combined with a totally negative attitude towards the future of Germany after Hitler was overthrown, was driving anti-Nazis to despair. 'Why is there this forgetfulness of the ideals by which our cause is inspired? . . . The Allies stand for something greater than power. The chief name inscribed on our banner is "Law".'[57] In the debate, Lang strongly supported Bell, criticized the change in bombing policy and deplored recent public gloating about the destruction of German cities. Temple was unable to be present.

On 24 February, Temple writing to Bell as 'My dear George' expressed his 'immense admiration' for his courage but disagreed with his speech. He might have to reveal this divergence in public. On 26 February Bell began his letter 'My dear William'. He was distressed because he had thought that Temple agreed with him. Hamburg and Berlin had been marked out section by section and systematically bombed. 'If this is really defensible, are you not inevitably led to the adoption of the principle that the end justifies the means; and that anything – poison gas or anything else you like to mention – is justifiable if it is going to secure military victory?' Temple responded that he believed that the basic moral principles were being observed.[58] Bell continued to remind the public of the distinction between Germany and the Nazis, criticized the policy of unconditional surrender and spoke of the need for post-war Europe to be reconstructed on a Christian basis with the help of all the churches. Bell knew at first hand, in a way that Churchill and others did not, the integrity and extent of the anti-Nazi opposition in Germany.

Bell was a very dull speaker, deficient in the subtler arts of persuasion, but the courage of his war-time witness endures when more eloquent speakers are now forgotten. The churches have never lacked captivating orators – 'poor little talkative Christianity' E. M. Forster scoffed in *A Passage to India*. But all too rarely have these orators possessed that integrity and fearlessness which Bell so supremely exemplified. Rolf Hochhuth, the German playwright, recognized this when he chose Bell to be Churchill's adversary in a recreation of the moral issues involved in obliteration bombing, in his play *The Soldiers* (1977).[59]

In March 1963 D. M. MacKinnon wrote in *Theology*: 'The historians of the Church of England may yet recognise that the worst misfortunte to befall its leadership in the end of the war was less the premature death of William Temple than his succession by Fisher of London, and not by Bell of Chichester.' The post-war history both of Britain and the Church of England confirms the wisdom of that observation. Bell's war-time ministry of dissent may have destroyed his chances of succeeding Temple at Canterbury, though Temple himself saw Fisher as his natural successor. Nor was Bell chosen for London in 1945 or York in 1956. But then he had been passed over for London in 1939. It is not clear that the more recent method of nomination, in which the church has a decisive voice, would have ensured a different decision. Lord Woolton and others pressed the Government, when Bell retired, to confer some honour (such as a C.H.) but met with silence. Kenneth Slack comments: 'there were some in the governing élite of this country who remained too vindictive and mean to honour a greatness of heart and spirit that had been acclaimed throughout the Christian world'.[60] During the war, when an RAF chaplain asked for transport for Bell who was coming for a confirmation, the adjutant initially replied 'Let the bugger bike'.[61] Ironically both Bell and Churchill derived their attitudes from first war experiences. Bell had learned about the moral limitations on warfare from Davidson and so condemned the massive loss of German life caused by Allied bombing. Some airmen expressed to Bell their moral revulsion at having to bomb civilians. Churchill resorted to heavy bombing partly to avoid the numbing British casualties of the first war. But though British service casualties in the second war were less than half those in the first, the number killed in Bomber Command greatly exceeded the number of British officers killed between 1914 and 1918.[62]

Though Temple declined to support Bell's protests about obliteration bombing, he refused to regard the war as a 'crusade'. The war was a judgment on the churches for failing to be a world-wide, united and effective fellowship, and on the nations for their self-centred policies.[63] In July 1944 he suggested that the Victory Service at the end of the war ought to hold together 'two different emotions' – penitence and thanksgiving. It should begin with the penitential Psalm 51, followed by an exhortation 'in which it was explained that at all times when our hearts are lifted up we should none the less approach God in penitence'. In September, he suggested that the congregation might begin by standing for the *Te Deum*, then be asked to kneel for Psalm 51. Inevitably his advisers told him that this idea would be unacceptable.[64] On 30 October it was Psalm 51 which the choir chanted as Temple's body was brought into Canterbury Cathedral prior to the funeral the next day, the Eve of All Saints.

There is a slight indication that by 1944 Temple was beginning to have qualms about Allied bombing policy. One of Temple's contemporaries at Balliol was Stephen Hobhouse, a well-connected Etonian. Hobhouse became a Tolstoyan pacifist in 1902 at Oxford, left the Church of England and joined the Society of Friends. During the first war he was imprisoned as an absolutist. After a breakdown in 1920–22 he and his wife lived largely on trust funds established by his wealthy family.[65] In the 1940s he engaged Temple in regular correspondence about the conduct of the war. In 1944, with Temple's warm approval, he returned to the Church of England as a communicant, while retaining his membership of the Society of Friends. On 26 March 1944 Temple conveyed to Hobhouse his readiness to write an introduction for his pamphlet *Christ and our Enemies*. SPCK, the venerable Church of England society, published it in 1944 because it carried Temple's commendation. Temple decided to break his rule not to write introductions because as an 'anti-pacifist' he wanted to express his sense of unity with pacifists. In his Introduction, dated 25 March 1944, Temple explained his understanding of repentance and forgiveness. 'The love that offers forgiveness may also and at the same time inflict punishment if forgiveness is not accepted.' He went on:

> To me it seemed at an earlier stage of the war that the peace terms must for a limited period include a penal element, if justice were to be done. But the intensification of the bombing of German cities seems to me to have altered that. Those of us who believe that this intense bombing is justified as a military measure, aiming at the checking of Germany's power to produce war material, must also recognise that it constitutes a penalty for German aggression so great that no other can be called for.

Temple's secretary, Miss Dorothy Howell-Thomas, in a letter to Temple's widow of 1 January 1945 expressed surprise that he had written these sentences and wondered whether they were composed under stress. When Hobhouse wrote to Geoffrey Fisher, Temple's successor, on 20 February, pointing out Temple's withdrawal of earlier views, Fisher was alarmed. He asked Hobhouse to be careful how he used Temple's statement. He told Hobhouse punishment was necessary for discipline.[66] Hobhouse secured a circulation of 20,000 for his pamphlet, partly because through a gift from a Methodist minister he was able to send copies to Anglican clergy, Free Church ministers and to all chaplains in Germany.

The bombing of Britain

In 1937 the Imperial Defence Committee predicted that in the first two months of a war, bombing would cause 1,800,000 casualties in Britain, a third of them fatal. In 1938 the Ministry of Health was warned to expect up to four million mental cases in the first six months. Both predictions proved to be false. In fact, during the second war 60,000 civilians were killed in air raids, two thirds of them in 1940–41. Half of those who died lived in London. In the event bombing proved exciting as well as frightening, and many people discovered a new personal significance, a new purpose and a new comradeship as they faced the common challenge. Though remote areas were unaffected, air raid warnings disrupted life in regions which, though rarely bombed, were used as flight paths by the German bombers. It was of course the cities which suffered the worst. An elderly air-raid warden in Hull described with unforgettable pathos the experience of returning from his post to discover that his street had been flattened. His wife, who had been making him a cup of tea, had been killed:

> I'd 'ave lost fifteen homes if I could 'ave kept my missus. We used to read together. I can't read mesen. She used to read to me like. We'd 'ave our arm-chairs one either side of the fire, and she read me bits out o' the paper. We 'ad a paper every evening. *Every* evening.[67]

Social and religious barriers were eroded by the air raids. Employers and employees, masters and servants shared the same shelters. A service in the largest of the tube shelters was conducted jointly by the Bishop of London, a Roman Catholic priest, a Nonconformist minister, a Rabbi and a Salvationist. The war created novel forms of ministry. In Leeds there was a shortage of tram drivers and conductors. The vicar of the Venerable Bede, Wyther, asked a former tram driver from the congregation to drive trams in and out of Leeds to transport the workers. The vicar acted as the conductor and so met people of his parish whom he would not normally have encountered.

The Chislehurst Caves in Kent had long been a favourite place for outings for Londoners. During the war thousands from South London slept there. For those who had been bombed out it was their only home. Initially the organization was in the hands of the local parish priest and two laymen, but soon the shelterers demonstrated the capacity of ordinary people for self-management. Electricity was installed entirely by voluntary labour, a system of marshals established, and doctors, canteens, evening classes and even a barber were laid on. A church was created in one of the caves. Every night an evening service was held, and on Sundays, Communion, Mattins and Evensong. People were prepared for baptism and confirmation. Two women arriving for the first time on a November Sunday evening in 1940 joined between three hundred and four hundred at Evensong. 'Rock of ages' was appropriately the first hymn.[68]

In Stepney, Fr John Groser, the Christian socialist vicar, gathered an interdenominational group which ministered comfort, cocoa and compline to the people in the shelters. When shops were bombed and food was short, Groser characteristically smashed open a local food depot, lit a bonfire and fed the hungry. Garbett, Bishop of Winchester, in 1940 regularly visited Southampton. 'I know I can do nothing practical or useful on these occasions, but I feel that in a way I am a kind of symbol of the Church's pity and concern.'[69] He was also anguished by the fate of the clergy and people of the Channel Islands which were occupied by the Germans on 1 July 1940, and which lay within his diocese. During an air-raid on Brighton, Bishop Bell discovered that a number of unexploded bombs had fallen near St Peter's, but the crowd of frightened people refused to leave the crypt. He picked up a sleeping child and led them all to a place of greater safety.

In 1940 the basement of Westminster Methodist Central Hall was turned into a shelter. The minister, Dr W. E. Sangster, arranged a wide range of activities: lectures on current affairs, films, concerts, table tennis, cookery classes, religious groups. But he waited to be asked before he began public prayers. Early in 1941, as the bombs crashed nearby, a man asked 'Oughtn't we to be talking to' im up there?' and so Sangster began a regular short evening service. He was placed in charge of all the Westminster shelters. When occasionally he had to be absent, people were very uneasy. As long as he was there, they believed they were safe. When he heard that his home had been bombed he went to inspect the damage. His neighbour, Dr Luke Wiseman, the Methodist scholar, walked in, Greek Testament under his arm. Spontaneously they began to sing the hymn by Charles Wesley, with which Methodist Conferences have opened since the eighteenth century:

> And are we yet alive,
> And see each other's face?

Nearly half a million people spent a night or the whole five years in the shelter beneath the Central Hall. When the time came for it to be closed, some begged to be allowed to stay, not wanting to return to the loneliness of their previous existence.[70]

F. R. Barry, a Canon at the Abbey nearby, assisted Sangster in his shelter work. He felt closer to the people than he had ever done through parochial visiting. Conducting a funeral at the Abbey with the bombs coming nearer and nearer, the words of the lesson 'we shall all be changed, in a moment, in the twinkling of an eye' took on a new significance for him together with the whole of New Testament eschatology. In May 1941 his house was bombed and he and his wife lost all their possessions. They had to struggle with a bullying official to obtain extra coupons for essential clothing. 'I learnt then how the poor and most defenceless can be hectored by petty officials . . .' When later that year he became Bishop of Southwell, friends had to collect money and furniture to equip their new home.[71]

In December 1940 the Hammersmith clergy produced a statement deploring the miserable and insanitary conditions in public shelters, some of which they said, were also badly constructed.[72] In 1940–41 all these matters created a sharp controversy in several cities, urged on by left-wing activists. Before the war Bishop Barnes of Birmingham had expressed concern about the inadequate provision for air-raid precautions in the city. In 1940 there was a shortage of cement for shelter construction because large quantities were required for military purposes. Barnes' clergy reported to him that shelters were often overcrowded and insanitary, and that some were vulnerable to anything like a direct hit. Barnes was invited by two fellow-pacifists, H. G. Wood and Leyton Richards, to open an exhibition in November 1940 to publicize a new steel and concrete shelter. Barnes took the opportunity to accuse the cement manufacturers of using their near-monopoly to restrict output and to make large profits.

Barnes' motives were mixed. He was concerned for the safety of his people. He desired to serve Birmingham in one of the few ways open to him as a pacifist in war-time. The attack also provided an outlet for one who, though charming in private, all too often in public combined advocacy of pacifism with aggressive outbursts. On 3 December the Cement Makers' Federation issued a writ for slander. Undeterred, on 18 December Barnes repeated his accusations when opening a debate in the Lords about the provision of shelters. Meanwhile he relished discussing how he would administer the diocese from prison. He lost his case. But many thought his accusations just and friends clubbed together to find most of the £1,600 damages he was ordered to pay.[73]

Big Business now joined his other 'causes'. One of these was eugenics. In 1937, declining an invitation to him and his wife to attend a Christmas entertainment at Queen's College Birmingham he explained 'We are both pledged to go to the meeting on Voluntary Sterilisation that evening. I wish that all of you were coming to that meeting also.'[74] In May 1940, when the Germans were advancing to the Channel ports, Barnes told Garbett that he would preach that Sunday on the theme that even defeat could not destroy the inner life of a nation, provided it preserved its best stocks by careful breeding. After the war he continued to be an ardent advocate of eugenics, despite its associations with Nazism.

During the war about 15,000 ecclesiastical buildings of all types were damaged and many thousands destroyed. Methodism, for example, had to contend with 2,607 cases of major war damage. The Bishop of London (Fisher) created a Reconstruction Committee which included Roman Catholic, Free Church, Salvation Army, Quaker, Jewish as well as Anglican representatives, in order to co-ordinate repairs and applications for the licences needed for them.

At St Paul's Cathedral a twenty-four hour fire-watch was inaugurated in August 1939. After the first air raid warnings in September 1939, services were never again interrupted. Daily services continued throughout the war except for a brief period when forbidden by the police. The cathedral received its first direct hit on 10 October 1940. One of the fire-watchers often walked round the Golden Gallery at midnight saying the Lord's Prayer and the opening petitions of the Litany. The Collect 'Lighten our darkness' took on new meaning when said with the fire-watchers each night.[75] The survival of the cathedral, standing alone in blackened nobility in the largest single area of devastation in Britain, was to many an indestructible symbol of hope. A city printer remarked: 'You know, mate, I ain't a religious bloke – I never go to church, and I don't pray or anything. But I should hate to see dear old St Paul's hurt or damaged . . . well, blast it all, it's *London*, ain't it?'[76] For the Dean, W. R. Matthews, 'there were moments . . . in those days of terror, when the only hope seemed to be that God was undefeatable . . .' The experience forced this liberal theologian to drop 'the optimism about the future of mankind in this world' and to face 'the problem of evil in a realistic manner' which made his previous essays in theodicy look 'almost trivial'.[77] On 10 May 1941, the whole of Westminster seemed to be on fire and the Abbey was in great danger. The central tower was burning. Red hot lead was pouring from the roof. F. R. Barry phoned Downing Street at 3 am and said that only the Prime Minister's authority could save the Abbey. As a result, a fire brigade arrived to deal with the blaze which was beyond the control of the volunteer fire watchers. At the Elephant and Castle that night St Mary's blazed, and the great bells crashed down from the tower. Christopher Veazey, the curate, and his wife struggled to save what valuables and church records they could. In spite of being pregnant, Joan Veazey found strength to carry over forty-two buckets of water down five flights of stairs. But 'it was like pouring a thimbleful of water onto Hell itself' and the church was gutted.[78]

A war, like a strike, provides a common cause, a common enemy, drama for dull lives and positions of authority for those normally at everyone's beck and call. To the ordinary people who faced the blitz with courage and humour, sudden catastrophies, shortages and overcrowding had always been a part of normal working-class life. In 1943, when regular bombing was a thing of the past, thousands of Londoners still spent the nights in the tubes because they enjoyed the community life. A London factory worker who had been bombed out, was offered evacuation. 'What, and miss all this?' he exclaimed. 'There's never been nothing like it! Never! And never will be again.' A woman described 'the feeling that it was perfectly wonderful, to be on the right side in this stupendous conflict between good and evil. Oh! I am so glad my lot fell to the twentieth century.'[79]

Hensley Henson had strong aggressive instincts – in November 1939 he dreamed that he was in the Lords laying about himself with a hammer. In the impotence of old age and retirement in his journal and letters he indulged in wild tirades against the Nazis. He imagined Julius Streicher being smothered by copies of his own anti-semitic periodical. As early as 1936 he had privately advocated the assassination of Hitler and Mussolini as moral acts. Now in 1942 he suggested the trial and public shooting of Hitler. He dedicated his third volume of his *Retrospect* in fulsome language to Churchill ('Pater Patriae') with whose pugnacity he easily identified himself.[80]

War-time religion

The war revealed much about English patterns of belief. It brought together sections of the population which hitherto had never met. Roman Catholic families were evacuated from Liverpool to rural Wales where Roman Catholics were few. The large size of Roman Catholic families and the neglected state of some of the children (they often came from the poorest parts of cities) reinforced popular dislike of Rome. Jewish children billeted with Gentile families had a hard struggle to explain and maintain their dietary laws.

In 1941, forty to fifty per cent of people confessed to a belief in astrology. By the end of the war the proportion had fallen to under twenty per cent. Similarly in 1940–41, when invasion and defeat seemed imminent, apocalyptic had particular appeal. Brother Edward, an itinerant Anglican priest and evangelist, faced the crisis of 1940 strengthened by his faith that the war was hastening the End which would also include the conversion of the Jews.[81]

Widespread bereavement led to an increase of spiritualism, as in the first war. But this time there was much less concern with the after-life. Then belief in judgment and hell was much stronger and many first war sermons aimed to assure the bereaved that their loved ones, having fought in God's cause, had died with a place in heaven secured.[82] But popular liberal religion between the wars completed the virtual banishment of judgment and hell from English Christianity, except for the ultra-orthodox and Roman Catholics. (According to David Lodge's black comic novel *How Far Can You Go?* (1980), it was not until the 1960s that hell disappeared for Roman Catholics too.) In 1940 Percy Hartill, Archdeacon of Stoke, asked to preach on life after death, resorted to Browning's 'Abt Vogler': 'There shall never be one lost good! . . .'

The belief in fate and luck which had enabled many soldiers to remain relatively calm in the trenches, surfaced again. A third of those in the services carried a mascot. In the blitz, people believed that once you had had a near-miss you were unlikely or even unable to experience another and that two bombs could not fall in the same place. 'If it's got your number on it you get it' was once again often quoted. Thus people struggled to find some pattern or meaning in catastrophes. The following was heard in a Stepney shelter in 1940:

> Woman of 60: 'If we ever live through this night, we have the good God above to thank for it!'
> Friend: 'I don't know if there is one, or he wouldn't *let* us suffer like this.'[83]

After the war in a sermon Geoffrey Lampe, the theologian, wrestled with the meaning of providence from his own experience as a chaplain. Lampe under fire, was invited by a doctor to join him in his dugout. But he had 'a very strange and irrational compulsion' to remain where he was. An hour or two later the doctor was killed. Lampe was saved. Was this 'providence'? Or should providence be thought of as God's creative use of all sorts of complicated circumstances, including both human sin and human responsiveness to him?[84]

What about prayer? A woman explained: 'I heard the bomb coming and I prayed to God as hard as I could to push it a bit further down the street and he did.'[85] A popular shelter hymn began:

> God is our refuge, be not afraid,
> He will be with you all through the raid.

Had not millions prayed for peace and God had given them the Munich agreement? No sooner had they given thanks to God, and war was again imminent. On 5 January 1940 a letter-writer to the *Guardian* was dismayed by 'the total failure of the prayers of the Universal Church to arrest the awful sufferings' of so many people all over Europe. On 21 June it printed two articles, side by side, one entitled 'Why Does Not God Intervene?' and the other claiming that the Dunkirk deliverance 'was a miracle in which forces above and beyond man's agency and control – tide, wind and water – played their part'. The conservative evangelical Bishop Chavasse regarded it as a miracle and James Parkes, the liberal theologian, as an answer to prayer. The Rector of Lowestoft wrote in a letter to the *Times* of 6 June 1940: 'It is worth remarking that this great calm has persisted ever since the Day of Prayer.' In the *Guardian* during June and July 1940 the story of the Angels of Mons was recalled as proof of divine intervention in war-time.[86] General Sir William Dobbie, Governor of Malta, a member of the Plymouth Brethren, believed that divine mediation had saved the island. In *A Very Present Help* (1945) he worked out a direct connection between Days of Prayer and military successes. R. R. Williams of the MOI preaching at St Paul's in 1943, quoted a commanding officer who claimed that, because his destroyer had been blessed by a bishop, this provided a source of 'Heavenly Guidance' for the crew.[87]

In December 1939 Leslie Weatherhead was more frank than most about the problems of prayer in war-time. Can prayer 'deflect a bullet or protect a loved one against a bursting bomb?' We have to pour out our needs and doubts to God. In answering prayer, God would not exercise favouritism, violate his own laws, or do for people what they should do themselves. 'I don't know, to be quite honest, what is the effect of a prayer for the safety of a loved one.'[88] William Temple thought it best not to pray directly for victory, though it would be permissible if the petition were qualified by 'If it will be thy will'. Garbett thought this sophistical. So did Henson, who though nearly seventy-seven was brought back by Churchill to the Abbey in 1940 to be eloquent in the national cause. Temple was particularly concerned that prayer should promote catholicity not nationalism.[89] In England ordinary people often displayed an extraordinary capacity for forgiving their enemies. A bereaved father said of the German who had aimed the fatal bomb: 'He didn't know what he was doing'. People in the raids remarked of the bomber crews overhead: 'They're only doing their job' – a striking example of working-class solidarity. Fr Harry Williams remembers council flat tenants in Pimlico saying, as British bombers flew overhead to Germany, 'Poor wretches, I'm afraid that they're going to get it tonight'. He wondered who was the more Christian, these compassionate non-churchgoers or the devout Anglo-Catholic clergy agitating at that time with such hatred against church union in South India?[90]

Some churchmen thought that the war was reviving religion. The reporters for Mass Observation did not, though some people were praying more than usual because of stress. Much religion was designed to provide comfort and security in a frightening world.[91] Nevertheless, religion was still interwoven with national life to a degree which now seems surprising. Some war-time Sunday cinema performances began with a short service conducted by one of the local clergy. The King's broadcasts were more explicitly Christian than royal broadcasts since then. When in his Christmas broadcast of 1939 he quoted 'I said to the man who stood at the Gate of the Year . . .' the subsequent demand for the poem was enormous. One incumbent added the poem to the 'Comfortable Words' at Communion and introduced it by 'Hear also what King George VI saith'. People during the war met the clergy in new situations – in the ARP and Home Guard, when evacuees used church or parish hall for school lessons, calling at the vicarage because it was a First Aid post. Many people said they missed the sound of church bells, which were only to be rung to announce an invasion.

In 1942 the President of the Board of Trade, Hugh Dalton (son of a Canon of Windsor) felt it vital to invoke the church's authority to bind and loose. He asked Temple to announce that, because of war-time shortage of materials, 'women could, without impropriety, come hatless and stockingless to church'. After discussing the request with the bishops, the two Archbishops issued a statement that St Paul's regulation, which required women to be veiled, had 'long ago fallen out of use'. Women and girls should not hesitate to enter a Church 'uncovered'.[92] The *Church Times* on 13 November tortuously argued that the manner of the announcement was contrary to Catholic custom. When on 19 August 1944 a clerical correspondent told Temple that older people were disgusted by the change, Temple quoted Bishop Gore's remark that 'St Paul would not be in the least propitiated by a little hat'.[93]

Some war-time films conveyed the conviction that Britain was fighting for values which were rooted deep in its history and supremely expressed in Elizabethan England. These traditional values could be symbolized by, for example, an ancient village parish church or by Shakespeare. During the war Kingsley Martin was astonished to see the correspondence columns of his left-wing *New Statesman* being filled by letters urging the importance of Christian doctrine as a means of saving the world from Fascism and Communism. In 1944, the year of the Allied invasion of Europe, Laurence Olivier's film *Henry V* appeared. On the actual D-Day crossing, one commander read to his troops from the play itself. Churchill's war speeches relied on echoes from Shakespeare and the Authorized Version. Hollywood's tribute to war-time Britain, *Mrs Miniver* (1942), concluded with a patriotic sermon by a rector in a village church. A documentary film, promoted jointly by the British and Americans, *The True Glory* (1945) combined a highly realistic visual presentation of the fighting for the liberation of Europe with the use of quasi-Shakespearian blank verse for the film's emotional climaxes. The film ended:

> Now the time has come to put our victory to the tests of peace, in company with men of many lands to sift from ashes what the struggle taught. In the rebuilding of a broken earth may we keep in our hearts this ancient prayer: 'O Lord God, when thou givest to thy servants to endeavour any great matter, grant us also to know that it is not the beginning, but the continuing of the same until it be thoroughly finished, which yieldeth the true glory.'

This 'ancient prayer' used for the title for the film, was in fact composed for the National Day of Prayer of 21 March 1941 by Eric Milner-White, Dean of York. (Milner-White had returned from a chaplaincy in the first war proclaiming himself a revolutionary, but then devoted himself to the composition of liturgical evocations of traditional England, supremely exemplified in 1918 by his creation of the Carol Service at King's College Cambridge.) In 1941 Milner-White characteristically based this special prayer on a phrase used by Sir Francis Drake which he saw posted up on a notice-board in a War Operations Room. British propaganda cultivated the legend that this was the prayer composed by Drake as he embarked on his voyage to destroy the Spanish fleet at Cadiz.[94]

The hope for a post-war social order which would continue the war-time experience of 'fair shares' and a sense of common purpose was expressed in the 1940 Peace Points and other statements from religious leaders during the war. This hope also found expression in war-time films, both commercial and documentary. *The Life and Death of*

Colonel Blimp (1943) with its satiric portrayal of the old diehards of Britain was toned down at the insistence of the MOI. Churchill disliked it. But the officially sponsored documentary *The World of Plenty* (1943) directed by Paul Rotha, savagely depicted the pre-war world of scandalous inequalities between classes in Britain and the rich and poor nations in the world. By contrast, films usually upheld traditional sexual morals. Noel Coward's *This Happy Breed* (1944) had as its central theme the stability of the family in a world of change. Of course film-makers (and others too) in their desire to portray a united nation were sometimes romantic and far-fetched. Priestley hymned the Dunkirk evacuation as the work of civilians in small craft when in fact it was achieved principally by the Royal Navy.[95] But British propaganda which celebrated the contribution of ordinary people to the war effort, in the process seemed to secure for them a new and valued place in the life of the nation.[96]

Like these film makers, the church thought about the nature of post-war society as well as acting as a guardian of national memory. William Temple, enthroned with ancient ceremony at Canterbury in 1942, called his first collection of speeches as Archbishop, *The Church Looks Forward* (1944). This was the title of a major speech by Temple given at a meeting in the Albert Hall on 26 September 1942, the first of a series arranged by the Industrial Christian Fellowship and addressed by Temple. These meetings carried the message of COPEC and Malvern to the wider public, showing the church to be in earnest about post-war reconstruction. It was the ICF Director who suggested what became the Malvern Conference, as an Anglican contribution to reconstruction. (The Church of Scotland was thinking and acting upon similar lines.[97]) In the Albert Hall Temple told nearly nine thousand people that they were there to affirm 'the right and the duty of the Church . . . to lay down principles which should govern the ordering of society' (a theme of his *Christianity and Social Order* published that year). The war had united 'the two nations' of Britain, but unless 'a new way' was taken once the war was over the divisions would reappear. He called for a fairer distribution of resources, for an end to the 'canker' of unemployment and for public interest to take precedence over private profit. (His criticisms of the banking system caused much controversy.) The eucharist was the paradigm, for it represented the consecration of work. At the same meeting, Garbett argued for a gigantic post-war housing programme and the public planning of land use. Unemployment, bad housing, malnutrition and poverty were contrary to the will of God. Sir Stafford Cripps, Lord Privy Seal, who was regarded then (apart from Eden) as the only credible successor to Churchill, said he looked to the Church of England to provide the moral force for social reform. Christian principles must so permeate public opinion that no government could act against them.[98] (Cripps' father, Lord Parmoor, had been Vicar-General of Canterbury, Lord President in the first Labour Government and had attended COPEC. Cripps was attracted towards Christian socialism by the headmaster of Winchester, H. M. Burge, later Bishop of Southwark, and by Temple himself. R. H. Tawney, the Anglican socialist, deeply influenced both Cripps and Temple.[99])

The left exulted. The *Sunday Pictorial* wrote on 27 September: 'Something has happened in Britian at last. Until yesterday, those of us who insisted on a new deal for the people were rated as cranks and visionaries.' But now 'the Church has jumped into the ring, and the militant cry of the two Archbishops cannot be stifled'. But in private, Garbett was uneasy about being identified with what he described as 'rather like a political programme'.[100] (Headlam had repudiated Temple's policies in the *Guardian* on 28 February 1941).

In fact, Temple, Garbett and Cripps, were articulating the emerging national consensus. The *Times* on 1 July 1940 after Dunkirk, wrote in a leader: 'The new order cannot be based on the preservation of privilege, whether the privilege be that of a country, of a class, of an individual.' Paul Addison, in *The Road to 1945* (1975), drew attention to the growing number of groups which in the late 1930s advocated state control of land use, better housing, education and a health service. The détente with the trade unions, promoted early in 1939 by the likelihood of war, was sealed by the coalition of 1940 and the entry of Ernest Bevin into Parliament and the Government. The evacuation opened many eyes. Chamberlain, who had been Minister of Health, in September 1939 confessed with shame that he had not known how his neighbours had been living and pledged himself to improve social conditions. Public opinion blamed the disasters of 1940 on the Conservatives of the 1930s. In 1940 J. B. Priestley became the popular spokesman of the conviction that we must never return to the 30s: the war was a 'huge collective effort' which was changing our habits of thought; 'we're all in the same boat'.[101] So between Dunkirk and El Alamein there were many signs of a leftward movement reinforced by roseate accounts of Russian life purveyed by Anglo-Soviet weeks, the reports of Mass Observation, *Picture Post*, the *Daily Mirror* and the Army Education programmes. In the popular film *Dawn Patrol* (1941) a member of the Home Guard declared that the great war effort must be followed by 'a fine big peace effort' – no more unemployment, slums and 'half-starved kids'. 'We found out in this war as how we were all neighbours, and we aren't going to forget it when it's all over . . . "The old men shall see visions, and the young men shall dream dreams." '[102] A Baptist girl in Coventry entered the invasion of Holland and Belgium in her diary for 10 May 1940 and then wrote: 'It was a relief to go in the afternoon to see the City Architects' exhibition "City of Tomorrow" . . . small scale models of ideal buildings and cities . . .'[103]

William Beveridge broadly agreed with the letter from church leaders outlining Christian social standards in the *Times* of December 1940. Beveridge's Report of 1942 gave the consensus more detailed shape. Temple, who had been at Balliol with Beveridge (and Tawney) was enthusiastic. While Churchill was concentrating on the war-effort Labour leaders spoke more about the home front. Churchill failed to convince the public that he was really committed to a new society.

It was Temple who first used the term 'Welfare State'. In Lecture IV of *Christianity and the State* (1928) dedicated to Tawney, and in Chapter II of *Citizen and Churchman* (1941) he used it to draw a contrast between a state which used power over the community and one which existed for the community. Temple's approach to social problems was characterized by personalism, a general optimism that a common interest existed and social progress could be achieved by rational means.[104] The agreement between the churches and the government expressed by the Education Act of 1944 owed much to Temple's personal friendship with R. A. Butler, the Minister,[105] and to the war-time conviction expressed by the *Times* on 14 August 1943 that there was a value in national Christianity: 'unless the future of Christian knowledge and training can be secured the Christian basis of our society cannot be preserved'. The settlement was also a fruit of war-time ecumenism. It revealed the decline of the political power of the Free Churches and the rise of the political influence of the Roman Catholics. On 23 February 1942 Professor Henry Clay, the economic historian, wrote a letter to his old friend William Temple, which cut right across the consensus:

> I believe this war is the outcome of and punishment for our materialism; and I feel that social reformers like ourselves are largely to blame. We have encouraged people to concentrate on economic reforms to the forgetting of ultimate values . . . on balance your influence helped to confirm the English people in the view that the chief object of politics was to improve social conditions.[106]

Yet beneath the apparent commitment of the church to a planned society, the rural nostalgia and anti-industrialism dating back to the

Romantic Revival still continued. So the report *Towards the Conversion of England* attacked the Industrial Revolution and the Machine Age for producing an attitude of mind hostile to ideals and incapable of abstract thought (echoing remarks made at Malvern). Perhaps (it said) the religious revival would begin in rural England?[107] (According to many of the popular songs of the period it was rural England – and Home Counties England at that – for which Britain was fighting.)

If the state was to be reformed, why not do something about the Church of England which was still a thicket of anomalies and individualism, ripe for clearance? Temple, who in his young days had organized Life and Liberty, quelled his doubts about living at Bishopthorpe when he was Archbishop of York by concluding 'but that is for the Church to decide'.[108] When he moved to Canterbury he was determined to live at Lambeth, despite its devastation by the bombing. It was his old home and 'Lambeth' had a historical ring. In his enthronement sermon he did not mention church reform, one of the main themes of Garbett's enthronement sermon at York. Bell who, like Garbett, wanted a readjustment in the form of the establishment, felt frustrated by the lack of interest shown by his brother bishops.

Canon Roger Lloyd in the *Guardian* for 23 August 1940 argued that the 'Socialist revolution' in the state should be paralleled in the church. Every deacon should be paid the same salary (say £200) increasing to (say) £400 after fifteen years. This system should apply to everyone from deacons to bishops, though the differing expenses of office should be allowed for. Both freehold benefices and large vicarages should disappear. A group working with Leslie Hunter, (Bishop of Sheffield from 1939) proposed extensive reforms set out in: *Men, Money and the Ministry* (1937) and *Putting our House in Order* (1941). Hunter told his diocese in 1940: 'Absolute freehold, and indefensible inequalities between benefices, have tended to produce a temper which is at variance with the idea of Christian community in the New Testament.' Hunter had served on the committee which produced *The Army and Religion* (1919). Its analysis of the alienation of most Englishmen from institutional religion continued to haunt him, and in 1944 Hunter created the Sheffield Industrial Mission to begin some bridge building.[109] But the Church of England was slow to move. In 1939 clergy of the Convocation of York again voted against allowing lay readers to administer the chalice, and in 1940 the bishops decided they had no time to consider admitting women as readers because of the imminent danger of invasion.[110] Though during the war attempts were made to ensure a minimum stipend, the Paul Report of 1964 showed that stipends still varied enormously, and it was not until 1977 that, with the pooling of benefice endowments and glebe, the Church of England began to move towards equal stipends for incumbents.[111] First war chaplains had to contend with regular criticisms of episcopal palaces and salaries. In 1942 the Radio Padre began a broadcast interview with Archbishop Temple for the forces by asking him about exactly these topics.[112]

How much of what religious leaders did and said actually filtered down to people in the local church? At this level, the main possible sources of distinctively Christian teaching (for example about the ethics of warfare) were sermons and the parish magazine. Few people took either church periodicals or quality newspapers, the only places where (say) a speech by Bishop Bell would receive a balanced report. BBC Religious Broadcasting made a strenuous effort during the war to educate the churches, but the rule that religious controversy must be avoided was one reason why audiences for educative material tended to be small.

What do the parish magazines for St Michael's Headingley, Leeds, reveal? It was then a parish of 10,000, with an electoral roll of 650, and a mixture of professional and working class people. The vicar was Canon R. J. Wood, a cautious and moderate Anglo-Catholic, very suitable for the devout, reticent church designed by Loughborough Pearson. The curate during the war was C. W. Odling-Smee, a member of FOR, APF and PPU whom the Bishop of Ripon (Lunt) was happy to ordain in 1940, knowing him to be a pacifist. Wood told his curate that, though he must not preach pacifism from the pulpit, he was free to discuss it in the parish.

The magazine included the 'Ripon Diocesan Messenger' and 'The Sign', a national inset with a circulation of about 600,000. Between Munich and the outbreak of war, neither bishop nor vicar in their monthly letters made any real effort to discuss the theological and moral issues at stake. Yet in the 'Messenger' for July 1939 there was this chilling item: 'In the event of an air raid everyone will be cleared from the streets except the military police, special constables and ARP workers.' Only rarely during the war did the Bishop, in his monthly letter, take seriously his teaching office. In February 1940 the Bishop began: 'This letter is actually being written in Torquay whither I have brought Mrs Lunt for a fortnight's convalescence, in search of the sun.' (Admittedly this is a particularly crass example.) 'The Sign' throughout the war continued to offer its customary nostalgic fare. The monthly 'Query Corner' unfailingly explored the footnotes of ecclesiastical life – Why there is no vigil for St Luke's Day? Should flower vases stand on the altar? What is the correct number of sidesmen? In the first issue to be printed after the war began (November 1939) 'The Sign' explained its policy:

> Our readers will look elsewhere for news of the conflict and for direct comment upon it; for those things which concern their earthly citizenship. A parish magazine is for those who desire to be reminded of their heavenly citizenship . . . It is our hope that our readers may find some degree of encouragement or solace in pages that take them a little apart from what may now necessarily become their daily reading.

The war nudged the wary vicar along lines being articulated by Temple, Bell and the *Christian News-Letter* (the latter was commended and quoted in the magazine). So in October 1939 he wrote that the church must not turn itself into 'a department of the State' echoing 'the State creed' – one of the evils of Nazism. Later on he quoted Cardinal Galen of Münster and commended his courage and condemned Nazi anti-semitism. After the war we must be prepared to divert food from Britain to Europe. Parishioners were warned to avoid worshipping the tribal God of the previous war, when some people refused to listen to Beethoven or Wagner. He welcomed the release of Oswald Mosley in 1943: detention without trial was one of the practices Britain was fighting against. At the end of the war he wrote. 'The courage and military skill of the Russians has earned our unstinted admiration and gratitude.' A missionary article praised the contribution of coloured people to the Allied forces. The vicar asked the parish to contribute to the fund for the stricken churches of Europe. There was no mention of the atomic bomb.

Canon Wood approved of J. B. Priestley for focussing attention upon post-war reconstruction. How tragic that it had taken a war to make Britain tackle unemployment. Though he commended the interdenominational co-operation of Religion and Life weeks, he advised against too rosy a view of the prospects for reunion. He had no wish for a complete equality of clerical stipends but would welcome a reform of the present haphazard system. In February 1945 he was glad to report his move into a smaller house from the large vicarage designed to be served by four maids.

Pacifism

The experiences of 1939–40 weeded out many pacifiers from among pacifists. In addition, some pacifists modified their beliefs or abandoned them altogether. Maude Royden, who had worked closely with Dick Sheppard, resigned from the Peace Pledge Union in September

1939. Leslie Weatherhead was a pacifist up to about 1937 then became an ardent pacifier. But by mid-September 1939 he was asking 'Is evil to go entirely unrestrained because we have perfected no way of restraint?'[113] In 1940 the pace of renunciations quickened. Three PPU Sponsors resigned: Bertrand Russell, Philip Mumford and Storm Jameson. Storm Jameson, president of the British section of PEN, had travelled extensively in Europe and had heard accounts of Nazism from many refugees in Britain. In 1941 she felt she must explain her resignation from PPU:

> A pacifist who says, 'Come let us reason together' is guilty of a deep refusal of honesty. The way of reasoning together is not open to us. What is open to us is submission, the concentration camp, the death of our humblest with our best, the forcing of our children's minds into an evil mould.

Among the many hundreds who wrote in response was William Temple: 'We have at all costs to avoid two things: the tendency through sheer fatigue to shirk the responsibility which military success will involve, and the eagerness of the bosses to reconstitute an order which gives them power and wealth . . .'[114] Middleton Murry remained an a-political Christian pacifist, and edited *Peace News* successfully during the war. But by 1944 the behaviour of radical pacifists who joined his farming community was leading him to abandon his pacifist faith in human goodness.

C. J. Cadoux, the Vice-Principal of Mansfield Congregational College Oxford, had been a pacifist since before the first war. In 1940 at the end of *Christian Pacifism Re-examined*, he confessed that he had now been forced to modify his absolutism because of the totalitarian nature of Nazism with its concentration camps and its persecution of Jews and Christians: 'no-one can plead with any show of reason that the rectification of Germany's grievances' justified its conduct.[115] He claimed to be still a pacifist but wrote: 'If one recognizes, as I hold one might do, that the war is *relatively* justified . . . I do not see how one can refuse to admit that it is better that it should be victoriously carried through, than that it should be discontinued before the undertaking is completed.'[116]

Nathaniel Micklem, the Principal of Mansfield, had resigned his pastorate during the first war rather than refrain from preaching pacifism. During the 1930s he had been deeply involved in the German church conflict and (much to Cadoux's dismay) had moved to neo-orthodoxy. *May God Defend the Right!* the title of Micklem's book dated 27 September 1939, expressed his complete change of mind.

However horrible war is (he wrote) 'The destruction of "Hitlerism" will be the victory of God . . .'[117] He not only quoted from Pius XI's encyclical *Mit Brennender Sorge* (1937) but also from his own experience, in depicting the terrible persecution of the German church. In *The Theology of Politics* (1941), Micklem, while paying tribute to the Nonconformist struggle for social reform, pointed out that the Church of England was no longer the Tory party at prayer, and gratefully quoted Temple on social as well as theological questions. In Chapter IX Micklem stated that his pacifist assumption that nations were open to moral persuasion had been destroyed by the character of Nazism. It is true that we cannot imagine Jesus wielding a bayonet. But nor can we picture him as a policeman, judge or Foreign Secretary. We had to choose between the evil of war or the greater evil of passivity. The pacifist must follow his own conscience: 'But the judgement of most men of moral seriousness will be against him, and he may not safely claim that the New Testament is on his side.'[118] In November 1939, when Lambeth asked Micklem's advice as to how to answer pacifist correspondents, Micklem replied that Christ embodied the virtues as a Saviour; but we have to exhibit them as sinners and citizens.[119]

Other war time books did not substantially further the debate. Percy Hartill edited two Anglican symposia: *Into the Way of Peace* (1941) and *On Earth Peace* (1944). In the latter R. H. Le Messurier contemplated a Nazi invasion with horror but added: 'I believe that a great deal of the excessive brutality which is at present bound up with the Nazi system would tend to disappear as it found no opposition on which to feed.'[120] *This War and Christian Ethics* (1940) edited by Ashley Sampson and Edwyn Bevan's *Christians in a World at War* (1940) rehearsed arguments we have already described.

Those who remained pacifists became more a-political. It was no longer possible to urge pacifism as the way to avoid war. The impotence of pacifists encouraged public tolerance, which in its turn eroded the impact of their witness. The specifically religious pacifist groups grew during the war, but the diffused humanitarianism of PPU was a cause of its decline. Christian pacifists talked of the importance of bearing an individual witness, of being a redemptive minority, even if this seemed to have no visible results. Some pacifists won public admiration for their heroism as stretcher-bearers under fire, or as workers during the raids, but not because of their actual convictions. Pacifists who wanted to express their faith politically, appealed for a negotiated peace and attacked Allied bombing policies, but most were anxious not to appear subversive.

If several leading pacifists abandoned their faith, others like Charles Raven, Vera Brittain, Leyton Richards, Bishop Barnes, Stuart Morris, Percy Hartill and Donald Soper remained steadfast. Donald Soper went on courageously preaching pacifism in the open air. Though he granted that the persecution of the Jews pre-dated the war, he argued that the war had increased Nazi violence against the Jews.[121] In 1944 he wrote that the old utilitarian arguments had lost their power. 'I am alone sustained by the Christian faith which assures me that what is morally right carries with it the ultimate resources of the universe . . .'[122] At the beginning of the war Barnes told his clergy to preach from the New Testament not from the newspaper. Regularly he pleaded for just treatment of COs, even the Jehovah's Witnesses whose theology he abhorred. He called for the free importation of foodstuffs in to Germany and condemned obliteration bombing. Though he desired an Allied victory he would not pray for it. He continued to recommend Cadoux's book *The Early Christian Attitude to War* (1919). He resigned from the Modern Churchmen's Union, which he regarded as nationalist and socially reactionary. Guy Rogers, Rector of Birmingham, a first-war chaplain, found Barnes' belittling of chaplains, his refusal to dine with the army and his unwillingness to allow discussion of his pacifist speeches at diocesan conferences, all hard to bear.[123] Leyton Richards, the Congregationalist, became warden of a Quaker International College in Birmingham. Pacifists seemed to him voices crying in the wilderness. In 1946 he joined the Society of Friends but was allowed to remain on the list of Congregational ministers.

When in 1940 Gandhi appealed for Britons to adopt non-violence, Raven replied that in this 'moment of supreme peril' the appeal would meet with little response. Pacifists had failed to convince Britain of the 'value and practicability' of non-violence. But Christian pacifists believed that passive resistance was not enough: society must be radically reformed.[124] Eric Gill, the Roman Catholic sculptor of Nonconformist stock, imagined himself confronting a tribunal, in a piece written in September 1939. He was still as convinced that war was caused by big business, as when his Leeds University war memorial was unveiled in 1923. In any case, 'Our hands are no cleaner than any one else's.'[125] Ralph Partridge, a Bloomsbury humanist and pacifist, withdrew during the war with his wife to the private world of their Wiltshire house. When he learned of the annexation of Denmark, he tried to restore the world to sanity by listening to Monteverdi and Haydn. Yet however much he tried to remain detached from the war, when he heard of the gas chambers and saw pictures of the corpses he felt that 'the world's sanity had received a fatal blow'.[126]

How did the leaders of the Church of England treat pacifist clergy during the war? Percy Hartill, Chairman of the Anglican Pacifist Fellowship, regularly wrote to Lambeth about issues which troubled him. Lang and Temple were always ready to write to Government departments about alleged cases of ill-treatment of COs. Hartill concluded a letter to Lang of 3 November 1939: 'we gratefully recognize the sympathetic spirit of all your Grace's references to those who hold the pacifist position'. In 1940 the Archbishops were at first reluctant to meet an APF deputation, for both, on occasion, found pacifists 'tiresome' (Temple's adjective). However, on 11 June 1940, a group representing 2,571 members, including 371 priests, met the Archbishops at Lambeth. Raven warned of a possible rift between pacifist and non-pacifist. Hartill was worried about the treatment of COs and the apparent identification of an Allied victory with a victory for Christianity. Temple replied that pacifism was a genuine vocation for some. We could never declare that we were fighting for the gospel, but we could claim that we were fighting for the opportunity of living the Christian way of life. He had not heard of many cases of bad treatment of COs. COs should be prepared to change their occupations to do some work of service. Pacifist clergy, in their ministry, should be sensitive to their congregations. Lang said that he had deliberately accepted a pacifist for ordination. Pacifism should be debated by the clergy.[127] When an agreed report of the meeting was published by APF, the deputation expressed 'its deep sense of gratitude to the Archbishops for their unfailing courtesy and understanding in their treatment of *a rather obscure minority*' (my italics).

Though Dean Malden in his preface to the 1941 *Crockford's* crudely accused pacifists of cowardice, he was unrepresentative. In cases I have encountered, bishops treated pacifist ordinands and clergy with understanding. On the other hand, parishioners could be hostile.[128] In 1939, John Kingsnorth, was an ordinand at Cuddesdon (later he became Archdeacon of Northern Rhodesia). In mid-September he wrote to his bishop (Lunt of Ripon) to tell him he was a pacifist. Lunt wrote at length assuring him of his deep respect for his position, though explaining his disagreement with it. Kingsnorth was not an absolutist, but holding firmly to Just War principles, considered that in this war the means were not proportionate to the end, and later, obliteration bombing strengthened this conviction. His pacifism caused no controversy with his fellow clergy or in the Leeds parish to which he was ordained in 1940. His 'guru' was Bishop Bell. J. R. H.

Moorman was Rector of Fallowfield, Manchester, when in 1942 refusing attractive offers of promotion, he resigned his living to become a farm worker. (His first book on St Francis had been published in 1940.) His decision was not a political protest, but a desire, as a pacifist, to share something of the hardship being asked of other men. He believed that the war was widening the gulf between the secure 'little world' of the clergy and that of laypeople. The Bishop of Manchester (Warman) was most sympathetic but could not quite follow his reasoning. Opinion in the parish was divided. During his two years as a farm labourer, at first he found it difficult to get used to tough manual work, primitive conditions and being ordered about. At weekends he helped the local vicar. In 1946 Bishop Bell asked Moorman to become Principal of Chichester. In 1959 he became Bishop of Ripon.[129]

During the second war there were 59,000 COs compared with about 16,500 in the first.[130] The proportion of objectors declined sharply as the war progressed. Not all COs were pacifists; some objected for political reasons. COs were predominantly white-collar workers. Tribunals were more fairly constituted than in the previous war, and paid particular attention to the religious and ethical convictions of the objectors. Those who asked for unconditional exemption found it very difficult to convince tribunals. To refuse to work on the land, join the Non-Combatant Corps, or to help in civil defence seemed a total refusal of responsibility to society. If a CO was connected with a church whose leaders supported the war, he was asked why he differed from their views. The Quaker appeal to the 'inner light' was hard for tribunals to understand. Christadelphians were disliked because they often read from standard statements. The report of the South-West tribunal in 1942 revealed that of 4,056 cases, seventy-one per cent had objected on religious grounds: 170 Christadelphians, 439 Plymouth Brethren, 155 Jehovah's Witnesses, 662 Methodists, 187 Baptists, 143 Congregationalists, 302 Quakers, 12 Presbyterians, 9 Unitarians, 18 Jews and 64 Roman Catholics. Half the 531 Anglicans were not communicants. Thus religious and political dissent were still linked.

Henry Carter, a pacifist, was for many years Secretary of the Methodist Social Welfare Department. In October 1939 the *Methodist Recorder* published his article advising COs how to prepare for tribunals; later his department published it as a pamphlet. Soper considered that in ninety-nine cases out of a hundred the tribunals' judgments were right. Hartill wrote to Lambeth on 14 December 1939. One CO had spoken 'in the most glowing terms' of the sympathy displayed by the Birmingham tribunal.[131] The government, determined to avoid creating martyrs, made some modifications in policies from time to time. Once again British society discovered a way of neutralizing dissent.

However the BBC took a harsher line with pacifists. 'With the coming of war, the Corporation was to control the churches just as it was itself to be subject to nation and Government.'[132] James Welch, Director of Religious Broadcasting, believed that in any controversy both sides should be heard. In the first months of the war he invited not only Archbishop Temple and Cardinal Hinsley to broadcast, but also the pacifists George Macleod and Charles Raven. However, in February 1940, Leyton Richards, unlike MacLeod and Raven, and against Welch's advice, broadcast an explicitly pacifist sermon. On 6 June the Governors decided that Religious Broadcasting should be in full accord with the national effort, and those who disagreed should not broadcast. Most members of the Central Religious Advisory Committee, including its chairman, Garbett, and many of the bishops, supported Welch in the ensuing controversy. Eventually the BBC relented slightly: pacifists could be invited if they were not publicly known to be opposed to the war effort. Welch made strenuous efforts on behalf of Raven and Soper, but to no avail. Even the non-pacifist Dean of Lichfield, F. A. Iremonger, the former head of Religious Broadcasting, was not allowed to broadcast his review of the biography of his old friend Dick Sheppard.

Chaplains and the armed services

Of all the clergy perhaps it was the military chaplains who were in the greatest danger of becoming auxiliaries of the state.[133] A second war chaplain defined his role: 'primarily a link with home and a link with God – and through his own non-combatancy, a link with peace'.[134] But does this go far enough? What about the chaplain's ministry of creative dissent towards the institution he serves? Too often that element has been confined to protests about dirty songs at concerts or unjust treatment of servicemen by authority. Can it be right (for example) for a priest to say mass on a bomb (as happened)? Does this not proclaim a simple alignment between Christianity and war against which Temple protested so constantly?

Why is it that no second war chaplains became household names as did (say) Studdert Kennedy and Tubby Clayton after 1918? One answer is that in the second war, the chaplaincy service was better organized leaving much less room for individual initiatives. Certain chaplains after 1918 became the focus for either attempts to prolong comradeship (Tubby Clayton) or for disillusionment (Studdert

Kennedy). Nor did second war chaplains or servicemen produce the searing, memorable literature of their predecessors. Soldiers in the first war 'pondered, in their letters, on profundities of theology, complexities of politics, convolutions of psychology and a hundred other topics almost completely absent from the letters of soldiers one generation later'.[135] Certain first war chaplains continued to be paradigms. Maurice Wood, RNVR chaplain 1943–46, (later Bishop of Norwich) has spoken of how much his own ministry owed to Studdert Kennedy. Perhaps only in the POW camps was there that intense comradeship which characterized the trenches and which afterwards Toc H and the British Legion attempted to keep alive.

At the peak of the second war there were 3,692 army chaplains of all denominations; of these 96 were killed compared with 172 in 1914–18. There was some tension between the Army Chaplains' Department (which tended to go its own way as a section of the War Office) and diocesan bishops. On 30 September 1941 Temple wrote to Lang: 'If we can put a very large bomb under the Chaplain General's department at the end of the war it would be useful.'[136] Eventually in 1944, Bishop Leslie Owen was appointed as the Archbishop's representative to the forces, and liaison and pastoral care of chaplains improved.

The file belonging to the Rev. H. D. Barton, an Anglican army chaplain throughout the war, reveals the outlook and methods of one chaplain. In an address in 1942 he looked back on that September as 'a remarkable month'. The National Day of Prayer had been observed in factories, cinemas and harvest fields as well as in churches. Lord Halifax, in a broadcast, had described St Paul's standing alone, now that the confused mass of surrounding buildings had been destroyed: what really matters remains. Barton rejoiced in the creation of the BCC, and that Malta had been saved by divine protection. W. H. Smith's had held a service of intercession for their staff. He quoted from the speeches at the Albert Hall by Temple, Garbett and Cripps. Press cuttings illustrated his belief that the church's leadership was rising to the challenge of war. Another section included addresses to new conscripts. The chaplain occupies 'a bridge position': an officer, but not 'in the military sense of the term'. Opportunities for worship were available for all Christians and for Jews. Breakfast would be kept for those who practised fasting Communion. He informed them of welfare provisions, explained discipline, warned against drunkenness, gambling and sexual immorality. In a second talk he sketched the history of the British Empire and told the recruits why the war was 'a crusade'.

In 1942 'Padre's Hour' was introduced. Servicemen asked 'Why

are there so many churches?'; 'Is Jesus God?'; 'Is God non-belligerent?'
The authorities gave permission for residential religious conferences.
'The Nails Movement' (Anglican), 'Sword of the Spirit' (Roman
Catholic) and 'The King's Way' (Free Church and Church of Scotland)
all emphasized (in Micklem's words) that 'Religion is essentially
churchmanship'.[137] The churches produced literature for religious
education in the forces. C. S. Lewis, through his books and broadcasts,
was providing apologetic material useful for chaplains and in the
parishes. In December 1939 the BBC created a Forces Programme.
James Welch ensured that it included a religious element. Hymns and
talks by Ronald Selby Wright, a Church of Scotland chaplain, the
'Radio Padre', were particularly popular.

Church parade was disliked by most servicemen and some chaplains
as a dreadful mix-up between religion and spit-and-polish, but
defended by many officers and some chaplains as a declaration of
corporate religious allegiance. To Eric Treacy, as for other chaplains,
only voluntarily attended Communions seemed genuine worship.
Anglo-Catholic chaplains who usually regarded the Chaplains' Department as erastian and protestant, tried to substitute a sung eucharist
for the truncated Mattins at church parade. They believed they were
striking a blow against the type of religion they regarded as ineffective
and narrowly English. John Collins, an RAF chaplain (later Canon of
St Paul's and Chairman of CND), reacted violently against compulsory
church parades punctuated by whistles and cat calls from men who
were perhaps soaked from waiting outside. He protested and the
compulsory church parades were abandoned.

Of course worship was very different on the eve of a battle, in the
Libyan desert or the Burmese jungle. In POW camps, worship was
often well-attended, partly because it reminded men of home and was
also a break from routine, partly because the men had often built the
chapel themselves and scrounged materials to make the furnishings.
In many Japanese camps, hymn sheets had to be written out by hand
and hidden between services. In 1942 the Singapore Race Club church
was built out of the stand. The bar became the altar. The Bishop,
Leonard Wilson, secured a pass to visit the camps through the help
of a Japanese Anglican officer. Interned in Changi jail in 1943 he still
managed to minister to the prisoners. During his beatings he tried to
imagine the torturers as they had been as children. But it was not
enough. Then he remembered the hymn:

> Look, Father, look on His anointed face,
> And only look on us as found in him . . .

Now he could forgive them. From his cell he could see the Methodist church and each day he said Wesley's hymn:

Christ, whose glory fills the skies . . .

In 1947 he baptized and confirmed one of his torturers.[138]

Chaplains in POW camps organized lectures as well as worship. George Millar, an agnostic officer, calculated that about thirty per cent of the officers and four per cent of the batmen 'took comfort from religion'. He thought that only about half of those who attended worship actually believed in God; others attended for a variety of reasons. Lectures given by the chaplain, Fr Hugh Bishop (then a Mirfield Father) were well attended. He was 'the finest and noblest speaker' he had ever heard. But Millar could not leap 'the gulf'.[139]

Battle made death, once a remote possibility, a daily reality. On the Burma and Siam railway it was not until cholera broke out and the chaplain ministered to the sick and buried the dead that the Japanese accepted him as a chaplain. Eric Treacy in Normandy buried British and Germans alike: 'It was a heart-rending business sorting out their personal effects. These nearly always contained photographs of the family and affectionate letters from their wives and children. Nothing was more unpleasant than extracting human remains from a truck that had been "brewed up" . . .'[140] The title of the most famous war-time memoirs *The Last Enemy* (1942) by Richard Hillary was derived from the lesson in the Burial Service. But Hillary was relieved that when he thought he was dying he did not resort to prayer. By contrast 'An Airman's Last Letter to His Mother' (*Times*, 18 June 1940) might have been written between 1914 and 1918: 'My death would not mean that your struggle has been in vain. Far from it. It means that your sacrifice is as great as mine. Those who serve England must expect nothing from her . . .' Within a month, half a million copies of the letter were sold.

The war created ecumenical opportunities. Bernard Pawley (later the Archbishop's representative in Rome) made friends with Copts in Cairo, Roman Catholics in Italy, Lutherans in Germany. In one POW camp in Germany the same altar was used in turn by Orthodox, Roman Catholics, Anglicans and French Reformed. But at Colditz, Ellison Platt, the Methodist chaplain, complained in his diary about the stiff-necked Anglican chaplains who seemed to be incapable of providing worship suitable for nominal Christians, but rather insisted on celebrating Communion at every opportunity.[141] When one Mirfield Father who was a chaplain, not only invited Nonconformists to communicate but also celebrated the eucharist in the evening, another member of the community, also a chaplain, strongly protested. Temple wanted a generous interpretation of regulations allowing non-Anglicans to communicate when cut off from their own churches, or when Free Church chaplains attended refresher courses run by Anglicans. But he could do little or nothing with those who took the exclusive attitude.[142]

If the war was breaking down some ecclesiastical barriers, it was also opening up more roles for women. In December 1941 it was decided to conscript women into the services or industrial work. Female chaplain's assistants were appointed to work in the women's services. 'Are the Churches going to set aside full time and highly responsible women for some sort of spiritual ministry when the war is over?' asked Micklem in the *Guardian* on 17 March 1944. Women played a large part in the various agencies like the Church Army, Salvation Army and YMCA which provided canteens for the troops. In the Spring of 1939 the Cathedral authorities at Ripon foresaw the need for a Services club, and the Rev. T. Garnett Jones was appointed to a nearby parish. During the war, he and his wife, with a host of helpers, served sometimes 7,000 meals a week. All sorts of visitors arrived – bargees from London, bedraggled and shocked troops from Dunkirk, even Italian prisoners and Russians liberated from POW camps.

The Rev. Peter Mayhew, Anglican chaplain 1939–46, in *The Ministry of an Army Chaplain*, warned new chaplains not to expect a keen body of churchmen. In the two units to which he was attached there was not one regular Anglican communicant. Out of 100 conscripts he received in 1939, 73 were 'C of E', but only 13 had been confirmed and none of them was a communicant. 'We are dealing with a pagan generation.' Field Marshal Montgomery, as a strong evangelical believer in the God of Battles, regarded chaplains as essential for the maintenance of spiritual morale and paid them high tributes. But two observers as different as Archbishop Garbett and John Collins were perturbed by the poor quality of some chaplains. Collins wrote: 'The work of the Church in the RAF often suffered because so many chaplains were afraid to challenge authority at those points where their integrity as ministers of the Christian religion was at stake'.[143] On 25 August 1944 the *Guardian* published comments on religion in the RAF from a Christian airman. He said that the men respect the padre and have no real hostility to religion, but the world of church and Bible is infinitely remote. 'Religion, in the Forces especially, is very much associated with the powers that be, and the padre, as he is an officer, with the officer class. And you know how removed that class is from the ordinary rank and file.' The chaplain who sent these extracts recalled that Donald Hankey had said much the same in 1916.

Frank Woods, vicar of Huddersfield was a chaplain throughout the war – later he became Archbishop of Melbourne. In a sermon in the *Guardian* (9 November 1945) he said that chaplains had discovered how wide was the gap between men and the church; that they were complete strangers to worship – 'the very idea of God just means nothing'; that they had no doctrinal basis for belief. Whereas the parish priest spent most of his time with the faithful, the chaplain shared every aspect of life with his men.

Thus the most perceptive chaplains of the second war discovered that the religious crisis, about which their predecessors had spoken with such urgency and passion thirty years previously, was just as intractable in 1945 as it had been in 1918.

10

THE COSTS OF VICTORY

Being a Christian in the Third Reich

Meanwhile in Hitler's Third Reich some Christians were strenuously trying to work out what form their discipleship could and should take. The following three Christians worked out their obedience in totally different but equally authentic forms.

Franz Jägerstätter was a Roman Catholic sexton in the village of St Radegund in Upper Austria. When Hitler's troops occupied Austria in 1938, Jägerstätter was the only man in the village to vote against the Anschluss. His spirituality was rigorist, biblicist and fiercely pietistic. In February 1943 he was called up. He refused to serve and was imprisoned. The prison chaplain tried to convince him that by taking the oath he would not be supporting the Nazis, just following the example of millions of fellow-Catholics, including seminarians. How could a peasant (he asked) presume to make a judgment about the war? He should place the welfare of his wife and family first. Jägerstätter's parish priest and his wife visited him and also tried to persuade him to change his mind. But he wrote: 'I cannot believe that, just because a man has a wife and children he is free to offend God by lying' and quoted Matthew 10.28 and 10.37. In August 1943 he was executed at the age of 36. His biographer, visiting the village nearly twenty years later, discovered that most of the inhabitants still did not understand his act of dissent. He had made a pointless sacrifice. Perhaps his piety had unhinged him. His action reflected badly on villagers who had obediently done their duty. The local bishop considered him 'a completely exceptional case, one more to be marvelled at than copied': 'those exemplary young Catholic men . . . who fought and died in heroic fulfilment of their duty', like Christian soldiers in the army of the heathen emperor, were 'the greater heroes.'[1] So Jägerstätter, like Jeremiah and Jesus, stood against the community, for the community, paradoxically also strengthened to do so by the religious resources which the community had provided.

The second example of a Christian response to Hitler is that of a Prussian aristocrat who served as a German officer in both wars. In 1945 the Belgian city of Louvain celebrated the end of the war with a torchlight procession. The people thanked the mayor who had brought the city through the occupation almost unscathed, whereas in 1914 it had suffered terribly from the German troops. But the mayor said that much of the gratitude should be passed on to the German commandant, Reinhold von Thadden-Trieglaff. It was an extraordinary moment. In 1947 Thadden was invited to return for a civic reception.

Thadden came from an ancient Prussian family. As an officer cadet in 1912 he made his first act of dissent by refusing to fight a duel. His superiors and fellow cadets were outraged and until his father intervened with the Kaiser he remained an NCO. After serving in the war, Thadden worked with the poor in Berlin. Rejecting pietist Christianity, instead he identified himself with the SCM, and became president of the German branch. Through the WSCF, his eyes were opened to the trans-national character of Christianity and he met Temple, Bell and Berggrav. When Hitler came to power, Thadden fought hard to prevent the incorporation of the SCM into the Nazi Student Unions. He became Chairman of the Pomeranian Confessing Church, and this brought him into contact with Bonhoeffer. Several times Thadden was arrested by the Gestapo.

In 1940 he was called up. His Prussian upbringing led him to obey, despite his distaste for serving in Hitler's army. However, as a Christian he was determined to work within the system to try to ameliorate its operation. As Regional Commissioner for the Louvain district, he consistently refused to take reprisals for acts of sabotage, and frequently saved innocent civilians from punishment or death. When the war was ending he rejected orders to shoot captured RAF officers, as contrary to both his faith and his officer's code. Before he evacuated the city he disobeyed orders to destroy food stocks and instead had them distributed to the people on condition that his troops would not be fired on as they withdrew.

The Russians arrested him on his estate in March 1945. They could not comprehend how he could be simultaneously a landowner, an anti-Nazi, a German officer and a Confessing Christian. Transported to a Russian camp, Thadden sustained a mixed group of Christians with stories of the world-wide church and by conducting services: 'life-giving springs in a desert of misery, despair and death' he described these gatherings. When in 1945 he returned to Berlin a sick man, an American officer, a former chairman of WSCF, smuggled Thadden and his wife through the Russian zone and into Switzerland. He began to work for the ecumenical movement. He accepted without reservation the statement of guilt made by the German churches. Asked how he could have served in Hitler's army, he replied: 'There is not one of us whose actions as a soldier in the war were always completely logical . . . there are plenty of opportunities for the Christian in an evil world to live by faith, and to affirm his obedience to the Will of God in each new actual decision.' In 1950 Thadden organized the first of the Protestant Kirchentag Assemblies for lay people, perhaps the greatest religious movement in post-war Europe. In 1961, the year of the Eichmann trial, one of the themes of the Berlin Kirchentag was 'Jews and Christians'. Thadden was a fine representative of the ancient European tradition which Christianized the best of the Graeco-Roman civilization.[2] Yet Barthians had maintained that only the 'pure Word of God' could sustain resistance to Nazism.

Dietrich Bonhoeffer was born in 1906 into a cultured and well-to-do family in Breslau. The family were not church-goers, but Bonhoeffer decided to be a pastor and theologian. In about 1929 he became a conditional pacifist, a stance which was very rare in German Protestantism which had no tradition of opposing the state. His Barthian theology made him question the erastianism of the German Church, but turned him against all forms of liberalism. His visit to Rome in 1924, his friendship with Bishop Bell (which dated from 1933) and his participation in the ecumenical movement gave him a vision of a world-wide church transcending national loyalties. He was ordained in 1931. As early as April 1933 he realized the theological absurdity of an Aryan Church, and in the next few years did all he could to support Jewish Christians. But his protests against the general persecution of the Jews were oblique.

By 1938–39 he was no longer predominantly concerned to sustain and protect the Confessing Church and began to launch into a more broadly based commitment to political action against Nazism. Should he emigrate? In June 1939 he travelled to the United States. But in July as the news grew more ominous he returned home. He wrote to explain his decision to Reinhold Niebuhr:

> I have made a mistake in coming to America. I must live through this difficult period of our national history with the Christian people of Germany. I will have no right to participate in the reconstruction of Christian life in Germany after the war if I do not share the trials

of this time with my people . . . Christians in Germany will face the terrible alternative of either willing the defeat of their nation in order that Christian civilization may survive, or willing the victory of their nation and thereby destroying our civilization. I know which of these alternatives I must choose; but I cannot make that choice in security.[3]

Soon after war began he applied to be an army chaplain to avoid serving at the front, but his application was refused as he had no military experience. By now Bonhoeffer believed that Christ would bless, not only those who suffered explicitly for him, but also any who suffered in a just cause. His brother-in-law, Hans von Dohnanyi, an anti-Nazi 'mole' in the Ministry of Justice, introduced him to conspirators and in 1940 arranged for him to become a voluntary member of Military Intelligence to protect him and to enable him to travel freely. Throughout this next period Bonhoeffer was conscious of his increasing isolation both from the church (which did not know of his double life) and from his own countrymen. Paradoxically, the fact that he was well-connected was invaluable to his work as a dissenter.

His views of the church began to change. In 1943 he said that the first use of the Law 'is not concerned with the christianization of worldly institutions or with their incorporation in the Church, but with their genuine worldliness, their 'naturalness' in obedience to God's word'.[4] He felt increasing misgivings about the biblicism of the Confessing Church which had led to a hostility towards culture and science. He was depressed that his own church, unlike those in Britain and America, was uninterested in post-war reconstruction. Meanwhile he was helping to smuggle some Jews to Switzerland. In May 1942, hearing that Bell was visiting Sweden, he decided to go to Stockholm, after consulting General Beck, the leader of the conspiracy. On 31 May Bell was astonished when Bonhoeffer arrived to see him. Bonhoeffer gave Bell the details of the resistance group to pass on to the British Government. When Bell returned to England he saw Anthony Eden, the Foreign Secretary. But Eden's attitude was negative. Though Bell could not divulge his sources in public, in the Lords and elsewhere he pressed for an Allied recognition of German resistance to Hitler.

In March 1943 a bomb which had been transported by Dohnanyi failed to explode in Hitler's plane. On 5 April Dohnanyi and Bonhoeffer were arrested, suspected of enabling Jews to escape from Germany. One day in the exercise yard at Tegel prison in Berlin a fellow prisoner asked Bonhoeffer how he, as a Christian and theologian, could participate in the resistance. Bonhoeffer replied that if he saw a drunken driver racing at high speed down the Kurfürstendamm, it was not enough to bury the victims and comfort the bereaved: he had to wrench the wheel out of the hands of the drunkard. At Christmas 1942 he had written about the moral ambiguities inherent in working for the resistance:

> The great masquerade of evil has played havoc with all our ethical concepts. For evil to appear disguised as light, charity, historical necessity, or social justice is quite bewildering to anyone brought up on our traditional ethical concepts, while for the Christian who bases his life on the Bible it merely confirms the fundamental wickedness of evil . . .

> It is infinitely easier to suffer in obedience to a human command than in the freedom of one's own responsibility. It is infinitely easier to suffer with others than to suffer alone. It is infinitely easier to suffer publicly and honourably than apart and ignominiously. It is infinitely easier to suffer through staking one's life than to suffer spiritually. Christ suffered as a free man alone, apart and in ignominy, in body and spirit; and since then many Christians have suffered with him. . .

> We have been the silent witnesses of evil deeds; we have been drenched by many storms; we have learnt the arts of equivocation and pretence . . . Will our inward power of resistance be strong enough, and our honesty with ourselves remorseless enough, for us to find our way back to simplicity and straighforwardness?[5]

As early as 1928 Bonhoeffer had felt an identification with Jeremiah. When Jerusalem was under siege, Jeremiah bought a plot of land in his home town as a gesture of faith in the future. So in January 1943 Bonhoeffer announced his engagement from prison.

On 20 July 1944, a bomb was exploded under Hitler's staff conference table, but did not kill him. The only church newspaper still licensed thanked God for Hitler's deliverance. Some one hundred and fifty alleged conspirators were executed. Now Bonhoeffer's participation in the resistance gradually came to light. In prison, deriving strength from the Bible, especially the Psalms, and Lutheran hymns, he ministered to his fellow-prisoners. He began a sketch for a new theology: 'The non-religious interpretation of Biblical terms in a world come of age'. He had become disenchanted with the Confessing Church which maintained the great doctrines but did not explain and interpret them and seemed preoccupied with itself. Bonhoeffer was in prison precisely because he had co-operated with many people who were remote from the church. When Bultmann proposed his programme of demythologizing, Bonhoeffer saw him as an ally against Barth, but believed that he did not go far enough.[6] Bonhoeffer, like Niemöller later, had been compelled by events to alter his whole way of looking at life. Before the war he had been chiefly concerned to express his solidarity with the Confessing Church and the ecumenical movement. Now he had a new sense of solidarity with all humanity. He began to read history from below, from the standpoint of the powerless and oppressed. It was as though his experiences had led him to re-appropriate elements of liberalism in his home background which in his Barthian period he had rejected. (But it was Barth who had taught him to be sceptical of religion.) Bonhoeffer wrote from prison in April 1944:

> How can Christ become the Lord of the religionless as well? . . . How do we speak . . . in a 'secular' way about God? . . . I often ask myself why a 'Christian instinct' often draws me more to the religionless people than to the religious, by which I don't in the least mean with any evangelizing intention, but, I might also say, 'in brotherhood'.[7]

A month before war ended, on 5 April 1945, Hitler decided that both Bonhoeffer and Dohnanyi must be executed. Bonhoeffer had been moved from Buchenwald where he had heard the American guns closing in. By request on Sunday 8 April Bonhoeffer conducted a service and expounded Isaiah 53.5 and I Peter 1.3. The next day at dawn he and some of the other conspirators were hanged. Dohnanyi was executed the same day at Sachsenhausen. Bonhoeffer's parents did not know of their son's death until on 27 July they listened to a memorial service on the BBC conducted by Bishop Bell. Bell said that it was Bonhoeffer's passion for justice which had led him into close partnership with others who, 'though outside the Church, shared the same humanitarian and liberal ideals'.[8] By contrast, Bonhoeffer's Church of Berlin-Brandenburg drew a sharp distinction between Christian martyrs like Pastor Paul Schneider and the political resisters and condemned the 1944 conspiracy. In 1970 Bethge wrote that Germans were still inhibited about fully integrating him and what he stood for.

Before Bonhoeffer was taken to be executed, he managed to give a last message to an English officer who was a fellow-prisoner. It was for George Bell:

Tell him that for me this is the end but also the beginning. With him I believe in the principle of our Universal Christian brotherhood which rises above all national interests, and that our victory is certain . . .[9]

When in October Bell led the first post-war deputation of English churchmen to Berlin, he visited the Bonhoeffer family. Bonhoeffer's mother took from a drawer a book which her son had used for his devotions in prison. It was *The Imitation of Christ.*

The victories of 1945

Three weeks after Bonhoeffer's execution Harold Macmillan was in Assisi. There he heard of the capitulation of the German forces in Italy. He wrote in his diary:

Hitler has lasted twelve years – with all his power of evil, his strength, his boasting. St Francis did not seem to have much power, but here in this lovely place one realises the immense strength and permanence of goodness . . .[10]

As the invading armies liberated the extermination camps it was not easy to believe, with Macmillan, in the 'permanence of goodness'. When the British liberated Belsen on 15 April, Richard Dimbleby of the BBC was the first correspondent to enter. The BBC in London, hardly believing his report, hesitated about transmitting it, until the enraged Dimbleby insisted. In the *Church Times* on 18 May, a British chaplain described children playing among the massed piles of bodies in Belsen. 'Tomorrow, with a Roman Catholic and a Jewish chaplain, I am burying over four thousand people in a communal grave.' Other graves were being dug in various parts of the camp. But the major article on that page was concerned with the South India scheme for church union, which had been the main source of anxiety for Anglo-Catholics during the war.

On VE Day Bishop Barry of Southwell stood beside the mayor of Nottingham when he read the proclamation from the balcony of the Council House. Twenty-five years later Barry recalled:

At his request I spoke through a microphone to the vast multitude in the Market Square 'a word in the name of the living God'. There was an almost audible silence, cigarettes were put out, hats were lifted, and the crowd felt like a worshipping congregation . . . But I wonder, could it happen like that today?[11]

In London, a total of 35,000 people attended almost continuous services at St Paul's. Churchill went with the Commons to St Margaret's, Westminster. He noted with particular pleasure the words of Psalm 124:

> Our soul is escaped even as a bird out of the
>   snare of the fowler:
> the snare is broken, and we are delivered.

A young Somerset woman wrote in her diary:

> 8 May. Glorious day! Sunshine, flags and happy crowds, and the marvellous feeling of relief. We made holiday all day . . . Mike and I went to church at 7.30 p.m., there was an immense congregation with people standing.[12]

On the same day in Church Stretton someone thought 'It's all over at last' and then saw three men from St Dunstan's blinded by the war. The following Sunday everyone in the Eighth Army in Italy attended religious services which began with a note of penitence. The lesson was Revelation 21.1–7 which includes the promise 'Behold I make all things new'. This was the text which had so gripped F. R. Barry and Mervyn Haigh as they returned from being chaplains at the end of the first war, full of optimistic hope of building a new church for a new world.

At the beginning of 1945 the Bishop of Liverpool, Clifford Martin, claimed that it was devotion to a common cause which had broken down barriers of class in war-time. After the war Britain would need the same spirit to tackle the problems of bad housing and inadequate health facilities and to create cultural facilities for the whole community. J. B. Priestley in his broadcast celebrating the end of the war, reiterated his message of 1940 that the war had taught Britain that it could be a community of neighbours. Such attitudes led people to vote Labour on 5 July. The Sunday after the result was announced, one priest said in his biddings: 'Let us pray for our King in the great sorrow that has come to him this week.' Lang thought Attlee 'the embodiment of the second-rate'.[13] But both comments were unrepresentative of general clerical opinion (though it is true that Attlee himself was widely underestimated). During the war those leaders of the Church of England best known to the general public had advocated many of the policies which appeared in Labour's manifesto in 1945. In addition much of the theology which had most influenced the clergy during the previous ten years had been corporatist. A. M. Ramsey in *The Gospel and the Catholic Church* (1936) urged the individual to die to his own experiences and live to those of the church, a theme reinforced by L. S. Thornton in his significantly titled book *The Common Life in the Body of Christ* (1942). Several books on the eucharist, from A. G. Hebert's *Liturgy and Society* (1935) to Dom Gregory Dix's *The Shape of the Liturgy* (1945), taught the clergy the benefits of corporate liturgy. That most characteristic Anglican expression of personal devotion, the 8 am Sunday Communion was therefore increasingly decried as selfishly individualistic. Thornton, Hebert and Dix all wrote out of the experience of the common life of the Anglican monastic communities to which they belonged. Thus, as a result of the war, probably more of the leading Christians in England expressed their faith through collectivist and socialist ideology than ever before. Cripps might have been addressing a war-time Religion and Life week when, as Minister of Economic Affairs, he told the Commons on 23 October 1947:

> I wish that today our country could refresh its heart and mind with a deep draught of that Christian faith which has come down to us over 2,000 years and has over those centuries inspired the peoples of Europe of fresh efforts and new hopes.

But there were nagging doubts about the stability of the peace which victory had brought. The *Guardian* on 4 May 1945 was thankful that peace was imminent, but the leader was headed 'It can happen again'. R. C. M. Howard in his poem 'The Voyage Back' written in August 1945 in the Far East notably qualified his sense of relief:

> To say it is done, for a few years at least, makes the heart want
> to shout . . .

The Japanese did not surrender until 14 August, after atomic bombs were dropped on Hiroshima (6 August) and Nagasaki (9 August). Most British people were only too glad that all hostilities were now over and did not stop to consider the moral implications of the use of atomic weapons. The war against Japan had never been as important to the British as it was to Americans. Japan was a very distant country in every sense. The British did not like the Japanese, and regarded them as purveyors of cheap, shoddy goods which before the war had put British people out of work. The Japanese were known to have treated POWs with great cruelty. By May 1945 only seven per cent of Japanese occupied territory had been liberated, so it looked as though a long struggle lay ahead which would cost many lives. Britain was weary after six years of war. Consciences had been blunted by the acceptance of obliteration bombing.

For once Henson found himself in agreement with the Vatican

which had condemned the use of atomic weapons. The justifications being offered were 'cynical'. He noted with satisfaction that Dean Thicknesse had refused the use of St Albans' Cathedral for a VJ Day Thanksgiving Service. Henson, who usually admired Churchill greatly, considered his apologia in the Commons to be 'faulty in logic, unsound in principle, and irrelevant in reference'. He told the village congregation that Sunday, that to use the bomb was 'deplorable and indefensible' and 'an essentially immoral action'.[14] By contrast, Geoffrey Fisher, the new Archbishop of Canterbury, was equivocal. 'This new discovery was not in itself either a catastrophe or a boon', he commented. However, in his sermon at the National Thanksgiving service in St Paul's on Sunday 19 August he told the congregation that they should not only thank God for victory but also pray for 'cleansing':

> We have fought for the light against spiritual darkness . . . But in so doing we have had to enter the darkness ourselves, to use the weapons of darkness, to turn every endeavour of mind and body to deadly and destructive ends. Physically the atomic bomb is a new thing. Morally it differs not in kind but only to a terrible degree from every other weapon of total war.

Garbett seemed more aware that a decisive line had been crossed. In November he declared that 'a very thin partition will separate our civilization from complete destruction'. The formula for the manufacture of atomic weapons should be handed over to an international organization which then would prevent any nation from making them.[15]

Bishop Chavasse of Rochester preached against the use of the bombs at a VJ Day service attended by Montgomery. In his Diocesan Chronicle he declared:

> From the Abyssinian war down to the present hour, we have vehemently denounced indiscriminate slaughter in war . . . Are we going to hang the Germans for doing what we ourselves have done so very much better than they?

But by 1958 the advent of the Cold War had changed his mind. Britain and America should hold '*the sword* of the hydrogen bomb' (my italics) to ensure the peace. Total destruction and a lingering death for survivors would be a lesser evil than totalitarian domination.[16] In a letter to the *Times* (14 August 1945) Bell recalled the condemnation of the bombing of Warsaw and Rotterdam. The Allied agreement of 8 August 1945 establishing the War Crimes Tribunal included the 'wanton destruction of cities' among 'War Crimes':

There are certain deeds science should not do. There are certain actions for which scientists should not be made conscripts by any nation. And surely the extermination of any civilian population by any nation is one of these.

Ronald Knox, the Roman Catholic priest, was so dismayed by the silence of his church leaders that he wrote *God and the Atom* (1945). Knox argued that both the use of the bomb and the revelation of the nature of atomic matter put a question against much traditional theology and ethics. Will not the use of the bomb produce a new age of atheists? Charles Raven, attending a Fellowship of Reconciliation Conference, threw aside his speech at hearing the news, and spoke in apocalyptic terms. It was particularly agonizing for him to see the scientific discoveries of Rutherford (whom he had known and admired) used for the slaughter of the innocent. Others were numbed and silenced. Edith Sitwell in 'The Shadow of Cain' was one of the very few poets who tried to find words to express what had happened.

On the other side, Lord Vansittart (*Times*, 18 August) asked if victory had cost another half million British and American lives, would Dean Thicknesse have allowed his Cathedral to be used for a service? In a sermon reported on 22 August, the Dean of Ely commented that the critics seemed a value the lives of 'a cruel and barbarous people' above the lives of our own forces.

Geoffrey Fisher distrusted emotion and saw life as a series of fascinating crossword puzzles awaiting solution. He described committee work as 'entrancing'. Instinctively he identified with those in authority and therefore usually gave any dissenters short shrift.[17] It was therefore wholly characteristic that he replied to the many protesting letters which arrived at Lambeth with cool detachment. Among chaplains who wrote to express their horror at the use of atomic weapons was John Collins. As an RAF chaplain he had been reprimanded by his commanding officer for preaching that we should not be prepared to achieve victory by means which sacrificed moral integrity. He had been increasingly tormented by the moral revulsion felt by some airmen at the obliteration bombing they were ordered to undertake. 'Why' asked a Christian airman 'do the Churches not tell us we are doing an evil job?'[18] Fisher replied to Collins on 18 August that the *Times* correspondence showed that honest men may honestly differ about the use of the bomb. It was not morally in a separate category. But if it were used again he would protest. Collins on 21 August was grateful for Fisher's readiness to protest about any further use of the bomb. Percy Hartill reminded Fisher of the Archbishops' assurances of 1940 that there were moral limits to warfare. Bishop Mann, a former bishop in Japan, pointed out that Lang and others had condemned the Japanese bombing of Chinese cities in 1937. On 16 August Fisher explained his position to Newton Flew, the Methodist minister, then Moderator of the Free Church Federal Council. Now that the war was over it was not 'necessary' to debate whether the bomb should have been used. 'I find it difficult to decide precisely on what grounds the use of it can be condemned apart from the general grounds which condemn other forms of bombing just as much.' In his diocesan leaflet, Fisher contented himself with putting the arguments on both sides, but added that every conscience was shocked and ashamed. At this early stage both Collins and Hartill believed that Fisher's position was close to their own. (Later Collins said that he was converted to pacifism on the day the atom bomb was dropped.) In October, Fisher decided to support the appointment of a BCC group to consider the moral and spiritual implications of modern methods of warfare. Its subsequent report *The Era of Atomic Power* (1946), and that of a group appointed by the Church Assembly, showed that from the first, Christian opinion was deeply divided about both the possession and use of atomic weapons.[19]

Rebuilding Europe

In February 1945, the Church Assembly appealed to the dioceses to contribute £250,000 to the national appeal for one million pounds for Christian reconstruction and refugee work in Europe. As soon as the war ended, Bell began to organize a renewal of contacts with the churches in Germany, many of whose leaders were exhausted physically and spiritually. In September, Niemöller, recovering after nearly eight years in prison, bluntly told a group of Evangelical church leaders: 'Had there been a German victory, we should none of us be here today.' In October Bell and Dr Gordon Rupp, the Methodist scholar, travelled to Germany. They joined a WCC delegation for a meeting with leaders of the Evangelical Church. The WCC delegation included representatives of countries which had particularly suffered from German occupation – France, Holland and Norway. At the meeting Niemöller handed the visitors a document on behalf of the Evangelical Church which became known as the 'Stuttgart Declaration'.

> We are the more grateful for this visit, as we with our people know ourselves to be not only in a great company of suffering, but also in a solidarity of guilt. With great pain do we say: through us has

endless suffering been brought to many peoples and countries . . .
True, we have struggled for many years in the name of Jesus Christ
against the spirit which has found its terrible expression in the
National Socialist régime of violence, but we accuse ourselves for
not being more courageous, for not praying more faithfully, for not
believing more joyously and for not loving more ardently. Now a
new beginning is to be made in our churches . . .

Bishop Dibelius had drafted the text, but only with difficulty accepted
the insertion of the crucial section written by Niemöller: 'With great
pain we say . . . made in our churches'. The Declaration was a great
act of courage and humility. Those who signed it, anticipated that
many of their fellow countrymen would accuse them of agreeing to
another Versailles, as indeed happened. Bell's presence made all the
difference. It was, said one of the WCC delegates 'more easy for the
Germans to give the Declaration to a personality like the Bishop of
Chichester whom they trusted and loved, than to any other man'. (For
example, Bishop Wurm, one of the signatories, who had protested to
Hitler about the euthanasia programme and the extermination of the
Jews in 1943, had been quite unable to look forward to the defeat of
his own country.) The act of reconciliation at Stuttgart was sealed by
an invitation to the Germans to send a delegation to the WCC
Committee in Geneva in February 1946.[20]

The German Roman Catholics made no such declaration. Cardinal
Galen, known as the 'Lion of Münster' for his outspoken attacks on
Nazism, felt like Bishop Wurm, a painful conflict between Christian
conscience and love of country. So Galen declared during the war:
'We will continue to do our duty in obedience to God, out of love for
our German *Volk* and *Vaterland* . . . But not for those men who wound
our hearts and bring shame upon the German name before God and
man by their cruel acts . . .'[21] Nor could German church leaders at
that stage face their share of guilt for the extermination of the Jews.
The Jews were not even mentioned in the Stuttgart Declaration. The
churches in the Allied countries recognized the Declaration as a
courageous and unprecedented ecumenical response, but it also made
it easier for them to evade their own share of responsibility.

Remembering the dead

How did the British commemorate their dead after the second world
war? After 1918 every community erected a memorial: a simple cross
on a village green or a colossal monument like that at Southport
with a huge obelisk flanked by colonnades – within were inscribed

remorseless lists of names, above epitaphs such as 'Faithful to her we fell and rest content'. It was very different in 1945. By the time communities were considering memorials, the Cold War was beginning. No one thought, as in 1918, that it had been a war which had ended war. So many a community and church simply cleaned the first war memorial and added 'Also 1939–45' and the extra names. The British in 1945 often preferred to raise money for 'something useful' like playing fields, a new heating system for the church or a new library for school or college. Attitudes to death itself had changed. Cremations were increasing. More and more people preferred to scatter the ashes at the crematorium rose garden rather than to bury the coffin in the churchyard. A new benign pantheism was replacing the anxious concern about the fate of loved ones so common in the first war. In 1917 the Cabinet contemplated building a 'Hall of Honour' in London, as the central feature of a National War Museum. In the Hall would be inscribed the name of every serviceman who had died for the Empire. By contrast, in 1946 the Government decided to give fifty million pounds to establish a National Land Fund for the recreational and cultural enjoyment of the British public. The decision to observe Remembrance Day on the Sunday nearest Armistice Day rendered it much more marginal to national life. Gone were the days when traffic stopped and the whole nation paused for the two minutes silence. But the basic ethos and rituals of Remembrance Day remain those evolved after 1918. There seemed nothing distinctively new to say or do. At Remembrancetide 1982, the television programme 'Songs of Praise' invited Mrs Thatcher to select a hymn to commemorate the Falklands dead. She chose 'O Valiant Hearts' published in 1919.

A few special second war memorials were erected, particularly by regiments and service associations. Stained glass windows in Westminster Abbey commemorated the Battle of Britain. In Durham Cathedral a window dedicated to the Royal Air Force, depicts an airman flying over Durham on the wings of an eagle. Underneath is the striking inscription from Isaiah 31 'As birds flying so shall the Lord of Hosts protect Jerusalem'. But many, particularly in the North of England, relied on first war precedents for inspiration. The Book of Remembrance in Bradford Cathedral is inscribed with lines from Rupert Brooke 'These laid the world away . . .' For the memorial at Ambleside parish church someone chose the line from Kipling: 'Who dies if England live'. In Wakefield Cathedral a regimental memorial is flanked by statues of St Michael and St George in armour.

In 1944 a new incumbent arrived in Langthwaite, North Yorkshire. He had been a chaplain in both wars and his son had been killed during the second. He compiled a Book of Remembrance which included photographs of the dead of the first war and of all who served in the second. A new reredos was erected to commemorate the 1939–45 war. Its three panels depict a sailing ship, a sword and angel's wings – not we note a destroyer, a machine gun and a bomber. Nearby, in Richmond parish church, a side chapel was dedicated as a memorial to the Green Howards. Its reredos is more realistic than the one at Langthwaite and portrays soldiers digging, walking, on sentry duty and playing a mouth organ. A central crucifix stands on a hill behind them. They wear battle dress and tin hats, not armour. But no soldier is actually fighting. All these memorials indicate the great difficulty their creators experienced when trying to reconcile Christianity with modern warfare.

Many churches contain individual memorial plaques erected during the first war by the local industrialist or squire to commemorate a son. The more egalitarian ethos of the second war was reflected in the advice given by the Chancellor of the Carlisle diocese in 1944: 'it seems inconsistent with the principles for which the war is being fought that some of those who fall should be singled out, by the accident of material prosperity, for particular commemoration'.[22]

When France was being liberated in 1944, the Imperial War Graves Commission began to inspect the damaged and overgrown cemeteries and to recruit staff to add to the thirty-four gardeners who had continued their work during the occupation. Now it had to care for 24,000 sites all over the world. The name panels on the Menin Gate had been chipped by bullets, the causeway destroyed and the bronze entrance gates had vanished. Some cemeteries had been bombed or ploughed up. There were 370,000 new graves to be dug and 250,000 missing to be commemorated. There was not the emotional or financial support for its work that there had been after 1918. By October 1956 ninety per cent of the new graves had been marked with headstones.[23]

> People change, and smile: but the agony abides.
> Time the destroyer is time the preserver . . .
> (T. S. Eliot, 'The Dry Salvages')

There is a strange and poignant contrast between the capacity of human beings to devise such ugly and disorderly deaths, and their determination afterwards to take infinite trouble to locate the bodies and place them in such ordered rows.

EPILOGUE

11

BEYOND TRAGEDY?

Humiliation

During the twentieth century the English churches have been humiliated by their own impotence, though they have not usually admitted either to the humiliation or the impotence. In 1906 Bishop Gore spoke of

> . . . the powerlessness of the Church, in spite of even splendid exceptions in this or that parish, to produce any broad, corporate effect, to make any effective spiritual appeal by its own proper influence, in the great democracy of England today.[1]

In 1969 David Edwards wrote about the urgent need of the church for renewal and the apparently insuperable difficulties of ever achieving it:

> Conferences have come, and conferences have gone; books have exploded, and books have been forgotten; and the local churches, sullenly resentful or cheerfully ignorant, have remained much as they were before the prophets arose . . . The humiliation of the Christian Church is the great fact which stands out . . .[2]

The half century of church life which we have surveyed in this book leaves me with two dominant impressions. First: never in its long history has the church in England, through all its branches, tried so hard to be faithful, to proclaim and re-interpret the gospel, to pray, to serve the community and to engage in self-examination. Never before has it included so many Christians prepared to stand against the prevailing forces of public opinion. But second: despite the church's many notable achievements, some of which have been chronicled in this book, the church has been like a boat firmly stuck on a sandbank, lapped and sometimes shaken by the waves, but never able to free itself to sail out into the open sea.

What have been some of the main sources of this powerlessness and humiliation?

During the twentieth century the English churches have experienced catastrophic decline – though the Roman Catholic church, until the last decade or so, because of its special history, has been an exception. This decline may be shrugged off by reminders that in the eighteenth century church attendance in England was also low, or that the high level of allegiance in the Victorian period was wholly untypical. But at the local level such explanations mean nothing to you when your much loved parish church is demolished or your chapel, which used to be so thriving, is turned into a carpet warehouse. Some of the statistics of decline were presented at the beginning of Chapter 3. But statistics are cold and abstract, and need to be fleshed out. I know of no more poignant reminder of what decline really means, than the following advertisement which appeared in the *Methodist Recorder* on 3 December 1970:

CATHEDRAL OF METHODISM. Elswick Rd. Newcastle-upon-Tyne. Closing Service December 30th. Available cheap: organ . . . new electric boiler . . . 6 beautiful stained glass windows . . .

This sense of powerlessness and humiliation is deepened if one accepts the analysis of Currie, Gilbert and Horsley in *Churches and Churchgoers* (1977) that church policy is less significant, when assessing reasons for growth or decline, than such external factors as: secularization, industrialization, urbanization, trade fluctuations, political changes and war. If this is true, then there is little likelihood that the fortunes of the churches in this country will improve until external factors become more favourable to growth.

What is so striking is that this period of continuous decline has in fact been characterized by strenuous movements for renewal and large numbers of varied types of evangelistic effort. The National Mission of Repentance and Hope of 1916 represented an unprecedented effort by the Church of England to bring Christianity to the nation. But its effect on church attendance, like that of the Free Church 'Come to Church' campaign of 1915, was imperceptible. Yet between 1914 and 1918 many Christians were convinced that the war had created a religious revival. Neville Talbot, a first war chaplain who became Bishop of Pretoria in 1920, in the Preface to his book *The Returning Tide of Faith* (1923) rejected the famous lines of Matthew Arnold's 'Dover Beach' about the 'melancholy, long, withdrawing roar' of the sea of faith. Instead he claimed: 'the ebb-tide of faith has turned'. Between 1917 and 1920, much energy was devoted to, and many high hopes were raised by, Life and Liberty – but did it help one more person to believe in God? On 17 January 1929 the *Methodist Recorder* claimed that 'a Revival will coincide with the coming of Methodist Union . . . with the consummation of union a great forward movement on quite unprecedented lines is anticipated; is indeed inevitable'.[3] But decline continued after Methodist Union in 1932. Or again: what did the Archbishop of Canterbury's 'Recall to Religion' of 1937 achieve? In the midst of the international crisis of September 1938 Dr Robert Bond, Moderator of the Free Church Federal Council, for many years Secretary of the Methodist Conference, asserted: 'For a considerable time a big section of the nation had been drifting away from God, but there were signs of this drift being checked . . .'[4] On the eve of the war, Frank Buchman, leader of the Oxford Group movement, broadcast a starkly simple message to the nations: 'moral rearmament is the only permanent cure for crisis'.[5] (The hopes and fervour then engendered by Buchmanism were broadly similar to those created by the Charismatic Movement in the 1970s.) The Church of England Report *Towards the Conversion of England* (1945) sold well and produced a few tangible results but the actual conversion of England remained as elusive as ever.[6] W. E. Sangster throughout his ministry enthusiastically engaged in many evangelistic campaigns. 1953 was designated by Methodism as a 'Year of Evangelism'. But at the end of the year Sangster sadly confessed 'No sweeping revival has come'.[7] In 1959 J. A. T. Robinson in his first confirmation sermon as Bishop of Woolwich told the candidates:

> You are coming into active membership of the Church at a time when great things are afoot. I believe that in England we may be at a turning of the tide. Indeed, in Cambridge, where I have recently come from, I am convinced that the tide has already turned.

When he quoted this in 1969 he commented ruefully 'How wrong can one be?'[8] Yet in the 1960s the radicals (including Robinson himself) believed that if only the church's theology, liturgy and structures could be modernized the tide would turn.

No doubt the churches would have declined even more without all these efforts. But each campaign was, and had to be, inaugurated with large claims and high hopes in order to win enthusiastic support. Yet each ended with the usual apologetic explanation that even if the hoped for revival had not arrived, at least the faithful had been strengthened and that such-and-such a chapel or church was now full of converts. But many at the local level, repeatedly hurt and bewildered by the failure of evangelistic and ecumenical hopes to materialize,

have (in effect) increasingly echoed D. H. Lawrence's angry plea 'send
no more saviours'.[9]

In Chapter 3 we have already given some examples of the powerfully
corrosive effects of secularization, pluralism and modernity on
religious faith and allegiance between the wars. Since then all three
movements have become even more powerful and pervasive in British
society.[10] First, Britain has become a much more secular society
despite a good deal of residual religion and superstition. In the winter
of 1882–83, bad weather was seriously affecting agriculture. The
Bishop of Norwich told his diocese that this was a direct punishment
from God and called all parishioners to attend services of prayer,
humiliation and repentance. But when in 1982 a village in North
Yorkshire was devastated by floods, no one even hinted to the vicar
that this might be anything to do with God or religion. Secondly,
Britain has gradually become a pluralist society during the last 150
years. In the nineteenth century the Anglican monopoly in England
was decisively broken. In the twentieth century immigration and
humanism have permanently ruptured the Christian monopoly.
Thirdly, modernity discourages people from looking to the past for
guidance and faith. The past is for nostalgia and tourism, and religion
is part of that past. The churches' response to modernity has been to
engage in programmes of modernization, of which the lamentable
Alternative Service Book (1980) and the self-important bodies created
by synodical government are prime examples in the Church of
England. But modernization starkly exposes, but in no way solves,
the deepening crisis which faces Christianity: that the Christian
revelation was expressed through a culture which has become percept-
ibly even more remote during the twentieth century. So modern
liturgies and new translations of the Bible are often banal or hollowly
rhetorical because the modern English language is incapable of
conveying the old faith convincingly. The authentic faith of poets like
T. S. Eliot, Edwin Muir or R. S. Thomas can be expressed in genuinely
modern English because their faith is oblique, wry and constantly
sensitive to the integrity of doubt. In 1934 in *Choruses from 'The Rock'*
T. S. Eliot summed up the religious crisis of modern Britain:

> Men have left GOD not for other gods, they say, but
> for no god; and this has never happened before . . .

The English churches have also been humiliated and rendered
impotent by their failure to exercise prophetic discernment about the
questions that affect the lives of ordinary people. The most obvious
example of this has been the failure of the churches to do or say

anything distinctively Christian about war. The words, judgments and deeds of both pacifists and non-pacifists (with a few notable exceptions) have often been almost indistinguishable from those of secular people of like mind, because ideology has been more determinative than theology. Karl Barth asked in 1959: 'How do you explain the fact that the large Christian bodies cannot pronounce a definite yes or no on the matter of atomic war?'[11] Robin Gill in *Prophecy and Praxis* (1981) argues that on social questions the churches tend to follow rather than lead public opinion. Recently Gill asks why the churches are not at least 'prepared to display some of the paradoxical attitudes towards war apparent in the New Testament and in the history of the earliest church'.[12]

The churches have also proved notably incompetent about anticipating and sensitively evaluating changing patterns of sexuality (though many Christian leaders showed much more understanding of homosexuality in the 1950s than most other leaders in British society). As a result the churches have got themselves into all kind of humiliating muddles. Women obtained the right to be members of the new legislative bodies created by the Church of England in 1919. But they owed their membership not to theology but to changed attitudes to women created by the war. In January 1917 the majority of a House of Commons committee recommended that women should be given the vote. It was in September that year that the first woman was ordained in England – as a Congregational minister at King's Weigh House London where Dr W. E. Orchard was minister. Therefore when eventually the Church of England and the Roman Catholic church ordain women as priests, it will be the reverse of a prophetic sign. The 1923 edition of Mrs Beeton's *Book of Household Management* dropped its opening quotation from Proverbs 31 depicting the virtuous woman managing her household, as inappropriate to the modern world. In 1980 the ASB included it among the eucharistic lections of the Church of England for the first time in its history. In 1920, the bishops of the Lambeth Conference condemned contraception. But two years earlier, the publication of *Married Love* by Marie Stopes had led Anglican clergy and their wives to begin to consult her, not the bishops, about contraception and their sexual problems. When eventually in 1958 the Lambeth Conference gave its approval to contraception, most Anglican laity (and indeed most Anglican clergy) had already decided the issue for themselves many years before.

During the period since *Humanae Vitae* (1968) the Roman Catholic Church has been experiencing a humiliating, dramatic collapse of its traditional pattern of authority. A survey of English Roman Catholics who attended six of the major events during the Pope's visit in 1982 concluded:

> The majority of the Catholics we interviewed who dissented at least partially from the teaching of the Pope, appeared to do so without any sense of guilt, fear or shame. Arguably a generation ago this would not have been the case. The threat of religious sanctions which previously intimidated many Catholics into compliance no longer has the power to convince or persuade . . . The Pope is seen as a 'great guy' to be welcomed warmly as a celebrity, whose heart is in the right place, but no more. When it comes to responding to his teaching in the absence of any coercive sanctions the ordinary Catholic may treat him as a guide but not as an 'ethical prophet' in Weber's sense and he will, in the last analysis, make up his mind on moral issues pragmatically and common-sensically and, to a greater or lesser degree, in such a way as to favour his own convenience and self-interest.[13]

Yet ecumenical negotiations are conducted between the churches as though their respective theological and ethical formulae are totally representative and authoritative within their own churches. The maintenance of this fiction is one reason why ecumenical schemes founder, and why, for example, it is not easy to recognize the empirical reality of either the Roman Catholic or Anglican churches from the agreed ARCIC documents.

How have the churches reacted to their humiliation and increasing powerlessness? Some believe there is a simple solution. Theology and spirituality should become more liberal or more biblical or more charismatic. The structures should be made more efficient or more participative or more simple. Those who advocate such easy solutions have not heeded what either the best of first war chaplains or Bonhoeffer discovered after much travail. Others act as though by attacking the church they will endear themselves to the public. A cartoon in the 1960s pictured the church as a group of flagellants lashing one another, with the caption 'Like us, please like us'. Another group reacts to humiliation and powerlessness in a schizoid fashion. 'If you, the public, won't attend our churches, we will refuse to baptise your children and mock your weddings and funerals as pagan rites. We will take away the forms of the Our Father and Psalm 23 which you know, and provide so many alternatives in public worship that if you come to church you will feel a total outsider. And we will recite very loudly "We are the Body of Christ" every Sunday to show that Jesus belongs to us.'

There is another possible reaction. It involves the churches accepting their powerlessness and marginality, staying with their bewilderment and continuing to try to hold together truths and experiences which seem contradictory. Therefore, like the Psalmists the churches would allow for doubt and questioning in worship as well as affirmation.[14] The churches would recognize that their penchant for enthusiasm and their dislike of ambivalence isolates them from crucial areas of human experience. Such a new way should not be confused with sectarianism, self-pity, masochism, a cult of failure, cowardice or a lack of faith. It would involve a readiness to recognize gratefully and without envy that other people have different tasks in the human community but that the Christian task is to keep the rumour of God alive, to be alert for signals of transcendence.[15] As R. S. Thomas put it in his poem 'The Priest':

> 'Crippled soul', do you say? looking at him
> From the mind's height; 'limping through life
> On his prayers. There are other people
> In the world, sitting at table
> Contented, though the broken body
> And the shed blood are not on the menu'.
>
> 'Let it be so', I say. 'Amen and amen'.

This is (to use the title of W. H. Vanstone's book) 'The Stature of Waiting' and it requires a Benedictine-like stability, rooted in faith in God, and God alone. For, as David Jenkins wrote (long before he became Bishop of Durham): 'the near-panic which seems to develop in many quarters in the church when old authorities seem to be resolutely questioned does suggest that faith *in God* is not a very dominating element in the life of the church'.[16]

Holocaust

The Second World War faced the human race with two main revelations, both particularly alarming for Christians. The first was the discovery of the near-bankruptcy of both the Just War tradition and Christian pacifism, as sources of ethical guidance in modern warfare. The second revelation was the holocaust.

Perhaps no text in the Bible has had such catastrophic consequences as Matthew 27.25: 'His blood be on us, and on our children'. Through the ages Christians have talked much about sharing Christ's crucifixion, but it is the Jews who have been crucified. Christians have preached about being outcast and rejected, but the Jew knows more than the Christian about the inside of that experience. It is one of the searing ironies of Christian history that it was Holy Week which Jews always dreaded most. For it was then that Christians, inflamed with love for Jesus, sometimes went into the ghettos to destroy and kill. Jews who fled to Britain and America from eastern Europe dreaded the sound of church bells, for that is how the beginning of a pogrom was often announced. It is another tragic irony that a people whose religion includes the story of a God who refuses the human sacrifice of Isaac, should have been so cruelly persecuted by a people whose religion is focussed on a story of a God who accepts the sacrifice of his son. The very word 'holocaust' contains an almost intolerable paradox. In 1942 a Jew in the Warsaw ghetto wrote in his diary: 'We are like rams and sheep bound for sacrifice.'

Most ordinary Christians simply blame Hitler and the Germans for the holocaust. But we have to go back beyond Hitler to liberal German theology which despised the Old Testament and beyond that to Luther himself. Anti-Judaism is also very evident in the collect for Good Friday in the old Roman Missal and in the Book of Common Prayer. (Even in the Good Friday collect in the ASB, Jews are classed with those 'who have not known you, or who deny the faith of Christ crucified'.) The Eastern Orthodox Liturgies have always described the Jews in the blackest terms. In his book on Christian-Jewish relations, Peter Schneider, a Jewish Christian, placed in parallel columns Hitler's measures against Jews and those taken by the church from 306. 'Can any Christian now say another word in the presence of a Jew?' he asked.[17] The humiliation of Christianity is deepened when it is realized that Christian anti-Judaism was not only active in every era of the history of the church, but inculcated by the foundation documents of Christianity. John Austin Baker writes: 'Recent scholarship has opened our eyes to the way in which anti-Judaism, and anti-Jewish propaganda, have infected so much of the New Testament.'[18] What all this led to is summed up by Alan Ecclestone in one sentence: 'The train-loads of Jews on their way to the death-camps passed through countrysides dotted with Christian spires.'[19] For the Christian nourished on such texts as 'No man cometh unto the Father, but by me' (John 14.6) and 'at the name of Jesus every knee should bow' (Phil. 2.10), every Jew has seemed an affront, the archetypal dissenter, a perpetual question against the all-sufficiency of Christianity.

In September 1938 Pius XI in a broadcast condemned anti-semitism: 'Spiritually we are Semites.'[20] But in Germany all but a handful of churchmen turned a blind eye to the attempt to exterminate the Jews.[21] In 1947 an Emergency Conference of Christians and Jews drew up

'The Ten Points of Seelisberg' which aimed to root out Christian misrepresentation of Judaism. It is one God who speaks through both Testaments. Jesus and the first disciples were Jews. Christians should avoid telling the Passion Story in such a way that blamed Jews alone.[22] The holocaust deeply influenced the section on Judaism in the documents of Vatican II. But its preparation proved one of the Council's most difficult tasks. All references to the conversion of the Jews were removed. The Council repudiated the beliefs that the Jews were a perpetually accursed race and that the Jews were alone responsible for the crucifixion. But the declaration lacked warmth and many Jews were deeply disappointed by it.

Anne Frank's question of 1944 is still unanswered: 'Who has inflicted this upon us? Who has made us Jews different to all other people? Who has allowed us to suffer so terribly up till now?'[23]

Ulrich Simon depicts the victims of the camps as in the image of the Suffering Servant: 'the ancient pattern of defeat, of the sheep before the shearer, the victim before the slaughter'. To Simon this is no abstract problem – many of his relations died in the camps. There can be no forgiveness for the 'evil-doers of Auschwitz' for they are 'as hard as steel and as dark as pitch'. Though there cannot be any resurrection for them, there are signs of it elsewhere: in the fact of Israel itself and the ending of the old hatreds between Christian and Jew.[24] Alan Ecclestone trusts that 'Jew and Christian alike . . . may find in Him whom they have in all their various ways rejected, despised, spat upon and mocked, their one hope of life for mankind'.[25] Pinchas Lapide is one of the few Jews who is sympathetic to the Christian focus upon the crucified Jew as a key to the holocaust: '*Eli, Eli lama sabachthani* is not merely a psalm of David and a word of Jesus from the cross, but – I would almost say – the leitmotive of those who had to go to Auschwitz and Majdanek . . . Is not this rabbi, bleeding on the cross, the authentic incarnation of his suffering people . . .?'[26] Jonathan Magonet, the Jewish reviewer of Alan Ecclestone's book in *The Month* (April 1980), was deeply moved by it, and recognized the highest tribute was being paid by this comparison between the sufferings of the Jews and the sufferings of Christ:

Yet to a Jew the analogy is grotesque. For it was a Christian world that killed not one Jew on a cross, but six million, and to make that equation, however well intentioned, is akin to a confidence trick, a takeover bid of that suffering, a cheapening and falsifying of those six million separate and private tortures and deaths under one convenient and somehow comforting symbol. A Christian world

that has hardly begun to come to terms with its responsibility for
that event, let alone past centuries of persecution of Jews, has not
yet earned the right to trade on the memory of the dead in this
way . . .

Christians should also recognize that their analogy between the
crucified Jesus and the sufferings of the holocaust, rests upon an
identification of the Jew as a victim. Since the holocaust, some Jews
have sadly reflected that their willingness to accept this role over the
centuries probably stimulated the sadism of their persecutors. Some,
both Christians and Jews, have likened the creation of the state of
Israel to the resurrection. But much of Israel's foreign policy has been
based upon a pugnacious determination never to be victims again.

Tragedy

Niebuhr said boldly: 'Christianity is a religion which transcends
tragedy. Tears, with death, are swallowed up in victory. The cross is
not tragic but the resolution of tragedy.'[27] But even if all that is
intractable and tragic is ultimately redeemed, here and now the tragic
perspective is an important element in the Christian assessment of
life. We cannot possibly know whether tragedy comes within the
experience of God, but much twentieth-century theology has only
managed to develop a theodicy in any way adequate to the two world
wars and the holocaust by believing that God suffers in and with the
world. Jeremiah's experience at the house of the potter (ch. 18), the
haunting mystery of Judas, the possibility of hell (however defined):
all point to the possibility of a type of failure in the divine as well as
the human experience. Jim Garrison's bold neo-Jungian attempt to
incorporate evil into God as his shadow does violence to the reality of
evil as evil, but at least Garrison demands that we face the fact that
Hiroshima must be allowed to say as much about God as it does about
man. If (as Garrison and others argue) God is more contingent than
we usually like to admit, then chance and tragedy would fall within
his experience.[28]

But whatever may be the case with God, it is dangerous for Christians
to assert unequivocally that Christianity is beyond tragedy. Christians
are too prone to appeal to the resurrection or eschatology whenever a
really intractable problem presents itself. The Fourth Gospel softens
the jaggedness of Jesus by projecting backwards the Easter light, and
this gospel has contributed to both Christian triumphalism and to a
readiness to slide away from facing the full impact of those characteristic human experiences which characterize Jesus in the Markan

tradition: fear, anxiety, bewilderment, struggle, disappointment, dereliction. In his poem, 'The Transfiguration', Edwin Muir portrayed the Second Coming as a return of the wooden cross to its place as a tree in Eden, and continued:

> And Judas damned take his long journey backward
> From darkness into light and be a child
> Beside his mother's knee, and the betrayal
> Be quite undone and never more be done.

But would Christians be wise to relax towards such a touchingly reassuring vision in the age of Auschwitz, Hiroshima and the holocaust? Una Kroll wrote about a tragically failed relationship and also pondered the mystery of Judas. Unusually for a Christian she accepted the category of failure:

> Let failure
> stand
> as failure,
> unredeemed
> by phantasies
> of reconciliation,
> resurrection,
> hope of second chances,
> second coming . . .[29]

Only then, she believes, is resurrection a possibility. For those Christians who hurry past the Garden, Judgment Hall and Cross and try to live wholly in Easter light, the great literary tragedies are particularly important. Nicholas Lash makes an important distinction between optimism, despair and hope. Optimism and despair both assume that the end of the story is known. Whereas optimism leaves behind tragic experience, hope includes it. Hope is 'inherently unstable' and 'precarious' because it focusses on the middle distance. But the optimist gazes to the far horizon which is attractive because it is invisible.[30]

In a nuclear age, hope is necessarily precarious and provisional, for there is no way we can know how the story will end. Faith has to take into account the possibility that what Freud called man's instinct towards death will conquer his instinct towards life, and that God will have on his hands and conscience what to human eyes would be accounted as 'failure'. So it is more than ever important for the classical characteristics of tragedy to be given a place in Christian theology and spirituality.

1. Tragic irony (*peripeteia*) The cross has been used by Christians as a reason for killing Jews to avenge the Jew who hung upon it. Jingoists, pacifists and neo-orthodox have conducted their very different campaigns with the sign of the cross. But there is tragic ambiguity even in the victory of Christ himself, and not just in the ways in which human beings have misused it. Donald MacKinnon writes:

> To Christian faith, Jesus is without sin; yet from his life, as a matter of historical fact, there flows a dark inheritance of evil as well as good. One has only to think, for instance, of the infection of anti-Semitism present in the Christian church from the earliest years . . . A gushing woman once remarked to the great Duke of Wellington 'A victory must be a supremely exhilarating and glorious experience.' The old man replied: 'A victory, Madam, is the greatest tragedy in the world, only excepting a defeat.' There is a profundity in this comment by a great soldier which, in the world of theology, is sadly absent in the writings of those theologians who write and speak glibly of Christ's victory.[31]

2. Tragic error (*hamartia*) How is it that such short phrases as 'His blood be on us' (Matt. 27.25) or 'Compel them to come in' (Luke 14.23) could lead to so many centuries of torture and so many deaths? Cordelia says only the three words 'Nothing, my Lord' to King Lear and a tragedy is unleashed.

3. Pity and fear leading to *catharsis*. The tragedies teach us that breakdown and failure reveal the true nature of things. The Bible emphasizes that only those who are broken open can fully know God: Jacob at the ford; Job; the Prodigal Son; Jesus himself.

4. We might add another element: the experience of being trapped. Job cried 'God has . . . closed his net about me' (19.6). Balaam and his ass were trapped in the narrow way. The soldiers were trapped in the trenches, and Jews in the gaschambers. One of the recurring themes in the novels of Solzhenitsyn is that of the trapped man who creates freedom in its total absence. Jesus, as W. H. Vanstone suggests in *The Stature of Waiting* (1982), is the one who walks into the trap, and is then handed over to be acted upon.

It would be possible to end with some majestic eschatological organ peal from (say) E. C. Hoskyns. But though we have had necessarily to listen much to the leaders of church and state, we have tried to remember that it was 'the common people' who heard Jesus 'gladly'. Storm Jameson travelled to devastated Warsaw in August 1945. There she observed that a Pole had 'cobbled together a room without light, heat or water on the upper floor of a tottering building, reached by fragments of a staircase jutting precariously from the shaky wall'. But on the window-sill blackened by fire he had set a pot of bright geraniums, a defiant gesture of fierce hope. [32]

NOTES

Preface

1 Harold Bell and John Bell (eds), *Wilfred Owen: Collected Letters*, Oxford University Press 1967, p. 461.

1. The Dilemmas of Dissent

1. Don Cupitt, *Explorations in Theology 6*, SCM Press 1979, p. x.
2. See H. Richard Niebuhr, *Christ and Culture*, Harper & Row 1951; F. W. Dillistone, *Religious Experience and Christian Faith*, SCM Press 1981.
3. See Bryan Wilson, *Religious Sects*, Weidenfeld & Nicolson 1970.
4. See Robin Gill, *The Social Context of Theology*, Mowbray 1975 and *Theology and Social Structure*, Mowbray 1977.
5. See Alan Wilkinson, 'Are we really the Body of Christ?' *Theology*, March 1983.
6. See Don Cupitt, *Crisis of Moral Authority*, Lutterworth 1972, reissued SCM Press 1985, Ch. 3; Brian Heeney, 'The Beginnings of Church Feminism', *Journal of Ecclesiastical History*, January 1982; Alan Wilkinson, *The Church of England and the First World War*, SPCK 1978 (hereafter *CEFWW*).
7. R. Currie, A. Gilbert and L. Horsley, *Churches and Churchgoers*, Oxford University Press 1977, p. v.
8. Rupert Davies et al. (eds), *A History of the Methodist Church in Great Britain*, Vol. 2, Epworth Press 1978, p. 45.
9. See R. P. Carroll, *When Prophecy Failed*, SCM Press 1979; Robin Gill, *Prophecy and Praxis*, Marshall, Morgan & Scott 1981.
10. *Richard Baxter: Autobiography*, ed. J. M. Lloyd Thomas, Dent 1925, p. 110.
11. 'Sesame and Lilies', para. 140 in *The Works of John Ruskin*, ed. E. T. Cook and Alexander Wedderburn, Vol. XVIII, George Allen 1905.
12. J. T. Wilkinson, *Arthur Samuel Peake*, Epworth Press 1971, p. 158.
13. Ruskin, 'The Two Paths', para 137 in *Works*, Vol. XVI.
14. See Mark Girouard, *The Return to Camelot: Chivalry and the English Gentleman*, Yale University Press 1981.
15. J. T. Wilkinson, op. cit., p. 48.
16. Dorothea Price Hughes, *The Life of Hugh Price Hughes*, Hodder & Stoughton 1904, p. 562.
17. On Samuel Smiles see Asa Briggs, *Victorian People*, Odhams 1954, ch. 5. In the Pelican edition of this book Briggs draws attention to the amount of Victorian

literature available on how to succeed in life, some of it specifically addressed to young men (p. 310).

18. *Primitive Methodist Leader*, 13 February 1913.

19. See Martin J. Wiener, *English Culture and the Decline of the Industrial Spirit*, Cambridge University Press 1981.

20. Cf. Ruskin's contrast between Rochdale and Pisa in 'The Two Paths', para 91.

21. For a balanced account see John Rae, *Conscience and Politics: The British Government and the Conscientious Objector to Military Service 1916–1919*, Oxford University Press 1970.

22. See G. H. Hardy, *Bertrand Russell and Trinity*, Cambridge University Press 1970; John Barnes, *Ahead of His Age: Bishop Barnes of Birmingham*, Collins 1979, pp. 63–67; Barnes was Russell's chief champion in Trinity.

23. *Manchester Guardian*, 31 October 1916.

24. See Boyd Litzinger, *Time's Revenges: Browning's Reputation as a Thinker 1889–1962*, University of Tennessee 1964.

25. Hutton, *Guidance from Robert Browning in Matters of Faith*, Oliphant, Anderson & Ferrier 1905, pp. 16–17; see also his *Further Guidance from Robert Browning in Matters of Faith*, Hodder & Stoughton 1929.

26. R. F. Horton, *The Dissolution of Dissent*, Free Church Library 1902, p. 20.

27. *Proceedings of the First National Council of the Evangelical Free Churches*, James Clarke 1896, p. 37.

28. William Peterson, *Interrogating the Oracle: A History of the London Browning Society*, University of Ohio 1969, pp. 60–64, 111–13.

29. For other estimates of Browning as a religious thinker, see William Boyd Carpenter, *The Religious Spirit in the Poets*, Isbister & Co 1900; W. R. Inge, *Studies of English Mystics*, Murray 1906; Henry Jones, *Browning as a Philosophical and Religious Teacher*, Nelson 1891; B. F. Westcott, *Essays in the History of Religious Thought in the West*, Macmillan 1891. Browning deeply influenced other such diverse figures as Bishop Barnes, Dr John Clifford, Donald Hankey, G. A. Studdert Kennedy and Dr Leslie Weatherhead.

30. Private communication.

31. J. H. Shakespeare, *The Churches at the Crossroads*, Williams & Norgate 1918, p. 13.

32. F. R. Leavis, *New Bearings in English Poetry*, Chatto & Windus 1932, p. 20.

33. On this theme see Wilkinson, *CEFWW*, pp. 172–3, 244–7.

34. Gerard Manley Hopkins, *Selected Prose*, ed. Gerald Roberts, Oxford University Press 1980, p. 97.

35. D. W. Bebbington, *The Nonconformist Conscience: Chapel and Politics 1870–1914*, Allen & Unwin 1982, p. ix.

36. John Kent, 'Hugh Price Hughes and the Nonconformist Conscience' in G. V. Bennett and J. D. Walsh (eds), *Essays in Modern Church History*, A. & C. Black 1966, p. 182.

37. Rupert Davies et al. (eds), *A History of the Methodist Church in Great Britain*, Volume 3, Epworth Press 1983, pp. 146–47.

38. Bebbington, op. cit., pp. 14–15, 97, 115–17, 152–7.

39. Ibid., pp. 121–4; Stephen Koss (ed.), *The Anatomy of an Anti-War Movement: The Pro-Boers*, University of Chicago Press 1973; James Marchant, *Dr John Clifford*, Cassell 1924, pp. 145–53; for Anglican attitudes to the Boer War, see Wilkinson, *CEFWW*, pp. 10–11.

40. Bebbington, op. cit., pp. 106–21.
41. *Proceedings of the First National Council*, op. cit., pp. 75–8.
42. Marchant op. cit., p. 128.
43. Jose Rodo, *The Motives of Proteus*, quoted in Michael Foot, *Aneurin Bevin*, Macgibbon & Kee 1973, Vol. II, p. 585.
44. Bebbington, op. cit., Ch. 7 and pp. 76–80; Stephen Koss, *Nonconformity In Modern British Politics*, Batsford 1975.
45. Marchant, op. cit., p. xii.

2. Dissent and the First World War

1. Donald Read (ed.), *Edwardian England*, Croom Helm 1982, p. 37.
2. See Keith Robbins, *The Abolition of War: The 'Peace Movement' in Britain 1914–1919*, University of Wales Press 1976, ch. 1;
3. *Proceedings*, op. cit., p. 37.
4. Marchant, op. cit., p. 149.
5. Randall Davidson (ed.), *The Five Lambeth Conferences*, SPCK 1920, p. 329.
6. See Wilkinson, *CEFWW*, pp. 21–3.
7. Marchant, op. cit., pp. 131–32.
8. *Christian World*, 8 January 1914.
9. *British Weekly*, 20 August 1914.
10. *Annual Register*, 1914, p. 203; *Baptist Times*, 18 September 1914.
11. *Baptist Times*, 25 September 1914; see Keith Clements, 'Baptists and the Outbreak of the First World War', *Baptist Quarterly*, April 1975.
12. On Winnington Ingram, see Wilkinson, *CEFWW*, passim.
13. *British Weekly*, 6, 13 August 1914; John Harries, *G. Campbell Morgan*, F. H. Revell & Co 1930, pp. 126–27.
14. Clyde Binfield, *So Down to Prayers: Studies in English Nonconformity 1780–1920*, Dent 1977, p. 245; see also F. W. Dillistone, *C. H. Dodd*, Hodder & Stoughton 1977, p. 84. For Anglican support for recruiting, see Wilkinson, *CEFWW*, pp. 32–42.
15. John Briggs, *St George's Newcastle-under-Lyme*, North Staffordshire Polytechnic 1978, pp. 46–7.
16. *Manchester Guardian, Times*, 11 November 1914; T. H. Darlow, *William Robertson Nicoll*, Hodder & Stoughton 1925, pp. 241–2; Koss, op. cit., p. 131.
17. Stuart Mews, 'Urban Problems and Rural Solutions: Drink and Disestablishment in the First World War', in *Studies in Church History*, ed. Derek Baker, Vol. XVI, 1979.
18. John Briggs, op. cit., pp. 46–7.
19. Marchant, op. cit., pp. 230–31.
20. See Wilkinson, *CEFWW*, pp. 24–31.
21. *Primitive Methodist Leader*, 25 June 1914.
22. John G. Bowran, *The Life of Arthur Thomas Guttery*, Holborn Publishing House 1922.
23. See 'Arthur T. Guttery as Preacher', *Primitive Methodist Leader*. 9 July 1914.
24. Cf. this sentence from the much-quoted book by J. A. Cramb, *Germany and England*, Murray 1914; 'Corsica, in a word, has conquered Galilee', p. 119.
25. On the Angels of Mons, see Wilkinson, *CEFWW*, pp. 194–5; John Terraine, *The Smoke and the Fire*, Sidgwick & Jackson 1980, pp. 17–19.
26. See Girouard, op. cit., pp. 3–4, 14, 258. 'Greater love hath no man than

this' commented Vera Brittain in her diary – a text frequently quoted on First World War memorials (Vera Brittain, *Chronicle of Youth*, Fontana 1982, p. 32).

27. Bowran, op. cit., pp. 164–7.

28. *British Weekly*, 14 March 1918.

29. H. B. Kendall, *History of the Primitive Methodist Church*, Joseph Johnson 1919, pp. 169–70.

30. For a discussion and reproduction of this popular picture, see Wilkinson, *CEFWW*, pp. 191, 328, plate 2.

31. See C. E. Osborne, *Religion in Europe and the World Crisis*, Unwin 1916; Wilkinson, *CEFWW*, pp. 198–9; Albert Marrin, *The Last Crusade*, Duke University Press 1974, pp. 90–134.

32. See J. A. Cramb, *Germany and England*, Murray 1914 – lectures given in 1913.

33. In the *Aldersgate Magazine* for January 1917, Peake argued that the war had raised no *new* difficulties for theology, but old problems had been given a new thrust: suffering, the fate of those who die without explicit Christian faith, the meaning of non-resistance in Christ's teaching, the role of conscience. On theology during the war, see Wilkinson, *CEFWW*, ch. 10.

34. See Wilkinson, *CEFWW*, Ch. 2.

35. See ibid., pp. 71–9, 159–65, 292–3; Alan Wilkinson, 'Searching for Meaning in Time of War: Theological Themes in First World War Literature', *Modern Churchman*, New Series Vol. XXVII, no. 2, 1985.

36. John Smyth, *In this Sign Conquer: The Story of Army Chaplains*, Mowbray 1968, pp. xviii-xix, 202–3; E. K. H. Jordan, *Free Church Unity: History of the Free Church Council Movement*, Lutterworth 1956, pp. 141–2.

37. Gerald Studdert Kennedy, *Dog-Collar Democracy*, Macmillan 1982, pp. 53–4.

38. See Michael Moynihan, *God on Our Side*, Secker & Warburg 1983; Wilkinson, *CEFWW*, Chs 5–7; Wilkinson, 'The Paradox of the Military Chaplain', *Theology*, July 1981.

39. Quoted in Smyth, op. cit., p. 161.

40. For accounts of these chaplains see Wilkinson, *CEFWW*, passim.

41. See also P. J. Fisher, *Khaki Vignettes*, Joseph Johnson 1917; Kingscote Greenland, *Cameos from Camps*, National Free Church Council n.d.; William Sellers, *With Our Fighting Men*, Religious Tract Society 1915; Thomas Tiplady, *The Kitten in the Crater and Other Fragments from the Front*, Kelly 1917; R. F. Wearmouth, *Pages from a Padre's Diary*, published by the author privately 1958.

42. *British Weekly*, 14 March 1918.

43. Anthony Eden, *Another World*, Allen Lane 1976, p. 75.

44. Clements, op. cit., p. 90.

45. Alfred O'Rahilly, *Father William Doyle*, Longman's Green & Co. 1920.

46. Quoted by Clyde Binfield in 'Mill Hill School and the Great War', in *Studies in Church History*, ed. W. J. Sheils, Vol. XX, Blackwell 1983, p. 378.

47. See e. g., *The Crown of Wild Olive*, Lecture III, paras 87, 94, *Works*, Vol. XVIII.

48. H. H. Henson, *War-Time Sermons*, Macmillan 1915, sermon xiv.

49. H. B. Elliott (ed.), *Great Thoughts of Horatio Bottomley*, Holden & Hardingham 1918, p. 8.

50. Darlow, op. cit., p. 251.

51. Ibid., pp. 165, 166, 251, 375, 416–17.

52. For Roman Catholic attitudes see, Ernest Oldmeadow, *Francis Cardinal Bourne*, 1944, II, Chs XIV, XV and XVII.

53. Wolfgang Huber, 'Evangelische Theologie und Kirche beim Ausbruch des Ersten Weltkriegs', in *Studien zur Friedensforschung*, 4, Stuttgart 1970.

54. R. Tudur Jones, *Congregationalism in England 1662–1962*, Independent Press 1962, p. 356.

55. For the effect of the war on attitudes to death, bereavement, heaven and hell, see Wilkinson, *CEFWW*, Ch. 8.

56. See Wilkinson, *CEFWW*, pp. 70–90, 317; David Thompson, 'War, the Nation and the Kingdom of God: The Origin of the National Mission of Repentance and Hope', in *Studies in Church History*, ed. W. J. Sheils, Vol, XX, Blackwell 1983.

57. Jordan, op. cit., p. 149.

58. Kendall, op. cit., pp. 163, 168.

59. Christopher Hill, *God's Englishman*, Weidenfeld & Nicolson 1970, pp. 267–8.

60. Roy Strong, *And When Did You Last See Your Father?: The Victorian Painter and British History*, Thames & Hudson 1978, pp. 146–51.

61. Robert Horton, *Oliver Cromwell*, James Clarke 1897, pp. v-vi, 208.

62. Michael Foot, *Debts of Honour*, Picador edition 1981, p. 13; cf. Kingsley Martin, *Father Figures*, Penguin 1969, pp. 20–21.

63. D. R. Davies, *In Search of Myself*, Geoffrey Bles 1961, pp. 61–71.

64. Nathaniel Micklem, *The Box and the Puppets*, Geoffrey Bles 1957, pp. 58–60.

65. Edith Ryley Richards, *Private View of a Public Man: The Life of Leyton Richards*, Allen & Unwin 1950.

66. Letter in possession of Dr F. W. Dillistone, 12 April 1918.

67. C. J. Cadoux, *Christian Pacifism Re-Examined*, Blackwell 1940; Dillistone, *Dodd*, pp. 153–5; N. Micklem, *The Theology of Politics*, Oxford University Press 1941.

68. Elaine Kaye, *The History of King's Weigh House Church*, Allen & Unwin 1968, Ch. VIII (I am indebted to Miss Kaye for providing information about Orchard and Cadoux); W. E. Orchard, *From Faith to Faith*, Magani & Son 1933.

69. P. T. Forsyth, *The Christian Ethic of War*, Longmans 1916, pp. 21, 23, 37, 39, 71. See also Forsyth, *The Justification of God*, Duckworth 1916; Stuart Mews, 'Neo-Orthodoxy, Liberalism and War; Karl Barth, P. T. Forsyth and John Oman, 1914–18', in *Studies in Church History*, ed. Derek Baker, Vol. XIV, Blackwell 1977.

70. Private communication.

71. Elfrida Vipoint, *Arnold Rowntree*, Bannisdale Press 1955, pp. 68–9.

72. Alfred E. Garvie, *Memories and Meanings of My Life*, Allen & Unwin 1938, p. 169; Jordan, op. cit., p. 143.

73. J. T. Wilkinson, op. cit., pp. 152–5; text of resolution in Appendix to *Prisoners of Hope*.

74. Marchant, op. cit., pp. 154, 231.

75. David M. Paton (ed.), *Essays in Anglican Self-Criticism*, SCM Press 1958, p. 180.

76. Robbins, op. cit., p. 195.

77. G. K. A. Bell (ed.), *The War and the Kingdom of God*, Longmans 1915, p. 40; see also, Henson, *War-Time Sermons*, pp. viii, 18–21.

78. See Margaret E. Hirst, *The Quakers in Peace and War*, Swarthmore Press 1923; Anna B. Thomas, *St Stephen's House: Friends' Emergency Work in England 1914–1920*, Friends' Emergency Committee n.d.

79. David Thompson in Rupert Davies (ed.), *The Testing of the Churches 1932–1982*, Epworth Press 1982, pp. 88, 114.

3. The Assimilation of Dissent

1. Bebbington, op. cit., pp. 29–30.
2. Shakespeare, op. cit., p. 67; cf. Kendall, op. cit., p. 172.
3. Marchant, op. cit., p. 235.
4. Private communication.
5. See Wilkinson, *CEFWW*, pp. 290–93.
6. Daniel Jenkins, *The British: Their Identity and their Religion*, SCM Press 1975, p. 103.
7. Currie, Gilbert and Horsley, op. cit., pp. 17–18.
8. *Proceedings*, p. 37.
9. For the connection between Anglican pluriformity and the tolerant pluralism of English society in the twentieth century, see Arthur Marwick, *British Society since 1945*, Penguin 1982, pp. 16, 264, 270.
10. R. F. Horton, *The Dissolution of Dissent*, pp. 10–11, 37.
11. Quoted by Read, op. cit., p. 25.
12. See Trevor Wilson, *The Downfall of the Liberal Party 1914–1935*, Collins 1966, ch. 1.
13. See William Pickering, 'Religion – A Leisure-Time Pursuit?' in *A Sociological Yearbook of Great Britain*, Vol. 1, SCM Press 1968, and 'The Secularized Sabbath', in ibid., vol. 5, 1972.
14. See Joseph Darracott and Belinda Loftus, *First World War Posters*, HMSO 1972, p. 22.
15. 'Hymns in a Man's Life' in D. H. Lawrence, *Selected Literary Criticism*, Heinemann 1956.
16. For Dickens' picture of a Victorian Sunday see e.g., *Little Dorrit*, Ch. III.
17. Owen Chadwick, *Hensley Henson*, Oxford University Press 1983, pp. 53, 121; see also Wilkinson, *CEFWW*, pp. 102–4.
18. David B. Clark, *Survey of Anglicans and Methodists in Four Towns*, Epworth Press 1965, pp. 86–7. See also John M. Turner in *A History of the Methodist Church*, Vol. 3, pp. 353–56; Bebbington, op. cit., pp. 46ff.
19. Beatrice Webb, *My Apprenticeship*, Penguin 1938, vol. 1, p. 194.
20. See John Kent, 'A Late Nineteenth-Century Renaissance' in *Studies in Church History*, ed. Derek Baker, Vol. XIV, Blackwell 1977.
21. *A History of the Methodist Church*, Vol. 3, p. 364.
22. For some examples see Jeffrey Cox, *The English Churches in a Secular Society*, Oxford University Press 1982, pp. 229–42.
23. See Robert Currie, *Methodism Divided*, Faber 1968, pp. 125–40; Alan D. Gilbert, *The Making of Post-Christian Britain*, Longman 1980, pp. 111–12.
24. J. B. Priestley, *English Journey*, Heinemann 1934, p. 174.
25. H. R. L. Sheppard, *God and My Neighbour*, Cassell 1937, p. 117.
26. Priestley, op. cit., pp. 397–401. On these themes see Peter Berger, *The Heretical Imperative*, Collins 1980; Gilbert, op. cit.; James Walvin, *Beside the Seaside: A Social History of the Popular Seaside Holiday*, Allen Lane 1978, and

Leisure and Society 1830–1950, Longman 1978; Marion Yass, *Britain Between the Wars 1918–1939*, Wayland 1975.

27. On Shakespeare's ecumenical thinking, see Roger Hayden, 'Still at the Crossroads?' in K. W. Clements (ed.), *Baptists in the Twentieth Century*, Baptist Historical Society 1983.

28. See Currie, op. cit., p. 187; W. A. Visser't Hooft, *The Genesis and Formation of the World Council of Churches*, WCC 1982, pp. 1–8.

29. For unity as ecclesiastical rationalization for the sake of evangelism, see Shakespeare, op. cit., passim; Currie, op. cit., ch. 6 and p. 299. For the argument for industrial rationalization and the programme of the Industrial Christian Fellowship for social reconciliation, see Studdert Kennedy, op. cit.

30. For the Brotherhood Movement, see Studdert Kennedy, op. cit., pp. 145–7.

31. Marchant, op. cit., pp. 100–1, 207–8. Cf. e.g. Bishop Barnes, quoted in Barnes, *Ahead of His Age*, p. 94.

32. Quoted in Joe Riley, *Today's Cathedral*, SPCK 1978, p. 108.

33. F. W. Dillistone, *Charles Raven*, Hodder & Stoughton 1975, p. 147.

34. *The Listener*, 14 April 1937. Most of the information in the rest of this section on Dwelly and Liverpool Cathedral is derived from my father's papers and press cuttings.

35. See Nathaniel Micklem, *Box and the Puppets*, pp. 92–9; Horton Davies, *Worship and Theology in England*. Vol. 5, Oxford University Press 1965, pp. 184–6.

36. F. A. Iremonger, *William Temple*, Oxford University Press 1948, p. 494.

37. Gilbert, op. cit., pp. 74–5.

38. Ibid., pp. 86–91.

39. See Stuart Mews, 'The Churches', in Margaret Morris (ed.), *The General Strike*, Penguin 1976.

40. Dillistone, *Dodd*, p. 29.

41. Quoted by Oliver Tomkins, *The Church in the Purpose of God*, SCM Press 1950, p. 80.

42. W. E. Orchard, *The Outlook for Religion*, Cassell 1917, pp. 128–30.

43. Darlow, op. cit., p. 375.

44. Paul Sangster, *Doctor Sangster*, Epworth Press 1962.

45. Sydney Pickering, *Kirkstall as I Knew It 1896–1914*, Kirkstall Village Community Association, Leeds 1982.

46. Aneurin Bevan, *In Place of Fear*, Heinemann 1952, p. 7.

47. See Michael Foot, *Aneurin Bevan*, Vol. 2, 1973, p. 581.

48. See J. T. Wilkinson, *The Romance of the Century*, John Chatwin, Cradley Heath 1927.

49. 'Wesleyan Methodist Church' first appeared on class-tickets in 1893; in 1902 'Primitive Methodist Church' first appeared in the *Minutes* and on class-tickets: *A History of the Methodist Church*, Vol. 3, pp. 156n., 177.

50. *Third National Congress of the Evangelical Free Churches . . . Official Report*, James Clarke 1895, pp. 30–31, 35, 38, 64.

51. *Proceedings*, pp. 28, 30–31, 33.

52. Christopher Driver, *A Future for the Free Churches?*, SCM Press 1962, p. 8. For other descriptions of the contemporary situation of the Free Churches, see Paul Sangster, *A History of the Free Churches*, Heinemann 1983; J. T. Wilkinson, *1662 – And After*, Epworth Press 1962.

4. Never Again!

1. *The Brown Book*, Lady Margaret Hall, Oxford 1978, p. 48.

2. Samuel Hynes, *The Auden Generation: Literature and Politics in England in the 1930s*, Faber 1979 edition, p. 24.

3. G. K. A. Bell, *Randall Davidson*, Oxford University Press 1952 edition, p. 1208.

4. Robert Speaight, *The Life of Eric Gill*, Methuen 1966, pp. 254–8.

5. Kenneth Rose, *The Later Cecils*, Weidenfeld & Nicolson 1975, p. 159.

6. John Oliver, *The Church and Social Order: Social Thought in the Church of England 1918–1939*, Mowbray 1968, p. 178.

7. *The Proceedings of COPEC*, Longmans 1924, pp. 287–9.

8. For the ecumenical influences on Lambeth 1930, see Ruth Rouse and Stephen Neill (eds), *A History of the Ecumenical Movement*, SPCK 1967, pp. 564–5.

9. See *Arms and the Churches*, published by the LNU and the World Alliance in August 1931, which included draft resolutions for congregations and individuals, supporting disarmament.

10. *The Guardian*, 12, 19 June, 18 December 1931, 5 February, 21 October 1932. For other examples of post-war Christian optimism about both the international and national orders, see Wilkinson, *CEFWW*, ch. 11.

11. H. H. Henson, *Bishoprick Papers*, Oxford University Press 1946, p. 46; Henson quoted from Book X of *The Ring and the Book*.

12. See also Martin Ceadel, 'Christian Pacifism in the Era of the Two World Wars', in *Studies in Church History*, Vol. XX. I am greatly indebted to Ceadel's writings.

13. Ceadel, *Pacifism*, Oxford University Press 1980, pp. 3–6, 60–64; Michael Pugh, 'Pacifism and Politics in Britain 1931–1935', *The Historical Journal*, 1980, Vol. 23, pp. 642–3.

14. Martin, *Father Figures*, p. 102.

15. Neville Thompson, *The Anti-Appeasers*, Oxford University Press 1971, pp. 42–3.

16. F. A. Iremonger, *William Temple*, p. 376. Temple had failed to persuade Davidson to agree to a statement in 1924 about Britain's share of responsibility – see Bell, *Davidson*, p. 1209.

17. Percy Dearmer (ed.), *Christianity and the Crisis*, Gollancz 1933, p. 601.

18. Chadwick, *Henson*, p. 238.

19. Franklin R. Gannon, *The British Press and Germany 1936–1939*, Oxford University Press 1971, p. 288.

20. Martin, *Editor*, Penguin 1969, p. 36.

21. *Hansard*, Commons, Vol. 270, col. 632.

22. Ibid., Vol. 295, col. 858.

23. G. M. Young, *Stanley Baldwin*, Hart-Davies 1952, p. 214.

24. A. J. P. Taylor (ed.), *Lloyd George: A Diary by Frances Stevenson*, Hutchinson 1971, p. 309.

25. Hynes, op. cit., p. 21.

26. See Wilkinson, *CEFWW*, Ch. 12, 'Remembrance'.

27. See John Terraine, *The Smoke and the Fire: Myths and Anti-Myths of War 1861–1945*, Sidgwick & Jackson 1980, for an analysis of how the descriptions and interpretations of the First World War by politicians, historians and writers encouraged appeasement.

28. Ceadel, *Pacifism*, p. 81.

29. Gannon, op. cit., pp. 87–8, 227.

30. Martin Gilbert and Richard Gott, *The Appeasers*, Weidenfeld & Nicolson 1967 edition, pp. 23, 63.

31. Percy Dearmer, *Songs of Praise Discussed*, Oxford University Press 1933, pp. xxiv, 44, 79, 286; see also Wilkinson, *CEFWW*, p. 267.

32. H. H. Henson, *Retrospect of an Unimportant Life*, Oxford University Press 1943 edition, Vol. 2, pp. 317–18.

33. Barnes, *Barnes*, pp. 89, 193, 212, 222, 316.

34. Leslie Paul, *A Church by Daylight*, Geoffrey Chapman 1973, pp. 100–101; for another assessment, see G. W. H. Lampe's introduction to the 1982 edition of the Report.

35. C. G. Jung, *Memories, Dreams, Reflections*, Fontana 1967, pp. 360, 363; see also Eric Fromm, *The Fear of Freedom*, Routledge & Kegan Paul 1960 edition, Ch. VI.

36. Henson, *Retrospect*, Vol. 2, p. 408; see also Hynes, op. cit., pp. 88, 109, 191.

37. Owen Chadwick, 'The English Bishops and the Nazis', in *Annual Report of the Friends of Lambeth Palace Library*, 1973, p. 16.

38. Richard Griffiths, *Fellow Travellers of the Right: British Enthusiasts for Nazi Germany 1933–39*, Constable 1980, pp. 129–30.

39. Gilbert and Gott, op. cit., p. 36.

40. Adrian Hastings (ed.), *Bishops and Writers*, Anthony Clarke 1977, pp. 114–23; John C. Heenan, *Cardinal Hinsley*, Burns & Oates 1944, pp. 92, 102; Stuart Mews, 'The Sword of the Spirit', in *Studies in Church History*, Vol. XX, pp. 414–16.

41. Rouse and Neill, op. cit., pp. 530, 565, 579–92; Dillistone, *Raven*, pp. 225–7; J. H. Oldham (ed.), *The Churches Survey their Task*, Allen & Unwin 1937.

5. Christian Pacifism

1. Ceadel, *Pacifism*, Ch. 2 and pp. 74, 78, 84, 98.

2. George Orwell, *The Road to Wigan Pier*, Penguin 1980, p. 152.

3. On the Leeds University war memorial, see Malcolm Yorke, *Eric Gill*, Constable 1981, pp. 220–25.

4. Walter Shewring (ed.), *Letters of Eric Gill*, Cape 1947, p. 425.

5. C. J. Cadoux, *The Early Christian Attitude to War*, Allen & Unwin 1919, p. 46.

6. Ibid., pp. 263–4. Cf. William E. Wilson, *Atonement and Non-Resistance*, Swarthmore Press 1914, 1923 edition: a Quaker reinterpretation of atonement, supportive of pacifism: 'Jesus Christ dies as a non-resistant; His death came to Him because he testified to the principle of non-resistance' (p. 32).

7. In *The Early Church and the World*, Clark 1925, Cadoux reiterated his case that the church's rejection of pacifism was part of a general surrender to the spirit of the world.

8. John Graham, *Conscription and Conscience*, Allen & Unwin 1922, p. 23.

9. Ibid., pp. 31–2.

10. For Percival and Hicks, see Wilkinson, *CEFWW*, pp. 24–7.

11. James Carpenter, *Gore: A Study in Liberal Catholic Thought*, Faith Press 1960, p. 268.

12. See Wilkinson, *CEFWW*, pp. 140–42, 182.

13. C. E. Raven, *Musings and Memories*, Martin Hopkinson 1931, pp. 162, 163, 170, 173; *A Wanderer's Way*, Martin Hopkinson 1929, pp. 84–5, 156–7; *Good News of God*, Hodder & Stoughton 1943, p. 48.

14. 'Liberal Christianity and the War', *The Modern Churchman*, January–February 1919.

15. 'The Liberal Tradition in Theology', *The Listener*, 8 March 1951.

16. *Musings and Memories*, p. 148; *A Wanderer's Way*, pp. 63–5.

17. 'The Holy Spirit in the Evolution of Mankind', *The Listener*, 13 May 1948.

18. Dillistone, *Raven*, pp. 252–3. I am indebted to this fine biography for much of my assessment of Raven's personality and theology.

19. Raven, *Is War Obsolete?*, Allen & Unwin 1935, pp. 182–3.

20. Ibid., p. 160.

21. Ibid., pp. 39–40.

22. Raven, *War and the Christian*, SCM Press 1938, p. 49.

23. Ibid., p. 67.

24. Ibid., pp. 120–21.

25. Ibid., p. 153.

26. Ibid., p. 156.

27. Raven, *The Cross and the Crisis*, Fellowship of Reconciliation 1940, p. 19.

28. Ibid., p. 89.

29. Ibid., p. 83.

30. Raven, *The Theological Basis of Christian Pacifism*, FOR 1952, pp. 15, 22n.

31. Ibid., p. 11.

32. Ibid., p. 3.

33. The literature about Dick Sheppard includes: *Hugh Richard Lawrie Sheppard 1880–1937*, St Martin's *Review*, December 1937; C. H. S. Matthews, *Dick Sheppard: Man of Peace*, James Clarke 1948; R. J. Northcott, *Dick Sheppard and St Martin's*, Longmans 1937; R. E. Roberts, *H. R. L. Sheppard*, Murray 1942; Carolyn Scott, *Dick Sheppard*, Hodder & Stoughton 1977; *Dick Sheppard*, by His Friends, Hodder & Stoughton 1938.

34. Roberts, op. cit., pp. 91–2.

35. Quoted in Gordon E. Harris, *A Ministry Renewed*, SCM Press 1968, p. 116.

36. Roberts, op. cit., p. 158.

37. Roger Lloyd, *The Church of England 1900–1965*, SCM Press 1966, p. 249.

38. See Robin Gill, *Theology and Social Structure*, Mowbray 1977, pp. 74–5, 124–5.

39. H. R. L. Sheppard, *The Impatience of a Parson*, Hodder & Stoughton 1927, pp. 182, 214–20.

40. Iremonger, op. cit., p. 289.

41. H. R. L. Sheppard, *If I Were Dictator*, Methuen 1935, p. 12; *Impatience*, pp. 28, 104, 156, 172.

42. Sheppard, *God and My Neighbour*, Cassell 1937, pp. 73, 196.

43. John Habgood, *Church and Nation in a Secular Age*, Darton, Longman & Todd 1983, p. 105.

44. E. F. Braley (ed.), *More Letters of Herbert Hensley Henson*, SPCK 1954, p. 48.

45. On Peter Green see Wilkinson, *CEFWW*, passim.

46. William Temple, *The Recall to Religion*, Eyre & Spottiswoode 1937, pp. 119–53. On Smyth see Maurice Cowling, *Religion and Public Doctrine in England*, Cambridge University Press 1980, pp. 77–91.

47. See his letter to Dean and Chapter, Roberts, op. cit., pp. 307–8.

48. Lang, Letters to Wilfred Parker, Lambeth Palace Library, 8 January 1938.

49. Roberts, op. cit., p. 314; Vera Brittain, *Testament of Experience*, 1979 Virago edition, p. 186.

50. *Impatience*, pp. 45–7.

51. Dora Pym, *Tom Pym*, Heffer 1952, p. 139.

52. *St Martin's Review*, December 1937, p. 7.

53. Martin, *Editor*, p. 211.

54. *Impatience*, p. 170.

55. Laurence Housman (ed.), *What Can We Believe? Letters exchanged between Dick Sheppard and L. H.*, Cape 1939, p. 88.

56. Ceadel, *Pacifism*, pp. 93–100; Conrad Noel, *Autobiography*, Dent 1945, p. 107.

57. Ceadel, *Pacifism*, pp. 223f., 263; William Purcell, *Odd Man Out: A Biography of Lord Soper of Kingsway*, Mowbray 1983 edition, p. 133.

58. Roberts, op. cit., p. 305.

59. Adelaide Livingstone, *The Peace Ballot: The Official History*, Gollancz 1935; Pugh, op. cit., pp. 652–5; *Guardian*, 18 January 1935; see also Winston Churchill, *The Gathering Storm*, Cassell 1949 edition, p. 152.

60. Brittain, *Testament*, pp. 164–73.

61. Sheppard, *We Say 'No'*, Murray 1935, p. x.

62. Ibid., p. 6.

63. Ibid., p. 7.

64. Ibid., p. 54.

65. Ibid., p. 94.

66. Ibid., p. 108.

67. Ibid., p. 156.

68. See Ceadel, *Pacifism*, pp. 188–90 on Lansbury's last years.

69. Housman, op. cit., p. 240.

70. *Guardian*, 12 February 1937.

71. *We Say 'No'*, p. 126.

72. Lang to Parker, 10 November 1937.

73. Ceadel, *Pacifism*, pp. 247–8; Anthony C. Deane, *Time Remembered*, Faber 1945, p. 177.

74. Ceadel, *Pacifism*, pp. 251, 279–80; Purcell, op. cit., p. 79.

75. Kingsley Weatherhead, *Leslie Weatherhead*, Hodder & Stoughton 1975, p. 83.

76. J. G. Lockhart, *Charles Lindley, Viscount Halifax*, Geoffrey Bles 1936, Vol. 2, p. 37.

77. Ceadel, *Pacifism*, pp. 69, 212; Ceadel, art. cit., p. 404.

78. A. M. D. Ashley, *Joyful Servant: The Ministry of Percy Hartill*, Abbey Press 1967.

79. Ceadel, *Pacifism*, pp. 230, 238–40.

80. Ibid., p. 142.

81. Leyton Richards, *The Christian's Contribution to Peace*, SCM Press 1935, p. 9 and Ch. IX.

82. See also a letter from a number of clergy (including Dick Sheppard and Stuart Morris) attacking military sanctions as 'contrary to the mind of Christ', *Guardian*, 25 October 1935.

83. Richard B. Gregg, *The Power of Non-Violence*, Routledge 1935, p. ix.

84. Ibid., pp. 26–9.

85. Leyton Richards looking back to Gregg's book more than a decade later, criticized it for not being Christian in inspiration and commented: 'the very endeavour to reduce Christian love to a technique only emphasises the failure; for a technique follows a prescribed routine, while love takes any course which achieves its redemptive purpose', *Christian Pacifism After Two World Wars*, Fellowship of Reconciliation 1948, p. 38.

86. Ceadel, *Pacifism*, pp. 251–6; cf. the programme of non-violence and its training methods adopted by Martin Luther King outlined in Martin Luther King, *Why We Can't Wait*, Signet 1964. King, like Gandhi, depended for the success of his campaigns upon the fact that the authorities were sensitive to world opinion.

87. Ceadel, *Pacifism*, p. 278.

88. Purcell, op. cit., p. 124.

89. Barnes, *Barnes*, pp. 146, 301–2, 344–52; Oliver, op. cit., p. 178; Address to Modern Churchmen's Union, 1937, *Guardian*, 3 September 1937.

90. Ashley, op. cit., pp. 88–90; Church Assembly, *Proceedings*, 1939, p. 168.

91. Dillistone, *Dodd*, pp. 153–4.

92. G. H. C. Macgregor, *The New Testament Basis of Pacifism*, James Clarke 1936, p. 50.

93. Ibid., p. 98.

94. Ibid., p. 143.

95. Macgregor, *The Relevance of the Impossible*, Fellowship of Reconciliation 1941, p. 83.

96. Ibid., pp. 90–93.

97. Speaight, op. cit., pp. 282–3; information from 'Pax Christi' of Pottery Lane, London W1.

98. Ceadel, art. cit., p. 404; Purcell, *Soper*, p. 134.

6. Can Dictators Be Pacified?

1. E. F. Braley (ed.), *Letters of Herbert Hensley Henson*, SPCK 1950, p. 128.

2. Keith Feiling, *The Life of Neville Chamberlain*, Macmillan 1970 edition, pp. 455, 462.

3. Most of the factual material for this section on Lang is derived from J. G. Lockhart, *Cosmo Gordon Lang*, Hodder & Stoughton 1949.

4. See Ruth Hall (ed.), *Dear Dr Stopes: Sex in the 1920s*, Penguin 1981.

5. Rose, *Later Cecils*, p. 171.

6. Edward Carpenter, *Cantuar*, Cassell 1971, p. 447.

7. See also Keith Briant and Lyall Wilkes, *Would I Fight?*, Oxford University Press 1935, p. 43; Beverley Nichols, *The Fool Hath Said*, Cape 1936, pp. 238–41; both quoted (like Bedborough) from the same war-time sermon by Winnington Ingram. For text of sermon see Wilkinson, *CEFWW*, pp. 217–18. *Guardian*, 15 May 1936 printed a protest by the Rev. Dr A. J. Macdonald, Rector of St Dunstan-in-the-West, against Nichols' treatment of the Bishop of London.

8. See Gerald Studdert-Kennedy, *Dog-Collar Democracy*, Macmillan 1982.

9. Harold Owen and John Bell (eds), *Wilfred Owen: Collected Letters*, Oxford University Press 1967, p. 467.

10. *Guardian*, 4 September, 2, 9, October 1931.

11. Charles Scott Gillett, *Herman Leonard Pass*, Mowbray 1939.

12. Eberhard Bethge, *Dietrich Bonhoeffer*, Collins, Fountain Books 1977, pp. 261, 282, 446.

13. Percy Dearmer (ed.) *Christianity and the Crisis*, Gollancz 1933, p. 11.

14. On Burroughs, see Wilkinson, *CEFWW*, pp. 30, 73, 282.

15. Burroughs, in *Christianity and the Crisis*, pp. 27, 31.

16. Oliver, op. cit., p. 185.

17. Andrew Sharf, *The British Press and Jews under Nazi Rule*, Oxford University Press 1964, pp. 8–9.

18. The editor of *Crockford's Clerical Directory*, R. H. Malden, Dean of Wells, kept up a regular and sardonic commentary on German church affairs, and consistently condemned Nazi actions: see *Crockford Prefaces*, Oxford University Press 1947.

19. R. C. D. Jasper, *Arthur Cayley Headlam*, Faith Press 1960, pp. 8–9.

20. Henson, *Retrospect*, Vol. 2, p. 413; see also Edward Norman, *Church and Society in England 1770–1970*, Oxford University Press 1976, pp. 360–61.

21. S. C. Carpenter, *Duncan-Jones of Chichester*, Mowbray 1956, pp. 84–90.

22. Jasper, *Headlam*, pp. 290–301; e.g. *Times*, 24 October, 24 November 1933, 24 February 1937, 14, 20 July 1938; Chadwick, 'English Bishops and the Nazis', pp. 22, 26.

23. *Guardian*, 11 August 1933.

24. *Guardian*, 12 June 1931; 12 February 1932; *Times*, 24 October 1933; *Guardian*, 29 June 1934.

25. See Keith Robbins, 'Church and Politics: Dorothy Buxton and the German Church Struggle', in *Studies in Church History*, ed. Derek Baker, Vol. XII, Blackwell 1975.

26. R. C. D. Jasper, *George Bell*, Oxford University Press 1967, p. 219n.

27. James Bentley, *Martin Niemöller*, Oxford University Press 1984, p. 42.

28. J. S. Conway, *The Nazi Persecution of the Churches*, Weidenfeld & Nicolson 1968, p. v.

29. Nathaniel Micklem, *The Box and the Puppets*, p. 100.

30. Keith Robbins, 'Martin Niemöller, the German Struggle, and English Opinion', *Journal of Ecclesiastical History*, April 1970.

31. Bethge, op. cit., p. 430.

32. See J. R. C. Wright, '*Above Parties': The Political Attitudes of the German Protestant Church Leadership 1918–1933*, Oxford University Press 1974.

33. Conway, op. cit., pp. 20, 65, 115.

34. Karl Barth, *The German Church Conflict*, Lutterworth 1965, p. 75.

35. A. G. Hebert, *Liturgy and Society*, Faber 1935, p. 13.

36. Ibid., pp. 188–9, 197.

37. See James Bentley, 'British and German High Churchmen in the Struggle against Hitler', *Journal of Ecclesiastical History*, July 1972; 'The Most Irresistible Temptation', *Listener*, 16 November 1978; Gordon Wakefield (ed.), *Crucifixion – Resurrection*, SPCK 1981, on Hoskyns.

38. Chadwick, *Henson*, p. 264.

39. Robbins, op. cit., p. 163.

40. Ibid., p. 165.

41. Ibid., p. 164.

42. Bentley, *Niemöller*, passim.

43. See Haddon Willmer, 'Otto Dibelius: A Missing Piece in the Puzzle of Dietrich Bonhoeffer?', in Derek Baker (ed.), *Studies in Church History*, Vol. XV,

Blackwell 1978; Otto Dibelius, *In the Service of the Lord*, Faber 1965, p. 138; Gutteridge and others criticize Dibelius' anti-semitism.

44. Peter Berger, *The Heretical Imperative*, Collins 1980, pp. 73, 143, 157.

45. Keith W. Clements, 'A Question of Freedom? – British Baptists and the German Church Struggle', in Keith W. Clements (ed.), *Baptists in the Twentieth Century*, Baptist Historical Society 1983, p. 108.

46. Barth, op. cit., p. 45.

47. *Listener*, 25 December 1929.

48. Jasper, *Bell*, p. 243.

49. Bentley, *Niemöller*, p. 137; Griffiths, *Fellow Travellers*, pp. 251–3. A. C. Don, Archbishop of Canterbury's chaplain, was invited to meet von der Ropp at a dinner in 1937 and reported sympathetically the idea of a deeper spiritual understanding between the Germans and English (Diary of A. C. Don, Lambeth Palace Library, 9 March 1937).

50. Quoted in Clements, op. cit., p. 97.

51. *Guardian*, 30 June 1933, 22 November 1935, 23 December 1938.

52. Chadwick, *Henson*, pp. 255–62, 267, 325.

53. W. R. Matthews, *Memories and Meanings*, Hodder & Stoughton 1969, pp. 373–5.

54. Bentley, *Niemöller*, pp. 66, 164–5.

55. Jasper, *Bell*, pp. 135–45.

56. Robert Kee, *The World We Left Behind: A Chronicle of the Year 1939*, Weidenfeld & Nicolson 1984.

57. *Guardian*, 11 October 1935, 10 July 1936.

58. Ibid., 8, 22 May 1936.

59. In September 1935, Hinsley courageously appealed to the Vatican, in a private letter, to dissociate the church from the actions of the Italian government. (Thomas Moloney, *Westminster, Whitehall and the Vatican: The Role of Cardinal Hinsley 1935–43*, Burns & Oates 1985, p. 49.)

60. Heenan, *Hinsley*, pp. 55–62; J. C. Heenan, *Not the Whole Truth*, Hodder & Stoughton 1971, pp. 98, 197; C. H. Smyth, *Cyril Forster Garbett*, Hodder & Stoughton 1959, p. 235n.

61. Weatherhead, op. cit., pp. 83, 113.

62. *Guardian*, 3 June 1938.

63. Hynes, op. cit., pp. 242–63, 414.

64. Dean of New York (ed.), *Modern Canterbury Pilgrims*, Mowbray 1956, pp. 40–41; cf. George Orwell, 'Looking Back at the Spanish War', 1943, *Collected Essays*, Mercury Books 1961.

65. D. R. Davies, *In Search of Myself*, Geoffrey Bless 1961, pp. 165–85.

66. *Guardian*, 4 September 1936.

67. *Guardian*, 19 February 1937.

68. *Guardian*, 1 October, 3 September 1937.

69. Moloney, *Hinsley*, p. 71.

70. Smyth, *Garbett*, pp. 232–4.

71. Diary of A. C. Don, 30 March 1938.

72. *Times*, 28 September 1938.

73. *Guardian*, 30 September 1938.

74. Studdert Kennedy, op. cit., pp. 35–6, 183–5. This offer from the British Legion was criticized; see letter in *Daily Telegraph*, 7 October 1938.

75. *Guardian*, 7 October 1938.

76. Clyde Binfield, *Pastors and People: The Biography of a Baptist Church: Queen's Road, Coventry*, Queen's Road Baptist Church, Coventry 1984.
77. *Guardian*, 7 October 1938.
78. *Guardian*, 5 December 1918.
79. *Guardian*, 28 October 1938.
80. Adam Fox, *Dean Inge*, Murray 1960, p. 243.
81. Weatherhead, op. cit., p. 115.
82. *Times*, 28 October 1938.
83. Lang Papers, Vol. 77.
84. Koss, *Nonconformity*, pp. 220–21.
85. Carpenter, *Duncan-Jones*, p. 91.
86. Kenneth Brill (ed.), *John Groser*, Mowbray 1971; see Wilkinson, *CEFWW*, pp. 142–3, 201, 290.
87. Feiling, op. cit., p. 375.
88. Keith Robbins, *Munich 1938*, Cassell 1965, p. 330.
89. Lang, Letters to Wilfred Parker, 4 November 1938.
90. *Listener*, 5 January 1939.
91. T. S. Eliot, *The Idea of a Christian Society*, Faber 1939, pp. 63–4; see the letter from J. H. Oldham to the *Times* of 3 October 1938, quoted on pp. 85–7.
92. F. R. Barry, *Period of My Life*, Hodder & Stoughton 1970, pp. 127–8. On Barry as first war chaplain, see Wilkinson, *CEFWW*.
93. Ulrich Simon, *Sitting in Judgement 1913–1963*, SPCK 1978, pp. 62–3. The Dean of Lincoln was the Very Rev. R. A. Mitchell.
94. Robbins, *Munich*, pp. 4–5, 348, 350–51, 355.
95. A. J. P. Taylor, *English History 1914–1945*, Penguin 1975, pp. 537–9.
96. Don, Lang's chaplain, regretted the speech as unadvisedly bellicose – Diary, 22, 31 March, 5 May 1939. Don was also Chaplain to the Speaker of the House of Commons.
97. *Guardian*, 26 May 1939.
98. Lang Papers, Vols 77, 78.
99. *Guardian*, 26, 12 May 1939.
100. Kenneth Harris, *Attlee*, Weidenfeld & Nicolson 1982, p. 555; cf. Arnold Toynbee quoted in Gannon, op. cit., pp. 126–7.
101. *Guardian*, 7, 14 July 1939.
102. The Earl of Birkenhead, *Halifax*, Hamish Hamilton 1965, pp. 368, 372, 423, 606–7.
103. Chadwick, 'English Bishops and the Nazis', pp. 12–14.
104. Robbins, 'Niemöller', p. 157.
105. Jasper, *Bell*, p. 239.

7. The Retreat from Liberal Optimism

1. Martin, *Editor*, p. 162.
2. C. E. M. Joad, *Guide to Modern Wickedness*, Faber 1939, p. 72.
3. Ibid., p. 233.
4. Joad, *God and Evil*, Faber 1942, p. 68.
5. David Martin, *A Sociology of English Religion*, SCM Press 1967, pp. 103–4.
6. Bernard Crick, *George Orwell*, Secker & Warburg 1981 edition, pp. 405–6.
7. Hynes, op. cit., p. 339.
8. Stephen Spender (ed.), *W. H. Auden*, Weidenfeld & Nicolson 1974, pp. 101–2, 108.

9. A. M. Ramsey, *From Gore to Temple*, Longman 1960, p. 142.

10. Karl Barth, *The Epistle to the Romans*, ET Oxford University Press 1933, pp. 98–99.

11. Ibid., p. 187.

12. Ibid., p. 269.

13. Ibid., p. 432.

14. Ibid., p. 471.

15. Micklem, *Box and the Puppets*, p. 93.

16. Karl Barth, *A Letter to Great Britain from Switzerland*, Sheldon Press 1941, p. 11.

17. E. G. Selwyn (ed.), *Essays Catholic and Critical*, SPCK 1926.

18. Ramsey, op. cit., pp. 132–3, 137. Hoskyns influenced the historian Herbert Butterfield, whose *Christianity and History*, G. Bell & Sons 1949, with its strong emphasis on sin and judgment, impressed a generation. See Noel Annan in *Twentieth Century*, February 1955. Maurice Cowling in *Religion and Public Doctrine in England*, Cambridge University Press 1980, sets Butterfield within the anti-liberal movement of the 1920s of which P. T. Forsyth, T. E. Hulme, G. K. Chesterton and J. N. Figgis were initiators.

19. E. C. Hoskyns, *Cambridge Sermons*, SPCK 1938, p. 219.

20. Ibid., pp. 35, 37, 40, 87, 164, 167–8.

21. E. C. Hoskyns, *We are the Pharisees*, SPCK 1960, p. 30.

22. On Donald Hankey, see Wilkinson, *CEFWW*.

23. Gordon Wakefield (ed.), *Crucifixion-Resurrection*, p. 39.

24. Ibid., pp. 64–6.

25. Reinhold Niebuhr, *Leaves from the Notebook of a Tamed Cynic*, Willett, Clark & Colby, New York 1929, pp. x, 42, 74, 182.

26. Niebuhr, *The Nature and Destiny of Man*, Nisbet, I 1941, p. 285, II 1943, pp. 69, 121, 263, 289; *Christianity and Power Politics*, Scribners, New York 1940, p. 58.

27. Niebuhr, *An Interpretation of Christian Ethics*, SCM Press 1936, p. 26.

28. *Beyond Tragedy*, Nisbet 1938, p. 167.

29. *Nature and Destiny* I, p. 241.

30. *Discerning the Signs of the Times*, SCM Press 1946, p. 33.

31. *Nature and Destiny* II, p. 113n.

32. *The Children of Light and the Children of Darkness*, Scribners, New York 1944, 1972 edition, p. xiii.

33. *Moral Man and Immoral Society*, Scribners, New York 1932, 1960 edition, pp. 21–2.

34. *Discerning the Signs*, p. 84.

35. Charles W. Kegley and Robert W. Bretall (eds), *Reinhold Niebuhr*, Macmillan, New York 1956, 1961 edition, p. 52.

36. *Discerning the Signs*, pp. 92–3.

37. *Nature and Destiny* II, p. 44.

38. *Interpretation of Christian Ethics*, p. 200.

39. *Discerning the Signs*, p. 40.

40. *Interpretation of Christian Ethics*, p. 49.

41. Stanley Hauerwas, *The Peaceable Kingdom*, SCM Press 1984, pp. 135–41, 172.

42. Niebuhr, *Christianity and Power Politics*, 1940, p. 6.

43. Ibid., p. 31.

44. *Nature and Destiny* II, p. 75.
45. *Modern Churchman*, new series, XXV, No. 2, 1982 – letter in reply to Richard Harries' Re-Review of *Moral Man and Immoral Society*, in XXV, No. 1, 1982.
46. For these and other criticisms, see Kegley and Bretall, op. cit., passim.
47. A. R. Vidler, *Twentieth-Century Defenders of the Faith*, SCM Press 1965, p. 95.
48. Vidler, *God's Judgment on Europe*, Longmans 1940, pp. 70, 73.
49. Ibid., pp. 99–100.
50. Ibid., p. 101.
51. Vidler, *Scenes from Clerical Life*, Collins 1977, pp. 122–30.
52. *Listener*, 6 March 1980.
53. See Alan Suggate, 'William Temple and the Challenge of Reinhold Niebuhr', *Theology*, November 1981.
54. Iremonger, *Temple*, p. 524.
55. Ibid., pp. 537–8,
56. *Malvern 1941*, Longmans 1941, pp. 14, 76, 96, 105, 107, 197. See also Alan Suggate 'Reflections on William Temple's Christian Social Ethics', *Crucible*, October 1981.
57. William Temple, *Christianity and Social Order*, Penguin 1942, p. 21.
58. Cited by Edward Norman, *Church and Society*, p. 371.
59. *Modern Canterbury Pilgrims*, pp. 83–7.
60. Davies, *Down Peacock's Feathers*, Centenary Press 1942, p. 1.
61. Davies, *In Search of Myself*, pp. 190–93.
62. Vidler, *Twentieth-Century Defenders*, pp. 99–100.
63. Davies, *Onto Orthodoxy*, Hodder & Stoughton 1939, p. 17.
64. Ibid., p. 39.
65. Frank H. West, *FHB – A Portrait of Bishop Russell Barry*, Bramcote 1980, p. 92.
66. Temple Papers, Lambeth Palace Library, Vol. 10.
67. *Midnight Hour*, 1942, p. 9.
68. Ibid., pp. 148–9.
69. Ibid., p. 66.
70. *Towards the Conversion of England*, 1945, p. 8.
71. Ibid., p. 10.
72. Ibid., pp. 13–14.
73. Hans Ehrenberg, *Autobiography of a German Pastor*, SCM Press 1943, p. 8.
74. Ibid., p. 9.
75. Ibid., pp. 50–51.
76. Ibid., p. 138.
77. Raven, *Good News of God*. 1943, p. 20.
78. Ibid., p. 30.
79. Ibid., p. 104.
80. Ibid., p. 55.
81. Ibid., p. 81.
82. Dillistone, *Raven*, Ch. 17 and p. 437.
83. Hildebrandt, *This is the Message*, Lutterworth 1944, p. 110.
84. Ibid., p. 27.
85. Ibid., p. 41.
86. Ibid., p. 109.

87. Ibid., p. 83.
88. Ibid., pp. 89–90.
89. Ibid., p. 96.
90. Dillistone, op. cit., p. 312.
91. John Hadham, *God in a World at War*, Penguin 1940, p. 27.
92. Ibid., p. 45.
93. Ibid., p. 74.
94. Peter Berger, *The Heretical Imperative*, pp. 79, 81, 90, 139.

8. A Very Different Kind of War

1. Clive Aslet, *The Last Country Houses*, Yale University Press 1982, p. 82.
2. *Guardian*, 26 May, 14 June 1939.
3. Adam Fox, *Dean Inge*, p. 244; W. R. Inge, *Diary of a Dean*, Hutchinson 1949, pp. 125, 164.
4. Henson, *Retrospect*, Vol. 3, p. 47.
5. Don, *Diary*, 14 January, 27 September 1938; 5 February, 4, 23, 30 August, 6 September 1939.
6. Jasper, *Bell*, p. 86.
7. Max Warren, *Crowded Canvas*, Hodder & Stoughton 1974, pp. 101–3.
8. Kenneth Clark, *Another Part of the Wood*, Murray 1974, p. 277.
9. John Peart-Binns, *Eric Treacy*, Ian Allan 1980, pp. 54–5.
10. Norman Longmate, *How We Lived Then: A History of Everyday Life during the Second World War*, Arrow Books 1973 edition, p. 59n: a valuable source of information used in this chapter.
11. Vera Brittain, *England's Hour*, 1941, Futura 1981, Chs XXIV–XXV.
12. *Guardian*, 8, 15 September 1939.
13. A. R. Vidler, *Scenes from Clerical Life*, pp. 114–16.
14. Macdonald again demonstrated his patriotism when just after D-Day he called for 'prayer and more prayer for victory' (*Guardian*, 16 June 1944).
15. G. K. A. Bell, *The Church and Humanity*, Longmans 1946, Ch. II.
16. Brittain, *England's Hour*, pp. 17–18, 28, 35, 71, 81, 144, 195–6, 209.
17. See Jasper, *Bell*, Ch. 7.
18. Hynes, *Auden Generation*, pp. 389–91.
19. Henson, *Retrospect*, Vol. 3, p. 85.
20. See Alan Wilkinson, 'Searching for Meaning in Time of War: Theological Themes in First World War Literature', *Modern Churchman*, XXVII, No. 2, 1985.
21. Desmond Graham (ed.), *The Complete Poems of Keith Douglas*, Oxford University Press 1978, p. 124.
22. Stephen Spender, *World Within World*, Hamish Hamilton 1951, pp. 286, 303ff.
23. On the arts and literature in war-time, see Ronald Blythe (ed.), *Writing in a War*, Penguin 1982; Angus Calder, *The People's War: Britain 1939–45*, Cape 1969, pp. 501–23; Brian Gardner (ed.), *The Terrible Rain: The War Poets 1939–1945*, Magnum 1966.
24. William Temple, *Thoughts in War-Time*, Macmillan 1940, pp. 53–5.
25. Hadham, *God in a World at War*, p. 86; cf. Henson, *Retrospect*, Vol. 3, p. 104; Harold Nicolson, 'Then and Now', *Listener*, 14 September 1939.
26. Temple, *Thoughts*, p. 85.
27. See Christopher Andrew, 'Secrets of the Kaiser', *Listener*, 7 June 1984.

28. A. J. P. Taylor, *Europe: Grandeur and Decline*, Penguin 1983, preface; *A Personal History*, Coronet 1984, pp. 298ff.

29. Temple, *Thoughts*, p. 7.

30. J. Danielou, A. H. Couratin and John Kent, *The Pelican Guide to Modern Theology*, Vol. 2, 1969, p. 314.

31. See Cate Haste, *Keep the Home Fires Burning: Propaganda in the First World War*, Allen Lane 1977.

32. Brittain, *England's Hour*, p. x.

33. J. B. Priestley, *Postscripts*, Heinemann 1940, pp. 26–7.

34. Martin, *Father Figures*, p. 23, Ch. 4; *Editor*, pp. 289–93, 303.

35. Charles Carrington, *Soldier from the Wars Returning*, Hutchinson 1965, p. 14.

36. See Wilkinson, *CEFWW*, pp. 156–7, 210–11.

37. R. H. S. Crossman (ed.) *New Fabian Essays*, Turnstile Press 1952, p. 8.

38. Taylor, *English History*, pp. 727, 774.

39. Clements, *A Patriotism for Today*, p. 90.

9. War-Time Ministries

1. Rouse and Neill, *History of Ecumenical Movement*, pp. 699–711.

2. Kenneth M. Wolfe, *The Churches and the British Broadcasting Corporation 1922–1956*, SCM Press 1984, pp. 283–95; Francis House, 'Inter-church Relations in Wartime', *Crucible*, January 1981.

3. G. K. A. Bell, *The Kingship of Christ*, Penguin 1954, p. 38.

4. Jasper, *Bell*, p. 244.

5. John S. Peart-Binns, *Defender of the Church of England: The Life of Bishop R. R. Williams*, Amate Press 1984, pp. 1, 19–23, 31.

6. Ian McLaine, *Ministry of Morale*, Allen & Unwin 1979, pp. 151–3.

7. *Guardian*, 30 April 1943.

8. Books published during the war about Christian resistance to Hitler included: Eivind Berggrav, *With God in the Darkness*, Hodder & Stoughton 1943; Bjarne Höye and Trygve Ager, *The Fight of the Norwegian Church against Nazism*, Macmillan, New York 1943; Hugh Martin et al. (eds), *Christian Counter-Attack: Europe's Churches against Nazism*, SCM Press 1943; Henry P. Van Dusen, *What is the Church Doing?* SCM Press 1943.

9. Temple, *The Church Looks Forward*, Macmillan 1944, p. 9.

10. Don, *Diary*, 28 July 1939.

11. John C. Heenan, *Not the Whole Truth*, p. 212.

12. Rupert Davies (ed.) *The Testing of the Churches*, Epworth Press 1982, p. 18.

13. On the Sword of the Spirit, see Moloney, *Hinsley*, Ch. 10; Stuart Mews, 'The Sword of the Spirit', *Studies in Church History*, XX, 1983; Michael Walsh, 'Ecumenism in War-Time Britain: The Sword of the Spirit and Religion and Life, 1940–1945', *The Heythrop Journal*, Vol. XXIII, 1982.

14. Heenan, *Hinsley*, pp. 183, 186.

15. Moloney, op. cit., p. 187.

16. *Church Times*, 5, 12, 19 July, 16, 30 August, 4 October 1940; see also Gavin White, 'The Fall of France', *Studies in Church History*, XX.

17. J. H. Oldham (ed.), *The Churches Survey Their Task*, 1937, pp. 116–17. The historian and Conservative MP, Kenneth Pickthorn attacked the joint letter as naively idealistic in the *Guardian* for 10 January 1941.

18. Moloney, op. cit., p. 200.

19. *Guardian*, 20 July 1945.
20. Temple, *Church Looks Forward*, p. 2.
21. Temple, *Thoughts*, p. 44. Niebuhr wrote to thank Temple for the 'Christian character' of his October broadcast on War Aims (Temple Papers, Vol. 51).
22. *Guardian*, 23 October 1942.
23. *Guardian*, 13 October 1944.
24. Brittain, *England's Hour*, pp. 218–20.
25. Jasper, *Bell*, pp. 146–54; Bell, *Church and Humanity*, Ch. IV; *Church Times* 7 June, 26 July, 9 August 1940.
26. For this section I am indebted to Matthew Barry Sullivan, *Thresholds of Peace: German Prisoners and the People of Britain 1944–1948*, Hamish Hamilton 1979.
27. Jürgen Moltmann, *Experiences of God*, SCM Press 1980, p. 7.
28. Sullivan, op. cit., p. 375; Gordon Hewitt (ed.), *Strategist for the Spirit: Leslie Hunter, Bishop of Sheffield 1939–1962*, Becket 1985, pp. 81, 151, 173–4.
29. *Orkney's Italian Chapel*, Stromess, Orkney n.d.
30. Lang Papers, Vol. 78, Hanson to Lang, 29 June 1940.
31. Lockhart, *Lang*, pp. 405–6; E. F. Braley (ed.), *Letters of Herbert Hensley Henson*, SPCK 1950, p. 99; John Wheeler-Bennett, *King George VI*, Macmillan 1958, p. 310.
32. Wolfe, op. cit., p. 298.
33. Lockhart, op. cit., pp. 440–41; Don, *Diary*, 28 February 1942.
34. Iremonger, op. cit., p. 475; F. S. Temple (ed.), *William Temple: Some Lambeth Letters*, Oxford University Press 1963, p. 57; Smyth, *Garbett*, p. 290.
35. Carpenter, *Cantuar*, p. 467.
36. Braley (ed.), *Letters*, pp. 138, 158, 159, 240; Henson, *Retrospect*, Vol. 3, p. 240.
37. David Dilks (ed.), *The Diaries of Sir Alexander Cadogan*, Cassell 1971, p. 675.
38. W. R. Matthews et al., *William Temple: An Estimate and An Appreciation*, James Clarke 1946, p. 98.
39. A. R. Vidler, 'The Limitations of William Temple', *Theology*, January 1976, p. 37.
40. Guardian, 20 July 1945.
41. Iremonger, op. cit., pp. 536, 543, 544; Temple, *Thoughts*, p. 9; cf. H. F. Woodhouse, 'Can Compromise be the Will of God?', *Crucible*, January 1982.
42. Dearmer (ed.), *Christianity and the Crisis*, p. 600.
43. *Guardian*, 1, 8 November 1935.
44. Temple, *Thoughts*, pp. 7, 28–9.
45. Taylor, *English History*, pp. 628–30, 649, 670, 717; McLaine, op. cit., pp. 159–66; Geoffrey Best, 'The Bishop and the Bomber', *History Today*, September 1983.
46. Lang Papers, Vols 78 and 80; Temple Papers, Vol. 57; cf. Don, *Diary*, 29 September 1938.
47. *Lambeth Letters*, p. 102.
48. Temple Papers, Vol. 51.
49. F. R. Barry, *Mervyn Haigh*, SPCK 1964, pp. 135–8.
50. Temple to Bell, 24, 28 February 1944 (Temple Papers, Vol. 57).
51. W. E. Rose, *Sent from Coventry: A Mission of International Reconciliation*, Oswald Wolff 1980.

52. For Just War principles, see Sydney D. Bailey, *Prohibitions and Restraints in War*, Oxford University Press 1972; for Davidson's attitudes during the First World War, see Wilkinson, *CEFWW*, passim.

53. Jasper, *Bell*, Ch. 14.

54. Temple Papers, Vol. 57. The Bishop of Lichfield also protested: see Oliver Tomkins, *Edward Woods*, SCM Press 1957, p. 148.

55. Jasper, op. cit., p. 277.

56. Dresden, full of refugees fleeing from advancing Soviet armies, was devastated by massive bombing, 13–14 February 1945. Some claimed it was a vital communications centre. Some believe Churchill wanted to demonstrate Western power to, and in support of, Soviet forces.

57. Bell, *Church and Humanity*, Ch. XIV. In May 1941 Lang had criticized calls for retaliation and urged the Government to continue to reject indiscriminate bombing (*Guardian*, 30 May 1941). For reactions to Bell's speech, see Jasper, op. cit., pp. 278–9.

58. Temple Papers, Vol. 57.

59. See D. M. MacKinnon, *The Stripping of the Altars*, Fontana 1969, pp. 83–94; Lancelot Mason, ' "Soldiers" and Bishop Bell', *Crucible*, March 1969.

60. Kenneth Slack, *George Bell*, SCM Press 1971, p. 123 and Ch. 7; see Lloyd, *Church of England*, pp. 460–64.

61. Gordon C. Zahn, *Chaplains in the RAF*, Manchester University Press 1969, p. 167n.

62. Terraine, *Smoke and the Fire*. p. 208.

63. *Lambeth Letters*, p. 25; *Thoughts*, pp. 5–6.

64. *Lambeth Letters*, p. 176; Matthews, *Estimate*, p. 49.

65. Stephen Hobhouse, *Forty Years*, James Clarke 1951; see also Wilkinson, *CEFWW*, pp. 48–51.

66. Temple Papers, Vol. 51; Fisher Papers, Vol. 5.

67. Tom Harrison, *Living Through the Blitz*, Penguin 1978, p. 266.

68. *Guardian*, 24 October 1941; Harrison, op. cit., p. 130.

69. Smyth, *Garbett*, p. 262.

70. Paul Sangster, *Doctor Sangster*, 1962, Ch. XII.

71. Barry, *Period*, pp. 134–8.

72. *Guardian*, 13 December 1940.

73. Barnes, *Barnes*, pp. 351, 364–79; A. R. Vidler, 'Bishop Barnes', *Modern Churchman*, Spring 1975.

74. *Church Times*, 22 January 1971.

75. W. R. Matthews, *St Paul's Cathedral in Wartime*, Hutchinson 1946.

76. Quoted in Susan Briggs, *Keep Smiling Through: The Home Front 1939–45*, Weidenfeld & Nicolson, p. 68.

77. Matthews, *Memories*, p. 263.

78. Michael Moynihan (ed.), *People at War 1939–1945*, David & Charles 1974, p. 148.

79. Harrison, op. cit., pp. 127, 257 (for criticisms of the war-time ministry of the church see pp. 161, 226–7, 307–8); Calder, *People's War*, p. 338.

80. Henson, *Retrospect*, Vol. 3, pp. 57, 60; *Letters*, pp. 236–7; Chadwick, *Henson*, p. 263.

81. *Guardian*, 23 February, 12 April 1940; Kenneth G. Packard, *Brother Edward*, Geoffrey Bles 1955.

82. See Wilkinson, *CEFWW*, Ch. 8.

83. Harrison, op. cit., p. 63.
84. C. F. D. Moule (ed.), *G. W. H. Lampe*, Mowbray 1982, p. 24.
85. William Purcell, *Fisher of Lambeth*, Hodder & Stoughton 1969, p. 83; cf. 'In Westminster Abbey' by John Betjeman.
86. *Guardian*, 21 June, 19, 26 July 1940.
87. *Guardian*, 10 December 1943.
88. Weatherhead, *Thinking Aloud*, Ch. 7.
89. Temple, *Thoughts*, pp. 43–4, 48; *Lambeth Letters*, pp. 71, 145–6; Henson, *Last Words in Westminster Abbey*, Hodder & Stoughton 1941, pp. 86–8.
90. Harrison, op. cit., pp. 260, 316; H. A. Williams, *Some Day I'll Find You*, Mitchell Beazley 1982, pp. 109–10.
91. See for example, the hymn produced by Thomas Tiplady, superintendent of the Lambeth Methodist Mission, for the National Day of Prayer, September 1941 (*Guardian*, 22 August 1941).
92. *Lambeth Letters*, pp. 33–5.
93. Temple Papers, Vol. 57.
94. Wilkinson, *CEFWW*, pp. 168, 232; Adrian Leak, 'Eric Milner-White's Prayers', *New Fire*, Autumn 1984.
95. Peter Fleming, *Invasion 1940*, Hart-Davies 1957.
96. On war-time films see, Roger Manvell, *Films and the Second World War*, Dent Barnes 1974; Geoff Hurd (ed.), *National Fictions: World War Two in British Films and Television*, British Film Institute 1984.
97. Duncan B. Forrester, *Christianity and the Future of Welfare*, Epworth Press 1985, pp. 38–41.
98. Temple, *Church Looks Forward*, pp. 105–14; *Times*, 28 September 1942.
99. Colin Cooke, *The Life of Richard Stafford Cripps*, Hodder & Stoughton 1957; Forrester, op. cit., pp. 27–33.
100. Smyth, *Garbett*, p. 293.
101. Priestley, *Postscripts*, p. 38.
102. Quoted in Briggs, *Keep Smiling*, p. 221; see also posters, p. 231.
103. Binfield, *Pastors and People*, p. 252.
104. See David Nicholls, 'William Temple and the Welfare State', *Crucible*, October 1984.
105. Lord Butler, *The Art of Memory*, Hodder & Stoughton 1982, 'William Temple and Educational Reform'.
106. Temple Papers, Vol. 51.
107. *Towards the Conversion of England*, pp. 13, 81; *Malvern 1941*, p. 142; cf. M. B. Reckitt (ed.), *Prospect for Christendom*, Faber 1945, 'Nature and Rural Man'.
108. Iremonger, op. cit., p. 511.
109. Hewitt, *Hunter*, p. 73 and Ch. 11.
110. *Guardian*, 27 January 1939, 26 July 1940.
111. See Paul Welsby, *A History of the Church of England 1945–1980*, Oxford University Press 1984, Chs 2, 7 and 14.
112. Quoted in Wolfe, *Churches and BBC*, Appendix 3.
113. Weatherhead, *Weatherhead*, pp. 117–18.
114. Ceadel, *Pacifism*, p. 297; Storm Jameson, *Journey from the North*, Virago 1984 edition, Vol. 2, p. 96.
115. C. J. Cadoux, *Christian Pacifism Re-examined*, Blackwell 1940, p. 208.
116. Ibid., p. 216.

117. Nathaniel Micklem, *May God Defend the Right!*, Hodder & Stoughton 1939, p. 41.
118. Ibid., p. 139.
119. Lang Papers, Vol. 80; cf. Micklem's critique of pacifism, *Guardian*, 20 July 1945.
120. Percy Hartill (ed.), *On Earth Peace*, James Clarke 1944, p. 86.
121. Purcell, *Soper*, p. 136.
122. Ceadel, op. cit., p. 212.
123. Barnes, *Barnes*, pp. 353–63; Guy Rogers, *A Rebel at Heart*, Longman 1956, pp. 208–9.
124. Dillistone, *Raven*, pp. 230–33.
125. Speaight, *Gill*, pp. 303–7.
126. Frances Partridge, *A Pacifist's War*, Hogarth Press 1978.
127. Lang Papers, Vol. 80.
128. Arthur Hopkinson, *Pastor's Progress*, Michael Joseph 1942, p. 51; Ernest Raymond's novel, *The Chalice and the Sword*, Cassell 1952.
129. Parish Magazine of Holy Innocents, Fallowfield, October, November 1942; private communication. In 1956 Moorman took another independent line by writing a highly critical article about Archbishop Davidson, to which Bell's former chaplain replied (*Theology*, July, September, October 1956). In 1972 Moorman dissented from the majority of the bench by voting against the Anglican-Methodist union scheme.
130. This paragraph is indebted to Rachel Barker, *Conscience, Government and War . . . 1939–45*, Routledge & Kegan Paul 1982.
131. Lang Papers, Vol. 80.
132. Wolfe, op. cit., p. 173; see pp. 170–204 for the BBC's attitude to controversy in war time.
133. See Zahn, *Chaplains*; Alan Wilkinson, 'The Paradox of the Military Chaplain', *Theology*, July 1981.
134. Smyth, *In this Sign*, p. 243.
135. John Laffin, *Letters from the Front 1914–1918*, Dent 1973, p. 5.
136. Lang Papers, Vol. 79.
137. *Guardian*, 4 June 1943.
138. Roy McKay, *John Leonard Wilson*, Hodder & Stoughton 1973.
139. George Millar, *Horned Pigeon*, Heinemann 1946, pp. 92f.
140. Peart-Binns, *Treacy*, p. 77.
141. Margaret Duggan (ed.), *Padre in Colditz*, Hodder & Stoughton 1978.
142. Lang Papers, Vol. 79; Temple Papers, Vol. 51.
143. L. John Collins, *Faith under Fire*, Leslie Frewin 1966, p. 85.

10. The Costs of Victory

1. Gordon Zahn, *In Solitary Witness: The Life and Death of Franz Jägerstätter*, Geoffrey Chapman 1966.
2. Werner Hühne, *A Man To be Reckoned With*, SCM Press 1962.
3. Bethge, *Bonhoeffer*, p. 559.
4. Ibid, p. 614.
5. Dietrich Bonhoeffer, *Letters and Papers from Prison*, Revised and Enlarged Edition, SCM Press 1971, pp. 4, 14, 16.
6. J. A. T. Robinson in *Honest to God*, SCM Press 1963, p. 25 asserted that Bultmann had 'in the first instance' been drawn to write his essay 'New Testament

and Mythology' (1941) because it had proved impossible to communicate the gospel to German soldiers at the front. Professor Günther Bornkamm, a pupil of Bultmann's, writes in a private communication, that Bultmann's ideas had been in gestation for some time, and that though contacts with German chaplains may have strengthened Bultmann's determination, these contacts cannot have been the primary impetus for his demythologizing programme.

7. Bonhoeffer, *Letters and Papers*, pp. 280–81.

8. Bethge, op. cit., p. 833.

9. Ibid., p. 830n. The foregoing account of Bonhoeffer draws upon Bethge's biography; Wolf Dieter-Zimmermann (ed.), *I Knew Dietrich Bonhoeffer*, Collins 1966; K. W. Clements, *A Patriotism for Today*, Bristol Baptist College 1984.

10. Harold Macmillan, *The Blast of War*, Macmillan 1967, p. 706.

11. Barry, *Period*, p. 155.

12. Moynihan, *People at War*, p. 172.

13. *Crucible*, January 1982, p. 14; Lang to Parker, 17 September 1945.

14. Henson, *Retrospect*, Vol. 3, pp. 300–301.

15. *Guardian*, 24 August, 2 November 1945.

16. Selwyn Gummer, *The Chavasse Twins*, Hodder & Stoughton 1963, pp. 159, 217–18.

17. Purcell, *Fisher*, pp. 32, 35, 87, 108.

18. Collins, *Faith*, pp. 85–100.

19. Fisher Papers, Vol. 2. See also Margaret Thrall, 'The Bishops and the Nuclear Deterrent', *Theology*, August 1972. For newspaper reactions in 1945 to the atomic bomb, see Robert Kee, *1945*, Hamish Hamilton 1985, Ch. 24.

20. Jasper, *Bell*, pp. 289–95; Stewart Herman, *The Rebirth of the German Church*, SCM Press 1946, p. 138; Wright, *Above Parties*, pp. 167, 170n.

21. Quoted in Gordon Zahn, *War, Conscience and Dissent*, Geoffrey Chapman 1967, p. 212.

22. *Guardian*, 7 July 1944.

23. Philip Longworth, *The Unending Vigil: A History of the Commonwealth War Graves Commission*, Constable 1967.

11. Beyond Tragedy?

1. *Church Congress Report*, Bemrose & Sons 1906, pp. 21–6; C. F. G. Masterman, *The Condition of England*, Methuen 1909.

2. David Edwards, *Religion and Change*, Hodder & Stoughton 1970 edition, pp. 270–71.

3. Quoted in Currie, *Methodism*, p. 299.

4. *Times*, 20 September 1938.

5. *Guardian*, 1 September 1939.

6. See Welsby, *Church of England*, pp. 44–50.

7. Sangster, *Sangster*, p. 181.

8. J. A. T. Robinson, *On Being the Church in the World*, Penguin edition 1969, p. 9.

9. D. H. Lawrence, 'When Wilt Thou Teach the People?'.

10. John Stevenson, *British Society 1914–45*, Penguin 1984, provides a comprehensive and sensitive account of modern Britain.

11. Quoted by Jim Garrison, *The Darkness of God: Theology after Hiroshima*, SCM Press 1982, p. 1.

12. Robin Gill, *The Cross Against the Bomb*, Epworth Press 1984, p. 82; cf. Haddon Wilmer, 'Forgiveness and Politics', *Crucible*, July 1979.

13. Michael P. Hornsby Smith, 'English Catholics and Papal Authority: Reflections on the Pope's Visit 1982', pp. 39–40: an unpublished paper presented to the Sixth Consultation on Implicit Religion, 1983; quoted by permission.

14. See Robert Davidson, *The Courage to Doubt: Exploring an Old Testament Theme*, SCM Press 1983.

15. See Peter Berger, *A Rumour of Angels*, Allen Lane 1970.

16. David Jenkins, *Living with Questions*, SCM Press 1969, p. 209.

17. Peter Schneider, *Sweeter Than Honey*, SCM Press 1966, p. 38.

18. 'Racism and the Bible', in Kenneth Leech (ed.), *Theology and Racism*, Board of Social Responsibility 1985, p. 11.

19. Alan Ecclestone, *The Night Sky of the Lord*, Darton, Longman & Todd 1980, p. 76.

20. J. Jocz, *The Jewish People and Jesus Christ*, SPCK 1954, p. 95.

21. Conway, *Nazi Persecution*, pp. 261–7.

22. Schneider, op. cit., pp. 71–3.

23. Anne Frank, *The Diary of a Young Girl*, Pan Books 1954, p. 174.

24. Ulrich Simon, *A Theology of Auschwitz*, Gollancz 1967, pp. 44, 71–5, 91–3.

25. Ecclestone, op. cit., p. 39; see also Jürgen Moltmann, *The Crucified God*, SCM Press 1974.

26. Hans Küng and Pinchas Lapide, *Brother or Lord?*, Fount 1977, p. 20.

27. Reinhold Niebuhr, *Beyond Tragedy*, p. 153; cf. Karl Jaspers, *Tragedy is Not Enough*, Gollancz 1953; E. J. Tinsley, *Christian Theology and the Frontiers of Tragedy*, Leeds University Press 1963.

28. Garrison, op. cit., pp. 51, 118.

29. Una Kroll, *Lament for a Lost Enemy*, SPCK 1977, p. 122.

30. Nicholas Lash, *A Matter of Hope*, Darton, Longman & Todd 1981, pp. 268–70.

31. Donald MacKinnon, *Explorations in Theology 5*, SCM Press 1976, pp. 65, 192–5.

32. Jameson, *Journey*, p. 151.

INDEX

Index

ADDITIONAL BIBLIOGRAPHY

Relevant recent publications include the following:

Chandler, Andrew (ed.), *Brethren in Adversity: Bishop George Bell, the Church of England and the Crisis of German Protestantism 1933-1939*, Boydell Press 1997.

Gregory, Adrian, *The Silence of Memory: Armistice Day 1919-1946*, Berg 1994.

Hastings, Adrian, *A History of English Christianity 1920-1985*, Collins 1986.

Hughes, Michael, *Conscience and Conflict: Methodism, Peace and War in the Twentieth Century*, Epworth, 2008.

Kent, John, *William Temple : Church, State, and Society in Britain 1880-1950*, Cambridge University Press 1992.

Foster, Paul (ed.), *Bell of Chichester (1883-1958)*, University of Chichester 2004.

Kirby, Dianne, *Church, State and Propaganda: The Archbishop of York and International Relations, A Political Study of Cyril Forster Garbett, 1942-1955*, University of Hull Press 1999.

Lawson, Tom, *The Church of England and the Holocaust: Christianity, Memory and Nazism*, Boydell Press 2006.

Louden, Stephen H., *Chaplains in Conflict: The Role of Army Chaplains since 1914*, Avon Books 1996.

Snape, M. F., *God and the British Soldier: Religion and the British Army in the First and Second World Wars*, Routledge 2005.

Spencer, Stephen, *William Temple : A Calling to Prophecy*, SPCK 2001.

Wilkinson, Alan, 'Searching for Meaning in Time of War: Theological themes in First World War Literature', *Modern Churchman*, XXVII No. 2, 1985

———, 'The Poetry of War', *Theology*, November 1986

———, 'Bishop Bell and Germany', in Peter Catterall and C.J. Morris (eds), *Britain and the Threat to Stability in Europe, 1918-47*, Leicester University Press 1993.

———, 'Is Poetry a Part of History?', *Modern History Review*, April 1996

———, 'Changing English Attitudes to Death in the Two World Wars', in P. Jupp and G. Howarth (eds), *The Changing Face of Death*, Macmilliam 1997

Lightning Source UK Ltd.
Milton Keynes UK
UKOW051757170213

206416UK00001B/33/P